The Evolving Role of Central Banks

The Evolving Role of Central Banks

Editors

Patrick Downes
Reza Vaez-Zadeh

Papers presented at the fifth seminar on central banking,
Washington, D.C., November 5-15, 1990

Central Banking Department
International Monetary Fund
Washington • 1991

Cover design by IMF Graphics Section

Joint Bank-Fund Library Cataloging-in-Publication Data

The Evolving role of central banks: papers presented at the fifth seminar on central banking, Washington, D.C., November 5–15, 1990 / Patrick Downes, Reza Vaez-Zadeh, editors.
p. cm.
Includes bibliographical references.
ISBN 1-557-75185-4
1. Banks and banking, Central—Congresses. I. Downes, Patrick, II. Vaez-Zadeh, Reza.
HG1811.E95 1991 CIP

Price: US$28.50

Address orders to:
International Monetary Fund, Publication Services
700 19th Street, N.W., Washington, D.C. 20431, U.S.A.
Telephone: (202) 623-7430
Telefax: (202) 623-7491
Cable: Interfund

Foreword

The art of central banking has evolved over time and continues to change, but the principles of sound central banking practice have remained largely unchanged. This is the message that has emerged from a series of central banking seminars for senior officials of the Fund's member countries that have been held at the International Monetary Fund (IMF) since 1983. These seminars have provided a forum for an open and lively exchange of views between the participants, speakers, and the staff of the Fund about the evolving role of central banks. While there was lively controversy on almost all the issues discussed in the seminars, a remarkable measure of support emerged for the idea that the central bank should have a degree of autonomy in pursuing single-mindedly the objective of price stability, which is generally agreed to be an important factor contributing to long-run growth and prosperity.

The success of the seminars owes a great deal to the participants, who come from an ever-widening range of countries. Their questions and active participation enriched the discussion and helped us to obtain a better grasp of the major concerns among member central banks, which will enable us to focus our own efforts. We are grateful to the many distinguished guest speakers who invested their time in preparing for the seminar and participating in stimulating discussions. Finally, I would like to thank the members of the Fund's Executive Board, who assisted in the recruitment of speakers.

The papers in the present volume were presented at the fifth seminar in this series, held November 5–15, 1990. The theme was the interdependence of central banking functions and the role of central bank autonomy viewed against the background of economic transition, financial sector reform, and banking system crisis. As a former central banker, I believe that the issues raised in this volume are important, thought-provoking, and exciting. They are both relevant to the day-to-day art of central banking and important for the evolving role of the central bank in an ever-changing world.

MICHEL CAMDESSUS
Managing Director
International Monetary Fund

Preface

The organization of the seminars on central banking—which is done jointly by the Central Banking Department and the IMF Institute—is an important aspect of the work of the Central Banking Department. The main responsibility of the department is to assist member countries improve their capacities to implement sound economic policies through financial systems reform. This is a broad term that includes a revamping of the institutional and regulatory framework. It means, for example, establishing or restructuring a central bank with an appropriate degree of autonomy that can operate a market-oriented monetary policy; introducing modern instruments and operating procedures for implementation of monetary and foreign exchange market operations and banking supervision; promoting a sound and robust financial system designed to deliver an appropriate range of financial services; and establishing a legal and accounting framework and effective payment and clearing systems that allow the proper functioning and adequate monitoring of the operations of the financial institutions in a market-based economy.

We see the seminar as a forum for the exchange of ideas—to learn from the participants and our invited speakers, and to share with them the experience we have gathered from our operations in member countries. On each occasion, we have adapted the content of the seminars to reflect the concerns and experiences of member country central banks and those of the staff of the Central Banking Department in responding to the requests for technical assistance. We have tried to incorporate the views and suggestions of the past seminar participants. In the latest seminar, which focused on the role, functions, and independence of central banks, the objective was to present the evolving views about the proper role of the central bank and about the design of monetary and regulatory policies, and to review and analyze the developments in financial markets around the world. The major objective of the Central Banking Department in the 1990s is to help strengthen the role of monetary policy in member countries, and this seminar was the first installment toward that goal.

Within the Fund, many people have contributed to the successful organization of the seminar and the production of this volume. I would mention in particular the teamwork of Patrick Downes, Reza Vaez-Zadeh, and Hannah Faux of the Central Banking Department, which has guided this project from start to finish, and the editorial assistance provided by Juanita Roushdy of the External Relations Department of the IMF.

J.B. ZULU
Director
Central Banking Department
International Monetary Fund

Contents

Background Papers

Introduction

PATRICK DOWNES AND REZA VAEZ-ZADEH

This volume brings together papers submitted by speakers at the fifth seminar on central banking. The seminar came at a time of unprecedented change in the world economic and political order, with many countries moving toward market-based economic systems and democratic government. These countries are placing emphasis on a well-functioning central bank as one of the most essential management tools in a market economy and on the need for a sound legal and regulatory framework to underpin the effective development of market-oriented financial systems. Many central banks in Asia, Africa, Eastern and Central Europe, and Latin America are being established or reorganized in the context of the restructuring and modernization of the financial sector, to reflect this new orientation. These developments reflect a general awareness in these countries of the need to strengthen competitive forces and promote sound financial systems, in order to be better placed to achieve the goals of economic policy. There is little doubt that, in this new environment, monetary policy will take on a greater significance, and central banks will be called upon to play a more crucial role in economic management.

Indeed, the trend has already started. Recent years have seen central banks growing in influence and stature. This reflects, in large measure, the fact that, in major industrial countries especially, central banks have shown more assertiveness in dealing with economic problems. The fruit of these actions has been less inflation and a long period of sustained growth in many countries. Out of this experience has emerged a growing recognition that achieving price stability should be a cornerstone of any program to redress economic problems; that credible monetary policy—supported, of course, by other policies, particularly fiscal—has an important contribution to make to this process; and that the central bank should be given sufficient autonomy to conduct monetary policy in a manner conducive to achieving this goal. Nowhere is this recognition more apparent than within the European Community, where the debate on the formation of a monetary union seems to be leading to support for the idea that the crucial component of such a union would have to be an operationally independent central bank with a strong mandate for price stability.

Against the background of these momentous changes occurring in world economic and political relationships, the seminar program was prepared to reflect the current concerns of central bankers about the appropriate role, functions, and degree of independence of central banks in market-based economies and their input to the formulation and implementation of economic policy. The presentation of the papers dealing with these issues in the present volume generally follows the order in the seminar program and is organized in four parts: a) the functions normally performed by a central bank and their interaction; b) the importance of central bank independence for the conduct of central banking functions; c) the role of the central bank in dealing with financial system crises; and d) the role of the central bank in financial reform, particularly in countries in transition from a centrally planned to a market-based economy.

What should be the role of a central bank in a market economy? There is little disagreement among practitioners that the conduct of monetary policy and the parallel development of the money market should be the primary responsibility of the central banks. Foreign exchange management is also usually accepted as a closely interrelated central banking function. Views diverge, however, on the extent to which the central bank should take on other responsibilities in such areas as prudential supervision, domestic debt management, and clearing and payments system. These functions are seen by some as complementary to, and by others as potentially in conflict with that of preserving the value of the currency. The first part of the volume is devoted to a discussion of these alternative points of view.

Perhaps the most controversial issue considered in this part of the volume is the role of the central bank in prudential supervision. Supporters of the idea that central banks should have responsibility for prudential supervision view this function—defined broadly to include also the oversight of clearing and payment systems and money and securities markets—as analytically interconnected and mutually reinforcing with the monetary policy function of the central bank. They argue that these linkages enhance, in the long run, the capacity of the central bank to implement monetary policy in an effective manner. Others, however, argue that the portfolio restrictions imposed for prudential purposes, and the occasionally conflicting interactions between prudential supervision considerations and monetary policy objectives—especially in relation to the central bank's role as a lender of last resort—could detract from the effectiveness of monetary control. Thus, they suggest that having monetary policy and prudential supervision functions both performed by the central bank could compromise monetary policy and undermine a central bank's independence from the political process. Nevertheless, there is little disagreement between the two groups that, when the responsibility for the two functions is separated, economies of scale in information gathering and the efficient implementation of supervisory and monetary actions call for close coordination by the supervisory and monetary authorities.

There can also be important interactions between various other functions performed by the central bank. For example, the issuance of government debt instruments for fiscal purposes or as an instrument of sterilization, and the limits on central bank lending to government, directly influence monetary aggregates and the development of financial markets. Clearing and payment arrangements managed in varying degrees by central banks around the world have implications for both monetary policy and prudential supervision. The use of indirect instruments of monetary policy by the central bank, and the development of the financial system can be greatly facilitated by establishment of efficient payment clearing and settlement arrangements. However, such arrangements could necessitate new prudential rules, such as those aimed at control of systemic risk in the payments system, daylight exposure, etc. Moreover, such rules would have to be taken into account in designing the mechanism for the implementation of monetary policy by the central bank.

The need for prudence by the central bank in taking on additional responsibilities is especially apparent in the case of quasi-fiscal activities performed by the central bank in support of government policies. Such activities—which include, for example, preferential refinancing of banks' loans to priority sectors, foreign borrowing for on-lending to government, and coverage of foreign exchange risk of loans to public entities—have resulted in substantial losses for many central banks around the world. It may be argued that central bank losses do not matter because a central bank cannot become insolvent in the conventional sense of the word. The experiences of many countries indicate, however, that central bank losses can entail adverse implications for the economy as they can undermine the effectiveness of monetary control, depending on the way that they are financed. These adverse effects are to some extent related to the fact that often the losses of a central bank are both a symptom of its lack of independence and a source of further erosion of its independence.

The second part of the volume is devoted to a discussion of the appropriate degree of central bank independence; a question that boils down to how much freedom should a central bank have in managing the constituent items of its own balance sheet. The advantages and disadvantages of providing a central bank with autonomy from the political process in carrying out its different function relate to the question of monetary policy credibility and the impact of autonomy on the overall effectiveness of economic policy in achieving its objectives. The desirable degree of a central bank's autonomy has to be assessed with due regard to the level of development of the country and its institutional and political structures. Indeed, it is probably more salutary to talk about conditions for successful central banking rather than the ideal attributes of an independent central bank: an independent central bank is unlikely to be any more effective than a dependent one if the legal and institutional structures are inadequate, political institutions unstable, the financial system repressed, fiscal policy out of line, and the household savings rate insufficient. Moreover, in practice, the effective degree of independence and public acceptance of a central bank will depend crucially on how well it defines and performs its role over time.

Several Eastern European countries are currently debating these issues, and the question of independence also lies at the center of discussions concerning the establishment of a central bank for Western Europe. This volume presents views on these issues from the perspective of several eminent central bankers around the world, dealing with the experience of their own countries. In this regard, the much-debated evolution of the autonomy of the Reserve Bank of New Zealand, which culminated in innovative legal arrangements—the so-called policy target agreement—governing the operations of the Bank, provides an especially interesting case study.

The role of central banks in banking crises is examined in the third part of the volume. Recent years have seen a sharp increase in the number of financial institutions in distress, owing to such factors as economic mismanagement, adverse external shocks, and—some will argue—inadequate prudential supervision of the financial institutions. Many central banks now confront the challenge of developing new initiatives—such as "bad banks" and the Resolution Trust Corporation established in the United States—to deal with financial institutions in distress. An important issue in this regard relates to the desirable degree of cooperation among supervision agencies around the world in dealing with banking crises. Of particular interest is how to apply prudential supervision and regulation to prevent financial crisis.

The last part of the volume considers a range of issues relating to the role of the central bank in financial reform and economic transition. Governments in many countries have been pursuing reforms of the financial sector to increase savings, enhance intermediation, and raise the productivity and the level of investment—with the ultimate objective of improving the growth performance of the economy. Financial sector reform has constituted an important element of adjustment programs supported by the International Monetary Fund. The reform programs have focused on the monetary control framework, especially the design of instruments that would facilitate a switch away from direct controls; institutional and regulatory reforms to improve the soundness and efficiency of the financial system; and measures to promote market-based interest rates. The central bank has a paramount role to play in the reform process, especially to determine its content and the sequencing of specific financial sector reforms. The reform process also presents a challenge to the central bank in setting up new organizational structures, facilities, and operating procedures in all areas of central banking (monetary management, money market development, research and analysis, prudential supervision, foreign exchange operations, accounting and audit, and clearing and payment systems) and, generally, in ensuring adequate monetary control during the reform period.

Nowhere has the process of financial sector reform been more sweeping than in the formerly centrally planned economies. The spotlight shines most brightly on the Eastern and Central European countries. But, many developing countries in other parts of the world have been following a similar path, albeit, in some cases, at a slower pace. In Asia, the Lao People's Democratic Republic, and Viet Nam come to mind, countries with planned economies that have embarked on far-reaching reforms. In Africa, there are several countries where elements of central planning are being dismantled and replaced by market-based strategies, such as Algeria, Guinea, and Madagascar. And in Latin America also, there is growing acceptance of the need for market-based systems of economic management, and for strong central banks with a greatly reduced role in financing budgetary deficits. The volume presents the case of several of these countries.

A great deal of discussion took place on all of the above topics in the course of the seminar presentations and during panel discussion sessions. The papers presented in this volume—and, indeed, the discourse in this introduction—do not, therefore, necessarily reflect the consensus of the seminar. Rather they could be viewed as starting points for an analysis of issues which central bankers and many government officials have to deal with in the day-to-day task of managing an economic system.

Part I

Role and Functions of Central Banks

1

Government Financing, Domestic Debt Management, and Monetary Policy: Some Lessons from the Italian Experience

CESARE CARANZA*

The relationships and potential conflicts between monetary and fiscal policies have been widely debated in the economic literature. A number of important contributions to this debate appeared during the 1970s and the 1980s in the wake of the tidal wave of fiscal deficits in some major industrial countries and the successive efforts for fiscal consolidation. As always, the facts of life set the tune for economic research.

The economic consequences of high and persisting public deficits have been extensively analyzed. It is well known that monetary accommodation of fiscal deficits may fuel inflation, maintain excessively low real interest rates, and, in the end, distort the allocation of resources. On the other side, the attrition between a lax fiscal policy and a restrictive monetary policy may crowd out private investment and, in the extreme case of noncooperative solutions à la Sargent-Wallace, to an unsustainable situation of ballooning public debt fueled by the growth of interest payments.

But I do not want to lecture about the economic theory of government deficits. As a former central banker, I rather want to analyze the impact of government deficits on monetary policy learning, from the practical experience of my own country. Italy makes an interesting case for study because of the potential for conflict between fiscal and monetary policy. With a public debt that roughly equals gross domes-

*Former Executive Director at The World Bank.

tic product (GDP) and a fiscal deficit of about 11 percent of GDP, the conflict is a fact of life.

I shall begin with some basic facts and figures that are essential for understanding the Italian experience. Then I shall describe the policy response of the monetary authorities, the strategy they followed to finance these growing fiscal deficits while maintaining a reasonably sound monetary policy. Third, I shall review the results of these policies and the problems still unsolved. Finally, I shall sketch the prospects for the future.

Public Debt in the 1970s and 1980s

We begin, then, with the facts and some figures. During the last two decades, Italy has experienced high and continuous public sector deficits and a ballooning public debt. At the same time, it has had a restrictive monetary policy aimed at maintaining the exchange rate of the lira within the European Monetary System (EMS) band. Although the lira has been devalued from time to time with respect to the deutsche mark, those changes did not compensate for the inflation differential with our major trading partners in Europe. In effect, Italy maintained a relatively strong exchange rate policy to reduce inflation to the level prevailing in our major European trading partners.

This objective of reducing inflation has been largely achieved. Consumer inflation peaked in 1980 at 21 percent. From that extremely high level at the beginning of the decade, it has declined over the last three years to an average of between 5 percent and 6 percent. At the same time, real growth improved. In the first half of the 1980s, GDP grew at an annual average of slightly less than 2 percent; in the second half of the decade, it grew at slightly more than 3 percent. More important, the productive sector of the economy recovered during the 1980s from the dark years of the 1970s. Private enterprises regained productive efficiency, competitiveness, and financial strength.

Meanwhile, the status of public finances deteriorated sharply. A few numbers will convey the basic scenario. The public sector borrowing requirement averaged 13 percent during the 1980s. From 14 percent in 1983, it decreased to the present level of about 11 percent. For 1991, the Government is aiming to reduce the deficit to about 9 percent, but that goal may prove elusive. As a consequence of these continuing high fiscal deficits, the stock of public debt grew rapidly. In 1990, it will roughly equal GDP, compared with about 50 percent at the beginning of 1980. Interest payments on public debt grew from 5 percent of GDP in 1980 to 9.5 percent in 1990. Primary deficits (that is, net of interest payments) climbed to 6.5 percent of GDP in 1983, then decreased gradually to 1 percent in 1990. Actually, the primary deficit, which is a key element in the story, has been cut. Yet, this improvement has been too slow and half-hearted to break the vicious circle of high deficits, higher debt, higher interest rates, and still higher deficits. That, in brief, is the scenario of the 1980s: a dramatically improving private sector; satisfactory real growth; a sharp reduction of inflation; but a heavier burden of public debt, with only partial improvement in the reduction of primary deficit.

The Two-Sided Coin of Monetary Policy

By what strategy have the monetary authorities tried to reconcile the financing of high deficits with an acceptable monetary discipline? The monetary authorities, and the central bank in particular, did not implement just a quantitative monetary policy, aimed at control of the monetary base, they tried to implement a structural or "qualitative" monetary policy, one that would develop the financial structure of the country in order to cope with the huge demand for funds from the public sector, while also modernizing the instruments of monetary control. They sought, of course, to keep the creation of the money base under control. At the same time, they sought to change the rules of the game for the financial sector. They tried to deepen and broaden the financial markets, to channel savings, and household savings in particular, into public securities.

A positive peculiarity of the Italian situation is the high saving propensity of the household. It is important to assess those high fiscal deficits of 11 percent or 12 percent of GDP against the high saving in the household sector, saving of between 20 percent and 21 percent of GDP. If a channel can be activated to transfer a major part of this saving into funding of the public debt, money creation can be reduced and kept under control.

In pursuit of more depth and breadth in the markets, the authorities introduced an enormous amount of financial innovation. They floated new kinds of securities: financially indexed securities and, short-term and medium-term securities. Many new instruments appeared in the financial markets, as well as new intermediaries. Some years ago, I wrote an article reviewing this process of financial innovation in Italy, which I called a lopsided process. It was lopsided because the public sector was the major, and almost the only, innovator. The reason was simply because its appetite for funds was so huge that it had to find new sources of funds.

So, this broadening of the markets, to channel more private saving into public debt, was the first major element of the monetary strategy.

The central bank, in particular, also tried to improve instruments of monetary control, to regain some maneuvering room for interest rate policy. One of the more significant developments in this direction was the so-called divorce in 1981 between the treasury and the Bank of Italy, whereby the central bank discontinued the commitment to act as the residual buyer of treasury bills at auctions of public securities. This divorce, which strengthened the role of the central bank in setting short-term interest rates, wrought a crucial change in the conduct of monetary policy in Italy.

These were the broad directions of policy; now we come to the results. The effort to channel private saving into public debt was a major success. The distribution of public securities in the economy changed dramatically. In the late 1970s, only about 20 percent of public securities in circulation was held in private sector portfolios; by the late 1980s, it had increased to more than 70 percent.

Of course, concomitant with the increase in private sector holdings was an equally dramatic decrease in the share of public securities held by commercial banks and the central bank. This redistribution meant less creation of base money and broad money. And in fact, money creation decelerated throughout the decade. In 1984, the Bank of Italy began to announce money targets, such as growth targets for M2 and for credit to the private sector. Although the credit target usually overshot, the M2 money target was almost always hit. The predominant tool for controlling money growth was interest rate policy, as permanent credit ceilings on bank loans were removed in 1983.

Real interest rates had, for the most part, been negative in the late 1970s. After the credit and monetary crunch at the beginning of the 1980s, real interest rates jumped to relatively high positive levels. Over the remainder of the decade, real rates remained high, although they showed a slight declining trend from the early highs. This was the precondition for marketing such a huge amount of public debt to the private sector. Even today, real interest rates in Italy remain a bit higher than in other major industrial countries. The differential, by the way, explains the huge inflows of capital into Italy during the more recent years. These relatively high real interest rates notwithstanding, Italy continued to enjoy a good performance of private investment.

Last, but not least, among the major results of the strategy has been the gradual liberalization of foreign exchange controls. We took the final step just this year, 1990. Since last May, capital controls have been completely removed, even on short-term capital movements. This liberalization is a crucial element of the story; from now on, our financial markets will not be protected from external competition by artificial barriers.

The increasing financial openness of the Italian economy has thus far brought huge capital inflows. The reason, simply enough, is the higher real interest rate, relative to other countries, combined with the prevailing expectation of exchange rate stability. For foreign investors, Italian financial markets provide good buys. Bonds, treasury bills, and treasury certificates, all with relatively high yields, are plentiful.

The results summarized above represent the positive aspects of the Italian situation. But the coin has a tarnished side. Of the two problems I want to discuss, one is more technical, the other is more general. The technical point concerns the implications of the shortened average maturity of Italy's public debt. To market that enormous amount of debt to the private sector during a period of high and variable inflation rates, the treasury had to accept a major shortening of maturities. This occurred not only as a direct shortening, by which I mean an increasing amount of treasury bills, for instance, but also as an indirect shortening. The treasury issued large quantities of so-called treasury certificates with maturities of between 4 and 7 years. Their yield is linked, however, to short-term rates, to the treasury bill rate; so the interest payments on them reflect the movement of short-term rates.

Today the average maturity on public debt is about 2.5 years. That is not drastically short, although it is much shorter than the average maturity some years ago. Still, a shorter average maturity of the public debt creates special pressures on monetary policy. At the same level of debt and of annual deficit, a shorter average maturity means that the debt stock must be recycled more frequently. The yearly gross issues of public securities in Italy reach 50 percent of GDP, against 10 percent in France, 5 percent in the United Kingdom, and 3 percent in Germany. Each month, Italy's public issues equal 4–5 percent of GDP—ten times the average stock of bank reserves. This high rate of turnover is a major threat to monetary policy. If a treasury bill auction is not completed satisfactorily, a serious problem of monetary control ensues. If not enough bills or bonds are sold in a month, bank reserves may get out of control. So refinancing of the debt becomes a continual and delicate game.

For the economy as a whole, the situation represents a high degree of financial fragility. The system is acutely exposed to external shocks from abroad and from changing expectations in domestic markets. This is one cost Italy has paid and will continue to pay for such a delicate equilibrium, which so far has been maintained but remains a cost and a threat for the future.

Now, to the second and more general point. Italy has had a primary deficit since 1965. In fact, for the last twenty-five years interest payments on the public debt have been covered not by taxes but by the issue of new securities. In this situation, public debt is no longer "irrelevant" in the Ricardo-Barro sense. Private agents in the economy consider their holdings of public debt as net wealth and its stream of interest payments as part of their disposable income, with expansionary effects on their spending decisions.

In addition, neither does the Keynesian description of interest payments measuring the conflict between producers and rentiers hold true. The absence of a conflict of interest between taxpayers and recipients of interest payments weakens the pressure of public opinion on government and parliament to cut the deficit and act to consolidate public finance.

Solutions

What solutions to these problems are possible? For a number of years now, the central bank has been insisting that the primary deficit must be cut and indeed, reversed into a primary surplus. If this first step is achieved, one can expect a reinforcing circle of improvements. Less demand pressure on the financial markets, because of the reduced deficit, would lessen pressure on interest rates. Since interest payments at short-term rates are a major component of the deficits, lower interest rates would further lower the overall deficit, and so on. It is easy to say that the starting point for readjustment should be cutting or even reversing the primary deficit, but it is difficult to do. In the end, the issues are sociopolitical and require a sociopolitical decision. If the country really wants to do this, it must choose to pay more in taxes or to cut public expenditure.

Italy has lately made some progress in the right direction. The Government plans to reverse the primary deficit into a (small) primary surplus the next fiscal year. The complete liberalization of capital movements, the decision to keep the lira within the narrow band of the EMS, and the expected further steps ahead in monetary policy coordination among European countries made it necessary to accelerate the process of fiscal consolidation. By the end of the so-called stage one of the European economic and monetary union, the monetary financing of fiscal deficits will not be allowed and deficits themselves will be limited to the financing of public investments.

Will this be the end of the story? The end of the conflict between fiscal and monetary policies? I do not think it will be an easy task to achieve this result, but certainly the proposed new rules of the game will make an appropriate policy mix easier to implement. If interest rates are given over to stabilizing the exchange rate within the EMS band, another instrument is needed to affect demand: fiscal policy. But the reabsorption of the structural deficit is the precondition for giving back to the fiscal instrument the degree of flexibility necessary for controlling the economy over the short term. With sound public finances and a monetary policy explicitly geared to maintaining price stability, we might see also in this area the end of the cold war, the long cold war, between the public sector and monetary discipline.

2

The Central Bank's Role in Financial Sector Development

DEENA KHATKHATE*

Ideas about the central bank and its role in the economy have gone through various phases during the last four decades. In the 1950s when economic development of the developing countries came to the forefront, the role envisaged for the central bank in the old vintage models of central banking in highly industrial countries was questioned on the ground that it would be too negative to deal with the problems of development. In regulating monetary expansion, earlier central banking principles and praxis used the interest rate as a price of saving and treated all borrowers uniformly, regardless of their ability to bear the burden of loans. It was soon realized that the reach of central banking in economies that are either modernizing or are about to do so would be limited without adequate development of the financial system, both in size and diversity.

It was this desideratum that shaped the concept of central banking in newly developing countries. The accent was on "the strategic or promotional objectives . . . relating to the development of the financial structure and improving the credit access of underbanked sectors." As one perceptive economist stated: "A central bank may be regarded as a highly specialized autonomous bureau for monitoring and developing the financial system which is akin to "octopoid," that is, spatially spread, public utility selling prized services to its customers."[1] Two sources provided support for this promotional role of the central bank—one is based on economic theory of externalities and the practices followed by some of the highly developed countries.

---

*The author is a Consultant at the World Bank.

[1]Chandavarkar (1988), pp. 4–5.

In the context of growth, money is treated as part of wealth, which is considered to compete with accumulation of physical capital. Since output growth is crucially dependent on physical capital, accumulation of money balances is deemed unproductive, and an appropriate policy contributing to output and growth is to tax the accumulation of money balances by expanding the money supply. The other is based on widespread recourse in most developing countries to low interest rate policies through ceilings on interest rates and credit allocation by guidance of the central banks of governments concerned. Both of these approaches to credit policy were motivated by the "market failures" arguments and the inadequacy of the financial environment to facilitate sharing the risks involved in new investment. Social rates of returns on investment tend to diverge from the private rates of return; they can be equalized only through intervention of one kind or another. Likewise, the type of financial system the developing countries have does not prevent risky investment. As a result, ceilings on nominal interest rates paid and received by banks and the allocation of credit were managed to benefit socially productive activity.

The practical rationale for promotional activities of the central bank emanated from what the central banks of advanced countries like Italy, Japan, the Netherlands, Sweden, and Germany had done, whether or not their central banking statutes permitted or prohibited certain types of activities. The central banks of these countries have used various techniques, such as asset reserve requirements and government borrowing and relending with or without interest rate subsidies to preferred sectors, such as agriculture, housing, exports, small businesses, and underdeveloped regions. These promotional measures are sought to be justified on the ground that the sectors are typically those that tend to suffer disproportionately from credit restrictions arising from deflationary policies.

As often happens in the real world, virtue carried to excess ceases to be a virtue. The same occurs with the promotional policies of a central bank. The preferential interest rates become pervasive to the extent that the central bank becomes the source of money for use by favored sectors of the economy. It also leads to the shrinkage of savings in the economy. Diversified credit programs not only exacerbate inflationary pressure but also grossly distort the economy, weaken the instruments of monetary control, and eventually involve the banking system in financial distress. As a consequence, a swing occurs in the opinion of both policymakers and academics away from the promotional aspects of central banking to "demotional" financial policies—if such an expression can be coined. The latter, well articulated in what is commonly described as financial liberalization, has taken central banking to the other extreme, so much so that it is likely to run the same risk of failure as earlier promotional policies of the central bank.

I will present in capsule form why financial sector development is an integral part of economic development, which is sought to be promoted by a central bank as a matter of deliberate policy. I will then emphasize how that policy leads to the command approach to monetary or central banking policy formulation and, finally, end by pointing out some danger spots in totally reversing promotional policies. The last point is important because the experiences of several countries, particularly those in Latin America, have conclusively shown that financial liberalization introduced at wrong times disregards the benign aspects of intervention for prudential purposes by the central bank and the government.

Money in the Development Process

There is renewed appreciation of the role of money in the development process, aided in part by recent theoretical and empirical insights derived from the accumulated experiences of several developing countries.[2] Importance is attributed to money as a conduit for savings from those who have it in excess to the potential investors so central to the development process. Money is one among many financial assets used to transfer savings, which means that development of a financial system that generates and diversifies financial assets is necessary for accelerating economic development; the central bank, at the apex of such a system, has a crucial role in shaping it.

Theories underlying money's role in the development process vary according to the view taken toward the determination of the investment rate in developing countries. In subsistence economies, savers and investors tend to be identical. In the absence of financial markets, private investment depends heavily on prior self-saving. Before accelerating the pace of development, internal financial constraints must be broken. Fiscal policies to encourage private saving and heavy reliance on government investment are typical efforts to overcome inefficient self-finance in developing countries.

Investment can also be initiated by recourse to credit creation, which renders money and credit more of a causal factor. With the conditions prevailing in developing countries, such credit-induced investment is a sure prescription for inflation. In theory, there can be counteracting forces. Given the level of money wages, profits would increase in relation to the gross national income when prices rise, and

[2]Khatkhate (1982).

if the propensity to save of profit earners is higher than that of wage earners, the aggregate saving ratio would tend to rise to catch up with the raised level of investment. But the mechanism by which the saving ratio moves is not so automatic and smooth as often implied. When prices rise, destabilizing price expectations tend to accentuate inflationary pressure, thereby depressing the profit and saving ratios.

If the return is unattractive, less is saved than might be. The return is usually low when saving is for self-investment or lending in the very limited "neighborhood market." Financial assets in this environment will be scarce and illiquid. On the other side, many potentially high-yielding investments are never made because funds are insufficient; what funds are available flow instead into less productive but more familiar and secure hands. Earlier analyses on aggregate saving and investment obscured these problems of efficiently utilizing what is saved. Individual economic units endowed with entrepreneurial talent and drive are not generally the same units that have surplus resources to invest. What is crucial, from the point of view of the development process, is the existence of channels through which the resources of surplus units can be transmitted to those in greatest need of those resources. Without such channels, economic growth fails to reach feasible rates as saving either remains sterile or is misallocated. It is in establishing such channels and in improving their efficiency that the central bank comes into its own.

Bank Intermediation and Economic Development

In the early stages of economic development, intersectoral flows take place through direct lending. That is, surpluses from savers in one sector are lent directly on the basis of close contacts with investors in other sectors; no paper, as such, is used in mediating these transactions. The market for credit by this direct form of lending is described as an unorganized credit market. As the economy expands, personal contacts dwindle and informal, direct forms of lending and borrowing are substituted more and more by indirect forms involving the use of money. Replacement of direct lending by bank intermediation raises the ratio of money to national income, which implies a release of real resources. It follows that in such a context money creation itself is the channel of transferring surplus saving to investing sectors. The real resources freed in this way reflect the real quantity of money willingly held and hence cannot be forced by simply supplying more nominal money. Monetization is a complex process, however, involving public habits, as well as the "quality" of the available monetary assets.

The saving units or sectors accumulate financial claims on the investing units, or on financial intermediaries which then transmit the funds to the investing units. Over time, these modes of lending lead to an ever-growing ratio of financial assets of all kinds to income and wealth with a concomitant rise in saving and investment ratios. Savers and investors, who hitherto have been scattered and isolated from each other, are joined together by various kinds of credit instruments and financial institutions. In brief, this implies that the market for credit becomes organized, wide, and unified—fully exposed to the price mechanism.

Issues of central banking policies are thus thrown into sharper focus. If the development of the economy is to be accelerated, it is essential that the resources saved by surplus sectors be put to the most productive uses and that the amount of such surpluses be increased. Since both of these require providing more attractive financial assets for surplus units as a repository of transferable savings, policies should be such as to supply the financial assets that are demanded by the surplus sectors.

The flow of funds between various economic units creates assets and liabilities in the process, but the structure of these assets and liabilities is not the same in every phase of economic development. Empirical evidence suggests that the income elasticity of demand for money, however defined, is inversely related to the state of development of money and capital markets. This means that in the early stages of development, when the economy is poorly equipped with a financial system, money is most sought after as a repository of wealth. As credit markets become better organized, the range of assets for holding saving is widened to include bonds, shares, etc. Desire for a variegated pattern of financial assets is motivated by such factors as risk aversion of savers (lenders) in addition to their transaction and liquidity needs. Hence, financial assets other than money need to be created if saving is to be fully mobilized for financing investment.

The objective is not simply to increase aggregate saving so much as to enlarge the amount of transferable saving. This can be achieved through altering the structure of saving of the surplus spending units, which in developing countries are, by and large, in the household sector. Most of the saving of the units in the household sector is generally invested in physical assets, such as goods or gold, which contribute little or nothing to economic growth. Much of saving invested in business enterprises is even wasted (i.e., it yields a lower return than it could), as fragmented or nonexistent financial markets force savers to invest excessively in their own activities. There is a compelling need for the ratio of financial assets to total saving of the household sector to grow as fast as possible.

Economic growth means increased productive capability. This requires more and better tools and equipment and a more skilled labor force; without resources being made available, these needs cannot be met. On the other hand, all the resources in the world will contribute nothing to economic growth if not used productively. The growth impact of given resources (saving) will reflect the efficiency with which they are utilized. Money and financial assets in general stand at the center of this process; they are the vital link.

Interest Rate and Credit Policies

As noted earlier, the promotional aspects of central banking took two predominant forms—subsidized interest rate policy and directed credit programs to boost the growth of the disadvantaged sectors of the economy. Both policies, however, stultified the growth of the financial system. During 1974–85, in developing countries with positive real interest rates, the ratio of gross domestic product (GDP) to M3, which can be taken as representing the depth of the financial system, increased by 40.3 percent as against 34.0 and 30.0 percent, respectively, in the case of countries with moderately and strongly negative real interest rates. The same could be said about the inflation rate in these countries, which was higher in those with subsidized interest rates than those without them. Similar is the story of the promotional policies directed toward priority sectors, which benefitted from lax lending standards and poor monitoring of use of credits.

Special credit programs were widespread in most countries. In Pakistan, about 70 percent of new lending by the leading national banks was targeted by the government through the central bank. In India, the technique of directed credit employed relies on setting margins—quantum in terms of proportion of total credit and the interest rate subsidy. The proportion of such credit has varied over the years, depending on public policy objectives, and is currently around 40 percent of total credit. These credits are costly operations, as they involve a heavy subsidy estimated to be about 6.6 percent of banks' earnings. The accumulation of bad and doubtful debts, estimated to be roughly 25–30 percent of deposits, has almost wiped out the entire capital base of several banks. In Yugoslavia, about 58 percent of short-term loans were directed credits; in Brazil, it was 70 percent.

Whatever the consequences of these directed credit programs for the growth of the economies and the distribution of income, their impact on the viability of the financial systems and their growth has been anything but salutary. Many directed credits have become nonperforming loans. The ability to borrow at cheap rates encouraged less productive investment. Those who borrowed for projects with low financial return could not repay their loans. In other cases, borrowers willingly defaulted: they believed that because their credit was in a favored category, no action could be taken. The distorted allocation of resources and the erosion of financial discipline have left financial intermediation unprofitable and, in many cases, have left financial intermediaries insolvent. Extensive refinancing schemes at low interest rates have reduced the need for intermediaries to mobilize resources on their own, leading to a lower level of financial intermediation. Moreover, by encouraging firms to borrow from banks, directed credit programs have impeded the development of capital markets.

Open Market Operations and Reserve Requirements

Perhaps the most deleterious impact of directed credit is felt on the effectiveness of central banking policy in developing countries. Central banking policy, or, broadly interpreted, monetary policy, has differed considerably from the normal concept of monetary policy that is identified with the regulation of cost and availability of credit. Its identity as an independent tool has been erased; it has come to be operated as an adjunct of an overall economic policy that remains always strongly interventionist in these countries. In actual practice, it has come to be only a penumbra of fiscal policy, with greater accent on direct methods of control. Occasional departures from this mold of monetary policy occur, but the basic tenor continues. In fact, such attempts at change only reveal how difficult it is to even slightly modify the command nature of monetary policy without having to liberalize the whole system.

This can be illustrated by referring to two familiar instruments of central banking policy—open market operations and reserve requirements. Of these, the first one, apart from having cosmetic value, serves more as a tool of fiscal policy rather than of monetary policy. It is a misnomer to describe open market operations in developing countries as a monetary policy instrument.

> Open market operations are conducted by a central bank mainly with a view to directly or indirectly affect the reserves of banks and thereby the extent of monetary expansion and in the process to create and maintain a desired pattern of yields on government securities and generally to help the government raise resources from the capital market. Thus, this policy instrument has two aspects viz. the monetary policy aspect and the

> fiscal aspect. For the conduct of open market operations as a monetary instrument, the market for government securities should be well organized, broad-based and deep, so that the central bank is in a position to sell and buy securities to the extent it considers desirable. A prerequisite for the emergence of such markets is that the rate of interest offered on government securities is competitive. Since these conditions are not met by the Indian capital market, open market operations are of minor importance as a monetary instrument though they serve as an adjunct of fiscal policy in India to some extent.[3]

Government securities are held mainly by the banking system and other institutions, such as government-owned insurance companies and provident funds, in compliance with statutory requirements. In a way, these holdings are a vehicle for providing priority credit; the priority sector in this case being the government and other public sector enterprises. Since government bonds bear a lower yield than that on other comparable financial assets, there is an implicit interest rate subsidy involved. It is clear that the directed credit programs tend to weaken monetary policy, apart from stunting the growth of the financial system.

When open market operations are not used as a monetary policy instrument and a subsidized interest rate regime is pervasive, the central bank relies on reserve requirements for monetary policy purposes. The reserve requirement is also the instrument available to governments for raising fiscal revenues; these aspects make its extensive use more convenient. Governments in developing countries perpetually need revenue sources for meeting their current and developmental expenditures. Fiscal authorities get round these inherent constraints on revenue by imposing reserve requirements. This is why high reserve requirements of 50 percent and more are imposed in most developing countries, especially those in Latin America. In this sense, reserve requirements constitute a tax on the banking system. There is, however, a constant conflict between two objectives of reserve requirements—that of monetary policy and of fiscal policy; experience shows that the fiscal policy objective emerges often as the winner, with an adverse impact on financial development.

Liberalization of the Financial System

What I have mentioned so far suggests that the excess of promotional policies adopted by the central banking authorities in several countries has repressed the financial system and enfeebled monetary

[3]Reserve Bank of India (1985), pp. 262–63.

policy instruments. For this reason, promotional policies need to be tempered by allowing the system to function in a more liberal atmosphere, unhampered by frequent and stifling interventionist policies; however, just as the excess of promotional central banking policies is undesirable, the excess of demotional policies, or financial liberalization, is also not warranted. The experience of countries with financial liberalization is not uniform nor always successful. There have been as stark failures, particularly in Latin America, as there have been impressive successes, as in Korea, Indonesia, and Malaysia. Much can be learned from these experiences by other countries who may like to replicate similar financial liberalization policies.

There are six lessons to be drawn from financial liberalization across countries. One of the most important is that price stability and, more broadly, macroeconomic stability, is the linchpin of successful liberalization, not the deregulation of interest rates per se, especially when the countries undergoing financial reforms have shallow financial markets.[4] The experiences of the Philippines, Malaysia, Indonesia, South Korea, and the Southern Cone countries underscore the importance of price stability in two different ways. In the first two countries, the level of inflation was a determining factor in attaining positive interest rates. The adjustment in real interest rates lagged when inflation was declining, although interest rates were fully liberalized. The resulting high interest rates led to widespread insolvency of firms with high-gearing ratios, as in Indonesia, or to an economy on a downward slope, as in the Philippines. In South Korea, although interest rates were administered by the Government, interest rates were substantially positive and stable because of price stability and the flexibility with which nominal interest rates were adjusted according to the movement of inflation. At the other extreme, the inconsistent macroeconomic policies of the Southern Cone countries rendered their economic system unstable and vulnerable to shocks; their economies could not inhale the whiff of financial liberalization policies. The resulting adverse expectations led to unsustainable high real interest rates.

Financial liberalization, if not properly designed, may cause instability of the financial system, which in turn may magnify macroeconomic instability. In Chile, Argentina, and Uruguay, preannounced exchange rate policies were reasonably credible at the beginning of liberalization, but once the monetary consequences of financial sector instability became clear, credibility began to crumble.[5] In Chile's case,

[4]Cho and Khatkhate (1989).
[5]Ibid.

it was clear that the Government could buttress the financial position of banks by borrowing abroad, but once it reached its limit (which it did in 1981 when it began losing its foreign reserves), the Central Bank extended massive financial assistance to financial institutions and contributed to the growth in base money. As a result, the inflationary expectations, curtailment of which was the main objective of the stabilization policy, resurged. In Argentina, it is true that the fiscal deficit was an important factor, but its impact was evident when the Central Bank had to infuse a large amount of credit to bail out the financial institutions.

Second, when capital movement is completely free in an economy where the financial market is relatively small, liberalizing domestic interest rates makes them sensitive to the pressures of expectations of foreign exchange movement. This often leads to volatile and high domestic interest rates, which may significantly diverge from the long-run equilibrium level. On the other hand, if a government attempts to control domestic interest rates, it may risk massive capital flight. The best approach may be to achieve a stable macroeconomic environment that will eliminate any abrupt changes in expectations about exchange rate movement. When this is not possible, a country with a small and vulnerable financial market may choose a second-best approach of continuing some restrictions on the capital account and maintaining interest rates. For example, Korea faced major macroeconomic imbalances and political uncertainty in the ear'y 1980s; had the Government fully liberalized the capital account and domestic interest rates then, it might have faced very high domestic interest rates, if not massive capital flight, and even more serious macroeconomic instability in the financial system. This suggests that when the domestic economy is unstable or when the depth of the domestic financial sector is inadequate, a country may maintain control over its capital account and domestic interest rates while flexibly adjusting the latter to the inflation rate and attempting to stabilize the inflation rate.

Third, financial liberalization centered on the banking system seems to have limitations. These are related to two important features of banking institutions; that is, the banking sector performs both the monetary and financial intermediation functions. The two functions do not work in the same direction, especially when macroeconomic imbalances arise. Often, the growth of liabilities and assets of the banking system is constrained by a tight monetary policy. When financial liberalization policy is pursued concurrently with stabilization policy, the intended goal of the policy—to enhance the financial intermediation role of banks—is weakened by the monetary policy directed toward containing inflation. In South Korea, the Government constrained domestic credit and controlled the growth of M2, although banks were privatized and allowed greater management autonomy and competition; however, owing to the policy of encouraging competition and innovation in the nonbanking financial institutions and securities market, growth of the financial sector was achieved through the expansion of the nonbanking financial sector. In the Philippines, the aggressive monetary policy to mop up liquidity, by issuing high-yield treasury bills and central bank bills, forced high interest rates in the banking system; to avoid massive disintermediation, the banks had to match their interest rates. The growth of the banking system was also directly limited by the tight monetary policy of the Government. In Malaysia, the liquidity of the banking system, which was greatly influenced by the restrictive monetary policy, determined the level of interest rates to a large extent, and their resulting high level deterred new investment. In Indonesia, a shrinkage of liquidity credits at the beginning of the reform accentuated the rise in interest rates, which in turn led to expansion of nonperforming loans via the profit squeeze on the borrowing corporate sector.

The other feature of the banking system stems from the banks' debt intermediation function whereby short-term fixed fee liabilities (deposits) are transformed into long-term fixed fee assets (loans). This function places banks at the risk of runs and insolvencies in the absence of appropriate government supervision and regulation. In addition, the dominance of debt intermediation in financial markets makes corporate firms (when they are highly leveraged) vulnerable to economic downturns and increases in interest rates. This has continuously called for some kind of government intervention in bank-oriented financial systems. The South Korean Government, despite its intention, maintained control over bank interest rates and intervened in credit allocation to prevent massive bankruptcies of corporate firms in the early 1980s when its economy was shaky and banks were burdened with increasing arrears. At the other extreme were the Latin American countries and the Philippines, which were involved in a massive restructuring of banks and corporate firms and experienced sharp credit and monetary expansion.

A fourth important lesson to be drawn from financial reform experiences is that excessively high positive real interest rates are as disequilibrating as are heavily repressed negative real interest rates. Experiences in the financially reformed countries have dramatized the contradiction between the need to maintain a high and positive real interest rate as a reward for savers and the imperative to lower the cost of funds to finance new investment. In the imperfect and oligopolistic money and credit markets characteristic of developing countries, a sudden dose of liberalization often leads to the overshooting of both nominal and real interest rates, unwarranted by the "fundamentals" when financial reform, especially interest rate deregulation, is undertaken amid high and fluctuating inflation rates. The resulting real interest rates often exceed the marginal return to capital, as happened in the Latin American countries, the Philippines, and Indonesia and led to increasing arrearage in the banking system. There is moral hazard when firms borrow to pay interest or simply to stave off bankruptcy rather than to invest or to finance working capital. Domestic investment tends to become hostage to high interest rates and, consequently, what is first the corporate sector's crisis becomes a system-wide crisis. South Korea tried to cushion high interest rates by slowing implementation of reform and maintaining interest rate controls and selected credit programs; the latter were gradually phased out. Indonesia backtracked in regard to phasing out liquidity credits under which loans to certain sectors were subsidized, and Sri Lanka persisted with special credit programs even to the present.

Fifth, financial liberalization assumes that the fully liberalized financial system will function optimally. It should be recognized, however, that in economies that have a long history of financial repression, the participants, be they bank managers, borrowers, lenders, or public servants, are not trained in new ways of dealing with a liberal and competitive system. For instance, it was suggested that in Chile's case some of the blame for a disastrous financial crisis resided "in little experience existing in the country in the management of a freer financial system."[6] The concept of "an associative heuristic" implies that the individual's caution is pronounced in the immediate aftermath of a disaster and tends to diminish as time passes and memory of disaster fades. Inability to asses risk and insufficient capacity to cope with adverse situations prevented the liberalization program from succeeding to the desired extent in Chile and other Latin American countries. Had these policies been unleashed gradually, those at the helm of the financial institutions (and others associated with them in some capacity) would have adjusted and become familiar with the new tasks over time. In Indonesia, training of public servants and financial managers before full and comprehensive liberalization has improved results.

Closely related to the above is the need to set up a well-planned financial infrastructure with provision for information flow, legal and accounting systems, and an appropriate regulatory system to monitor it carefully and continuously. Otherwise, financial liberalization will

---

[6]Cho and Khatkhate (1989), p. 104.

fail in its main purpose: to orient the financial system toward greater efficiency, competition, and effectiveness. For banks, it is not always possible to distinguish a necessary control for monetary stability purposes from a supernumerary regulation affecting credit allocation, but it is imperative that essential regulation be strictly enforced because of the oligopolistic nature of the banking system in several developing countries. It is now generally acknowledged that there is a widespread concentration of banking in developing countries. What is more, in some countries like Chile, the bank-holding company structure is more prominent and adversely affects competition, in opposition to the avowed objective of financial liberalization and deregulation. In the presence of such oligopolistic financial and industrial structures, freedom in transactions is often harnessed to increase the market share by price war. For instance, bank-holding companies increase interest rates on deposits to make inroads in the market for funds; this in turn results in higher loan rates. Since loans are provided to the interlocking firms in which banks have close interest, high interest rates do not affect credit demand. This encourages banks to be even more imprudent because they know that the government cannot allow them to go bankrupt without jeopardizing the entire monetary system. There is thus a moral hazard that provides incentive to banks to lend at very high interest rates in order to reduce liquidity strains. As McKinnon puts it, "the bank is beneficiary of an unfair bet against the government; it gets to keep extraordinary profits without having to pay the full social costs of unusually large losses from risky lending."[7] This underscores the need to strengthen the supervisory apparatus in liberalizing countries so that banks are disciplined in mobilizing deposit and lending operations.

Sixth, the financial reform experience in different types of economies raises a question about how authorities can remove the repressive characteristics of intervention without the disequilibrating shocks that emanate from the complete, once-for-all type of financial reforms. A pragmatic solution may be to evolve a certain set of market-oriented indicators based on fuller information from domestic and foreign sources while taking steps to build the financial infrastructure, reducing the monopoly element in the financial and industrial sectors, etc. In this respect, a great deal can be learned from the Korean and Japanese strategies of financial reform. It also should be recognized that liberalization, even in developed countries, has not brought unmixed blessings. For one thing, after financial liberalization real interest rates in those countries have reached very high levels by his-

---

[7]McKinnon (1988), p. 10.

torical standards and have afflicted their economies and those of the borrowing developing countries. For another, interest rates have been most volatile in recent years. As a result, interest rate risks have been transmitted from financial intermediaries to borrowers to a greater extent than before. The implication is that a gradual process of liberalization in developing countries is preferable to the sudden dismantling of all regulations recognized to be repressive.

Conclusion

We can generalize the role of central banks in financial sector development, thus: central banks can and should promote, by every possible means, the development of the financial system by answering the variegated needs of savers and investors. But in doing so, they should not exceed the limits of intervention dictated by prudence, efficiency, and effectiveness. If, perchance, limits are transgressed, the central bank should not swing to the other extreme of total withdrawal from the concerns for financial system development. What should be remembered is that "Nothing fails like excess."

Bibliography

Chandavarkar, Anand, "Promotional Role of Central Banks," *International Journal of Development Banking* (Bombay), Vol. 6 (January 1988), pp. 3–14.

Cho, Yoon-Je, and Deena Khatkhate, "Lessons of Financial Liberalization in Asia: A Comparative Study," World Bank Discussion Papers, No. 50 (mimeographed, Washington: The World Bank, 1989).

Khatkhate, Deena, "Practical Issues and Problems Facing a Newly Established Central Bank," paper presented at the IMF Central Banking Seminar held in Washington, June 1982.

———, "Use of Monetary Instruments and Management in Developing Countries," *International Journal of Development Banking* (Bombay), Vol. 6 (January 1988), pp. 15–23.

McKinnon, Ronald I., *Financial Liberalization and Economic Development: A Reassessment of Interest Rate Policies in Asia and Latin America* (Panama City: International Center for Economic Growth, 1988).

Reserve Bank of India, *Report of the Committee to Review the Working of the Monetary System* (Bombay, 1985).

World Bank, *World Development Report, 1989* (Washington, 1989).

3

Clearing and Payment Systems: The Central Bank's Role

BRUCE J. SUMMERS*

Two themes of the central banking seminar are directly relevant to consideration of payment system issues. One is the interdependencies of different functions normally performed by a central bank. In this regard, I know of no other aspect of the central bank's responsibility that requires more cooperation and coordination among the various central banking disciplines than the payment system does. A second theme is the role of the central bank in dealing with financial crises. Stress on a nation's payment system is often one of the earliest and most direct manifestations of financial crisis. Indeed, the payment system may be a direct channel through which liquidity and credit problems are transferred from one participant in the financial system to another. Such transfers have the potential to create systemic liquidity and credit problems that are of direct concern to the central bank. As a result, central banks are increasingly focusing on proper safeguards to allow payment system participants to control not only their risk, but also to prevent the contagion of systemic risk.

Because it has relevance for a range of central bank disciplines and functions and because it can become a focus of crisis management, the payment system does indeed deserve a prominent place in the thinking of central bankers. Yet, until the last decade or so, interest in payment system issues has been of secondary importance on the cen-

---

*The author is Deputy Director, Division of Reserve Bank Operations and Payment Systems, Board of Governors of the Federal Reserve System. The author has benefitted from comments made by colleagues in the Federal Reserve System and in several other central banks. Special appreciation is due to Jeffrey C. Marquardt and Patrick M. Parkinson for the critical review they have provided since the inception of the paper. A version of this paper was published in *Federal Reserve Bulletin* (Washington), Vol. 77 (February 1991), pp. 81–91.

tral banking agenda. The payment system has traditionally been almost the exclusive province of central bank staff members with operations and automation responsibilities, reflecting the view that the payment system is essentially a mechanical process. Along these lines, the literature on the payment system has traditionally been slanted toward analyses of economic efficiency, with much of the literature framed in the context of the economics of the firm. The payment system has now entered the mainstream for central bankers, although, admittedly, the degree of interest varies from country to country.

This paper has three parts. First, to provide a common frame of reference, I develop a conceptual model of the payment system, with special reference to the essential role of the central bank. Second, I discuss the implications of the public policy and supervisory roles of the central bank in the payment system. These implications include (1) the need to establish public policies to guide the structure of newly developing private clearing and settlement arrangements, in terms of both their integrity and efficiency, and (2) the need for supervision of private clearing arrangements, not only domestically, but also for cross-border systems, in close cooperation with foreign central banks. Finally, I examine the role of the central bank as operator of the large-value, interbank payment mechanism. Special attention is given to the implications of the central bank's role as a source of intra-day liquidity to the financial system and to the "safety net" attributes associated with access to the large-value transfer mechanism.

Model of the Payment System

In the simplest terms, the payment system is the apparatus through which obligations incurred as a result of economic activity are discharged through transfers of monetary value. The payment system is used mainly for simple day-to-day activities, such as retail transactions, that may be paid by using a very rudimentary, but nonetheless very effective, payment mechanism, such as cash.[1] If the obligation is not discharged immediately (or in "real time" to use technical language) by using cash, then an alternative payment instrument, such as a paper or electronic credit or debit order, must be used. For payment

[1]Although cash payments may appear rudimentary, they actually embody essential features that are sought in more sophisticated electronic payment mechanisms, including large-value funds transfer systems. When an obligation is discharged by using cash, and assuming there is confidence in the government issuing the cash, the payment and final settlement are simultaneous and immediate. Apart from the physical restrictions that make cash payments practical only for small-value transactions, much may be learned from the principles embodied in the use of this form of payment. See Goodfriend (1990).

orders, the process of discharging the obligation can be divided conceptually into two parts. The first part is the clearing process in which payment information is conveyed from the payor to the payee, probably through intermediary banks. The second part is settlement in which the actual transfer of value associated with the payment order is made, generally not with cash but with a claim on a bank.

The payment system is also used to settle complex and large-value transactions, such as those arising from trading in financial instruments and their derivative products, and for other "commodities." The markets for such instruments are very efficient: In some cases, assets are held for only a few hours or minutes. The size of individual transactions may also be very large: The average secondary market trade in U.S. Government securities, for example, is about $9 million. These markets therefore have rapid turnover of high-value transactions. Accordingly, while the model of clearing and settlement described here applies to large-value payments, the form the payment process takes has become rather specialized, often involving clearing organizations that ensure that payment in good funds is made against delivery for the contract in question (delivery-versus-payment systems) and that increasingly perform a multilateral netting of such contracts among those trading in the instruments to reduce the total value of individual deliveries and payments that must be completed.[2]

In this simple model of the payment process (Figure 1) economic activity gives rise to an obligation to perform on a contract. In many cases, the contract may specify the terms regarding the form of payment, including both timing and type of instrument used. As noted, discharge of an obligation using payment methods other than cash involves clearing the payment order, including the transfer, processing, and recording of payment instructions on the books of the institutions holding the accounts of the payor and the payee.

For most unspecialized transactions (right-hand side of Figure 1), each individual obligation is treated separately for purposes of clearing and settlement. When such obligations are handled and recorded individually, they are known as gross transactions, which receive gross settlement on the books of the settlement entity. Specialized transactions (left-hand side of Figure 1), which may include those for various classes of securities and equities and their derivative products, rely on traditional payment mechanisms for final settlement but increasingly involve the preliminary step of netting. Netting is a process in which gross obligations between two (bilateral) or more (multilateral) entities are settled by a single transfer of the net amount of funds or goods due

[2]See Parkinson (1990).

Figure 1. Conceptual Model of the Payment Process

Economic Activity

Assumption of an Obligation

Trading in goods, services, and financial instruments results in the assumption of an obligation to perform on a contract (to supply or pay for goods, services, or financial instruments). The contract may include specific terms regarding the timing and form of payment.

Payment

Discharge of the Obligation

Specialized ←	Cash or Payment order leading to the transfer of bank balances.	→ Unspecialized
Clearing organizations and systems. Net settlement is increasingly used.	1. Clearing: Transfer and recording of the payment instruction (can be gross, i.e., transaction by transaction, or, if channelled through a specialized clearing organization, net). 2. Settlement: Actual transfer of value to a deposit account at a bank based on the payment instruction. Timing can be • Immediate • Same-day (end-of-day) • Next-day	Traditional payment instructions through the banking system (paper or electronic credit or debit transfers). Gross settlement is the norm.

for each obligor. When properly performed, netting reduces significantly the total value transferred and the number of payment transactions. Properly executed, netting can result in significant reduction of risk, as described below.

Settlement involves the actual transfer of value based on payment instructions, whether gross or net, on the books of private banking institutions, through the use of bank balances, or on the books of the central bank. Commercial banks serve the primary role in the settlement step of the process. Banks are equipped to play the role of payment intermediary for two reasons. First, they hold the accounts of those engaged in economic activity. A second reason, often overlooked, is that banks can provide credit services to payors so that a payor's obligation can be discharged even though it may not have the funds available when the payment is due. If the payor is a good credit risk and agrees to the bank's credit terms, then the bank will complete settlement by transferring value even if the payor is short of funds, thus greatly facilitating the payment process. In essence, banks provide the liquidity to allow the payment process to run smoothly. As intermediaries, banks aggregate payments due to and from each other and often settle payments through their own intermediary, that is, the central bank.

The volume and value of payment transactions in a modern economy with well-developed financial markets have reached the level at which central banks are increasingly relied upon to provide final settlement among banks. Central bank settlement can be immediate, occurring directly upon the processing of a credit payment order, or on the same day, involving a delay until the end of the banking day.[3] As will be explained below, central banks may have a role in providing liquidity support to commercial banks by providing central bank credit either intra-day or at the end of the day, to ensure completion of payments on schedule. Such liquidity support should be consciously managed by the central bank because providing liquidity can easily get out of hand.[4] Short-term "daylight loans" to banks by the central bank, if not repaid by the end of the day, become overnight loans. Thus, a direct connection exists between a central bank's decision to provide daylight credit and the management of its discount or Lombard facility.

Public Policy and Supervisory Roles of the Central Bank

Central banks, although their role in the payment system varies from country to country, have several common areas of concern regarding their countries' payment systems as broadly defined, including both clearing and settlement.

[3]Some markets and central banks still rely on "next-day" settlement, in which the transfers of value nominally occur on a given day but remain provisional—that is, they could be reversed—until some specified time the next day. Next-day settlement is particularly common in securities markets and is being addressed by the Group of Thirty recommendation to move all securities to same-day settlement.

[4]As it has in the United States, where daylight overdrafts on the books of the Federal Reserve banks now total about $70 billion for funds transfers and another $90 billion for book-entry securities transfers.

Execution of Monetary Policy

One area of concern involves the relation between the payment system and the execution of monetary policy. The result of the clearing and settlement process is that an economic actor obtains a bank deposit, which is one component of "money," from another economic actor. The link between economic activity and money occurs via the clearing and settlement process, which in this manner can be seen as having a fundamental role in the execution of central bank policy.[5] Accordingly, central banks should have a special concern about clearing and payment systems for broad reasons of monetary policy implementation.

Stability of the Financial System

Another common area of concern among central banks has to do with the stability of the financial system. This concern leads directly to an interest in the integrity of the payment system, that is, the ability of the payment system to function safely and efficiently even during times of financial stress. Such financial stress may be related to generalized market factors, such as wide swings in asset prices that create difficulty for the "losers" in trading to meet their obligations. Or, financial stress may be related to specific problems with a large participant in the payment system, either a nonfinancial corporation or a bank, to meet its own and, in the case of a bank, possibly its customers' obligations.

As noted earlier, the payment system is one of the first places where financial stress can manifest itself—through the inability of payment system participants to meet their payment obligations. Serious problems involving one or several payment system participants, if contained, should not pose a threat to the safe and efficient functioning of the basic process. Such problems are properly the concern of the central bank in its bank supervisory role. Depending on the nature of the problem, however, financial stress suffered by one or more participants can translate into systemic problems that threaten the overall viability of the payment system. The celebrated case of the failure of

[5]Examples of the effects that malfunctions in the clearing and settlement process, even if due to mundane operational problems, may have for financial markets and central bank policy are not hard to find. In August 1990, a power outage on Wall Street led to disruptions in money market operations, including Fedwire. The disruptions resulted in interest rate swings owing to the inability of banks to move balances efficiently. Similarly, in November 1985 an internal software problem at the Bank of New York involving the securities transfer application led that bank to incur massive daylight overdrafts with the Federal Reserve and an overnight discount window loan of $23 billion.

Bankhaus Herstatt in 1974, for example, illustrates how just one institution's inability to discharge its payment obligations (in this case payment of dollars against deutsche mark in foreign exchange transactions) can seriously affect the positions of other payment system participants.[6] When the financial problems of one or several participants threaten the viability of the entire process, the possibility of systemic risk to the payment system becomes real.

Efficient Operation of the Payment System

The efficient operation of the payment system is another legitimate concern of the central bank and is important on at least two counts. First, the proper handling of payments is a resource-consuming activity that deserves attention on purely economic grounds. In the United States, for example, the annual cost of operating the domestic payment system is estimated at about $60 billion.[7] If the payment process involves substantial participation by the private sector, then we should have confidence that market forces will tend to enhance the efficient operation of the payment system. The introduction of newer technologies with high fixed investment costs, however, may entail some element of increasing returns to scale in the payment-processing aspects of clearing and settlement. To the extent that returns to scale are increasing, the payment process may assume natural monopoly characteristics. In the natural monopoly case, the central bank needs to be knowledgeable about payment-processing operations and the behavior of the natural monopolist that operates the system, including the fees charged and the fairness of the terms of access to the payment infrastructure.

The second reason for the central bank's concern about the efficiency of the payment system is that the functioning of the payment system has implications for the efficiency of the underlying markets that it supports. Some of these markets, such as those for certain

---

[6]The 1974 Herstatt case has given rise to the term "Herstatt risk," which describes the temporal dimension of the credit risk assumed by the counterparty in a foreign exchange deal when payment of one currency becomes final some time before the payment of the second currency is completed. Herstatt risk arises in part because the operating schedules of national payment systems are not synchronized. In addition, there is no mechanism today that offers the benefits of concurrence that could be derived from a delivery-versus-payment mechanism. In the case of the U.S. dollar, final settlement of roughly $425 billion in daily foreign exchange is delayed up to fourteen hours (for deals originated in the Far East) until the final settlement of Clearing House Interbank Payment System (CHIPS) transfers on the books of the Federal Reserve Bank of New York at about 5:30 p.m. eastern time in the United States.

[7]This estimate does not include any imputed cost associated with the risks assumed by banks (including the central bank) in granting credit as part of the payment process. See Humphrey and Berger (1990).

financial instruments, are worldwide. The location of the nucleus of activity for these markets may depend at least in part on the integrity and efficiency of the clearing and settlement process in different countries. Thus, countries that wish to play a role as financial centers must be concerned about the efficient operation of their payment systems.

Central Bank Payment System Operations

The actual operation of payment systems by central banks encompasses a broad range of experience. At one end of the spectrum is the example of the United States, where the Federal Reserve, through the twelve Federal Reserve banks, has been an active operator of both paper and electronic payment mechanisms since the passage of the Federal Reserve Act in 1913. It is estimated that the Federal Reserve handles one third of all checks cleared in the United States and the majority of automated clearing house (ACH) transactions (the ACH is a paperless, small-value, debit-and-credit transfer system). Moreover, the Federal Reserve handles about half of large-value funds transfers and all book-entry securities transfers of U.S. Government and certain agency securities over Fedwire. Since the passage of the Monetary Control Act of 1980, the Federal Reserve has established explicit fees for providing payment services. The Federal Reserve recovers the full costs of these services, including the imputed costs of capital, debt, and taxes a private firm would incur. Federal Reserve payment services are offered in direct competition with the private sector. Revenues generated from providing payment services now total nearly $800 million annually.

The Federal Reserve's dual role of competitor in and regulator of the payment system has been a difficult and almost chronically controversial one. The Congress of the United States mandated a very active operational role for the Federal Reserve in the payment system because of conditions arising from the fractionalized U.S. banking structure, in which true nationwide banking does not exist even today, and because of the geographic size and diversity of the nation. The geography and legal environment in the United States probably create a unique set of conditions. The conditions that influence the extent a central bank's involvement in payment system operations can change with time, however, so that the operating role of the central bank should not necessarily be taken as a constant, but rather as a matter of policy choice influenced by environmental factors.[8]

[8]See Johnson (1990).

Conditions other than geography and banking structure, however, may lead a central bank to play a significant operating role in a nation's payment system. For example, in some nations, such as France, the central bank plays a major operational role in the payment system on behalf of the banking system. In this model, which is probably influenced by economies of scale and national preferences regarding the degree of direct governmental involvement in management of national "utilities," the central bank is the logical entity to provide the payment infrastructure.

At the other end of the spectrum, some central banks play a very minor role in the operation of their nation's payment systems. In Canada and the United Kingdom, for example, payment processing is largely carried out by private enterprises and is governed by a ruling body composed of representatives of the financial services sector. The central bank, while not directly involved in the operations of the payment system, typically plays a coordinating role in governing these arrangements and, under certain terms and conditions, may make its books available for the settlement of payment transactions.

My purely personal point of view, which is conditioned by more than a decade of involvement in the payment system, both as a practitioner and as a policy advisor, is that the benefits of placing operations in the hands of the private sector should not be underestimated. Indeed, in virtually every other market for goods and services, the benefits of competition in ensuring a continuous high standard of performance are best attained through a free market approach. Assuming for the moment that principles governing the safe operation of the payment process are clearly laid out and adequately supervised by the central bank, then, all other things equal, the process should generally work best when ruled by competitive forces in a market environment.

I say "generally" because of the notable exception of the large-value payment mechanism that provides immediate settlement on the books of the central bank. This payment mechanism may be considered an instrument of financial policy and therefore is best controlled by the central bank. It is virtually impossible for the private sector to provide the degree of safety and liquidity for the transfer of money balances that can be provided by the central bank. Interbank systems for the transfer of large amounts of funds are discussed below.

Supervision of Private Clearing and Settlement Systems

The central bank's involvement in establishing principles for, and, when necessary, in supervising and regulating private clearing and settlement arrangements that support large-value transactions, is especially critical. I will not recount here the financial, structural, and operational features that should characterize these systems and in which the central bank must have an essential interest.[9] Most important, however, are features that commit the private participants in the specialized clearing systems, especially multilateral clearing arrangements, to provide guarantees for the final settlement of the net positions that arise from the clearing. Such guarantees must be founded upon carefully constructed entrance criteria for participation in the arrangements. Moreover, members of such clearing arrangements must have the incentives and capabilities to make their own credit judgments about the parties with whom they will do business. In addition, concrete commitments are needed in the form of loss-sharing arrangements backed by either collateral or lines of credit to ensure the liquidity and resources to guarantee settlement in the event of default by one or more participants.

A good deal of analysis is taking place in the United States at the Federal Reserve and in the private sector to refine the principles that should govern private large-value transfer systems, including delivery-versus-payment systems. Recently, the Federal Reserve has given regulatory approval for the operation of private clearing arrangements for U.S. Government securities (Government Securities Clearing Corporation) and for mortgage-backed securities (Participants Trust Company). An arrangement for converting from paper to book-entry form clearing and settling commercial paper transactions has been started by the Depository Trust Company. Finally, the members of the Clearing House Interbank Payment System (CHIPS) have adopted a system of settlement guarantees for that large-value funds transfer system.

The principles underlying the proper operation of private clearing and settlement arrangements are universal. Indeed, the central banks of the Group of Ten (G-10) countries have recently adopted international minimum standards to guide the operation of cross-border and multicurrency interbank netting and clearing arrangements.[10] The central banks of the Group of Ten have also recognized the need to oversee the operation of significant interbank netting arrangements and have established principles for cooperation among themselves when such arrangements operate across borders.

---

[9]For an excellent review of these features, see the May 1988 address given by E. Gerald Corrigan at the Williamsburg payments symposium sponsored by the Federal Reserve Bank of Richmond. See Corrigan (1990).

[10]See Bank for International Settlements (1990).

Clearly, a component of the financial system as important as the payment system should not go unsupervised. Active involvement by the central bank in developing the principles under which private clearing arrangements operate is the most important role in supervision of the payment system.

An important method for ensuring compliance with sound payment system principles is the regular commercial bank examination process, in which central banks or other governmental authorities conduct safety and soundness inspections of individual banks. A bank's participation in a private clearing arrangement can be scrutinized as part of the commercial bank examination process and effective influence can be applied to the clearing arrangement through the examination of the institutions that use it. In addition, the proper application of these principles can be accomplished through supervision of the privately operated clearing organizations that adopt these principles for the processing of specialized payment transactions, as described in Figure 1. Although central bank settlement of transactions processed through private clearing organizations provides a vehicle to ensure that such arrangements employ sound principles, the sole sanction of refusing to settle may be disruptive for established systems. Consequently, more flexible supervisory tools available to the central bank are desirable. Such supervisory tools involving clearing organizations might include review and approval authority over the rules of clearing organizations, rule-writing authority, and cease-and-desist powers to address in a timely manner serious problems that have implications for the safe and sound operation of the payments system.

Finally, in an interdependent world where goods, services, and financial instruments are traded routinely across national borders, the need for international payment mechanisms is increasing dramatically. Such cross-border systems may operate in many countries and time zones, thus presenting central banks with a variety of challenges that can only be met through cooperation in the development and execution of payment policy. The international payment system, therefore, should be a focus of our attention in the years ahead, as reflected in the recent actions of the central banks of the Group of Ten to adopt minimum standards to guide the operation of cross-border interbank netting and clearing arrangements, along with principles of cooperation among the central banks themselves for overseeing such arrangements.

Role of the Central Bank as Operator of Large-Value Payment Mechanisms

Another aspect of the role of the central bank in the payment system is, I believe, becoming increasingly important, if not essential. This role involves the operation of a large-value, real-time funds transfer mechanism to handle final settlement transfers on the books of the central bank.

Efficient financial markets are a perquisite to the development of modern financial systems. As noted earlier, the financial system is today characterized by high volumes of large-value transfers occurring each day. Experience has shown (for example, the Herstatt case and, more recently, the failure of Drexel, Burnham, Lambert, Inc.) that the payment system is best insulated from shocks that may have systemic risk consequences, such as the inability of one or more large participants to meet their payment obligations, by minimizing temporal risk and establishing private settlement guarantees to maintain confidence in the system. There is no surer way to provide finality and certainty of actual settlement than through the irrevocable transfer of value on the books of the central bank.

A large-value credit transfer mechanism run by the central bank can be flexible enough to support many types of payments, including net settlement transfers generated by specialized clearing organizations. Further, the transfer of value can occur through central bank operation of a delivery-versus-payment system for a subset of financial instruments, for example, government securities, in which gross transfers are settled as they occur. Or, the central bank can offer its real-time funds transfer capabilities to private book-entry settlement systems to settle the net positions of participants in these systems.

In summary, the availability of a final settlement vehicle that minimizes, to the theoretical limit of eliminating, the time delay between the initiation of a payment instruction and its final settlement is becoming more and more important. There is, in my view, no substitute for a central bank's playing the key role governing, if not operating, such a mechanism. Yet, caution must be exercised lest a central bank become the primary source of the intra-day liquidity needed for a smoothly functioning payment process. Along these lines, a relevant case study is our experience in the United States with daylight overdrafts on the books of the central bank occurring as a result of the operation of a large-value funds transfer mechanism.

As noted earlier, the practice of providing intra-day credit as part of the payment process is now recognized as a core banking function. In the United States, the Federal Reserve provides a huge amount of daylight liquidity to the U.S. payment system. Nearly 40 percent of these daylight overdrafts are incurred by the ten largest overdrafters, while approximately three fourths are incurred by the fifty largest overdrafters. There is also a private sector source of intra-day credit through CHIPS, with controls in place since October 1990 to help ensure timely end-of-day settlement should a participant with a large intra-day net debit position be unable to cover its obligations by the close of business.

Daylight credit is roughly analogous to the short-term working capital requirements of firms whose intra-day patterns of receipts may not exactly match their patterns of expenditure. A large, complex, market-oriented economy could not function effectively without a certain amount of intra-day liquidity to fund the gaps that result from the difficulty associated with synchronizing the timing of high volumes of payment transactions. In the United States, the central bank currently provides this liquidity at no explicit cost. In Switzerland, in contrast, the central bank does not permit overdrafts, and banks have managed to conduct their business without an intra-day market. Yet again, in Japan the central bank provides no intra-day liquidity, but a private market for daylight (morning and afternoon) credit has emerged.

Daylight credit is a valuable commodity. Extensions of daylight credit, however, have the economic cost of exposing the lender to default risk. For the central bank, a direct connection exists between the extension of intra-day credit and discount window or Lombard credit, because a borrower's inability to repay its daylight loan puts the central bank in the position of having to consider converting the loan to an overnight credit.

If something has value but is not priced, then it tends to be overused and wasted. The current high level of daylight overdrafts in the United States and the resulting exposure of the Federal Reserve to default risk suggest that intra-day credit is now being overused in the United States. Accordingly, the Board of Governors proposed in June 1989, and expects to implement once a scheme for measuring daylight overdrafts is adopted, an explicit fee be charged for the use of daylight credit extended by the Federal Reserve banks. The rationale for pricing daylight overdrafts is twofold. First, the Federal Reserve strongly favors market solutions to resource allocation problems. Second, we believe that the significant amount of daylight credit currently supplied should be controlled and reduced, without, however, disrupting the payment system. Charging a relatively low fee should permit users of payment services to make the necessary adjustments to reduce gradually the amount of daylight overdrafts they incur while avoiding abrupt changes in the supply of daylight credit.[11]

From a historical perspective, it seems clear to me that the Federal Reserve had no intention whatsoever of providing large amounts of daylight credit, priced or otherwise, when it began offering funds transfer services early in its history. The origins of the present day Fedwire system date to 1918, and the early designers and operators of the early system could not have anticipated the significant increase in the value and velocity of payments. In fact, it was not until the 1970s that the increase in the volume of funds transfers resulted in the rapid intra-day turnover of reserve balances, leading to material extensions of intra-day credit. Accordingly, I think it unlikely that the Federal Reserve would have positioned itself as a large provider of daylight credit had the nature of the modern day phenomenon been better understood when Fedwire was designed.

Consideration of the role of the central bank as the operator of a large-value funds transfer system leads naturally to the question of the "safety net" attributes of this role. Access to the payment system through clearing and settlement services provided by the central bank, including perhaps central bank credit, is one component of the safety net that central banks and governments place under their financial systems. In many countries, various implicit and explicit forms of deposit insurance designed to ensure public confidence in depository institutions and the safety of their deposits is also a component. Of course, the most essential component of the safety net is the emergency liquidity assistance that is available through the central bank.

Like any other part of the safety net, access to the payment system must be judiciously managed to ensure that it is not abused. Used properly, however, and in combination with the central bank's supervisory and regulatory oversight of the banking system, access to the payment system can be a useful regulatory tool in ensuring that depository institutions do not fail prematurely.[12] In essence, the central bank gives financial system participants confidence that the payments they may receive from a troubled institution are good value. With this confidence, they will be willing to continue to deal with that troubled institution, thus providing the time the bank regulatory authorities need to work out an orderly solution to the problem. Without such

---

[11]The Federal Reserve Board has proposed phasing in a charge of 25 basis points at an annual rate for daily average daylight overdrafts as an appropriate starting point for daylight overdraft pricing.

[12]See Board of Governors of the Federal Reserve System (1990).

confidence, a troubled institution, by being frozen out of the payment system, would be isolated and doomed to immediate failure.

Summary

The payment system is now recognized as an essential component of a smoothly operating market economy supported by an efficient and complex financial system. The central bank has a proper role (1) in establishing public policy to govern the structure of clearing and settlement arrangements in the payment system; (2) in supervising the payment system through the clearing organizations and banking institutions that play key roles in risk management; (3) in providing settlement across its books; and (4) in operating large-value payment mechanisms. Much is to be gained by permitting private entities to compete in the provision of payment services to the public. Because of the critical nature and "safety net" attributes of large-value payment mechanisms, however, operation of such a mechanism, alone or in parallel with similar privately operated mechanisms, is properly a role of the central bank. Central banks must take care in controlling the intra day liquidity they provide to the financial system and the payment system risk they absorb.

Bibliography

Bank for International Settlements, *Report of the Committee on Interbank Netting Schemes of the Central Banks of the Group of Ten Countries* (Basle, November 1990).

Board of Governors of the Federal Reserve System, *Policy Statement on Private Book-Entry Systems* (June 16, 1989).

———, "The Federal Reserve in the Payments System," *Federal Reserve Bulletin* (May 1990), pp. 293–98.

Corrigan, E. Gerald, "Perspectives on Payment System Risk Reduction," in *The U.S. Payment System: Efficiency, Risk and the Role of the Federal Reserve*, ed. by David B. Humphrey (Boston: Kluwer Academic Publishers, 1990), pp. 129–39.

Goodfriend, Marvin S., "Money, Credit, Banking, and Payment System Policy," in *The U.S. Payment System: Efficiency, Risk and the Role of the Federal Reserve*, ed. by David B. Humphrey (Boston: Kluwer Academic Publishers, 1990), pp. 247–77.

Humphrey, David B., and Allen N. Berger, "Market Failure and Resource Use: Economic Incentives to Use Different Payment Instruments," in *The U.S. Payment System: Efficiency, Risk and the Role of the Federal Reserve*, ed. by David B. Humphrey (Boston: Kluwer Academic Publishers, 1990), pp. 45–92.

Johnson, Manual H., speech delivered at the Annual Conference of the National Automated Clearing House Association, Washington, D.C., May 2, 1990.

Parkinson, Patrick M., "Innovations in Clearing Arrangements: A Framework for Analysis," paper prepared for the Conference on Bank Structure and Competition, Federal Reserve Bank of Chicago, May 9, 1990.

4

Foreign Exchange Management and Monetary Policy

C. FREEDMAN*

The paper is in four sections. The first defines what is meant by exchange rate policy. As will be seen, three types of policy directly affect exchange rates: (1) the choice of fixed versus flexible exchange rates (with and without managed floating), (2) monetary policy, and (3) intervention policy. The second section discusses the choice of fixed versus flexible exchange rates in broad brush fashion. The third section discusses in more detail the conduct of monetary policy and of intervention policy. The fourth discusses sterilization of reserve changes in a system of fixed exchange rates or a managed float. The paper concludes with a short addendum on intervention in the forward market.

Some Definitions

The term exchange rate policy is somewhat slippery because it focuses on the variable being affected by a variety of policies, rather than on the policies themselves. As such it differs from terms like monetary policy, fiscal policy, or commercial policy, which tend to focus on the "instrument" of policy (money or interest rates, taxes and transfers, government expenditures, tariffs, or quotas). Hence, rather than talking about exchange rate policy it is more useful to talk about the elements of policy that have a direct influence on exchange rates—choice of exchange rate system, monetary policy, and intervention policy. This is not to argue that other policies, as well as exogenous

*The author is Deputy Governor at the Bank of Canada. The views expressed in the paper are those of the author and no responsibility for them should be attributed to the Bank of Canada.

shocks, do not affect exchange rates, for example, fiscal policy, commercial policy, exogenous change in the world relative price of raw materials. They do, but it is the three policies that are under the control of the authorities and that have a more direct effect on exchange rates that are typically encompassed in the term exchange rate policy. The choice of exchange rate system is the fundamental decision; it has crucial implications for the scope of monetary policy. Intervention policy is the least important of the three and is much less powerful than monetary policy.

Fixed Versus Flexible Exchange Rates

Voluminous literature exists on the subject of fixed versus flexible exchange rates. Most applies to developed countries, but some applies to developing countries. The relative potency of monetary and fiscal policy under fixed and flexible exchange rates with various levels of capital mobility and asset substitutability,[1] the mechanism through which policies have their effects in the two regimes, the insulation properties of the different exchange rate regimes in response to various kinds of shocks, and the role of policy coordination and concerted intervention by the Group of Seven countries are among the important topics in the literature.[2]

Broadly speaking, a worldwide system of irrevocably fixed exchange rates (i.e., one currency) would have significant efficiency benefits. Most notably, transactions costs and the need to expend resources on coping with the risk of exchange rate changes would be eliminated. The advantages of flexible exchange rates arise from macroeconomic and adjustment considerations, in particular the ability of a country under a flexible exchange rate regime to achieve a better inflationary performance than its potential partners, and its enhanced ability to respond to real shocks that are specific to it.

In a world of fixed exchange rates, perfect asset substitutability, and no exchange controls, a small country has virtually no autonomy in monetary policy. This has two principal implications. First, a small country that fixes its exchange rate to the currency of a single large country or to a basket of currencies of a number of countries ties its inflation rate to that of its partner or a weighted average of its part-

[1]Capital mobility is defined as the absence of policy restrictions on the movement of funds between countries. Asset substitutability is defined as the willingness of investors and borrowers to shift between instruments denominated in different currencies in response to minute differences in expected returns.

[2]The Group of Seven countries comprise the major industrial countries: the United States, Japan, Germany, France, the United Kingdom, Italy, and Canada.

ners. Second, in the face of real shocks to the terms of trade, the real exchange rate adjusts through differential price movements rather than through nominal exchange rate changes.

A country that fixes its exchange rate (permanently) trades off its ability to influence domestic nominal variables in return for the rate of inflation of its larger partner. The greater the confidence a country has in the central bank of the country to which it is tying its currency and the greater the similarity of the shocks faced by the two countries, the more sensible is the decision. In the case of the European Monetary System (EMS), for example, other countries have been able to import the credibility of the Deutsche Bundesbank by tying their currencies to the deutsche mark. And, indeed, inflation rates have converged over time among those European countries (although with some lag as credibility is established). Another example is the francophone African countries that have maintained their ties to the French currency area.

Note that to obtain the full credibility benefit of the fixed rate in such circumstances, the country has to convince the market that the fixed rate is close to irrevocable. Having a fixed but adjustable exchange rate, in my view, does not yield the benefit of an irrevocably fixed rate—the country does not get the full advantage of the credibility, and it may be faced periodically with attacks on the currency followed by large discrete adjustments of the exchange rate peg with concomitant effects on prices of traded goods (or subsidies).

Choosing an irrevocably fixed exchange rate means that in the face of real shocks to the terms of trade, adjustment of the real exchange rate must take place through differential price movements rather than through changes in nominal exchange rates. A country should, then, tie its currency to that of a large credible country facing similar shocks to those it faces. This will permit its currency to float against those of other countries with differing external shocks.

Suppose such a match does not exist. That is, suppose a country faces sizable external shocks that are specific to it and that do not affect its potential partners, for example, a shift in raw materials prices relative to manufactured goods prices. In such a case, the movement in the exchange rate can act to offset in part the resulting changes in aggregate demand, to spread the costs and benefits of the change in raw materials prices throughout the economy, and to facilitate the movement in the real exchange rate toward its equilibrium. Of course, even with flexible exchange rates the adjustment is not easy. The risk always exists that a currency depreciation in response to a negative terms of trade shock will feed into a wage-price spiral. And flexible exchange rates will sometimes move away from equilibrium, not toward it. Indeed, misaligned exchange rates have prompted considerable discussion of currency zones, concerted intervention, EMS, and other ways of moving back toward the fixed exchange rate regime. Nonetheless, in a country subject to sizable periodic external shocks that are specific to it and do not affect its potential partners, it is difficult to argue that fixed exchange rates will dominate flexible exchange rates.

In this connection, it is worth noting the literature on optimal currency areas, where mobility of labor, the size and openness of the economy, the nature of shocks, and the flexibility of real wages are the focus. This reminds us that the decision regarding fixed versus flexible exchange rates is a multifaceted one, particularly for small countries.

I argued earlier that if there is perfect asset substitutability and no exchange controls, a country choosing fixed exchange rates will have no monetary policy autonomy. I now turn to the situation in a fixed exchange rate world with imperfect substitutability or exchange controls, or both.

Imperfect substitutability does permit a country to have some degree of autonomy in monetary policy even though its currency is fixed to another country's currency. The same holds true for exchange controls. Under these circumstances, a central bank can follow a somewhat different policy in the short run from its partner, but it has little longer-run autonomy unless it adjusts its exchange rate from time to time.

Consider, for example, a situation where small Country A chooses to follow a laxer monetary policy than large Country B to which its currency is tied. The lower interest rates in Country A can co-exist with higher interest rates in Country B since the capital outflow is not overwhelmingly large (because of imperfect substitutability or exchange controls). Over time, however, if Country A's inflation rate is higher than Country B's, its currency becomes more and more overvalued. This will induce capital outflows from Country A, as the public becomes more and more convinced of the inevitability of a future devaluation. Even if Country A's government is successful in preventing the outflow by using controls,[3] the overvalued currency will depress returns in the tradable goods sector, artificially increase the real wage rate (by keeping import prices low), make the inevitable adjustment harder to absorb, and raise the value of the rationed foreign exchange (raising the return to rent-seeking behavior).

---

[3]I would note that no controls are perfect. For example, black markets develop, and there are leads and lags in current account transactions.

In sum, the pure logic of the arguments thus far tends to lead one to support either an irrevocably fixed exchange rate (or one close enough to irrevocable so as to enable the authorities to obtain all the credibility benefits) or a flexible exchange rate (with or without management of the float), rather than an adjustable peg. The latter seems on the surface to have a variety of disadvantages without many compensating advantages. This particular judgment is stronger, the greater is asset substitutability and the less the reliance on controls. Having said this, I recognize that many countries have opted for this intermediate outcome. There are a number of reasons for such a result. Political considerations (in particular, concern about the perceptions of independence) may prevent a country from entering into a monetary union, while economic considerations (its lack of credibility) may lead it away from exchange rate flexibility. Also, experience under flexible exchange rates has made some countries wary of this structure. The second-best outcome in such a case might be to try to mimic monetary union by fixing the currency to that of a credible partner and holding tightly to that link. Moreover, a country may be nervous about tying irrevocably to another currency because the country to which it is tying may become less responsible in the future. Monetary union also precludes the adjustment of the exchange rate in case of a severe shock. Finally, the desire to capture the seigniorage tax may prevent monetary union.

Monetary Policy and Intervention Policy

In this section I consider more closely the conduct of monetary policy and intervention policy under fixed and flexible exchange rates.

Fixed Exchange Rate Regime

Consider first the short-run situation in a fixed exchange rate world. Continuing to use our example of small Country A and large Country B, let us suppose that Country A decides to relax its monetary policy and ease interest rates. What will be the effects on international reserves? The direct effect will be through capital outflows generated by the change in interest rate differentials (through transactions of both residents and nonresidents); the indirect effects will be through a deterioration of the current account as output and prices rise in Country A. The higher the degree of asset substitutability the larger will be the change in international reserves (i.e., the larger the amount of intervention needed) for a given change in interest rates. In the limit, with perfect asset substitutability, even a small change in interest rates results in an extremely large change in reserves, a reflection of the general point that there can be no autonomous monetary policy in a fixed exchange rate system with perfect substitutability.

Returning to the case of imperfect substitutability, I would repeat and amplify the point made previously that although a somewhat autonomous policy is possible in the short run, it is not possible in the long run without a parity adjustment. The easier monetary policy in Country A results in a capital outflow and a current account deterioration. If Country A persists in a more expansionary monetary policy, there will probably be further capital outflows (because of lagged adjustment to the earlier interest rate change) and the current account will continue to deteriorate, as domestic price inflation exceeds foreign inflation.

Domestic competitiveness will thus continually decline. The continuing and growing current account deficit will eventually exhaust the finite amount of international reserves available to Country A. Moreover, well before this occurs, the market will recognize that Country A's policies are not viable and that future devaluation is inevitable if they are not changed. The capital outflow driven by the expectation of a devaluation of Country A's currency can be considerably larger than the interest-rate-driven capital outflow, because the expected net returns from shedding investments in a currency that one expects will be devalued can be very high (since the discrete changes tend to be very large). In addition, if there is concern that the authorities will impose capital or exchange controls in such circumstances, the outward movement of capital will be even greater.[4] Experience suggests that residents play a prominent role in such capital outflows, and it is not just foreign investors that react.

In sum, in a fixed exchange rate structure a small country's monetary policy has to converge with that of its partner country in the long run even if asset substitutability is low, and in the short run if asset substitutability is high.

Flexible Exchange Rate Regime

I turn now to the case of a small country with flexible exchange rates. Monetary policy can be used autonomously by the authorities of the country. In the long run, autonomy enables the country to choose its own inflation rate and facilitates adjustment to real (terms of trade)

[4]Foreign borrowing by the authorities can provide more reserves, but market forces will eventually dominate.

shocks. At times, however, the market pushes flexible exchange rates too far in one direction or the other; adjustment costs for the tradable goods sector result. These erratic effects and bandwagon effects on the exchange rate provide the principal rationale for intervention in a flexible exchange rate system.

How does monetary policy get transmitted in a flexible exchange rate world? In a small open economy with flexible exchange rates, monetary policy is transmitted through changes in both interest rates and exchange rates. As economies become more open to foreign trade and foreign financial influences, the greater is the importance of the exchange rate channel. In the typical closed economy model, the tightening of monetary policy increases interest rates, and the higher interest rates, in turn, reduce interest-sensitive expenditures. Typically, the focus is on investment expenditures, residential construction, and consumer durables. In addition, spending on other forms of consumer goods is reduced via the wealth effect, at least in a world where long-term fixed-rate assets predominate. (In a world with Regulation-Q types of ceilings there would be disintermediation and credit rationing by financial institutions.) In the corresponding open economy model with flexible exchange rates, the tightening of monetary policy tends to increase the value of the domestic currency as well as to raise interest rates. The result is to reduce expenditures by foreigners on home goods and to shift expenditures by domestic residents from domestically produced goods to imports. In addition, the currency appreciation has a direct effect on prices, particularly in the case of the small open economy, where the prices of both exportable and importable products respond fairly directly to exchange rate changes.

It is important to note that the central bank has little influence on the split between interest rates and exchange rates of a given change in policy stance. Thus, a given tightening of policy may produce a significant interest rate increase and little appreciation, or relatively little interest rate change and a sharp appreciation. In large part, the split depends on expectations in the foreign exchange market, including expectations regarding the length of time the tighter policy and higher interest rates are expected to last and induced effects on expectations of future inflation. To assist them in the conduct of policy in these circumstances the authorities can use a "monetary conditions index," which tries to weight both interest rate and exchange rate changes in terms of their relative effect on aggregate demand.

Beyond the concern with its effect on aggregate demand, the exchange rate is also important in the conduct of monetary policy for a couple of other reasons. At a time of inflationary pressure, one would want to avoid a sharp depreciation of the currency, because it would feed into price changes fairly rapidly and have deleterious effects on expectations of future rates of inflation. And there is sometimes concern that markets will overshoot and push exchange rates too far, especially if they believe the authorities are taking a hands-off attitude to the exchange rate ("benign neglect"). Both monetary policy and intervention policy can be used to influence the exchange rate in such circumstances, although the former is clearly by far the more powerful influence.

I would emphasize, however, the distinction between responding in the short run to *changes* in the exchange rate and having an implicit or explicit target *level* of the exchange rate. The latter is not consistent (except by chance) with achieving a target value for some domestic nominal variable; the former, however, may assist the authorities in reaching the goal for the domestic variable.

More generally, in a world of flexible exchange rates with high asset substitutability, exchange market intervention is not likely to have long-run or even medium-run influence on the exchange rate although it may be useful in the short run. Thus, for example, the Canadian authorities tend to think of intervention as, first and foremost, a tool for promoting orderly markets and moderating exchange rate movements in response to shocks and temporary disruptions. The technique of leaning against the wind is used to dampen short-run volatility and to offset random movements. Even in the case of more persistent shocks and more fundamental pressures, intervention is used as a means of buying time in order to permit monetary policy to go to work. The Jurgensen report, prepared some years ago for the Group of Seven, also reached the conclusion that intervention policy could have some short-run effect on exchange rates but could not be expected to have any lasting influence.[5] Intervention can be sporadic or more continuous, the latter being the case in Canada.

Exchange market intervention could also be used to signal forthcoming monetary policy action, either automatic (in the case of unsterilized intervention), or discretionary (in the case of sterilized intervention). This role for intervention can be of particular importance when a belief has developed in the market that speculative forces have resulted in a considerable overshooting of the exchange rate. If market participants are already concerned about the viability of the currency at the prevailing exchange rate, strong intervention, which signals that the authorities hold the view that the currency is overpriced or underpriced and that they are likely to engage in more

[5]In a world with imperfect substitutability, intervention can have lasting effects but these are quantitatively small.

fundamental actions to move the rate, is likely to have a direct effect on market behavior. Without clear evidence of speculative overshoot, the signaling aspect will be less effective.

Sterilization of Changes in International Reserves

This penultimate section of the paper deals with the technical issue of sterilization of reserve changes. The details of sterilization will differ from country to country depending on the institutional structure (which, itself, is usually the result of the historical development of markets and institutions). The basic principle is, nonetheless, simple. Sterilization involves action (or no action in certain cases) by the authorities to prevent changes in international reserves from having secondary effects on domestic monetary conditions via their influence on the cash reserves of the domestic banking system.

Consider the following simple example. Suppose that international reserves are held on the books of the central bank (not a universal practice, as we shall see). The other asset of the central bank is domestic bonds, and the central bank liabilities are currency, the deposits of the banking system (bank reserves), and government deposits. Suppose that foreigners increase their desired holdings of domestic currency assets and that the authorities intervene to prevent an appreciation of the domestic currency. The central bank issues a check upon itself in return for the foreign currency (typically a check on a foreign bank). Whether the foreigner buys a bond from a resident or holds a deposit in a domestic bank, the domestic bank will obtain the claim on the central bank and its reserves at the central bank will rise. This will lead to downward pressure on short-term interest rates as the banks with excess reserves act to expand their portfolio of interest-bearing assets, and this downward pressure may be inappropriate.

There are a number of options available to the authorities to prevent the secondary effects: (1) The central bank can sell domestic assets on the domestic bill or bond market. (2) It can sell the foreign exchange to the domestic banks on a swap arrangement. (3) It can shift government deposits from the banks to the central bank. (4) The government can issue debt instruments and deposit the proceeds in the central bank. (5) The reserve-requirement ratio can be adjusted upward. Note that the first and fourth options assume the existence of a reasonably well-developed market for domestic instruments, while options two, three, and five do not.

It is sometimes argued that if the central bank or the government sells domestic instruments to sterilize the capital inflow, there will be upward pressure on domestic interest rates, further capital inflows, further need for open market sales for sterilization purposes, further upward pressure on interest rates, etc. This argument is fallacious because it does not take into account the destination of the original capital inflow. One possibility is that the foreign investor wants to hold domestic interest-bearing assets, with the result that the central bank indirectly ends up trading its own holdings of, say, treasury bills, to the foreign investor in return for foreign currency. A second possibility is that the foreign investor wishes to hold a deposit in a domestic bank. The central bank or government can then supply an interest-bearing asset for the bank to hold (treasury bill or swapped foreign exchange), or it can reduce other (i.e., government) deposits at the bank, or it can force the bank to hold more required reserves (either interest-bearing or non-interest-bearing), all of which actions prevent secondary repercussions. It is also possible for a country to impose a secondary reserve requirement, which would force banks to hold certain assets such as domestic treasury bills, in order to influence the demand by banks for the type of assets used in the sterilization operation.

In some countries, such as Canada, international reserves are held on the books of the government or a governmental entity and not on the books of the central bank. This does not change the logic of the above discussion but rather makes sterilization automatic rather than discretionary. In Canada, for example, international reserves are an asset in the Government's Exchange Fund Account and are financed in the short run by a reduction in government deposits at the banks and in the long run by an increase in treasury bills outstanding. The Bank of Canada acts as an agent. Note that if a government financed its increased holdings of international reserves by borrowing from the central bank, we would be right back to the earlier example.

I would note in conclusion that sterilization prevents certain automatic responses from taking place. Thus the autonomous capital inflow just discussed would, if unsterilized, have led to an expansion of the balance sheets of the banks, put downward pressure on interest rates, and, hence, induced a partly offsetting capital outflow. By engaging in sterilization, the authorities are trying to prevent the secondary repercussions on the interest rate and hence insulate the domestic economy from the capital inflow. Similarly, if the capital inflow were the result of a tightening of monetary policy, the sterilization tries to prevent downward pressure on interest rates, which would offset the original action. Recall, however, that in the limit in a fixed exchange rate system with perfect substitutability, fully sterilized intervention is not possible because of the infinite interest rate elasticity of capital flows, and unsterilized intervention simply reverses the original central bank tightening action (leaving the central bank with more foreign exchange and less domestic assets on its balance sheet).

An Addendum on Forward Exchange Market Intervention

Intervention in the forward market is virtually identical in its effects to intervention in the spot market. The only differences are first, that the authorities do not need foreign exchange to intervene in the forward market and hence are not limited by size of the stock of international reserves or the capacity to borrow and, second, that bank reserves are not affected by forward market intervention and therefore sterilization is not required. However, forward exchange market intervention may permit the authorities to take on too much risk since there is no obvious limit to intervention. One could argue that the authorities could always hold the exchange rate at a given level by an infinite amount of intervention in the forward market. At some point, however, the counterparties in such transactions would probably no longer be willing to transact with the central bank, because of the risk element.

5

Prudential Supervision and Monetary Policy

H. ROBERT HELLER*

Central banking and the supervision and regulation of financial institutions and markets are key governmental functions in any modern economy. In general, the government reserves for itself the right to issue money—a privilege that is often enshrined in the constitution itself. But in a modern mixed economy, monetary functions tend to be shared by the central bank and commercial banks, be they public or private institutions.

Typically, the country's central bank is given the exclusive authority to determine the quantity of currency in circulation. It also exercises authority over other types of money, such as demand deposits, that represent liabilities of other financial institutions. These financial institutions play important roles as depository institutions, sources of credit, and as financial intermediaries. In addition to being creditors and debtors to the rest of the economy, the financial institutions also perform payment services.

It is therefore appropriate to describe the financial system as the nerve center of a modern nation, without which it could not prosper. Given this key function of the financial system, it is not surprising that governments take a keen interest in the health of financial institutions and markets as well as the payments system.

The fundamental question to be addressed in this paper is whether the central banking function and the supervisory and regulatory functions should be combined in one institution, such as the central bank or the monetary authority, or whether supervisory and regulatory

*The author is President of Visa U.S.A.

functions should be delegated to a separate supervisory agency. Posing the question as a simple choice between the need for one or two institutions to exercise the central banking and supervisory and regulatory authority is an oversimplification of a complex set of problems and issues. A modern economy needs a broad range of financial institutions and markets, and the question as to which institutions should exercise, regulate, and supervise these functions is also complex. It is therefore no surprise that in a modern economy several regulators exercise these disparate functions. The search for a simple, all-encompassing framework will be difficult at best and lead to endless frustration at worst.

Policy Functions

First among the various financial functions that need to be exercised in a modern economy is the *monetary policy* function. Monetary policy encompasses the issuance of currency and the control of the monetary aggregates. Because liquid liabilities of depository institutions serve as money, the control over the aggregate amount of such monetary liabilities is a core element of monetary policy. Given the institutional structure of modern banking systems, this implies the need for control over reserve requirements and the total amount of reserves in existence. Without pursuing the point any further at this juncture, it is clear that whatever institution stipulates the required reserve ratio of depository institutions, it will be involved in the monetary policy-making process as well as the bank regulatory process.

Second is the lender-of-last-resort function. In a two-tier banking system, some institution has to be the banker's bank, by standing ready to supply high-powered money to the depository institutions. This function is tied intimately to the central bank's role as the issuer of a nation's currency. In nations without their own currency, the lender-of-last-resort function may be exercised by the central bank of the currency-issuing country or a large private bank of unquestioned standing.

Traditionally, the central bank performs this lender-of-last-resort function through the discount window. By setting the discount rate, a monetary policy function, the central bank sets the terms at which the individual banks have access to the central bank's resources. If the discount rate is set below the market rate at which reserves are traded in the free market, a need arises to administer the discount privilege. In turn, this may necessitate a need for information to verify that this below-market discount rate privilege is not abused. If the discount rate is set above the market rate, such a need will not normally arise as banks have an incentive not to use the discount window, except as a true last resort. Under such circumstances, the fact that a bank actually utilizes the discount window may be an important indicator for the supervisory agency.

Of course, if the discount window privilege is used not only for liquidity purposes, but also to hide the insolvency or impending insolvency of an institution, this would be cause for concern. If the central bank lends only against sound collateral, the danger is minimized because under the circumstances the act of liquifying an illiquid asset cannot help to hide insolvency. As long as the central bank lends only on the basis of sound collateral, the need for direct supervision to prevent the abuse of the discount window is thereby minimized.

Third is the role of the central bank as the *government's bank*. As such, it serves as depository for liquid funds owned by the finance ministry or the treasurer and manages and disburses these funds at the behest of the government. While these functions could also be exercised by private banks, governments need an institution of unquestioned integrity and reputation as their bank.

Fourth is the *payment systems* function, which encompasses the clearing and settlement of checks and electronic payments. Typically, central banks play an important role in the payment system, with transfers on the books of the central bank constituting final and irrevocable payment.

Clearly, some, or all, of these functions can also be performed by private sector financial institutions. Special precautions must be taken, however, to safeguard the system against the possible failure of a financial institution and the potential need to recast, or unwind a settlement. But while a nation's central bank can well serve as the backbone of a *national* payment system, the issues involved are not at all clear when it comes to the international payment system. Nations are by nature reluctant to let official agencies of other countries perform this function and hence there is an important role for the private sector or an international agency.

So far, we have discussed the functions of a central bank as they are more narrowly construed. We will now turn to the regulatory functions that may be exercised by the central bank or a supervisory and regulatory agency.

Bank Supervisory and Regulatory Functions

Rule-making authority is the broadest regulatory function that can be delegated to a bank supervisory agency. The legislature is the ultimate regular, rule-making authority in the country—save for a constitutional convention or the constitutional amendment process. Owing to the complexity of modern financial institutions and the ever-present need to adapt the regulatory environment to small institutional changes and market innovations, legislatures often find it convenient to delegate limited rule-making authority to regulatory bodies. This authority is generally confined to well-defined, narrow problem areas, but on occasion disputes regarding the legislative intent of the limits to an agency's rule-making authority may emerge. Rule making tends to follow a framework and set of procedures that are not unlike the legislative process itself. Typically, draft proposals are put out for public debate and comment and are implemented only after long and searching scrutiny.

In contrast, cases brought before the regulatory agency by various parties are handled in a manner that more closely resembles judicial procedures. Cases are brought either by regulated entities that wish to engage in additional activities or be relieved of restrictions imposed by previous regulatory decisions, or by other parties that wish to enjoin the regulated entities from engaging in certain activities or force them to offer additional services. By their very nature, cases are more closely related to the supervisory process and frequently arise out of the supervisory process itself.

Both rule making and case decisions can influence profoundly a country's banking structure. Over time, the cumulative effect of changes that are in and of themselves only marginal can be substantial, and the regulatory agency can thereby exercise quasi-legislative functions.

Key areas of regulatory activity are in defining the charter provision for banks and the granting of charters under these provisions; the ongoing administration of banking institutions, including capital adequacy, liquidity, and related balance sheet requirements; the authorization to engage in specified activities; and the approval of expansions, mergers, and acquisitions. Finally, the ultimate supervisory responsibility rests in the authority to withdraw the charter and force the dissolution of the banking organization.

Competing Interests

In addition to the regulatory and supervisory functions, financial institutions may also have to adhere to the rules and regulations established by other regulatory bodies. In particular, this may include the *insurance funds* for deposits in financial institutions. The interest of the insurance fund in regulatory issues will be heightened if the financial institutions to be insured have the option of seeking a charter from any one of several different supervisory and regulatory agencies. Under these circumstances, the insurance fund must make certain that the institutions are properly supervised and are adhering to certain minimum risk standards. This problem is less likely to arise in those countries where one single regulatory agency imposes a uniform set of standards upon all insured financial institutions. In that case, the insurance fund becomes a mere risk-pooling device rather than an agency that is concerned with the establishment of uniform standards.

Also, in many countries, a whole panoply of governmental agencies exists, such as the tax authorities, the securities and exchange commission (or its equivalent), and labor and employee health and safety commissions that also have a role in regulating financial institutions. It is therefore not surprising that in complex modern economies with sophisticated financial systems and high degrees of innovation, competing regulatory interests exist and maybe even a degree of tension and competition among various regulatory bodies. It is not surprising that competition is particularly evident in large countries with a federal structure and in countries that have a complex and differentiated financial system.

An extreme example is the United States, where competing regional and sectoral influences are further exacerbated by a governmental structure that emphasizes checks and balances at the federal level and the preservation of state's rights at the regional level. This has resulted in a web of regulatory agencies that has resisted numerous attempts at reform designed to produce a more unified and coherent structure. It would be interesting to speculate to what extent a unified Europe might eventually resemble the complex U.S. regulatory structure a few decades from now.

Basic Tenets

At this juncture it may be useful to establish some basic tenets that may guide us in arriving at an answer to the question of whether supervisory and regulatory authority should be exercised by the central bank or lodged in a separate institution, and—if so—where the dividing line should be drawn. One, the institutional structure of the regulatory, supervisory, and monetary authority should promote a safe and sound, stable financial system. It should also promote the development of dynamic markets. Two, the role of the government supervisory and regulating agency should not be to micro-manage the various financial institutions but to prevent *systemic* failures and the risk of contagion. Three, the freedom of action of the monetary, regulatory, and supervisory agencies should not be unduly impaired by conflicting goals and purposes.

The goal of a sound and stable financial system is the central focus of all governmental regulatory and supervisory activity, as well as of monetary policy. It should include the activities of the government itself, such as the conduct of the government's budgetary policy.

A stable financial environment necessitates the existence of a coherent and noncontradictory regulatory policy. Differences in regulatory and supervisory approaches lead to competitive advantages and disadvantages among financial institutions and thereby engender financial instability. For example, regulatory laxity is an aspect of regulatory diversity. It is easy for industry groups to plead that they should be accorded easier regulatory treatment when various regulators can be played off against each other. While the potential for competition in laxity among federal and state banking and regulatory agencies cannot be ruled out, the opposite—namely, competition in stringency—is also a real possibility when the government or even the public at large is looking for scapegoats in difficult times.

But competition on a regional basis, for example, between various state banking regulators, is difficult to control. On the one hand, there is the potential to attract entire branches of the financial service industry to one location by having a relatively permissive regulatory environment. This temptation on behalf of a state regulatory agency is particularly pronounced when the existence of a federal safety net provides protection to depositors lured by high interest rates made possible by a very lax state regulatory environment. On the other hand, the existence of competition among states and state regulators helps to avoid the creation of an overly powerful federal bureaucracy. In small countries, where there is no scope for the maintenance of several regional regulatory agencies, similar considerations may be brought into play by cross-border competition.

In sum, while a fragmented regulatory system may offer certain limited advantages by permitting experimentation and diversity in financial regulation, it is difficult to argue that regulatory diversity promotes stability, safety, and soundness of the financial system. For example, U.S. financial history provides little evidence to suggest that the existence of a multitude of regulatory agencies has served to enhance the safety and soundness of the U.S. financial system.

The potential conflict between macro- and micropolicy objectives is closely related to the question of whether the central bank or a separate bank supervisory agency should be involved in the day-to-day supervision of financial institutions. There are several reasons why one might argue that the central bank should be involved in the day-to-day supervision and regulation of financial institutions. First, the central bank can garner valuable insight into the overall state of the economy by being involved in the day-to-day supervision and regulation of financial institutions. Second, being able to influence bank policy through regulatory pressure might give additional force and impetus to monetary policy measures; however, in exercising this additional power, the central bank might easily cross the line from impartial macromanagement of the economy to credit allocation and micromanagement of individual institutions.

One may well argue that there is also the danger that impartial access to the discount window may not be given by a central bank that also has regulatory powers in case of a regulatory conflict between the central bank and a bank that it supervises. In other words, one can see certain advantages in the existence of the central bank as an independent and neutral lender of last resort, rather than as an institution that can leverage its own policy authority from one policy area to another policy area.

Central banks with supervisory and regulatory responsibilities have traditionally avoided such conflicts of interest by operating separate supervisory and monetary policy departments and have argued that the two functions are being conducted independent of each other. But if such "Chinese walls" exist within the central bank, then the argument that the supervisory and monetary policy functions should be exercised by one institution so as to take advantage of potential synergies does not hold water.

One can also easily envision situations where the monetary policy function and the regulatory function might result in a conflict of interest, for example, in times when the central bank is forced to pursue such a tight monetary policy that the very survival of many financial institutions is threatened. In such a situation, it may be difficult to separate the mandate for a sound monetary policy—which might drive interest rates so high as to threaten the existence of many financial institutions—from the mandate to maintain safe and sound financial institutions. In such a conflict, regulatory and supervisory actions may be delayed or not implemented so as not to exacerbate the impact of the monetary policy actions on the banking industry.

The alternative situation, namely, that monetary policy be conducted with excessive regard for supervisory concerns about the health of one or more financial institutions, would be potentially even more dangerous, as it might perpetuate inappropriate monetary policies that could, in the long run, actually worsen the problems confronting the nation. Of course, a central bank without supervisory responsibilities might also feel that it is limited in its freedom of action in a situation where the banking system is in a precarious situation; under these circumstances, however, the possibility of a direct conflict of interest is not present, and politicians and other observers cannot accuse the central bank of conflict of interest. Thus, it will be easier for the central bank to preserve its most cherished possession: its independence in the realm of monetary policy.

Preserving the Central Bank's Independence

This brings us to the essential point: preserving the independence of the central bank in monetary policy matters. In most countries, the central bank acts pursuant to authority granted to it by the congress or parliament. Whatever legislative powers the legislature grants, it can also take away.

Bank supervision and regulation is a function closely related to the exercise of general governmental authority, that is, the executive branch. It is not a function that is independent of the government, but governmental agencies—such as the Justice Department—are directly and substantially involved as well. To put the matter differently, *monetary policy* is a macroeconomic activity that touches individual economic agents only *indirectly*, while *regulatory* and *supervisory policy* involves *direct* control by governmental agencies.

If the central bank assumes daily regulatory authority, it will get involved in the day-to-day exercise of governmental authority, which may in extreme circumstances involve the central bank in partisan politics—thereby unavoidably endangering its independence. This does not imply that the central bank cannot do an outstanding job in regulating and supervising financial institutions. As a matter of fact, I believe that the Federal Reserve has done an excellent job in that regard and has managed to stay clear of controversy and partisan politics. This has not been true for some other supervisory agencies in the United States. Just imagine the potential damage to the reputation of the central bank that might have resulted if the Federal Reserve had also been the supervisory agency for the thrift industry. At best, its prestige would have been blemished, and at worst, its independence in monetary affairs might well have been challenged.

The Track Record

It may be interesting to compare the track record of central banks that have supervisory responsibilities with that of central banks without supervisory responsibilities in achieving the central goal of monetary policy: a low inflation rate. Table 1 shows the inflation rate, as

Table 1. Supervisory Responsibility of Central Banks and Inflation Performance

(Inflation rates are average annual rates for 1980–87, in percent)

	Central Banks *Without* Supervisory Authority		
Canada	5.0		
Germany	2.9		
Japan	1.4	4.9	(3.3 excluding Venezuela)
Switzerland	3.9		
Venezuela	11.4		
	Central Banks *Share* Supervisory Authority		
France	7.7		
Italy	11.5		
Netherlands	2.3	6.5	
United States	4.3		
	Central Banks *with* Supervisory Authority		
Argentina	298.7		
Australia	7.8		
Brazil	116.3		
Ireland	10.2	66.2	(9.6 excluding Argentina and Brazil)
South Africa	13.8		
Spain	10.7		
United Kingdom	5.7		

Sources: World Bank, *World Development Report, 1989*; and Price Waterhouse.

measured by the average annual increase in consumer prices during the period 1980–87, for central banks without supervisory responsibilities, for central banks that share the supervisory role, and for central banks that have main supervisory responsibilities.

Judging from the evidence provided by the limited sample of countries for which the evidence was readily obtainable, one may conclude that central banks without supervisory responsibilities were more successful in attaining a low inflation rate than central banks with shared or full supervisory responsibility. The average inflation rate for 1980–87 for countries with central banks without supervisory responsibility was 4.9 percent (or 3.3 percent if Venezuela, the only Latin American country in the group, is omitted). For the group of central banks that have shared supervisory responsibility, inflation averaged 6.5 percent, while it reached an annual rate of 66.2 percent for countries with central banks that have full supervisory responsibility (9.6 percent if the two Latin American countries in the sample, Argentina and Brazil, are excluded). This evidence supports the notion that central banks that concentrate all their energy on monetary policy tend to be more successful in achieving the goal of price stability than central banks that have major supervisory responsibilities.

Of course, this apparent association between a good performance in attaining price stability and the absence of supervisory responsibilities may also be caused by other influences. One possibility that comes immediately to mind is the degree of independence of the central bank from the government. It may well be that independent central banks are better in attaining the goal of price stability and that these independent banks also do not tend to have supervisory responsibilities. But in a way, this argument, if found to be true, would support the basic hypothesis, namely, that bank supervisory responsibility is a governmental function that is unlikely to be given to a truly independent central bank. In other words, the supervisory role for a central bank does tend to be associated with significant strings in terms of greater dependence on the government. Of course, exceptions to this general observation, like the highly independent Bank of the Netherlands, which also exercises supervisory authority, exist as well.

While the supervisory and regulatory function may impede the monetary policy function, the reverse is true as well, particularly if the central bank as regulator is empowered with rule-making authority. It is easy to conceive of situations where the rule-making authority of the central bank overlaps or comes into potential conflict with the legislative function itself. In those situations, it is not unheard of that legislators approach directly the central bank and make their views felt.

Once this direct contact is established, two dangers emerge: one, legislators may also attempt to influence monetary policy actions, and two, the central bank may defer regulatory action in order to preserve its monetary independence. Under these circumstances, the regulated entities will not be served as well as they would be served by a regulatory agency for which such considerations do not apply, thereby permitting greater regulatory freedom. Thus, one might conclude that, on balance, a central bank might be able to exercise its monetary policy responsibilities better if it is independent of primary supervisory and regulatory responsibilities. This has also been suggested by most of the task forces that have made recommendations regarding a possible restructuring of the U.S. monetary, supervisory, and regulatory authorities.

Role of the Central Bank in Supervision

Having stated that for various reasons the central bank should not be the primary regulatory agency, I believe that there is still an important role for the central bank in the regulatory process that will enhance and supplement its monetary policy function. One can see this role of the central bank in setting rules that establish appropriate liquidity levels for the financial institutions and in monitoring adherence thereto. This includes the setting of reserve requirements to be held against monetary liabilities of the financial institutions. The role would supplement the central bank's role as the lender of last resort and a monetary policymaker by extending the central bank's authority over that part of the bank's activities that has a monetary impact.

Such a split in supervisory functions between liquidity concerns, on the one hand, and general supervisory and solvency concerns, on the other, exists already in some countries, as well as in the international banking area. Here, the Basle Concordat provides for supervision of liquidity matters by the host country, while the home country, or the country of the bank's domicile, has general supervisory authority, including solvency matters.

The proposal would extend the international division of labor to the domestic arena, with the central bank in charge of liquidity concerns and the other supervisory agency in charge of solvency and general supervision and regulation. For internationally active banks, this proposal would imply no significant changes, except that the home country supervision and regulation would normally be undertaken by a bank regulatory agency, while the supervision of foreign branches and agencies would be the responsibility of the foreign central bank.

Conclusion

We may conclude that while central banks generally have a good track record as bank supervisor and regulator, a conflict may arise between regulatory and supervisory functions, on the one side, and monetary policy functions, on the other. Such a conflict could result in an inflation rate higher than might be achieved by a truly independent central bank without supervisory responsibilities. Nonetheless, it makes sense to give the nation's central bank limited supervisory functions in the liquidity area, as management of the money supply is a prime function of monetary policy. The supervisory and regulatory role pertaining to reserve requirements and liquidity ratios—as well as to the obligation of monitoring adherence thereto—can and should be exercised by the central bank.

This framework is similar to that agreed to in the Basle Concordat for international bank supervision, where the supervision of the liquidity position of foreign branches and agencies is delegated to the host country, while general supervision and regulation is performed by the regulatory and supervisory agency in the bank's home country.

By giving the major supervisory and regulatory responsibilities to a banking agency, while focusing the responsibilities of an independent central bank on monetary policy and supervision of liquidity, a possible conflict between supervisory and regulatory concerns and monetary policy objectives will be avoided and both national goals, the maintenance of a safe and sound financial system and an inflation-free environment, may be realized.

6

Implications and Remedies of Central Bank Losses

REZA VAEZ-ZADEH*

A central bank should normally make a profit because it is essentially a monopolistic enterprise supplying an essential commodity—that is, currency—the demand for which is inelastic—at least up to a minimum amount. Such privileged enterprises should not, under normal circumstances, make losses. Indeed, the notion of a loss seems so alien to the nature of central banking that its emergence on the books of a central bank may give the impression of a serious breakdown in financial discipline and raise doubts about the soundness of the entire financial system, and even the economy as a whole. Such an impression may not be fully justified, however. It is not necessarily a lack of financial discipline by the central bank that leads to losses; they often represent a hidden form of fiscal deficit, and, depending on how they are treated, they do not necessarily spell disaster.

A loss is, in principle, a possible outcome of central banking operations and can arise even in connection with the most basic of all central banking functions: currency issue. A loss will occur when the interest rate charged by the central bank on its loans is not sufficiently high to cover the printing, minting, and administrative costs of currency issue. More generally, losses could arise from a multitude of factors, and, in practice, many central banks have incurred persistent losses, for example, the Bank of Jamaica and the central banks

*The author is a Senior Economist in the Central Banking Department of the International Monetary Fund.

of Argentina, Brazil, Chile, Gambia, Ghana, the Philippines, and Turkey.[1]

In some countries, central banks have found themselves unprepared to deal with the losses, reflecting, in part, the inadequacies of the central banking laws. Indeed, many central banking laws do not incorporate adequate provisions regarding the financing of central bank losses.[2] Even where the provisions of the law are adequate, the practice in countries where the central bank has experienced losses has been to ignore them until their size becomes a significant macroeconomic and political issue.

This complacency in dealing with central bank losses could reflect the improbability of such losses in developed countries and a view that a central bank cannot become insolvent. According to this view, central banks, unlike other banks, can have a persistently negative net worth, so that their losses need not be funded.[3] The statement could be interpreted to mean that central bank losses are not important because they can be financed through creation of additional losses.[4]

This paper considers this proposition and concludes that central bank losses do matter, as they influence economic aggregates both directly and through their impact on monetary management. The sources from which central bank losses originate are reviewed in the next section. This is followed by a discussion of the problems posed by the losses and a few suggestions for preventing their emergence. Conclusions of the paper are summarized in the last section.

Sources of Central Bank Losses

In a discussion of the origins of central bank losses, it would be useful to distinguish current losses from capital losses. Current losses arise from imbalances in revenues and expenditures and capital losses result from differential changes in the value of assets and liabilities. Current losses (or gains)—whether realized or accrued—are always calculated into the financial results of the central bank, but certain capital losses are not. For example, a capital loss arising from an increase in net foreign liabilities due to a change in the exchange rate is usually excluded from the computation of annual profits and losses.

[1]In the case of Jamaica, losses in the last five years have exceeded 5 percent of gross domestic product (GDP) in each year. This has occurred at a time when the general government and public entities have recorded surpluses.

[2]A review of the central banking laws in some sixty countries revealed that almost one third did not have any specific provisions regarding the treatment of losses.

[3]See Robinson and Stella (1988) for a recent statement of this view.

[4]Losses could also be financed through inflation, but in that case the net worth will not remain persistently negative.

It is attributed to a valuation account, which is an item in the balance sheet. This approach allows the central bank's net worth and its reserves to remain intact as a result of such a loss until it is realized.

Current Losses

As in any kind of business activity, central bank current losses occur when earnings from assets are lower than the cost of operations. This observation can be translated into a relationship between the spread between average return on earning assets and the average charge on remunerable liabilities, the nonearning assets, and the base money.[5] To prevent losses, at any level of capital, the spread has to be larger, the larger are the nonearning assets and the smaller is the base money.[6] In other words, to prevent losses, the ratio of base money to nonearning assets would have to increase as the spread is reduced. This can be seen from the balance sheet relationships.[7] In a simplified and approximate form, the financial results of the central bank can be explained in the following way:

$$RES = (i + s).EA - i.RL, \tag{1}$$

where

RES = the financial result of the central bank (i.e., its profit or loss);

i = the average interest rate paid by the central bank on its remunerated liabilities;

s = the spread between the average return on earning assets and i;

EA = the stock of earning assets; and

RL = remunerated liabilities composed usually of foreign liabilities, deposits of government agencies and financial institutions, and financial instruments issued by the central bank.

[5]The nonearning assets could include revaluation accounts, non-interest-bearing government securities and loans, nonperforming loans, etc.

[6]In some countries interest is paid on all or part of financial institutions' deposits at the central bank, which are included in the base money. Strictly speaking, the relationship mentioned in the text holds for that part of the base money on which no interest is paid. This distinction is ignored in the paper.

[7]The discussion ignores the central bank's trading activities—such as purchases and sales of foreign exchange—its administrative expenses (including those associated with the provision of free services, such as banking supervision, payments mechanism, etc.), and the cost of issuing high-powered money, including the cost of printing and minting, as well as any interest paid on the interest-bearing part of high-powered money, which usually consists of financial institutions' deposits at the central bank.

Total assets can be decomposed into earning (*EA*) and nonearning assets (*NEA*). Total liabilities can be divided between remunerated liabilities, capital and reserves (*K*), and the base money (*RM*).[8] The balance sheet identity then becomes

$$RL = EA + NEA - K - RM, \qquad (2)$$

so that

$$RES = s.EA + i.K + i.RM - i.NEA. \qquad (3)$$

This equation indicates that any factor that constrains the ability of the central bank to vary its spread or the base money, or to contain its nonearning assets, contributes to the emergence of current losses.

The statement should not be interpreted as recommending that the central bank operate primarily to avoid losses. Even if it could control the factors that affect its losses, it should not behave as a profit-maximizing or cost-minimizing enterprise. By manipulating its spread, the base money, and nonearning assets, the central bank may reduce its losses, but at the same time, it may trigger undesirable changes in interest rates throughout the financial system, generate more inflation, or cause a depletion of foreign exchange reserves. Such developments are usually contrary to the objectives of economic policy, and their cost should be taken into account when formulating any policy to contain the losses of the central bank. This qualification notwithstanding, some of the factors that constrain the ability of the central bank to avert current losses are reviewed below.

Influencing the Spread

No central bank can exercise full control on the components of average spread, but it is fair to say that the central bank can exercise more control on the return on its assets than on the charges paid on its liabilities.[9] The charges on foreign liabilities are determined by developments in foreign financial markets and by the rate of change in the

[8]Currency is always considered as a liability of the central bank, but in fact it is not a liability in the usual sense. If currency is not convertible, it does not have to be redeemed and it entails practically no cost for the central bank. The only liability created for the central bank by issuing nonconvertible currency is to replace worn out or damaged notes and coins and to prevent forgery. If currency is not considered a liability, it would follow that the net worth of many central banks is larger than assumed, and that they can increase their net worth simply by issuing currency. See Fry (1990) on this point.

[9]The interest charged and the amount of credit provided by the central bank are, of course, interdependent. If there is no excess demand, the central bank's control on the level of its assets is limited. For example, it can put a ceiling on the access to its discount window, but the actual amount is demand-determined. Similarly, if the central bank overcharges the government, the latter may place its securities directly with the public.

exchange rate; the latter determines the variations in domestic currency value of these liabilities. The charges on domestic liabilities are determined to a large extent—in the absence of any coercion for holding financial instruments issued by the central bank—by public demand for such instruments. The central bank can usually manipulate the amount of such instruments in order to achieve the price it wants; however, the possibility becomes less probable as the size of its domestic debt grows.

The ability of the central bank to influence the return on its assets is, therefore, crucial to averting losses. The scope for such control is typically constrained by such factors as administrative restrictions on interest rates charged by the central bank. Such restrictions typically include an arbitrarily fixed discount rate, an obligation to provide subsidized loans to priority sectors, and low interest loans to the government. The latter is a common problem in many developing countries.[10]

Control of the Base Money

The central bank's ability to vary the base money in order to prevent losses could be constrained by its monetary policy objectives. For example, following a period of rapid monetary expansion, it may become necessary to withdraw large amounts of liquidity from the system. In the process, the central bank's income may fall, while its expenditure could rise, possibly resulting in overall losses. The decline in the central bank's income would result from a reduction in credit granted by the central bank, reflecting its contractionary stance. The increase in expenditure would reflect the rise in interest payments by the central bank, which would come about irrespective of whether absorption is carried out through the sale of the central bank's own financial instruments or through the sale of government securities.[11]

The above discussion points to the fiscal nature of central bank losses and to the inseparability of the central bank's activities from budgetary operations. For example, the sale of treasury bills from the central bank's own portfolio decreases its earning assets and, therefore, its income. If new treasury bills are issued for this purpose, the

---

[10]The case of Mexico is interesting in this regard because the rate of interest on government loans is determined ex post, once the cost of funding to the central bank is known.

[11]The above discussion also indicates that carrying out a transition from direct to indirect instruments of monetary policy would entail substantial costs for the central bank if there is a need to absorb large amounts of liquidity. The timing of such transition would have to be determined taking into account the implications of the losses for the attainment of macroeconomic objectives.

proceeds of the sale have to be deposited in the government's account at the central bank for the contractionary impact to be realized. The central bank may have to pay interest on these deposits to neutralize the adverse impact of the sale of new treasury bills on budgetary interest costs, and, thereby, on the budgetary deficit. The central bank's expenditure would increase and adversely affect its financial results.

Sources of Nonearning Assets

Activities that increase the nonearning assets of the central bank contribute to current losses. The sources of nonearning assets are usually non-interest-bearing government loans and securities held by the central bank, and its so-called quasi-fiscal activities carried out at the request of the government to support economic policies. These activities generally refer to central bank functions that are not directly related to the objective of safeguarding the value of the currency. They include such functions as domestic debt management, foreign reserves and exchange rate management, prudential supervision and deposit insurance, financial sector development, economic development, and improving income distribution.[12] For example, the takeover of nonperforming loans of bankrupt institutions as part of the supervisory functions of the central bank (as was the case in Chile and Uruguay) could contribute to the growth of nonearning assets of the central bank.

Foreign Exchange Operations

The above discussion of cash flow losses ignores the impact of what may be called trading activities of the central bank. These operations, especially those conducted in foreign currencies, could be a source of substantial losses for the central bank. In many countries, exchange control regulations give the central bank a virtual monopoly on foreign exchange operations. Exporters are required to surrender their foreign exchange receipts to the central bank—which is in turn obliged to purchase them—and the public can only purchase foreign exchange from the central bank. This monopoly position can be potentially profitable for the central bank as it can purchase foreign exchange from exporters at lower prices than it sells to importers. Exchange rate fluctuations, however, can erode such benefits and

[12]These activities also affect price stability, albeit indirectly. Therefore, the distinction between the quasi-fiscal and basic central bank activities may not always be clear-cut.

make the task of managing the foreign reserves of the country expensive for the central bank. The costs are higher if the central bank is also entrusted with the responsibility of defending the exchange rate. Many central banks also engage in forward operations in foreign exchange and borrow abroad in support of this policy, further exposing themselves to risk of capital losses arising from exchange rate variations.

Capital Losses

Capital losses usually originate from such factors as the impact of changes in the exchange rate on the foreign assets and liabilities of the central bank; the effect of fluctuations in foreign exchange parities on a diversified portfolio of foreign assets and liabilities held by the central bank; granting of exchange rate guarantees that are realized; rescue of troubled institutions by the central bank involving the purchase of their bad assets at inflated prices; and, generally, granting of loans and advances that turn out to be uncollectible. The most common sources of such losses for central banks in developing countries relate to their role in foreign exchange management. In implementing this role, many central banks accumulate large foreign liabilities, making them vulnerable to exchange rate fluctuations;[13] Jamaica, Argentina, and Turkey provide good examples of this problem.

The Bank of Jamaica has accumulated substantial net foreign liabilities in order to support the Government's exchange rate policy. These liabilities have made the Bank of Jamaica vulnerable to exchange rate movements, and the large devaluations of the Jamaican dollar during 1983–85 resulted in substantial losses for the bank.[14] At the end of March 1989, the bank's nonearning assets, which represent the counterpart of its losses, amounted to 78 percent of its assets.

In Argentina, the foreign assets of the central bank are sold to the Government in exchange for a government security denominated in foreign currency. The operation does not affect the central bank's net foreign assets as they appear in the balance sheet but does increase nonearning assets and reduce the central bank's income. This is because no interest is usually paid by the Government on its securities held by the central bank, nor can these securities be redeemed in

---

[13]The effect of devaluation on net foreign liabilities is also a common cause of accumulation of nonearning assets as explained in the following section.

[14]During August 1983–February 1985, the Jamaica dollar was devalued from 1.78 to 5.5 per U.S. dollar, more than tripling the domestic currency value of the Bank of Jamaica's foreign liabilities.

foreign currency when they mature. The potential loss is not reflected in the accounts of the central bank.

A capital loss could also be associated with the exchange rate guarantees or insurance schemes offered by the central bank that fix the debt service in terms of domestic currency. In Turkey, for example, the central bank's foreign exchange insurance scheme led to substantial losses during 1984–88. Under the scheme, the central bank on-lent funds borrowed abroad to domestic borrowers at interest rates that were substantially below the average rate of depreciation of the Turkish lira, thereby providing a large subsidy to them.

Impact of Losses

The losses of the central bank are likely to have an impact on its prestige and authority and may also influence macroeconomic developments. The perception that it may not be financially sound, however simplistic the view, could erode its authority to supervise the financial system and limit its ability to use moral suasion as an instrument of policy. Its independence in managing its internal affairs may be diluted by, for example, pressures to make the central bank's administrative budget subject to approval by the government or the legislature, as a way to limit its losses. Except in such extreme cases, the erosion of the central bank's authority would be difficult to measure. The losses would have a more tangible impact on economic aggregates and on monetary management. The macroeconomic effects could come about both directly—through the effects of the losses on monetary expansion—and indirectly—through their impact on the efficiency of monetary management.

Macroeconomic Impact

The expenditure of the central bank constitutes an injection of liquidity into the economy and its revenues, a withdrawal of liquidity. This statement holds for the central bank's operations in both domestic and foreign currency, but the impact of foreign currency operations on domestic liquidity may take time to materialize. Whenever foreign exchange resources used for a particular transaction are obtained from, or flow to, the domestic economy, the impact of the transaction on domestic liquidity will occur immediately. If, however, the central bank uses foreign exchange resources from its own stock, or borrows abroad, for a transaction, the operation will not immediately generate a domestic currency counterpart, nor will the impact on domestic liquidity be felt at the time of transaction. Nevertheless, even in this case, a monetary impact can occur over time if the use of foreign exchange for that transaction creates or widens excess demand for foreign exchange, forcing the public to hold more reserve money than desired, thereby putting pressure on the exchange rate and interest rates.[15]

From a macroeconomic point of view, losses of the central bank are a problem only if they endanger attainment of monetary targets. As the losses represent an injection of liquidity, the central bank may have to sterilize their impact partially or entirely in order to achieve money growth objectives. This would be the case if, in any period, losses lead to more rapid growth in the base money than desired, making it necessary for the central bank to issue interest-bearing liabilities, such as central bank certificates of deposit, to absorb the additional liquidity in the system.[16] This type of sterilization embodies a risk that future losses may grow exponentially. The point is further examined in Appendix I.

The vicious circle of rising losses and rising remunerated liabilities would be accompanied by increases in interest rates in each round. This would be necessary to reduce private demand and encourage the holding of certificates of deposit by the private sector. The prospect can be avoided as long as losses of the central bank are compensated by surpluses in other parts of the public sector. Surpluses may not be able to match the growing losses, however, and interest rates would have to rise, eventually leading to a reduction in profitability, investment, and growth.[17]

Problems Posed for Monetary Management

Losses of the central bank, especially if they are large relative to the monetary base, could erode the ability of the central bank to conduct monetary management efficiently, further compounding the adverse

---

[15]If resources for the transaction were borrowed abroad, the impact on excess demand for foreign exchange would materialize in connection with the eventual debt-service payments on the foreign loan.

[16]Using treasury bills instead of the central bank's own certificates of deposit would have a similar effect as the central bank losses, as discussed earlier.

[17]Fry (1990, p.8) defines a central bank to be insolvent "when it can continue to service its liabilities only through accelerating inflation." This implies that as long as the central bank can service its debt through accumulation of additional debt, thereby avoiding an acceleration of inflation, it cannot be considered insolvent. However, the public will only be willing to hold a growing volume of central bank debt at increasingly higher interest rates, entailing adverse implications for economic growth. A central bank should therefore be considered insolvent if it can only continue to service its debt through accelerating inflation or decelerating growth.

macroeconomic effects mentioned above. The experience of countries such as Jamaica indicates that persistent losses of the central bank could lead to inconsistent use of monetary policy instruments.

Growing losses create an environment in which the central bank would face the continuous task of sterilizing the monetary impact of its losses by absorbing liquidity from the financial institutions. To a large extent, this could be done through open market operations, but—as was the case in Jamaica—it may become necessary to reinforce the operations by raising the cost of access by financial institutions to the central bank's facilities. The Bank of Jamaica—which had accumulated substantial domestic interest-bearing liabilities (certificates of deposit) in order to contain monetary growth—raised the penalty rate on its liquidity support facility to 60 percent a year in 1989 and currently penalizes redemption of securities at very high rates. These measures made the management of day-to-day fluctuations in liquidity more difficult for the banking system and impeded the development of the money market. They were not, however, adequate to reduce liquidity to the desired level so that the Bank of Jamaica had to continue issuance of its own certificates of deposit.

At the same time as the central bank's domestic remunerable liabilities grow, so do pressures for expansionary monetary policy as a way to reduce losses, which would conflict with the objective of reducing liquidity in the system. Through an expansionary policy, the central bank can increase the proportion of nonremunerated debt in its liabilities portfolio, thereby reducing its losses. Thus, central bank losses embody an inherent bias toward generating inflationary surprises.

An analysis of the components of the term $i.RM$ in equation (3) shows that existence of nonearning assets on the central bank balance sheet increases the risk of inflationary bias in the central bank's behavior. This term represents seigniorage profits, that is, the amount that the central bank saves because of the public's willingness to hold the central bank's non-interest-bearing debt.[18] It can be decomposed into

[18]There is some debate in the literature as to the correct measurement of seigniorage (see Molho 1989 for an account of this debate). Nevertheless, it is generally agreed that it refers to the profits of the central bank resulting from its ability to purchase interest-bearing assets (government securities, loans to financial institutions, and foreign assets) by issuing non-interest-bearing (and in a sense nonmaturing), high-powered money. This could imply that the total amount of seigniorage should be the difference between the net amount earned by the central bank if it had to pay interest on its base money liabilities and the amount it earns because it can avoid such costs. These amounts would be equivalent to $s.RM$ and $ia.RM$, respectively, where ia is the average return on the central bank's assets. The difference between the two is $i.RM$.

two elements by replacing the nominal interest rate, i, with the sum of the real interest rate, r, and the inflation rate, p, in equation (3):

$$RES = s.EA + (r + p).K + r.RM + p.RM - i.NEA \tag{4}$$

Equation (4) shows the inflation tax, $p.RM$, as a component of seigniorage. Thus, the higher the nonearning assets, the stronger would be the incentive for the central bank to generate surprise bursts of inflation to finance its losses. Such policies, however, are likely to be self-defeating as they may lead the public to expect future inflations and devaluations, thereby helping to keep interest rates high.

Central bank losses are likely to complicate monetary management whether the central bank relies on market-oriented indirect instruments of monetary control or on direct instruments, such as bank-specific credit ceilings and administratively fixed interest rates. Under the indirect approach, as the losses lead to progressively higher interest rates and increase their volatility, interest rate management and financial programming become more complex. Interest rate volatility will also impede the development of the money market. These problems may eventually force the central bank to depart from its indirect approach, at the cost of distorting interest rates and impeding efficient resource allocation.

If the central bank relies primarily on direct instruments of monetary control, it can finance its losses through base money creation and then sterilize the impact by tightening the ceilings appropriately. The resulting excess reserve will lead to lower deposit rates, higher lending rates, or both, and pressures will intensify for evading the ceilings. To prevent this, the central bank may have to pay interest on the banking system deposits it holds, or to increase reserve requirements. The former will further increase its losses; the latter could have well-known undesirable effects on the financial system.

Possible Remedies

A conclusion of the discussion of the previous sections is that central bank losses are usually a substitute for larger fiscal deficits, and that their impact is the same as that associated with monetization of the budgetary deficits. Therefore, just as it would be necessary to contain the budget deficit to the levels that can be financed in a manner consistent with monetary targets, and just as this may require a transfer of resources from the public to the government, the losses of the central bank may have to be compensated through transfers from the public to the central bank. Against this background, a two-step approach to resolving the problem of the losses should be adopted. The first step would be aimed at eliminating the existing nonearning assets and improperly priced off-balance sheet items. The second would consist of putting in place procedures to avert emergence of losses due to increases in remunerated liabilities and assumption of nonearning and high-risk assets and exposures.

Dealing with Existing Nonearning Assets

The nonearning assets already on the balance sheet of the central bank should be eliminated by a transfer of negotiable treasury bills and longer-term government securities to the central bank in the amount of the latter's nonearning assets. It would be preferable if the transfer of these securities were intermediated through the private sector. This would ensure that the returns on these assets are market related and that the securities will be marketable—a characteristic that is important to preserve the integrity of the central bank's accounts. The mechanism could be for the government to raise cash by issuing securities through auctions or other appropriate selling techniques. The cash is then transferred to the central bank, and the latter will reduce its valuation account or other nonearning assets (or advances to the government, if past losses have been imputed to such an account) as well as its liabilities in the form of currency. The central bank can then sterilize the transaction by purchasing government securities on the secondary market as needed for monetary policy purposes.

In case this procedure cannot be implemented owing to the thinness of the secondary market for government securities relative to the size of the requisite transfer, negotiable securities should be transferred directly to the central bank, but the interest rates they carry should be market related. They can be set at a level consistent with the weighted average interest rate obtained from the latest treasury bill auction, if an auction mechanism is in effect. Otherwise, they should reflect international interest rates adjusted for expected rate of depreciation of domestic currency.

Many central banking laws would have to be amended to specifically permit and call for such transfers. Only a few of the central banking laws examined envisaged the possibility that the reserves of the central bank would not be sufficient to cover its losses, thus requiring a transfer from the government. Among these, only two require cash payments by the government (Jamaica and Solomon Islands), which is the only procedure that would guarantee a reduction in nonearning assets (canceled against a reduction in currency liabilities).[19] Others make the government responsible for compensating the central bank without specifying the mechanism (Japan, Nepal, Oman, the United Arab Emirates), or, as in Belize, require imputing the losses to a government advance account. In France, the law allows deduction of past central bank losses in calculating current year's net profits for distribution. In Somalia and Yemen, the law obliges the central bank to subsequently repay the amounts paid by the government to finance the losses. Neither of these operations would guarantee the elimination of nonearning assets.

Preventing Future Losses

The second step in addressing the problem of central bank losses consists of putting in place procedures that would help prevent the emergence of annual losses. A general principle in this regard is that, in its financial activities, the central bank should behave as much as possible like a well-functioning private institution. This does not necessarily mean that it should behave as a profit maximizer but that it should adequately cover its risks and adopt, as much as possible, a market-oriented approach to its operations.

Amalgamation of Central Bank Losses and Budgetary Deficits

The most important component of the above procedures is to rationalize the financial relationship between the government and the central bank.[20] This can be done by recognizing the fiscal nature of central bank losses by amalgamating them with the outcome of the government budget, thereby explicitly requiring government policies to cover the losses.[21] This procedure would impose a strong degree of budgetary discipline, as the government would have to choose an appropriate tax-spending mix to keep its debt on a nonexplosive

[19]Transfer of an interest-bearing security will also reduce nonearning assets, but—as experience in some countries shows—there is always a risk that interest due may not be paid by the government if the budgetary situation deteriorates. This would increase the nonearning assets again. This is an important consideration because, in most cases, the persistence of central bank losses are due to noncompliance of the government with its financial obligations to the central bank.

[20]See Leone (1990) for a discussion of the role of the central bank in financing government deficits and the role of the central bank budget constraint.

[21]Many governments may be reluctant to do so because it will inflate the deficit presented to the parliament. Some central banking laws, however, by prohibiting the government from making a further appropriation to pay for the losses of the central bank (Tanzania, Kenya, Republic of Yemen), in effect, call for amalgamating the losses in the government budget.

path.[22] The separation of the government budget deficit from the central bank's profits and losses does not alter the fact that, as noted by Fry (1990, pp. 13–14), what government saves today as a result of the expenditure incurred by the central bank, it will lose in the future through reduced transfers of central bank profits to the treasury.

Amalgamation has a further benefit in that it may reduce the incentive for the central bank to occasionally use such monetary policy instruments as the reserve requirement, for the sole purpose of reducing losses. For example, the presence of losses on the accounts of the central bank may create the impression that the primary beneficiaries of the losses are the main customers of the central bank, that is, the financial institutions. This could increase pressure to solve the problem of losses by taxing the financial sector—through, for example, an increase in reserve requirements.

Apart from the likely disruption of monetary management, such a policy would have other disadvantages. First, a one-time increase in the reserve requirement is unlikely to be sufficient to avert future losses since the bulk of the expenditure reduction due to a higher reserve ratio only occurs once, at the time of the increase. Further increases of similar proportions would be necessary in following years. Second, the cost of higher reserve requirements, would place a heavy burden on intermediation, with detrimental consequences for savings mobilization, investment, and economic growth.[23] Third, an increase in reserve requirements—which would allow the central bank to issue a larger volume of base money to support a given volume of deposits—for the sole purpose of reducing central bank losses could disrupt monetary management.

For the amalgamation of the losses into the budget to be more than a simple accounting arrangement, two additional procedures should be put in place.[24] First, at the time of the preparation of the budget, central bank losses should be included in the projected deficit. The magnitude of the combined deficit has to be judged on the basis of the implication of its financing for overall credit expansion and, if rele-

[22]The optimal size of the government's domestic debt is a subject of some controversy. It is generally agreed, however, that, sustainability of debt requires that the growth of annual debt-service obligations should not persistently exceed the growth of real GDP.

[23]Moreover, the revenue from the tax would be lower to the extent that deposits shift to the informal financial sector or to the institutions that are not subject to the reserve requirement.

[24]Inclusion of central bank losses in the budget requires defining a proper concept of deficit of the central bank as only losses that lead to a financing need should be included in the budgetary deficit. A devaluation, for example, does not immediately generate a financing need. There may also be a need to adjust the balance sheet of the central bank for the impact of inflation. For a discussion of such an adjustment see Teijeiro (1989).

vant, for domestic and foreign debt-service payments. If the deficit is deemed to be too large on these grounds the tax-spending mix may have to be changed to reduce the deficit. Second, in case the configuration of the budget is such that the losses of the central bank are to be compensated by surpluses generated in other parts of the public sector for the deficit target not to be exceeded, these surpluses should be deposited in the accounts of these agencies at the central bank as they are realized. In this way the requisite sterilization would occur and there would be no need for further measures by the central bank. If the surpluses are left elsewhere in the financial system, they would raise the banking system's liquidity and could lead to further unprogrammed credit expansion.

Complementary Measures

Whether or not central bank losses are incorporated into the budgetary deficit, specific procedures need to be put in place to rationalize the financial relationship of the government with the central bank. These procedures will be needed even more if amalgamation is not carried out. As a minimum, they should include the following.

First, although in practice it would make little difference whether the government receives low interest loans from the central bank or a share of its profits, it would be preferable for the central bank to charge market-related interest on its loans to the government. This would be beneficial from the point of view of maintaining the transparency and integrity of central bank accounts and in order to be able to ensure that the subsidy involved in central bank lending to the government would not result in overall losses for the central bank. The central bank should also rely on the securities issued by the government in conducting open market operations. This would help incorporate the cost of monetary policy implementation directly into the fiscal budget.

Second, in general, the central bank should not be a conduit for channeling financial resources to the priority sectors at below market prices. Such subsidization is best done through the budget, as in this way the cost of subsidies becomes transparent and their growth can be monitored clearly. If the central bank has to carry out such activities, it should impute the risk and the subsidy involved in its quasi-fiscal activities to its prudential reserves, thereby reducing its transfers to the government. The proper measure of these costs is the amount that would have to be paid to the private sector to carry out the function. This will help the central bank to maintain its financial integrity. In some countries, like Brazil, the government does make a provision for subsidies provided indirectly through the central bank. Typically, however, the amounts set aside have been inadequate.

Third, the central bank should not borrow abroad except for short-term balance of payments purposes, and the government should assume the entire exchange rate risk involved in all foreign borrowing by the central bank.[25] Central banks borrow abroad practically always in fulfillment of their role to preserve the value of the currency. In this sense, they are incurring obligations in support of government policy. Even short-term borrowing for balance of payments purposes is usually undertaken in support of a policy of exchange rate stabilization; an objective that is imposed on the central bank by government policy. In these cases, clearly, the government should bear any exchange risks involved.

The obligation of the government in this regard does not derive from the fact that there may be a subsidy involved in on-lending of foreign resources to the government by the central bank. If the central bank on-lends the funds borrowed abroad to the government at a market rate, no subsidy is involved.[26] The government should still be responsible, however, for any losses suffered by the central bank as a result of borrowing abroad. Such a loss would come about if actual devaluation exceeds expectations. This is because, in that case, the premium for devaluation expectations incorporated in the interest rate paid by the government on its credit from the central bank would not be sufficient to cover the entire cost to the central bank.

A foreign exchange risk is associated not only with transactions in foreign exchange, but with all the lending activities of the central bank. This is because, at any given level of demand for cash balances, any credit extended by the central bank will eventually create an equivalent demand for foreign exchange that—at an unchanged supply of foreign exchange—will put pressure on the exchange rate. If the exchange rate is then adjusted, the risk materializes. If it is not allowed to adjust, the additional demand will lead to an equivalent decline in the country's net international reserves, which in many countries are uniquely held by the central bank. Thus, a foreign exchange cost is involved in both cases.

---

[25]It would not be practical to expect that foreign borrowing should be done only by the government, although this is the preferable alternative.

[26]As a general rule, as long as the spot price of the foreign exchange at the time of transaction is equivalent to the discounted present value of services derived from it, no subsidy is involved. A market-determined exchange rate can be expected to incorporate this characteristic. Thus, if the foreign resources are evaluated at the market-oriented exchange rate and on-lent to the government at a market-related interest rate, no subsidy will be involved even if eventually the central bank makes a loss owing to a change in the exchange rate.

The central bank should be allowed to impute such risks—which are inherent in all its lending operations—to the interest rates it charges. Even if allowed to do so, however, the central bank's interest rate policy may at times dictate otherwise. For example, if monetary management is based on interest rate targeting, it may not be possible for the central bank to adjust the discount rate in order to take account of all the risks involved in its lending operations. In these circumstances, the likelihood of registering a loss increases, and the central bank should be compensated if a loss is actually realized.

Fourth, the central bank should set aside reserves against potential losses. Some central bank acts give the central bank discretion to set aside profits for this purpose. Thus the onus is placed on central bank management to have the foresight to provide adequately for eventual losses. Some central bank laws allow a (reserve) valuation account on the liabilities side of the balance sheet as a reserve against valuation losses arising from changes in the exchange rate. This account reflects net gains from valuation changes that are not distributed but set aside as reserve against future losses from exchange rate changes. When a valuation loss due to a change in the exchange rate occurs, the amount of the loss is deducted from the balance of the valuation account. In case the balance of this account is insufficient to cover the loss, these laws require a transfer of government securities to the central bank in the amount of the deficiency. In most cases, however, the law specifies that these securities should not be negotiable nor bear interest. Therefore, the transfer of these securities does not reduce the nonearning assets of the central bank, nor does it make it more probable that funds would be available when the foreign liability becomes payable.

An alternative but similar approach is to credit the gains from valuation into an interest-bearing blocked government account at the central bank and settle valuation losses by debiting this account. In case the credit balance is not sufficient to cover the losses, the government could transfer interest-bearing securities to the central bank. This would allow for a prudent distribution of the gains from valuation in the form of interest paid to the treasury and prevent the creation of nonearning assets.

Reserves are also necessary against contingent liabilities, such as foreign exchange guarantees. Under conventional accounting procedures no such provisions are made. There are differing points of view regarding the soundness of this practice. Supporters argue that provisions will reduce the net return on assets, while in fact the guarantee may never be realized. They point to the difficulty of deciding the amount of such provisions that have to be based on an evaluation of future gains and losses from foreign exchange changes. Critics point out, however, that this argument can apply equally to any kind of provisioning against future risk. Moreover, central banks do not usually charge an adequate premium or fee to cover the actuarial value of their liabilities should the guarantee come due. Thus, if the guarantee becomes binding, the central bank will incur an additional expense.

Timing of Transfers to the Central Bank

Should the central bank be compensated for losses at the time of their accrual (or at the time of a valuation change) or when the loss is realized?[27] Certainly, earlier payment will help assure the transparency and integrity of the central bank balance sheet—which is a public document. In general, however, the timing of compensation should be determined in a manner consistent with the budgetary cash flow requirements.

Compensation of the losses at the time of accrual will help soften the impact of the transfer on the budget.[28] To see this, assume that the payment is in the form of an interest-bearing security.[29] If the transfer of the security takes place at the time of accrual of the loss, its amount will be equal to the size of the loss. The government will have to pay interest on the security in regular intervals in an amount of, say, A, until the security matures. This additional interest earned by the central bank in the intervening period will be forgone if the transfer takes place at the time of the realization of the loss. The amount of the transfer at the time of realization will then have to be larger by a multiple of A. Thus, while the government will pay no interest in the period between the accrual and realization, a larger interest payment than A will be required from that point onward, reflecting the larger transfer that should be made.

In order to further ease budgetary cash flow problems, the transfer of central bank profits to the government could also be made more frequently than on an annual basis; however, it would also be most prudent to transfer only realized profits. Regular preparation of

---

[27]The question of when a profit or loss related to a foreign exchange operation is realized is controversial. Precise determination of the realized loss (or gain) requires relating each individual outflow (a sale or a repayment) of foreign exchange to a specific inflow (a purchase or a loan). This clearly requires detailed and cumbersome accounting. An alternative is to evaluate the unit of foreign exchange paid out on the first-in-first-out (FIFO) or last-in-first-out (LIFO) basis. The losses (or gains) would be larger if the FIFO procedure is used.

[28]Strictly speaking, a distinction should be made between the case where the operations of the central bank become profitable as a result of the transfer, and the case where the central bank continues to make losses following the transfer. The advantage mentioned in the text may not be valid in the former case. In this case, the discussion should also take into account whether or not the profits of the central bank are transferred to the treasury in their entirety.

[29]The transfer can also be in the form of a debit entry in a government deposit account at the central bank, but the impact on the budget remains essentially the same.

profit-and-loss accounts on a cash basis to complement the usual system of accrual accounting would be needed. This would help prevent an overestimation of the profits to be transferred to the treasury, which may raise government expenditure and be expansionary.

Concluding Remarks

A central bank is supposed to make profits because of the seigniorage involved in currency issue. However, many central banks make losses because the costs involved in trying to preserve the value of the currency, and in supporting government policy through quasi-fiscal activities, outweigh seigniorage.

This paper has argued that central bank losses cannot be ignored: They can undermine monetary management, slow down financial market development, and set back the attainment of such economic objectives as price stability and economic growth. In these regards, the impact of central bank losses is similar to that of the monetization of growing fiscal deficits. Therefore, their fiscal nature should be recognized and they should be incorporated into the government budget either directly, or—if this is not possible—by effectively assuring such an outcome through appropriate reform of central banking laws. At the same time, and especially if amalgamation is not possible, steps should be taken to remove any nonearning assets from the books of the central bank through transfer of earning assets from the government, and to rationalize the financial relationship between the government and the central bank. The latter would imply allowing the central bank to charge market-related interest rates on all its loans, including those to the government. This would mean that it should take the risk of exchange rate changes into account in setting its lending rates, to the extent allowed by monetary policy considerations. It should also rely on securities issued by the government in conducting monetary policy.

Appendix I

Path of Future Losses

This appendix considers the conditions under which central bank losses are likely to compound indefinitely to produce a path of future losses that grows explosively.[30] We begin by defining a simplified central bank balance sheet.

[30]This appendix was prepared by Alan MacArthur for the report: "Jamaica, Improving Monetary Management," by Reza Vaez-Zadeh, Alan MacArthur, and Ian Lamers, Central Banking Department, International Monetary Fund, May 1990.

Central Bank Balance Sheet

Assets	Liabilities
Credit to Government	Net foreign liabilities (*NFL*)
Interest-bearing (*TB*)	Reserve money (*RM*)
Non-interest-bearing (*LRS*)	Other liabilities (*OL*)
Credit to private sector (*CP*)	Net worth (*NW*)

Losses are defined as cash income less cash payments:

$$\text{Loss} = OL.i_{ol} + NFL.i_{nfl} - TB.i_{tb} - CP.i_{cp}, \tag{1}$$

where each i refers to the interest rate on the appropriate security. To simplify, we net all the interest-bearing securities into an aggregate, represented as the redefined *CD*.

$$\text{Loss} = CD.i. \tag{2}$$

At the moment that interest payments are made, the entire loss is converted into base money.[31] The central bank may need to sterilize a part of this injection in order to meet monetary growth objectives. Thus,

$$\text{Loss} = \Delta RM + \Delta CD, \text{ or} \tag{3}$$

$$\Delta CD = \text{Loss} - \Delta RM. \tag{4}$$

Interest-bearing liabilities grow from period to period if the losses outstrip programmed growth of the money supply. This raises the possibility that losses today lead to more losses tomorrow, resulting in an exponential growth path. The possibility is removed only if a desired money stock eventually becomes large enough to require a reduction of *CD*s rather than new issuance.

To show this, consider the following simplified system. From equation (2)

$$\text{Loss}_t = CD_{t-1}i_t, \tag{5}$$

where *CD* is the net quantity of interest-bearing liabilities of the central bank, and i is their average interest rate. Rewriting equation (4),

$$CD_t - CD_{t-1} = \text{loss} - (RM_t - RM_{t-1}), \tag{6}$$

[31]Payment of foreign interest by the Bank of Jamaica could also affect the liquidity of the banking system if demand for Bank of Jamaica foreign exchange exceeds supply. When the central bank makes an interest payment in foreign currency, it reduces foreign exchange available to agents outside the central bank. Thus, foreign exchange that would have been sold to other agents is not sold, and extra reserve money remains in the system.

substituting from equation (5) and rearranging,

$$CD_t = CD_{t-1}(1 + i_t) - (RM_t - RM_{t-1}), \tag{7}$$

defining programmed growth in the monetary base (g_t) as

$$g_t = (RM_t/RM_{t-1}) - 1, \tag{8}$$

we can rewrite equation (7) as

$$CD_t = CD_{t-1}(1 + i_t) - RM_{t-1}\,g_t. \tag{9}$$

The solution to this difference equation is

$$CD_t = CD_0 \prod_{j=1}^{t} (1 + i_j)$$

$$- RM_0 \sum_{k=1}^{t} g_k \sum_{n=k+1}^{t+1} \frac{(1 + i_n)}{(1 + i_{t+1})} \prod_{m=0}^{k-1} \frac{(1 + g_m)}{(1 + g_0)}. \tag{10}$$

We need to evaluate whether CD_t tends to explode or goes below zero as t gets large. This clearly depends on the relationship between money growth and the interest rate, as well as starting values of CD and RM. It is impossible to make any general conclusion about CD_t without knowing the exact path of interest rates and money growth; however, several fairly general cases will be considered.

Case 1: $g = i$; for all t.

That the growth of reserve money (g) and interest rate (i) should be equal is not so unlikely as it might at first appear, assuming a stable money multiplier. It requires that the growth of real GDP be equal to the real interest rate.

Given $g = i$, equation (10) becomes

$$CD_t = \left[CD_0 - RM_0 \sum_{k=1}^{t} \left(\frac{i_k}{1 + i_k}\right)\right] \prod_{j=0}^{t} (1 + i_j). \tag{11}$$

As t gets large, CD_t must go to zero as the term within brackets goes to zero. Thus, if $g = i$, no exponential path will develop.

Case 2: $g > i$; for all t.

In this case, CD_t declines even faster than in Case 1 as growth in money financing rises more quickly.

Case 3: $g < i$; for all t.

This case is mathematically the most interesting because, clearly, there is some value of g—as it goes toward zero—that will allow the quantity of liabilities to explode. Once again, there are infinite possible variants in this case; one representative, restricted solution is shown here. If g and i are fixed over time, then CD_t explodes as t gets large if

$$\frac{g}{i_0} < \frac{CD_0}{CD_0 + RM} \; . \tag{12}$$

As an example, we can construct one possible scenario for the growth of losses in the case of the Bank of Jamaica. Starting values for *RM* and *CD*, which roughly approximate their 1989 counterparts, and a possible path for interest rates and money growth are shown below:

CD_{1989} = \$J5 billion (value in *CD*s of interest-bearing liabilities less interest-bearing assets)
RM_{1989} = \$J4 billion

Parameter	1990	1991	1992	1993 and Beyond
i	.25	.20	.15	.11
g	.20	.15	.12	.08

Chart 1, below, shows the paths of the quantity of net liabilities, losses, and the base money that result from the above assumption. As the

Chart 1. Central Bank Losses: Hypothetical Path
(In millions of dollars)

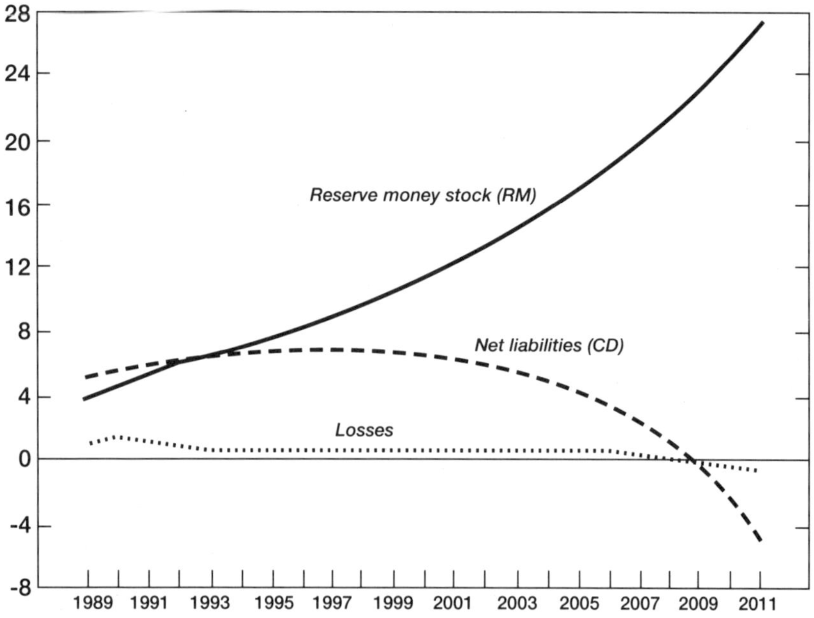

desired level of reserve money increases, the stock of net liabilities of the central bank starts to decline, reaching zero by 2009. In line with this development, the losses of the central bank decline throughout the period and are eventually eliminated.

Shortcomings of this analysis rest on its partial description of the macroeconomy, particularly in the assumption that i and g are exogenous to the size of losses. A more general analysis would make the interest rate dependent on the size of the losses and of other government borrowing, while the growth of the money supply might also depend on the size of the losses. Interest rates could depend on the losses in at least two ways: (1) as more public sector securities are held by the private sector, the interest rate on these securities would be expected to rise; and (2) the fact that past losses remain on the books may provide an inducement to raise the growth rate of money and reduce interest rates. Additional inflation might also lead to devaluation, and further valuation losses. Moreover, changes in the money multiplier would change the results. A full model should include all of these mechanisms, each of which would act to extend the period over which losses would be substantial, or even to make losses explosive.

Bibliography

Auernheimer, Leonardo, "The Honest Government's Guide to the Revenue from the Creation of Money," *Journal of Political Economy* (Chicago), Vol. 82 (May/June, 1974), pp. 598–606.

Fischer, Stanley, "Seigniorage and the Case for National Money," *Journal of Political Economy* (Chicago), Vol. 90 (1982), pp. 285–313.

Fry, Maxwell J., "Can a Central Bank Become Insolvent?" (unpublished, Washington: Fiscal Affairs Department, International Monetary Fund, May 1990).

Leone, Alfredo, "Effectiveness and Implications of Limits on Central Bank Credit to the Government" (unpublished, Washington: Central Banking Department, International Monetary Fund, October 1990).

MacArthur, Alan, "Monetary Operations, Financial Market Development, and Central Bank Independence" (unpublished, Washington: Central Banking Department, International Monetary Fund, October 1990).

Molho, Lazarus, "European Integration and Revenue from Seigniorage: The Case of Italy," IMF Working Paper, No. 89/41 (unpublished, Washington: International Monetary Fund, May 1989).

Robinson, David J., and Peter Stella, "Amalgamating Central Bank and Fiscal Deficits," in *Measurement of Fiscal Impact: Methodological Issues*, IMF Occasional Paper, No. 59, ed. by Mario J. Blejer and Ke-Young Chu (Washington: International Monetary Fund, June 1988), pp. 20–31.

Teijeiro, Mario O., "Central Bank Losses: Origins, Conceptual Issues, and Measurement Problems," Policy, Planning, and Research Working Papers, No. 293 (Washington: World Bank, 1989).

7

Managing a Central Bank: Goals, Strategies, and Techniques

T. O'GRADY WALSHE*

I have been asked to present a practical account of the experience of managing the Central Bank of Ireland. Why the Central Bank of Ireland? Because it is seen as a successful central bank in a small industrial country, and because it has evolved, within the relatively short span of my own career, from being a monofunctional currency board to a modern central bank exercising all of the key central banking functions, including market-based monetary management and prudential supervision of credit institutions. Meanwhile, the Irish economy has developed and expanded significantly, as has the financial sector. The country is a member of the European Community (EC) and of the European Monetary System (EMS), and the bank participates in the Exchange Rate Mechanism (ERM) of the EMS observing the limits of the so-called narrow band.

First, a few words about the Irish economy. Gross national product (GNP) in 1990 was about $40 billion, or $12,300 per capita. The economy is not only small, it is very open—total external trade in goods and services equals 140 percent of GNP. The rate of growth in 1990 was 5 percent and has been on that order in recent years. The annual rate of inflation in 1990 is estimated at 3.4 percent, and there is a surplus on the current external account equivalent to 3 percent of GNP. The official external reserves at the end of September 1990 were about $6 billion. The official external debt of about $16 billion, or 40 percent of GNP is due largely to imbalances in the late 1970s and the

*The author was General Manager/Director General, Central Bank of Ireland, from June 1985 to August 1990, when he retired. The views expressed in this paper are not necessarily those of the Central Bank of Ireland and are the personal responsibility of the author.

first half of the 1980s, which in turn can be laid largely at the door of excesses in the public finances. For example, the Exchequer Borrowing Requirement in 1981 was nearly 16 percent of GNP; in 1986, it was still nearly 13 percent but, owing to a remarkable reversion to "fiscal rectitude" in the most recent years, the Exchequer's borrowing is now down to 2 percent of GNP. Unemployment is the major negative in the economic picture; it stands at over 17 percent of the labor force.

In the financial sector of the economy, the full range of retail and wholesale banking services are provided by four multibranch clearing banks and their subsidiaries—two independent, indigenous banking groups quoted on the Stock Exchange in Dublin and London, which account for a major proportion of the domestic banking business, and two smaller banking groups, which are subsidiaries or branches of foreign banks. Twenty-three other banks are also licensed by the Central Bank, including branches or subsidiaries of U.S., Canadian, British, Belgian, Dutch, German, and French banks, which are significant competitors of the Irish banks in the wholesale banking markets. In addition, there are two small state-owned commercial banks and the Post Office and Trustee Savings Banks, which together account for not more than about 15 percent of bank deposits. Nine building societies (savings and loans institutions) account for about two thirds of home mortgages in Ireland; the other one third is provided by the banks. No intermediaries, such as discount houses, operate between the licensed banks and the Central Bank, but interbank markets in domestic currency and foreign exchange serviced by money brokers and market-making banks are active and effective.

The life insurance market, now an important competitor for personal savings, is largely catered for by indigenous companies although again there is significant foreign representation mostly in the form of branches of U.K. companies. General insurance has been a troubled sector in which the state has had to intervene twice in the past decade to salvage failing companies.

The securities market is dominated by government bonds, which account for about 85 percent of turnover on the stock exchange. Major holders of gilts are banks, building societies, insurance companies, pension funds, unit and investment trusts, commercial companies, and, to an increasingly large degree in recent years, external institutional investors in Germany and other EC countries. Trading is normally active and is effected through stockbroking firms acting as agents: there are no private sector market makers, but the authorities may intervene tactically through the official government broker. Equity markets are quite limited, as they are dominated by the stock of the two major banks and a handful of larger industrial and commercial companies. Outside the stock-exchange framework is a developing market in commercial paper.

I should mention, too, the development in the past two or three years of the International Financial Services Center at Dublin Port where, on the basis of a favorable tax regime, relatively low space-rental rates, advanced telecommunications technology, time-zone correspondence with London, and an abundant supply of well-educated computer-literate staff, and a joint public/private sector promotion agency have succeeded in attracting many international banks and other financial service entities to set up operations. These are conducted primarily with nonresidents and include banking, asset financing, reinsurance, fund management and administration, corporate treasury, corporate finance, etc.

Exchange controls have been largely dispensed with in Ireland; the principal remaining restrictions are that Irish residents may not hold foreign-currency bank accounts or short-term securities and that Irish-pound borrowing by nonresidents is not permitted except for trade, direct investment, or residential property purchase in Ireland. These restrictions will be removed before December 31, 1992, in accordance with Ireland's obligations to the EC. Finally, a recent survey shows that the banking, credit and insurance sector in Ireland contributes 5.5 percent of gross domestic product (GDP) and employs 46,000 people. While it is very small in absolute terms compared with other EC countries, its percentage contribution to GDP is similar, except in the predictable cases of Luxembourg and the United Kingdom where it is over 20 percent.

Having presented this short description of the economy and the financial sector environment in which the Central Bank operates, I will now turn to the bank itself.

Summary of the Bank's Functions

The following is an outline of each function that the bank performs.

(1) It conducts monetary policy, which is aimed at the maintenance of a firm exchange rate in the EMS primarily through the management of domestic liquidity and intervention in the foreign exchange market;

(2) engages in economic and monetary research and analysis to inform and support the bank's policies;

(3) acts as a bankers' bank, which entails maintaining accounts for the banks in respect of the variable reserve requirements, their "clearing" balances for interbank settlement purposes, any discretionary

time deposits, providing them with various forms of secured credits, and facilitating their exchange of clearing items;

(4) acts as banker to the Government, which entails the operation of the Government's major operational revenue and payments accounts, a deposit account for the Minister for Finance, and the occasional provision of restricted overdraft facilities;

(5) manages the official external reserves;

(6) manages the Gilt and Exchequer Bill Market in cooperation with the Department of Finance and stands ready to buy and sell exchequer bills at prevailing market rates and to intervene occasionally in the one- to five-year maturities in gilts in consultation with the department;

(7) provides a Gilt Settlement Office to facilitate dealings in the gilt market;

(8) acts as Registrar of Government Stocks, which entails recording transfers, the payment of dividends and redemption monies;

(9) supervises licensed banks, building societies, Trustee Savings Banks, money brokers, Futures and Options Exchange, and entities in the International Financial Services Center;

(10) produces, issues, and withdraws from circulation currency notes and coin;

(11) administers the remaining exchange controls as agent for the Minister for Finance; and

(12) maintains its own personnel and general administration services.

I should mention two functions that the Central Bank is not involved in which other central banks perform. It does not compile statistics other than those of a monetary or financial nature, and even then it is not responsible for the compilation of balance of payments data. These are compiled by the Government's Central Statistics Office, along with external trade statistics. Second, apart from the post-issue functions of Registrar and assisting market-making in exchequer bills and short bonds, it takes no part in public sector borrowing, external borrowing in particular.

Accounts of the Bank

The bank's latest balance sheet shows that its resources totaled £Ir4.4 billion at the end of 1989.[1] This comprised capital and reserves, £Ir1 billion, legal tender notes, £Ir1.4 billion, government deposits,

[1]*Annual Report*, report of the Central Bank of Ireland for the year ended December 31, 1989 (Dublin: Central Bank of Ireland, 1990).

£Ir1.1 billion, and bankers' deposits and other items, £Ir0.9 billion. The asset counterparts consisted of the official external reserves, £Ir2.6 billion, loans to banks, £Ir1.3 billion, and securities, etc. £Ir0.5 billion. It is interesting to note that 12 months earlier the external reserves were much higher, at £Ir3.2 billion, and loans to banks much smaller, £Ir0.2 billion. This reflects the fact that in 1989 the external reserves fell substantially, and coincidentally government deposits increased by a large amount; both of these actions reduced the banking system's liquidity, which the Central Bank offset by increasing its lending to the banks and by increasing interest rates by 1 percent on four separate occasions during 1989.

The shift from external to domestic assets, as between 1988 and 1989, dictated by external payments and domestic credit developments and the bank's response to them (including the 4 percentage point rise in interest rates) plus an increase in the rate of income earned on the external assets were together reflected in a 44 percent increase in the bank's net profit from £Ir120 million in 1988 to £Ir172 million in 1989. I will have more to say about this later. At this point, I want to say a little more about the performance of one or two of the bank's functions. I shall limit myself to monetary policy and the supervisory function.

Monetary Policy

The Central Bank did not have to concern itself very much with monetary policy matters for many years after its establishment because the fixed parity with sterling was underpinned by substantial holdings of that currency by the clearing banks and economic conditions were relatively stable. In the mid-1950s, minor liquidity difficulties for the banks led it to rediscount small quantities of commercial and exchequer bills and to introduce in 1958 a nonstatutory minimum liquidity ratio. A recurrence of difficulties in the mid-1960s caused the Central Bank to introduce an annual credit "advice" to the banks, and in 1971 the first quantified credit guidelines were issued. Throughout the 1970s and right up to the mid-1980s quantitative private sector credit controls were vigorously used, in the context of sometimes very large external payments deficits, high rates of inflation, and excessive fiscal deficits. Central bank deposit requirements in respect of capital inflows and penalties in the form of special deposits at penal rates in respect of excess lending, as well as sectoral credit controls, were also used. Quite apart from the well-known disabilities arising from the sustained use of quantitative credit controls, in Ireland, especially in the first half of the 1980s, monetary policy was seriously undermined by the very large fiscal deficits and their financing by foreign borrowing and recourse to the banks. Under the Central Bank's system of monetary budgeting the effect was largely the crowding-out or the curtailment of the private sector as far as Irish pound borrowing from domestic banks was concerned.

A number of developments over the past decade have together transformed the context in which monetary policy is now formulated and implemented. Accession to the EMS in March 1979 almost immediately put an end to the 150-year-old fixed parity with sterling. This necessitated the quick maturing of the previously limited interbank Irish pound and foreign exchange markets in Dublin, as well as the introduction by the Central Bank of an overnight credit facility for the banks in substitution of the ready access to the London markets that they had enjoyed up to then. The Central Bank subsequently added other lending facilities that could be used at its discretion to influence liquidity. These developments enabled the bank to adopt progressively the market-related methods of monetary management that were being widely adopted abroad, as rates of inflation declined and theoretical and political objections to direct controls became prevalent.

In recent years, the domestic inflation rate has fallen markedly, the current external account has been in surplus, and the fiscal deficit has been greatly reduced. These have been associated with a favorable international environment and political acceptance at home of the need to accept the discipline of a firm exchange rate policy in the EMS context as a condition for noninflationary growth.

Low inflation is indeed the ultimate objective of monetary policy in Ireland. To help achieve it, the Central Bank aims to maintain a stable exchange rate for the Irish pound in the ERM and to keep the external reserves at an adequate level for that purpose. To attain these objectives, it intervenes in the money markets as appropriate to influence the exchange rate and domestic interest rates. Among the instruments used are (1) varying (normally seasonally) the primary liquidity ratio deposits that banks are obliged to maintain at the Central Bank; (2) changing the rate of interest on the Short-Term Facility (STF rate), which is automatically available at the Central Bank to enable banks to balance their domestic currency market position at the close of each day; (3) effecting short-term swaps of Irish pound versus foreign exchange at the Central Bank's discretion; (4) entering into gilt sale and repurchase agreements (REPOS), which are also at the discretion of the Bank; and (5) modifying its daily interventions in the foreign exchange market to influence the markets' open position and hence the trend in the exchange rate—within the constraints of the ERM band.

Monetary policy is formulated at the beginning of each year on the basis of known or estimated data about money supply, economic developments, and financial flows, including in particular the budgetary position, exchequer funding, and inward and outward flows on the current and capital accounts. Having regard also to developments abroad, a target adequacy level is set for external reserves and a view is formed as to whether interest rates may need to be increased or reduced during the year so as to attain that level and maintain the position of the currency in the EMS. (Targets and views about necessary policy actions are, of course, kept under continuous review as the year unfolds.)

Policy formulation is the responsibility of the Monetary Policy Division of the Central Bank. Their analyses and proposals are considered by the Head of Economic Services, the rest of General Management, and the Governor before finalization and submission to the Board. With the Board's approval of the general thrust of policy, the Governor and General Management are in a position to implement it. Monetary policy developments are reviewed at the Board's monthly meetings and policy is also formally reviewed up to board level at least once during the year and on the occasion of any significant developments. Day-to-day implementation is the responsibility of the Market Sections of the Accounts Department and of the Foreign Exchange Department. They are guided by instructions emerging from weekly meetings of the Markets Committee. This is chaired by the Governor and is at general management level. Its function is to review developments in the foreign exchange, money, and gilt markets and to decide on market objectives and policy actions.

An Exchange Rate Policy Review Committee undertakes periodic assessments of the appropriateness of the current exchange rate policy, having regard to trends in competitiveness, major changes in fundamentals at home or abroad, and research findings in the bank or elsewhere. Finally, an Exchange Rate Policy Implementation Committee conducts a monthly review of developments affecting the major currencies and these and other currencies in the EMS and makes an assessment of possible developments in the coming months.

Supervision of Financial Institutions

The Central Bank's supervisory role began with the Central Bank Act, 1971, which gave it the task of licensing and supervising banks. In addition to the issuing of licenses, the bank was empowered to obtain information from banks about their business; to carry out inspections of banks' books and records; to require banks to publish information about their business; to require banks to maintain prescribed ratios between various categories of assets and liabilities; to attach conditions to licenses; to direct a bank to cease advertising for deposits for a time; and to direct a bank for a limited period to cease taking deposits or making payments if the Central Bank thought it was likely to become insolvent. The Bank was also empowered to refuse to issue a license or to revoke a license, but in either case the Minister for Finance's consent was required.

Following the legislation in 1971, the Central Bank immediately published a list of the standards and requirements it proposed to apply in assessing applications for licenses and in supervising banks on an ongoing basis. It made it clear that these were nonstatutory, but that they could be used as a point of reference if the Bank felt it necessary to attach a statutory condition to any license. The standards published included a minimum paid-up share capital requirement, a minimum own-funds-to-risk-assets ratio of 10 percent and limitations on risk-asset concentration, in particular, borrowers, or connected borrowers or particular economic sectors. (These standards were to become features of international supervisory practice and EC law fifteen years later.) Revisions and extensions of the licensing and supervisory requirements were published in 1975, 1981, and 1987. Implementation is based on the analysis of detailed monthly reporting by all banks, on periodic full inspections, and on twice yearly review meetings with bank managements. The Central Bank also keeps in close touch with the best practice and standards internationally and in particular has been closely involved in the development of banking standards and supervisory legislation in the European Community through participation in the EC Banking Advisory Committee, of which I had the honor to be Chairman in 1986–88.

Recent legislation (the Central Bank Act, 1989) has strengthened and extended the supervisory powers of the Bank. The result is that the Bank is now the supervisor of virtually all financial institutions in the country except insurance companies and those in the securities industry. It seems likely that securities firms and brokers will be brought under the Bank's supervision in the coming few years. There are also new deposit protection schemes for banks and building societies. I am confident that the Bank will be successful in discharging its greatly expanded supervisory role. There are two or three issues relating to this topic that I would like to address briefly.

First, views differ as to whether bank supervision should be a responsibility of the central bank since it is the lender of last resort. My own view is that this is a reason why it should be the supervisor. Another is that the efficacy of its monetary policy role, whether this entails direct controls or market-related methods, is likely to be improved by the additional insights into banks' operations, instruments, and markets that it will gain in the course of supervision, and by the greater assurance it will have that the banks can, for example, cope with restrictive monetary policy measures. In addition, the authority of the central bank in relation to the commercial banks is enhanced by having the dual role.

A further question is whether, as in the case of Ireland, it is beneficial that the central bank should have supervisory responsibility for such a wide range of financial institutions. First, this is more practicable in a small country where the number of entities to be supervised may be more than proportionately smaller than in, for example, the United States, Japan, or the United Kingdom. Second, with the breaking down and blurring of demarcation lines between different kinds of financial institutions in recent years a dilemma for policymakers is whether to focus on functions or on institutions so as to ensure comprehensive supervision. The single supervisor helps to resolve the problem and, incidentally, avoids the danger of lapses of liaison between separate supervisors. The single supervisor also entails a concentration of expertise in the one agency with mutually reinforcing insights, as well as greater economy in the use of resources. Of course, the wider and greater the supervisory responsibilities of the central bank, the greater must be the chance of its incurring criticism for some failure or deficiency in the system, which in turn might damage its standing or impair its independence.

The final observation I wish to make on this topic relates particularly to the prospect of the EMU in Europe and the emergence of a European Central Bank. It is already clear that if this institution is to emerge it will be on the basis of a concentration of monetary policy formulation at and execution from the center. Separate national financial markets would become progressively integrated and the role of existing national central banks may be drastically diminished. In such circumstances, the exercise of local supervision of financial institutions, widely defined, and of the payment system could be significant functions remaining with the national central banks.

The Management Challenge

At this point, it is necessary to bring into sharper focus what essentially the central bank is supposed to do. What is its core function? In Ireland, as elsewhere, one must look principally to the legislation governing the bank's role and operation. The Central Bank Act, 1942 (Section 6(1) and (2)) provides that the Central Bank has the general function and duty of taking such steps as it "may from time to time deem appropriate and advisable towards safeguarding the integrity of the currency . . . ," and that the Minister for Finance may, whenever he wishes, require the Governor or the Board to "consult and advise with" him in regard to the execution and performance by the Bank of its "general function and duty."

Of course, the bank has many other functions, which I have already described; however, safeguarding the integrity of the currency is the real justification for having a separate central banking institution. All other functions could in principle be carried out quite well by a ministry or department of the government, but maintaining the value of the currency domestically and externally is of such importance to the well-being of the economy that it is felt to be appropriate to give the task to an institution that can pursue it single-mindedly, without the danger of being thrown off course by some short-term economic or political objective.

These considerations underscore the logical necessity for ensuring that the central bank is "independent." It would be inconsistent to give the central bank the task of maintaining the value of the currency while interfering with its freedom of action in pursuit of that goal. Even then, the bank cannot hope to succeed in its task if the government pursues policies that are incompatible with monetary stability. Apart from the changing economic circumstances, and perhaps because of them, governments are prone to pursue policies from time to time that are expedient politically but harmful monetarily. And so the central bank must develop the art of marrying flexibility in responding to such economic and political circumstances with a single-minded dedication to the job it has been given. Inevitably, the bank will have encounters with government, but its success will be the more assured (1) if, because of the influence it has exercised on public opinion, for example, through the consistency of its policies and its published commentaries on economic matters, there is popular understanding of and support for the need to adhere to the principles and practice of sound monetary management, and (2) if the standing of the bank is such that the government would be reluctant to take issue with it publicly. In other words, the bank should be regarded as a consistent, dedicated, and effective organization whose dealings with the public are courteous and efficient (e.g., in dealing with inquiries as registrar of government stock issues, as administrator of exchange control regulations, as provider of currency notes and coin, or whatever).

All of the bank's functions, even secondary ones, must be fulfilled effectively and efficiently. Success in this will enhance its prestige and moral authority in the pursuit of its primary objective. It will also maximize the bank's financial return (profit) for the benefit of the Exchequer, or Treasury and, a fortiori, exclude any possible need for financial support from that quarter and thus reinforce the bank's authority or independence in relation to government and politicians in the exercise of its primary function.

The Management Response

How has the Central Bank of Ireland responded to the challenges mentioned earlier? I shall answer the question under five headings: organizational structure, human resources, management procedures, the financial dimension, and relationships.

Outline of Organizational Structure

The bank is headed by the Governor who is full-time head of the organization and Chairman of the Board of Directors. The Governor is appointed by the President of Ireland, on the advice of the Government, for a renewable term of seven years. He has considerable security of tenure and can be removed from office only by the President on the advice of the Government on grounds of ill health or at the unanimous request of the Board for a stated reason. Whereas by now it is almost always the case that the permanent Secretary of the Department of Finance moves on to become Governor of the Bank whenever that office becomes vacant, there is no legal or administrative requirement to the effect. The Governor's function is to chair the Board, to be ultimately responsible for giving effect to monetary and other major policies pursued by the Bank, to conduct the bank's relations with the Minister for Finance and Government, and to represent the Bank domestically and in international forums.

The Board consists of nine Directors and the Governor. Directors are appointed by the Minister for Finance; their term is normally five years (renewable), and they may not be removed from office. They have no executive role and meet every month. By tradition, the permanent Secretary of the Department of Finance is a member of the Board. The Board does not play a major role in running the bank, particularly since its operations have become increasingly technical in nature.

The legislation governing the bank did not envisage a purely supervisory or consultative role for the Board, such as one finds in other central banks, for example, De Nederlandsche Bank, which also has a statutory Executive Board. The Board has been empowered, however, by Section 5(5)(d) of the Central Bank Act of 1942, to delegate to the

Governor by formal regulation the exercise and performance of any of the functions, powers, and duties of the Bank or of the Board. In practice, the Governor, the General Manager, and the other members of top management act, in important matters, especially as regards monetary policy, as an informal Executive Board chaired by the Governor. In fact, I believe that central bank policymaking and implementation is such that a part-time nonexecutive board is not well placed to make a major contribution, especially nowadays when monetary policy is so market-focused and banking supervision (where it is the responsibility of the central bank) is becoming increasingly complex.

The General Manager heads the permanent management team of the bank. He is the Governor's principal adviser on policy matters and, subject to consultation with him on important matters, is responsible for the bank's administration and operations. Since the General Manager is invariably a career central banker, the recurring advent of new governors sometimes represents a stimulating challenge! The General Manager is supported by a Deputy who also acts as Secretary to the Board (they both participate as nonmembers at board meetings) and by a number of Assistant General Managers and the Senior Advisor (the head of Economic Services), to each of whom report the managers of several functional departments or divisions.

The total management complement, including deputy managers, numbered 40 people, at the end of June 1990 and below them a tiered structure of executive, clerical, and ancillary and support staff numbering 640 in all. Of these, about 225 were attributable to currency production and issue functions, which are carried out at a special currency center located some miles from Dublin city center. Including management, a total of 450 people are engaged in noncurrency functions, all performed at the bank's single-office premises in Dublin. It is not, therefore, a very big organization; a further advantage, from an administrative point of view, is that all functions are performed at just two locations in modern, high-quality premises.

Human Resources

The success of the bank depends ultimately on the quality and motivation of its staff. Obviously, motivation is important and needs to be worked at. The conservative and often reactive orientation of a central bank's work can have an impact on attitudes of middle and senior management. In recent years, innovation in commercial banking, in terms of engineering and marketing of new financial products, has relegated the role of the central banker to that of observer, learner, and perhaps worried supervisor; the central banker is rarely at the forefront of developments—normally, a step or two behind. This can lead to a loss of ambitious young managers looking to be in on the action. This particular problem is difficult to cope with. In my own experience I have consciously sought to have managers in the bank identify with the banking and commercial world and not be overidentified as part of a bureaucracy that appears to be at odds with the private sector ethos of the banks.

Other, more concrete, negative factors we have had to live with have been unfavorable pay and conditions compared with the commercial banks and the financial sector generally and, in recent years, a slowdown in promotional opportunities because of the age profile of the staff and a leveling off of the functional growth of the bank. Although the bank has the statutory independence to determine pay matters for itself, public service standards prevail because the Government sometimes exerts pressure on the bank to conform to public sector pay restraint guidelines; the bank itself is publicly committed to supporting pay restraint at the national level. As you can see, there is quite an incubus of negatives to contend with as far as morale is concerned. In recent years, the bank has lost a number of young promising staff, especially those who have gained experience as economists or in the foreign exchange dealing or money markets—to the extent that this has to be budgeted for in recruitment and training policies. Of course, the loss of such people to the domestic financial sector is not all bad. In a small country it is very effective in widening and deepening an understanding of the bank's role and of its techniques with respect to the markets. It is also not uncommon for former central bankers to occupy in due course very senior positions in some, including the largest, of the commercial banks. I should say too that those who stay on to form the management team in the Central Bank tend to be highly motivated and dedicated to what they are doing despite the less attractive reward system under which they operate.

I turn now to the question of maintaining the levels of skill and expertise in the staff, which is necessary if the bank is to do the best possible job. Against the background of a plentiful supply of high-grade, second-level school leavers and of constraints arising from the unionization of existing staff, the only general staff recruitment in the bank is clerical. In addition, well-qualified economists, accountants, and information technology specialists are recruited directly. All appointments are by open competition. Great care is taken to implement on-the-job training, interdepartmental staff mobility programs (which incidentally are continued right up to departmental management level), regular assessment, and impartially structured competitions for promotion. All staff are encouraged and rewarded for taking the examinations of the Institute of Bankers and very many do. In addition, an Academic and Professional Training Scheme (APTS) is in operation under which all fees are paid in advance by the bank and, as in the case of the Institute of Bankers exams, study and exam leave of absence is allowed. The list of university degree and professional courses covered by this scheme is extensive and the number of participating staff high. Excluding the cost of training on the job, I estimate that training related costs incurred by the bank in 1989 came to over 4.2 percent of total head-office payroll. Overall, there is a conscious management-led emphasis on expertise and professionalism, the influence of which on staff is reinforced by the prevailing ethos in the financial sector generally. Virtually all of the economists in the bank are recruited after academic qualification and often with some postgraduate employment experience.

Turnover of economist staff is high, and recruitment options, such as short-term appointments and project research contracts, are not excluded. Accountants to staff the supervisory side of the bank's work are recruited occasionally but most now come from within, having qualified professionally on the basis of the APTS and having benefitted from extensive training as members of inspection teams. Overall, the caliber of bank staff is high: virtually all of management are university graduates, many have higher level degrees in economics, business, statistics, or law, and many others of the staff are also university graduates or holders of the Certificate of the Institute of Bankers.

Management Procedures

I now turn to some of the management arrangements and procedures employed in the bank to enhance efficiency. First, a brief further word about the respective roles of the Board, the Governor, and senior management. In the early days of the bank, with the fixed sterling link, management's concern must have focused on how and when to implement the many functions bestowed by statute on the new bank. In that task, any significant decisions, and they were few, were effectively taken by the Governor. There was no significant management need or capacity in the bank. As the bank expanded the exercise of its role in the 1960s and 1970s, the Board, which at that time included representatives of the clearing banks, enjoyed its most active and influential period, while the Governors were active agents of change and development. From the late 1960s, the senior permanent staff of the bank began to have a progressively bigger role in management. This coincided with significant increases in staff numbers associated with currency manufacture and processing, credit policy formation, and implementation and the undertaking of banking supervision. In the late 1970s and through the 1980s, the work of the bank became more complex and technical; now, only major policy decisions are referred to the Board. Subject to the Board's endorsement, the Governor forms policy decisions in consultation with the general management, while control of the administration of the bank is largely in the hands of senior permanent management also.

The general approach to management in the bank is probably influenced by a feeling that the organization is not so big as to require or justify a bureaucratic, impersonal approach. Whereas administrative arrangements in the bank are comprehensive and systematically structured, the management ethos is relaxed and friendly. Considerable attention is devoted to effective internal communication. Each departmental manager completes a one- or two-page "Work Report" each two weeks itemizing and indicating the state of progress on tasks in hand in that department. All departments' Work Reports are circulated to all other departmental managers and to general management.

The General Manager, his deputy, the assistant general managers, and the head of Economic Services constitute a General Management Committee (GMC), which meets monthly to discuss and help make decisions on significant management issues including those reported on or referred up by the Departmental Management Committee (DMC). This group also meets monthly to deal with management issues that transcend departmental boundaries. A third committee, meeting regularly at general management level, is the Financial Control Committee, which pursues general or specific issues arising from regular monthly reports furnished by the Internal Auditor on his inspections of the records, control procedures, and systems operating in the various departments.

The work of these three committees has been productive. For example, it gave rise to an annual budgeting and planning system that has given a much sharper focus to management's efforts to run an efficient organization. Briefly, this entails the production each year by departmental management and final approval by general management, all within a three-month period (November–February), of reviews of each department's work during the year, its plans for the coming year, its budget outturns and proposals (centrally computerized), its space and other physical needs, and finally each department's staffing and skills requirements. Before final adoption of the integrated program, each departmental manager's input must be processed and agreed upon with the particular assistant general manager to whom the manager reports and this serves also as a personal assessment process. Finally, the staffing and skills requirements established for each department provide an input into a rolling three-year manpower planning process for which the Personnel Department is responsible.

The cost-budgeting exercise that is now operational has proved useful. It was realized from an early stage that ideally the process should be zero-based, but it was also realized that if this were adopted as a starting point for all departments the amount of work involved would be intolerable and the exercise counterproductive. We therefore decided that each year, in a cyclical pattern, two or three departments would be required to produce zero-based cost estimates. The experience with the departments first chosen has shifted the focus of the exercise from strict costing to what was termed an "Activity Based Review." This was done, with limited external consultation by multilevel teams within the departments radically examining all the significant tasks performed—why, how, alternative approaches, and so on. That the exercise was a self-examination and that junior staff participated as well as senior made it fruitful in a number of ways.

Before leaving "management procedures" I want to refer to information technology, which of course is now an indispensable tool of modern business. In 1986, the bank began to progressively upgrade and extend its computer installation to cover the operations of all departments. Installation of a satisfactory system is expensive and risky and needs careful management. It is extremely important to employ a carefully selected, project-oriented consultancy firm to advise and assist at every stage of planning and implementation. Top management must also be committed and fully supportive, and a high-level steering group is necessary to determine priorities and sort out interdepartmental rivalries. The project in the bank has been successful, every stage being satisfactorily completed within budget and in good time.

The Financial Dimension

Much of what I have been saying about human resources and management procedures is, of course, in effect about minimizing operating overheads consistent with effective discharge of our central banking tasks. The relevant figure in the Central Bank's accounts is £Ir17.3 million in 1989, comprising £Ir10.8 million in salaries and wages and £Ir6.5 million in nonpay expenses.

The other big outlay is the £Ir100 million interest paid on deposits, that is, government and bankers' deposits. When you consider that the bankers' deposits are almost all obligatory, in accordance with the "primary liquidity" (reserve asset) requirement, it might seem that the bank could readily increase its profits by reducing the market-related rate of interest it pays on such deposits. Account must be taken, however, of the knock-on effect on the commercial banks' profits or the net cost of their services to the public. In fact, when quoting loan rates for larger corporate clients, banks normally tend to build in an explicit reserve asset cost covering this element plus the alleged cost of the secondary (government stock) ratio requirement to which they are also subject. Likewise, the issue of whether to effect a change in the system of monetary control by reducing the level of compulsory reserve requirements runs into the question of the impact on the Central Bank's and commercial banks' respective profits—that is in addition to the overriding monetary policy implications.

The rate of interest paid by the bank on government deposits is ultimately of no account since the bank's annual profits are paid over to the Exchequer, but the Department of Finance would tend to want as high a rate as it can get from the bank, if only because it is an item of revenue with which that particular department will be credited in the system of government accounting.

I should mention here an element of the bank's resources on which it pays no interest, namely, the note issue. It would be interesting to observe the secular trend of the note issue as a proportion of the broader categories of money supply, or of, say, gross domestic expenditure, or to speculate about the effect thereon of the ever-growing use of plastic cards or electronic means of payment. I do not suppose there is much a central bank can do about that or would want to, perhaps, having regard to efficiency and security considerations affecting cash movements nowadays. On the other hand, the cost of currency production and, more particularly, the relative costs of note and coin production and the relative durability of notes and coins are matters to which the Central Bank directs attention for reasons of cost and profit, although other considerations such as aesthetics, hygiene, and the needs of the handicapped arise also.

I turn now to income. Disposition of the bank's assets, as between domestic and foreign (i.e., the external reserves), is really a function of what is happening to the level of the external reserves resulting from the net external flows of the economy on the current and capital accounts and of the bank's policy response. A net loss of reserves resulting from intervention sales of foreign exchange by the bank has its counterpart in a reduction in the banking system's domestic liquidity. Depending on its policy stance, the bank will restore more or less of the liquidity depletion, allowing the level of interest rates to increase less or more, correspondingly. In all likelihood, for sustained sizable flows, some central bank lending will take place but interest rates will also rise. The bank's normal experience is that a period of strain in the foreign exchange market tends to produce a substitution of higher-earning domestic assets for lower-earning external reserves with favorable implications for the bank's profits, as happened in 1989. This paradoxical result is entirely incidental—a by-product of monetary policy action. Likewise, a buildup of government balances in the bank, to the extent that it represents a seasonal or other temporary loss of liquidity to the banks, is likely to be compensated for by central bank lending to the banks (as a smoothing operation). This, incidentally, will entail a profitable temporary expansion of the bank's balance sheet.

On the other hand, purposeful management of the external reserves can produce profit increments for the Central Bank.[2] Obviously, liquidity and security must have priority, and there are many golden rules to follow here, relating inter alia to the choice of currencies, adherence to target ranges for the proportionate mix of currencies, the choice of investment instruments, observance of limits on certain instruments and maturities, and care in the choice and monitoring of banking depositories. The bank applies a considerable number of limits and rules dealing with these matters. The reserve-management staff are expected to maximize profit by the application of a number of conventional yield-enhancing techniques, notably by timely variations in the overall average life of the currency portfolios. I say "conventional" because I believe the Central Bank should be quite slow to employ new financial products and techniques in this area. Establishing satisfactory benchmarks for reserve-asset management performance is a difficult problem for which I do not have a ready solution.

Looking to other items of revenue, the Central Bank may, for example, charge, on a suitable cost basis, for agency work undertaken for government, such as maintaining the government stock register. Again, given the destination of the bank's profits, it may be felt that it does not matter very much, but there can be disciplinary merit in the costing and charging both for the bank and the Exchequer. Then, there is the question of charging banks and other credit institutions in respect of supervision costs. The Central Bank of Ireland is now empowered by the latest legislation to do so.

I turn now to the balance sheet. It is obviously necessary that this should show an impregnable position. In commercial banking, inter-

[2]On this subject, see a useful article by Patrick Downes, "Managing Foreign Exchange Reserves," in *Finance and Development* (Washington), Vol. 26 (December 1989), pp. 20–21.

nationally agreed capital adequacy ratios have been established through the work of the Basle Committee and of the Banking Advisory Committee of the EC. Applying capital ratios based on these formulations to central banks would be spurious. Yet, the concept does have validity for central banks, because a central bank could become insolvent technically. Rough calculation of the capital ratios of central banks based on their published accounts produces widely different results. Each central bank should look at this, because a weak position might oblige it to seek some form of support—financial or legislative—from its government, thereby undermining its independence.

How could a central bank's capital position be eroded? Principally by a strengthening of the domestic currency, which would necessitate writing down gold and foreign currency assets in its portfolio. (I am assuming that the central bank carries the official external reserves as an asset in its balance sheet, which is not universally the case.) Ironically, the bigger the proportion of foreign currency assets in the balance sheet and the greater the strengthening of the domestic currency, the bigger will be the capital (book) losses of the central bank expressed in domestic currency. Likewise, if foreign currency assets form a large proportion of the total and domestic currency weakens, there will be a significant capital gain in the books. The obvious protection for the central bank, in the face of such fluctuations, is to fortify its capital position by building up capital reserves as much as possible from profit retentions and retention of capital gains on appreciation of its assets. This depends on the statute governing the bank and the forbearance of the shareholder, normally the state.

In Ireland, the bank's capital position is strong notwithstanding having a large proportion of foreign exchange assets on average in its balance sheet and the Irish pound having a stable position in the EMS narrow band for a considerable time. This reflects the fact that, on the one hand, statutory regulations and the practices governing the disposal of its annual profits and the valuation of its assets have accommodated the retention of reasonable reserves.

A central bank should in principle wish to have the format of its accounts and their information content accord with the best commercial and standard accounting practices. This may be facilitated by the use of private sector auditors. In Ireland, the job is done by a public sector officer called the Comptroller and Auditor General, who can be quite demanding. The involvement of the state auditor, which is statutorily required in the case of the Central Bank of Ireland, can be helpful on balance in buttressing the independence of the bank by making or appearing to make it more publicly accountable.

Relationships

I come now to relationships. It goes without saying that all of the bank's relationships must be consciously directed at promoting the attainment of its primary objective of monetary stability. In some cases, the objective will be almost explicit, as in its relationships with the Minister for Finance; in other cases, it is more indirect, as when, in its dealings with the public, the bank is seeking to build a generally favorable image, which will come into play when monetary policy has to become restrictive.

The most important relationship is, of course, that with the Minister for Finance and the Government. The relationship with the Minister for Finance is statutorily based—most notably in connection with the "general exchange rate arrangements," "specific exchange rate adjustments," and the requirement of Section 6(2) of the 1942 Act under which the Minister may require the Governor or the Board to "consult and advise with" him in regard to the exercise by the Bank of its function of safeguarding the integrity of the currency. In practice, the Minister may informally invite the Governor to discuss some aspect of monetary policy with him or, indeed, the Governor may take the initiative. Such meetings are not frequent however; a possible alternative would be a firm arrangement for regular, but not too frequent, meetings between the Governor and the Minister. The practice in this regard varies from country to country, and apart from constitutional and political factors, the personalities of the Governor and the Minister are important considerations. For central banks, this is the most important relationship of all, and its nature can be strongly affected by the quality of the bank's other relationships, especially its standing with the public, because, in extremis, the bank's ultimate recourse is to the public, over the heads of the politicians. Their sanction is to change the law governing the bank.

The relationship with the Minister or the Government touches on the core of the bank's "independence." Whatever the degree of independence given by law or by practice to the Central Bank, in my view, it must continue to be worked for every day. The degree of independence will ebb and flow in a democracy with changes in governments and personalities and circumstances. Sustaining the bank's independence requires some delicacy of understanding and touch on the part of the Minister and, especially, his advisers. Likewise, in the bank itself it calls for something of an art—I have always so regarded it—the bank must not be so assertive as to test the natural reactions of the Minister and his advisers too far.

It needs to recognize that, ultimately, power rightly resides in the Government, acting in accordance with its constitutional status and responsibility. So the art in the bank is to know when to bend with the wind and when to stand ground, but not to the point of provoking a legislative curtailment of its powers; to recognize the legitimacy of politicians' primary concern with growth, employment, and perhaps resource transfers, but to be insistent on the perils of "short term-ism" and on the long-run benefits of monetary stability. In the "balance of powers" in economic management, the central banker's role is to be the conservative—the seeker after restraint, stability, and balance. We are likely to be more successful if we are adequately aware of the politicians' view of things, including their concern with growth, employment, and "economic and social cohesion."

Closely connected to the relationship with the Minister and the Government are the bank's relations with the Ministry of Finance and its officials. These call for vigilance on the part of the bank. First, it is important for the bank's officers to be seen domestically and externally as not being part of the central administration—this obviously relates to the question of independence and separateness from government. Second, the bank can relate more effectively to the financial sector, to the markets, and to other central banks if it is seen to be separate from the Ministry. Third, ministry officials may tend to be overintrusive in liaising with the bank on matters relating to the markets: they may be anxious at times to anticipate and, if possible, to head off changes that may create difficulty for their Minister.

In Ireland, relations with Parliament and politicians are generally not very active. The major factor in a democratic state such as Ireland, with changes of government parties and of ministerial personnel, is the cumulative buildup of relations with former ministers and governments. On the whole, these are favorable to the bank, reflecting a degree of respect for its integrity and the importance of its role. The annual report and accounts of the bank are required statutorily to be laid before each House of the Parliament every year.

The Central Bank of Ireland has a multifaceted relation with the commercial banks—as their licensing authority, their banker, their supplier of currency, the intervenor in their markets, and their supervisor. The bank's policy has always been to develop harmonious relationships, relying as far as possible on cooperation and persuasion rather than on the exercise of statutory powers. The shift of focus in monetary policy from credit regulation to reliance on market mechanisms on the one hand, and on the other, the extension of the bank's role as supervisor in the context of the development of more sophisticated markets and financial products has necessitated a widening and deepening of the bank's staff contacts with the commercial banks and the financial sector, generally. Familiarity with an expanding range of banks and financial institutions and markets (to which, e.g., the Bank of England or the Federal Reserve are accustomed by reason of the size of their financial centers and their history) is something the Central Bank of Ireland is consciously working to develop further. It is conscious that there is more to be done by way of formal and informal contacts with, for example, bank treasuries, fund managers, and other categories of market participants, not only to ensure that its market interventions are most effective but also, in the process, to preserve and enhance its standing and influence in a wider context.

Relations with the media are seen as important but as posing a number of dilemmas. Should they be pro-active or re-active? Should the bank have an in-house press office(r) or engage external public relations services—or neither? My own attitude has tended to be negative—based on a judgment that the bank's best interests and purposes are better served by saying less rather than more. The media in Ireland are voluble and fairly well informed about monetary matters and ad hoc or gratuitous comments by the bank are likely to be pursued and analyzed to discover a hidden significance that was never there. The bank's necessary reticence about market-sensitive policy intentions and actions creates a mystique, which is regrettable in some ways. I read a comment recently that said that a congressman had paid Chairman Greenspan an unwitting compliment when he described his testimony to the House of the U.S. Congress about monetary policy as "obfuscatory." Central bankers will understand why that was a compliment! Another aspect of media interest in the central bank is the independence or authority of the bank. It is better to have tacit acceptance of these than to have them the subject of public debate or comment, which might act as a provocation to a politician looking for a cause!

Other domestic categories calling for the management of relationships include special interest groups, for example, farming organizations, the Confederation of Industry, the trades union congress, the citizens at large (the bank has had a now-diminishing role in regard to consumer complaints against banks).

Finally, I should mention international relations. Mostly in the framework of the International Monetary Fund (IMF), the Bank for International Settlements (BIS), the EC committees, namely, the Committee of Governors, the Monetary Committee, and the Banking Advisory Committee, the bank has invested considerable management and staff resources in furthering its relations with other central banks. Leaving aside the direct purpose of these various institutions and forums, important incidental advantages flow from these relationships, for example, personal acquaintance with top bank supervisors in other countries, which can be of immense practical advantage in the event of a crisis affecting one of the banks in your jurisdiction. There is also the possibility of sharing knowledge and experience regarding, for example, management of external reserves, implementation of monetary policy, and aspects of relationships with government and banks.

Successful Central Banking

Is it possible to evaluate a central bank's performance? I believe it is, and I hope I have suggested a number of the more important criteria by which to form a judgment. As central bankers, it is to our advantage to cultivate a capacity for regular critical appraisal of what we are doing and why and how and how well, first to improve our effectiveness but also so that we can anticipate proposals for change from other quarters.

An objective evaluation must be relative. It must have regard to a host of attendant circumstances. The rate of inflation, even the direction in which it is moving, which might appear to be the ultimate test of a central bank's performance, cannot be so regarded given the multiplicity of factors, most of them outside the influence of the central bank, that contribute to it. Likewise the soundness of banks, if the central bank is the supervisor, is not a function only of its skill and diligence, but also of the performance and integrity of banks' management, not to mention macroeconomic developments and systemic trends and influences.

Given, therefore, these qualifications that must attend any appraisal of a central bank's performance, I thought it might be useful to attempt to outline the factors that appear to be most relevant to the successful exercise of a central bank's tasks:

(1) *The historical timing and pace of the central bank's evolution* in the context of the national political and economic development and that of the financial sector. Some central banks were born out of, or reborn out of, monetary crises, others from the sovereign's need for cheap finance, and others from an idealistic or theoretical perception of the economic or political benefit that would ensue. Those in the first category start with an advantage in that they are more likely to benefit from an endemic fear of monetary excess. Those in the last category, which include Ireland, have an advantage of starting out with a clean slate—no tradition of lending to government, for example.

(2) *The maturity of social and political structures.* This includes secure political institutions, reasonable stability of governments in office, and the integrity and competence of public administration. I would also advert to the advantage of a good general standard of literacy, education, and lawfulness, all of which imply a greater general receptivity to the concepts and principles the central bank wishes to impart.

(3) *The content and quality of central banking legislation.* The salient consideration here is the degree of independence explicitly or potentially bestowed on the bank. The elements to look for are: (i) whether the bank has an expressed obligation to protect the value of the currency, or similar, for example, minimize the rate of inflation; (ii) whether its duty in that respect is qualified or compromised by a parallel obligation to have regard to or to support the general economic policy of the government (which surprisingly is the case in Germany); (iii) whether the Governor and members of the Board of Directors have statutory security of tenure of office; (iv) the extent to which the Minister for Finance is directly represented on the Board; and (v) whether the Governor or Board has an obligation to take directions from or "confer with" the government and whether in the event of conflict, there are robust provisions to give reasonable support to the bank's position. The statutory provisions in this regard in the Netherlands are often held out as a good example. In this context generally, of course, the personal qualities of the Governor and of the board members can be at least as important as their statutory independence.

Another aspect of the governing legislation to be considered is the extent of the functions it bestows on the bank. My own view is that it is to the benefit of the bank in pursuing its core monetary functions that it should have responsibility for a wide range of related tasks, especially the issue of the circulating media, the secure functioning of the payments system, the supervision of all credit institutions and of the wholesale financial markets. The discharge of all these functions, with monetary policy, are mutually reinforcing and their effective and efficient discharge enhances the authority of the bank over the long haul.

Finally, on the legislative aspect, there is considerable advantage in the law not being overprescriptive as to how the central bank is to discharge its functions—that is, in allowing it to exercise flexibility in its administration.

(4) *The prevalence of "responsible" fiscal and economic policies on the part of government.* We would all agree that this is the sine qua non of success for a central bank. In the case of Ireland, with a broad-brush approach, I would say that in the period from the early 1970s to the mid-1980s fiscal policy was frequently or generally inimical to mone-

tary stability, failing particularly to adjust to external shocks, such as oil price hikes and economic slowdown in the United Kingdom, whereas in the past three years or so it has been quite favorable owing both to government commitment and to responsible support on the part of the main opposition party. There are those who would say that the real basis of the stable growth and exceptionally good economic performance in Ireland in recent years has been its membership in the EC and, specifically, in the narrow band of the ERM, which has forced a relatively tough economic discipline on the economy together with the fall in oil prices, an improvement in agricultural prices, and recovery in the United Kingdom. Regarding the bank, the seeds of its contribution were sown over many years, first, by constant insistence, in public and in private, on the need for adjustment and second, by its implementation of the discipline of the ERM.

(5) *The size and openness of an economy and of its financial sector and markets.* In Ireland, the extreme openness of the economy and the mobility of capital argue strongly for pegging the currency to that of a major trading partner with a low-inflation experience if the objective of low domestic inflation is to be achieved. The Central Bank can take some credit for the decision to adhere to the narrow band of the ERM, although this policy choice could not have been made without the wholehearted commitment of the Department of Finance, or obviously without a strong political will to take that road. The monetary policy consequences of such a choice, focusing essentially on central bank money creation, puts a premium on the bank's resolve in the face of possible government and public unwillingness to accept the necessary discipline.

(6) *Law and practice with regard to direct central bank funding of fiscal deficits.* If the bank is unable to extricate itself from such an obligation, its position is radically compromised.

(7) *The degree of freedom the bank enjoys to administer its operations efficiently and the extent of its financial independence.* Given the focus of my paper, I have already discussed these at length as far as the Central Bank of Ireland is concerned.

To sum up, all of the foregoing serves to remind us of the great variety of historical, social, political, economic, and legislative environments in which different central banks find themselves having to function. It is, therefore, not easy—nor is it indeed useful—to make judgments about their relative performance. It can be instructive, however, to focus on how an individual central bank has performed in its own environment.

Part II

Central Bank Independence

8

Role and Independence of Central Banks

ANTONIO FAZIO*

Toward the end of 1962, when the "monetarist controversy" was raging in academic circles, I was attending classes at the Massachusetts Institute of Technology. The graduate course of Monetary Theory was taught by Professor Samuelson, with the assistance of Albert Ando. One day a student came into class with a mimeographed copy of Friedman and Schwartz's *A Monetary History of the United States, 1867–1960.*[1] The manuscript was several inches thick. Professor Samuelson looked at it, weighed it in his hand, and said (more or less literally, I quote from memory): "Milton, Milton, we set up the Fed to adjust the quantity of money to the needs of the economy." It was a critique, but also, in a nutshell, a philosophy of central banking. I will return to this point later, at greater length.

Having implicitly declared my exposure—and my affiliation—to a vision of the economy that can be broadly defined as "Keynesian," let me nevertheless immediately state my conviction regarding (1) the importance of nominal quantities of money and credit (and not only of their relative prices with respect to other financial assets and liabilities, in other words, interest rates); and (2) the distrust of excessive activism in monetary intervention.

These two positions, together with the revival of the importance of monetary policy for the control of both output and prices, are certainly a product of what we may call a monetarist vision of the economy. I shall be more analytical and define the points I want to discuss and the arguments.

---

*The author is Deputy Director General of the Bank of Italy.

[1]See Friedman and Schwartz (1963).

What Is Money?

Let me begin by discussing what money is (not only what money does) in an analytical model, in which there are an independent state, a fiscal activity, a market, and a banking system. Modern economic theory has taught us that in such a context money may be a good that has no intrinsic value.[2] The amount of fiduciary money must be determined by forces that are outside the market. This requisite is necessary for units of money to have a determinate value.

Fiduciary money, circulating in the economy, embodies a credit on the authority that issues it. There must be reliance on some economic entity that is absolutely secure, that guarantees the value of money, or that has the authority to issue it. This requisite is necessary to ensure its general acceptability, in other words, to ensure its absolute or perfect liquidity. Since every private agent in a market economy can fail, the only authority that can guarantee all its debentures is the state—thanks to its power to levy taxes.

In ancient societies and early political organizations, money often circulated that had only conventional value.[3] It was when the authority of the state was not sufficiently strong that the circulating medium needed to have an intrinsic value (although even then the weight generally had to be certified by a sovereign). Within the state, money possessed clearly fiduciary characteristics. It was issued by the sovereign and circulated on the basis of confidence in his authority. It embodied a claim on the authority that issued it (to finance public expenditure), and accepted it back for tax payments. In this interpretation, there appears to be a close connection between public expenditure and money circulation and between sound fiscal policy and the value of money. (I am aware of the danger of simplifying complex historical phenomena by using modern analytical instruments, but I am confident that the interpretation is basically correct.)

In medieval times, there are instances of bankers issuing notes that were the certification of given quantities of precious metals deposited with them, first in Italy, and then in other important markets and cities in Europe.[4] In the loose institutional settings of the time, precious metals were the only internationally accepted medium of exchange. But, gradually, bankers' notes representing the value of the deposited metals began to circulate; they generally paid no interest and served as the basis for exchange and credit operations between different places. Bankers then experimented with the issue of notes that were backed

[2]See Patinkin (1956). For what money does, see Modigliani (1944) and (1963).
[3]See Crawford (1982) and Forzoni (1989).
[4]See Spufford (1988).

not by deposits of precious metals but by credits on merchants or, in some instances, on kings and foreign states.

The modern concept of banking activity began to emerge. Some credits to monarchs proved ruinous, both for the bankers and for their depositors. Modern states, which began to emerge in the seventeenth century with stronger institutional arrangements, "invented" the banks of issue. Some have evolved into what we now consider modern central banks.

The general acceptability of a medium of exchange can be established by decree. In this case, bank notes are raised to the status of legal tender for all payments, public and private. The imposition of the medium must be well received by the market and will become effective if there is confidence in the final debtor.

The Emergence of Central Banks

The origin and use of the expression "central bank" in academic literature goes back to the early decades of this century. In actual legislation, and in the usage of practical men and politicians, the term is a rather recent one. One definition describes the central bank as the "bank of banks." Other definitions are the bank of the treasury and the bank for the external sector of the economy, that is, the custodian of a country's foreign currency reserves.

If a central bank were only a bank of the banks, independence or degrees of autonomy would not be issues. Indeed, commercial banks are independent in their actions, subject only to legal limitations related to their special activity. For a central bank, the issue of independence arises when it is required—by law, by tradition, by the development of monetary theory, or by public opinion—to perform tasks that are considered to be of public interest. The institution charged with pursuing these particular public objectives is a bank of the banks, an institution that was historically generated by market forces. It would be difficult, I venture to say impossible, to assign those functions to a public body that was not so intrinsically linked with, and involved in, the working of the financial system.

The Bank of England during the nineteenth century emerged as a lender of last resort for the London bill market and progressively assumed the functions of a central bank.[5] Together with a response to the needs of liquidity control, there was, from time to time, the need to stabilize the value of the pound in terms of gold. All this presupposed and required a growing involvement of the bank with the market.

---

[5] See Hawtrey (1932).

The status of bank of issue was essential in performing these functions. Bank notes were considered a substitute for specie for certain classes of payments; the value of the bank notes was guaranteed by the gold reserve. When liquidity was tight, the government or parliament authorized, and basically guaranteed, an expansion in the volume of bank notes in circulation in excess of the rigid limits set by the gold reserve. The value of the bank notes, their liquidity, and their acceptability therefore rested ultimately on the existence of a gold reserve and on credit to the private sector, but in stringent periods an authorization and a guarantee from the political authority were also deemed necessary.

The U.S. Federal Reserve System was created in 1913 to act as a clearing house for the financial system and to provide liquidity to commercial banks under strain for cyclical or seasonal reasons by means of rediscounting. In practice, the system was also charged with the pursuit of public interest tasks of control over the circulation of the currency and of some operations of the banking system. Some of these functions had been previously performed by the U.S. Treasury.[6]

In Europe, several of what we now consider, and call, central banks were established as banks of issue: their bank notes had the status of legal tender and rigid provisions linked the volume of bank notes in circulation to the gold reserves; they also had special relationships with the treasury and the government.

Growing Need for Regulated Financial Systems

Financial crises that affect other economies and burgeoning financial markets have made authorities realize that financial systems need to be regulated.

Financial Instability

The Great Depression of the 1930s, with all its appalling social and political consequences, was partly due to a series of mistakes, lack of coordination, and rigidities in the conduct of monetary policy by the authorities and the central banks of the principal countries.[7] The restrictive impact of each reduction in bank credit, as a consequence of the crisis, on investment and production was amplified by the multiplier and by international trade.[8] In every country, the crisis led to,

[6]See Timberlake (1978).
[7]See Friedman and Schwartz (1963); Hawtrey (1932); and League of Nations (1944).
[8]See Keynes (1936).

and was amplified by, bank failures. The close relationship between economic and financial crisis and between macroeconomic regulation and banking stability became more evident.

The first consequence was the tendency of various economies to close their frontiers to international economic and financial dealings. Banking and financial legislation was adopted that regulated intermediaries and markets in a much more penetrating and detailed manner than ever before. Banks of issue acquired new powers; new government bodies were created to supervise and regulate the banking sector.

An unstable money supply, which included not only specie and bank notes but also banks' checking accounts, also emerged.[9] It became clear that the credit policies and behavior of banks affected and could upset monetary policy. Hence the dramatic proposal, coming from such a free-market-oriented center as the University of Chicago, of a 100 percent reserve requirement on checking accounts and the suppression of certain operations of private banking.[10]

Since World War II, growth and stability have been unprecedented. International trade has been liberalized and has become an engine of growth; it benefitted from the new monetary order provided by the Bretton Woods agreements. Public expenditure has grown considerably, even too much, providing a built-in stabilizer for the economic cycle. These conditions have drastically reduced financial instability by comparison with both the interwar period and the early years of this century.

Certainly, the economic environment and new international monetary arrangements have had a decisive effect on the performance of the financial systems, but monetary authorities and central banks have made good use of the expertise gained from earlier disastrous experiences.

Expanding Financial Markets

There are two macroeconomic aspects of the financial performance of national economies and of the international economy to which I want to draw attention.

First, the degree of financial deepening of the industrial economies has increased steadily over the last fifteen years. Table 1 shows how the volume of financial assets owned by the domestic private sector has evolved in relation to gross domestic product in six leading industrial

---

[9]See Keynes (1930). An explicit definition, the first to my knowledge, of the total quantity of money, as we usually consider it today, was given by Keynes in the *Treatise*, in particular, Volume I, *The Pure Theory of Money*, Book I, "The Nature of Money," p. 9, see Keynes (1930).

[10]See Simons (1934) and Hart (1935).

Table 1. Ratios of Domestic Financial Assets to GDP

	1975	1980	1985	1988
United States				
Households	2.2	2.4	2.5	2.6
Firms[1]	1.9	2.1	2.4	2.7
Total	4.1	4.5	4.9	5.3
Japan				
Households	1.1	1.3	1.8	2.2
Firms[1]	2.9	3.2	4.0	5.1
Total	4.1	4.6	5.9	7.3
Germany				
Households	0.9	1.0	1.2	1.2
Firms[1]	3.3	3.7	4.5	4.6
Total	4.2	4.7	5.7	5.9
France				
Households	1.0[2]	1.0	1.2	1.3
Firms[1]	2.5[2]	2.7	3.4	4.2
Total	3.5[2]	3.8	4.5	5.5
United Kingdom				
Households	1.3	1.3	1.8	2.0
Firms[1]	1.5	1.5	2.1	2.6
Total	2.8	2.7	3.9	4.6
Italy				
Households	0.9	0.9	1.1	1.3
Firms[1]	1.9	1.9	2.2	2.1
Total	2.8	2.8	3.3	3.4

Sources: Organization for Economic Cooperation and Development (OECD); *Financial Accounts*, for the United Kingdom; *CSO Financial Statistics*, for Italy, Bank of Italy.

[1]Firms include nonfinancial enterprises, banks, insurance companies, pension funds, and other financial institutions.

[2]Data are for 1977.

countries. In all the countries, the ratio has increased considerably, and constantly. In other words, the quantitative importance of the balance sheets of banks and other financial intermediaries has increased, and the financial markets have developed. This means that the expenditure behavior of households and firms is now dependent on the composition, nature, and yield of financial assets more than in the past.

The second aspect concerns the international economy. The size of the international financial markets, in relation to the world economy, as measured by available indicators, also grew dramatically in the last fifteen years. International banking activity, measured in terms of banks' total external assets, almost doubled. The international Eurobond market grew even more rapidly (Table 2).

Table 2. Growth of International Financial Intermediation

Year	Percentage Ratio of Banks' External Assets to GDP[1]	Percentage Ratio of International Bonds to GDP[2]
1975	10.6	0.5[3]
1980	17.0	2.2[3]
1985	30.9	6.3
1990[4]	33.6	8.4

Source: Bank for International Settlements (BIS).

[1]All banks in BIS reporting countries plus some offshore markets; end-of-the-year data. OECD area GDP at current prices and exchange rates.

[2]Total outstanding international bonds; end-of-the-year data. OECD area GDP at current prices and exchange rates.

[3]Estimates.

[4]Estimates based on second-quarter figures.

International banking activity is, as a first approximation, outside the monetary control of central banks. The performance of financial markets can be influenced only indirectly by the action of central banks and national regulatory agencies. All other things being equal, the growth of domestic and international financial markets increases the importance of, and the need for, financial regulation and control.

The "Weight" of Central Banks

If a central bank is to influence the behavior of financial aggregates and rates of interest, starting from its position in the market, one necessary condition is that its balance sheet be sufficiently large with respect to the dimension of the economy.

Assets

For various countries and periods, Table 3 shows the ratio of the total assets of the central banks to the money supply (a measure of the consolidated balance sheet of the banking system) and annual national product. Both ratios are significantly higher in Italy and in France, and lower in the United States and the United Kingdom. The ratios for Germany are between the two extremes. The situation does not change over time, except in the case of the United Kingdom, where the ratio of money to gross national product doubled in the second half of the 1980s, and the importance of the central bank remained unchanged in relation to the gross national product.

Table 3. Central Bank Assets, the Money Supply, and GDP: Selected Ratios
(Percentage ratios of annual averages)

	M2			GDP			M2/GDP		
	1980/83	1984/87	1988/89	1980/83	1984/87	1988/89	1980/83	1984/87	1988/89
Italy	36.20	34.30	31.70	25.70	22.80	21.30	70.90	66.30	67.30
United States	9.50	9.20	9.50	6.10	6.00	5.90	64.30	65.00	62.60
Germany	21.00	19.90	21.90	11.60	11.60	13.20	55.00	58.50	60.10
United Kingdom	—	19.90	10.50	9.40	8.70	9.60	—	43.70	90.90
France	35.20	30.50	27.50	18.50	16.20	13.40	53.00	52.60	48.90

Sources: Central bank bulletins; and International Monetary Fund, *International Financial Statistics*, (*IFS*).

Table 4 shows the weight of different categories of central bank assets and liabilities with respect to gross domestic product (GDP). On the assets side, it is evident that more than half of the high ratio found for the Bank of Italy is due to its financing of the treasury; the reserves of gold and foreign currencies are also remarkably high.[11] On the liabilities side, a large proportion is accounted for by the deposits of the banking system, that is, essentially compulsory reserves; given the amount of financing to the treasury and the amount of gold and foreign exchange reserves, these deposits increase the demand for monetary base and make it possible to maintain a minimum amount of refinancing to the banking system.

Other high figures on the assets side are the amount of treasury debentures of the U.S. Federal Reserve System and the refinancing of the private financial system for the Deutsche Bundesbank and the Bank of France. One tentative conclusion for such high figures is that in Italy and the United States, influence on market conditions is mostly transmitted via open market operations on, and financing of, the public debt. In Germany and France, there is a more direct influence on the financial sector, via lending to the banking system and the supply of liquidity to the private financial sector.

Liabilities

The central bank is part of the financial system; it intermediates a part of the flows of saving going through the same system. But the liabilities of the central bank are quite special; they are the money par

[11]The balance sheet shown here is the consolidation of the balance sheets of the Bank of Italy and the Ufficio Italiano dei Cambi.

Table 4. Central Bank Balance Sheet Aggregates and M2: Selected Ratios, 1989
(In percent)

	Italy	United States	Germany	United Kingdom[1]	France
Assets					
Foreign	11.62	1.65	7.42	5.05	14.05
Treasury	17.85	7.56	1.04	3.18	1.34
Financial system	0.67	0.08	13.01	0.11	8.45
Other assets	1.13	0.57	1.43	1.21	3.01
Total	31.27	9.86	22.89	9.54	26.85
Liabilities					
Currency	8.92	7.83	11.17	3.55	8.52
Bank deposits	14.12	1.24	4.96	0.34	2.68
Treasury	0.08	0.20	0.45	—	3.15
Capital and other liabilities	8.15	0.59	6.31	5.64	12.50
Total	31.27	9.86	22.89	9.54	26.85

Sources: Central bank bulletins; and International Monetary Fund, *International Financial Statistics, (IFS).*
[1]The monetary authorities' foreign assets and liabilities are based on those reported in *IFS*.

excellence, or monetary base. Because of their intrinsic qualities, legislative prescriptions, and long tradition, these liabilities have the features of absolute liquidity and general acceptability, and serve as means of payment, not only among individuals and firms but also among banks and financial intermediaries, which are, in turn, themselves creators of money.

Here again we meet the fundamental characteristic of the central bank as the bank of banks, and thus a natural candidate to influence their operations. This influence can be reinforced by obliging the banks to make special deposits, in other words, by imposing compulsory reserve requirements, which are now mostly enshrined in law. The reserves strengthen the link between the size of the central bank's balance sheet and that of the consolidated balance sheet of the banking system. The link would be perfectly rigid in the famous 100 percent reserve requirement proposed by the Chicago School in the 1930s. Worried by the excessive oscillations in the amount of money provided by the banking system and the disturbances to the economic cycle induced by banking activity, the Chicago School also proposed the abolition of private banking activity, in some extreme formulations.[12] Private banks have not been abolished; they are useful institu-

[12]See Simons (1934).

tions; they behave as free enterprises in their own field of activity. They are subject to special banking laws.

The point is that one can apply to banking activity, in order to preserve the value of banks' deposits, the same type of analysis that requires an outside limit on the amount of bank notes, in order to preserve their nominal value. The volume of banking activity, the output of the banking system as measured by the amount of credit and deposits, is not limited by the availability of some primary resource, as is the case with all other productive activities. In a closed economy, credit produces deposits, and deposits allow for further expansion of credit. This process affects real variables and prices.

Central banks did not fail during the Great Depression because they had sufficiently large gold reserves. Some analyses consider that it was precisely their sticking to the rules that was at the root of the crisis. Central banks were also mostly creditors of the state—which cannot fail— and had a sort of state guarantee.

A relation similar to that existing between the central bank and the banking system exists between banks and the financial system. This is made up of intermediaries that extend credit and collect liabilities that we do not generally consider as means of payments. The system also includes markets where debtors and creditors, investors and savers, meet directly. A bank can provide investors directly with means of payment, because its liabilities are considered as such. Other intermediaries, and financial markets, need at least a temporary credit, and then the money provided by the banking system. Expenditure by debtors stimulates economic activity and saving. Saving takes, in part, the form of bank deposits and financial assets, thus closing the financial circuit. The central bank, because of its special nature and position in the market, can understand what is happening in such a circuit and the velocity at which it operates, and can strongly influence its operation.

Discretion in Central Bank Action

In order to influence the volume, composition, and cost of financial transactions, the central bank needs to be able to manage the size and composition of its balance sheet, as regards both assets and liabilities. Because it has the monopoly of monetary base creation, it can set the nominal interest rate at which the monetary base is lent to the system.

In the monetarist approach to monetary policy, the central bank only needs to influence the amount of money, via the supply of monetary base and the money multiplier. It is assumed that the amount of money can be more or less perfectly controlled on the supply side.

The demand for money is stable in the long run; the underlying development of real variables is considered, per se, regular and stable. Prices are assumed to be sufficiently flexible; consequently, they respond to the quantity of money.

In a more realistic—and less doctrinaire—approach, monetary policy has a scope that is, in a certain sense, wider, though perhaps less definite and exclusive, less sharp edged. Monetary policy in this view can and has to affect first the behavior of the banking system, that is, bank credit, deposits, and the money supply. Specifically, by supplying the monetary base, the central bank will affect banks' willingness to lend, in other words, the supply of bank credit. This will be matched in the market with the demand for credit—for investment, for the financing of current production and sales, or even for the hedging of financial operations. All these uses of credit and the resulting amount of money affect the domestic economy in various ways, directly or indirectly, as well as the relationships with the foreign sector. The volume of foreign reserves held by the central bank will consequently be affected. And most important of all, so will the exchange rate.

The process I have just described is by no means a mechanical one. The reactions of different variables to the stimuli of monetary policy may vary considerably from one situation to another. Good qualitative and quantitative analyses can provide reliable indications of the effect of policy actions. It is not possible, however, at least in my view and experience, to cover all of this with simple rules, for example, merely by fixing the rate of money expansion.

Returning to what I said at the beginning, I believe that quantities of credit and money expansion have to be defined ex ante. The quantities can also be announced to provide markets with correct indications. But I do not think that there exist simple quantitative rules by means of which the price level can be controlled.

A lax monetary policy will certainly result in inflation. But monetary fine-tuning cannot be relied upon for close inflation control. Fine-tuning is difficult and probably impossible to achieve in such matters, mostly because of incomplete information, lags, and uncertainties regarding the size of the effect of the various instruments.

There is thus a grain of wisdom in the monetarist prescription of not seeking continuous correction of the economic cycle and avoiding over-activism in the use of monetary instruments.

Effectiveness of Central Bank Action in Italy

At the Bank of Italy, long experience has taught us to rely on a complex econometric model of the economy to understand how monetary policy affects all the variables we want to influence. The model is particularly detailed for the monetary and financial sectors. Numerical results provided by the model are only a basis for decisions. Judgment and other empirical evaluations complete the assessment of situations and influence decisions.

Technically speaking, reliance on the estimated coefficients of different equations of the model is limited to providing a starting basis for decisions. What is implicitly relied on, always, is the model, that is, the logical interconnections of all the variables. What the model, or more correctly the structure, says is that variables, such as internal demand, prices, employment, and the balance of payments, can be affected significantly, though not very much in the very short run, through the use of ordinary monetary policy instruments, such as open market operations, bank reserves, rediscount rates, and the like.

In some periods of high inflation, large balance of payments deficits, or exchange rate crises, it was necessary to resort to extraordinary administrative policy instruments, namely, credit ceilings and portfolio requirements, for which the Italian banking law provides. These extraordinary and harsh restrictive interventions were devised and graduated on the basis of the econometric model. They proved quite effective in stabilizing the economy.

Similar conclusions can be applied to all systems that find themselves under exceptional strain because of accelerating inflation, a balance of payments crisis, or rapid exchange rate depreciation. I have to remember, however, that in Italy, the adoption of direct or administrative methods of monetary control hindered, among other things, the efficient allocation of credit resources.

In conclusion, the central bank can and must first use its tools, its instrumental variables, to pursue the smooth and regular development of the economy, or, to paraphrase Professor Samuelson, to adjust the quantity of money to the needs of the economy, not merely to the demand of the economy.

Indeed, the behavior of real variables (including prices), that is, those variables that have a more or less direct impact on social welfare, could be unsatisfactory. In such cases, the central bank can use its instruments to correct the situation, via the supply of credit, interest rates, and bank money supply. In a deeper sense, if the correction is in the direction of stability, for the common good, it is an adjustment of the quantity of money to the more profound needs of the economy. We thus have a complete philosophy of central bank action.

Let me now turn to another more theoretical issue: whether it is the central bank that moves the economy or vice versa. From what has just been said, it is clear that over the long run a close correlation exists between the behavior of the economy and the evolution of the monetary aggregates. The parallelism, which is the result of close links between monetary, financial, and real variables, is for some periods the result of an adaptation of financial variables and monetary guidance to a satisfactorily smooth behavior of the economic system.

From time to time the system needs correction. The central bank has the power to enforce such corrections. The parallelism is now the result of active monetary policy intervention. In these cases, money and credit determine the evolution of the system. On such occasions, the quantitative relationships between real variables and financial variables are usually altered—a problem for the econometrician, but also for the central banker who has to use judgmental evaluation to graduate the strength of interventions. In this discussion, I have in mind mostly cases of restrictive monetary policy. Perhaps I continue to be influenced by the dictum that monetary policy is like a rope that you can pull but not push.

Economic Objectives of the Central Bank and the State

The central bank must coordinate its action and its economic policy interventions in the general context of the state's economic policy. Given the macroeconomic objectives of the political community, which can be defined, depending on the level of generality and constancy over time, either by law or by the government, the central bank has to deploy all its tools to achieve those objectives. Some are more immediately within the reach of the central bank; others require the central bank to cooperate with other institutions or agencies. Ensuring financial stability and the proper functioning of the financial system is certainly a primary duty of the central bank. When stability depends on an adequate supply of liquidity, the central bank is endowed with all the necessary powers.

Regulation of the structure of the banking system and achievement of a good performance by that system generally require powers that go beyond those relating to the supply of liquidity. These powers are granted by banking legislation, which recognizes the particular character of banking activity, within the institutional system. The central bank is at the center of the system; it understands and participates in the working of the system. It is natural to use its status and technical skills to enact banking legislation and to discipline the behavior and working of this important sector of the economy.

Within the banking sector, important pieces of information are necessarily possessed only by individual banks; consequently, their assets are not marketable. So the working of competitive markets can be relied upon only within certain limits. The central bank is then empowered with supervision and inspection duties and possibilities of intervention in order to prevent instability.

In current macroeconomic policy, maintaining the purchasing power of the currency is the primary duty assigned naturally to central banks. As I said before, to do this the central bank must control, in complete freedom, the size and composition of its balance sheet. The pursuit of macroeconomic objectives must be related to the overall economic policy. As far as monetary matters are concerned, the ways and means of achieving the objectives should be, and generally are, left to the judgment of central bankers. Central banks themselves can help define some of the economic objectives of the nation. An executive power of the state that affects directly the process of money creation generates a conflict of interest between different powers of the state. The executive power does not have to interfere with the process of money creation. This does not mean that the central bank cannot facilitate the financing of the treasury, in ways that do not conflict with the stability of the currency. Indeed, one traditional and fundamental task of central banks is to cooperate actively in the management of the public debt.

Managing Public Debt: Inflation Control

The mere existence of a budget deficit, and of a public debt, means that parliament has chosen not to cover a part of public expenditure through taxation. This can be done for structural, redistributive, or allocative reasons, or even just for cyclical reasons. Such a superior will of the parliament is, at least in the short run, a dictum for all public bodies and institutions within the state.

I have examined the operations of the central banks' of all the main industrial countries: all of them have special arrangements with the treasury for the placing and management of the public debt. There are functional and historical reasons for the central bank to perform such a role. In the first place, an important part of monetary control is implemented via purchases and sales of government paper and, as I said before, government debentures constitute an important component of the central bank's assets. Moreover, in a system where fiduciary money is the norm, confidence in central bank money is in some fundamental way related to the authority of the state. It would be difficult to think of sound money in a fiscally bankrupt state, unless we assume, for example, a money circulation strictly related to gold or foreign assets.

Sound money cannot exist without a sound fiscal system. In countries where most of the tax revenue comes from seigniorage, money is deprived of its most intrinsic features. In a hypothetical, unsound fiscal system, one could imagine, for a while, a monetary system based directly or indirectly only on credit to the private sector. Such an equilibrium is illusory, and at best temporary. In such circumstances, the bad government debt might take on some of the functions of a monetary standard and tend to displace the sound money. More realistically, the crisis of the state would entail that of the private sector.

The question is sometimes discussed whether the central bank, or more generally monetary policy, can be assigned the objective of absolute price stability. It is certainly true that good monetary management is a necessary prerequisite for price stability. However, our knowledge of the working of modern economic systems suggests that in some cases an objective defined in precise quantitative terms, for example, zero price growth, can be difficult or even impossible for the central bank to achieve.

In an open system, central banks may have considerable scope for influencing the external value of the currency—in the short run, through intervention on foreign exchange markets and, more basically, by controlling the expansion of credit and money. The external value of a currency is, in turn, an important component of the currency's domestic value, its internal purchasing power.

In a large and complex economic system, the level of prices is strongly affected by other variables and circumstances, first of all fiscal policy and labor costs. In such cases, relying solely on monetary policy to achieve monetary stability can be extremely costly in terms of other economic objectives. Monetary policy, including exchange rate policy, can make a large and essential contribution to the achievement of price stability. Other policies, namely fiscal and wage policies, have to join forces in the same direction.

Institutional Status of the Central Bank

One fundamental issue remains to be discussed, namely, that of the institutional setting of the central bank in relation to other powers of the state.[13] Is there room for defining, within the state organization, a money-regulating power that flanks the traditional powers: the Legislature, the Judiciary, and the Executive?

---

[13]See, for example, Friedman (1962).

The problem did not arise in the past, because the purchasing power of money was usually thought of as being anchored by law to a circulating medium having an intrinsic value, namely, gold. But, over the last sixty years or so—especially over the last ten or twenty years—the value of money has relied only on the limitation of its nominal quantity and on its good management by central banks and monetary authorities.

I confess my difficulty in deciding on the basis of economic analysis alone what is the appropriate solution for the institutional position of the central bank in the state organization. The solution has to be sought with reference to social and constitutional theories of political organization. The existence of international treaties conferring monetary powers on international or supranational organizations complicates the problem, or, perhaps, just adds another dimension to it. Economic analysis, nonetheless, has a duty to suggest some guidelines, or at least minimum prerequisites, for the appropriate institutional setting.

First of all, there must exist, at the constitutional level, a broad, explicit or implicit, delegation of authority by a sovereign state, which has the power to levy taxes, to the central bank, to provide the fiduciary standard for the economy. Second, there must be independence from other powers of the state in the process of money creation and control, in the sense that the amount of money and the channels of creation have to be decided only on the basis of the achievement of the general objectives of economic policy. Within this framework, the central bank will seek the best ways to achieve those objectives.

A closely correlated proposition is the implausibility of creating a system separated from the fiscal authority and the value of the public debt. The points of contact and the degree of involvement in this field are a very delicate issue. I simply wish to express my fears about the emergence, where there is absolute separation, of a sort of parallel monetary system in the event of an uncontrolled public debt; as Gresham said, bad money drives out good.

Finally, there must be a functional, legally sanctioned connection between official money, created by the central bank, and the money produced by the banking system. In effect, central banks and monetary authorities control money creation indirectly, on the basis of banking legislation giving central banks powers to exercise wide control over banking activities. This amounts to recognition, at the institutional level, that money is a component of the financial process. It is also an indispensable element for the correct and stable unfolding of the whole process. Given all these conditions, a bank of issue becomes the central bank of the system.

The International Dimension

Up to now I have made reference to economic systems that are independent of each other, not only politically but also to a large degree economically. I would like to add a few considerations about a central bank's position in the international economy.

As I have already indicated, in the last few years a feature of the evolution of the international economy has been the rapid development of banking and financial activities outside national boundaries. Underlying this development has been a steady growth of international trade in goods and services, but more important still has been the rapid growth in transactions for purely financial purposes. Industrial countries, during the 1980s, removed many restrictions on such transactions, and on capital movements in general; stable exchange rates are once again being valued, after the skepticism of the 1970s; and computing and communication costs have fallen dramatically. These factors have created favorable conditions for the expansion of international financial transactions.

The implications and advantages of this development in terms of economic growth, employment, and economic stability are not yet clear; however, this trend, given the fiduciary character of money in circulation, poses formidable new problems for the regulation of the economic cycle and for international, financial, and economic stability.

Central banks and national monetary authorities find themselves rather disarmed in this field. In some respects, a sort of free banking exists in international markets, in a context in which there is no reserve having an intrinsic value and no lender of last resort. Freedom of capital movements and relatively stable exchange rates tend to create an international monetary system that is deprived of overall quantitative limits. Until now, risks of various kinds have somewhat checked the expansion of the markets—but at a cost.

Central banks are in the market. By virtue of their participation in the foreign exchange markets, in particular, they are in a position to perfectly understand what is happening in the international banking and financial markets. Since the abandonment of the Bretton Woods system in the early 1970s, national monetary authorities have been trying to restore their control of the international monetary order by means of closer cooperation and various reform proposals at regional or world level.

Summary

Central banks emerged, with their present role and functions, from the tormented political and monetary history of the twentieth century.

In the great economic and financial crisis of the 1930s, the close connection between financial stability and economic activity became dramatically apparent. Problems have persisted and reappeared at various times since then, though less dramatically.

Solutions included imposing restrictions on international trade and finance, introducing banking legislation, engaging in more active central bank intervention, and, after World War II, establishing a new monetary order. The Bretton Woods system stressed new aspects of the importance of the objective of the external value of the currency.

The development of unrestricted international banking activity and the more recent reciprocal opening of financial systems, in a context of money circulation based on purely fiduciary standards, pose new problems for national central banks and national monetary authorities. They are being attacked through closer cooperation and projects of reform.

Central banks play an important and sometimes exclusive role in preserving the value of currencies and in ensuring the overall stability of banking and financial systems; they contribute to the achievement of governments' economic objectives. The central bank's ability to preserve the value of the currency rests, explicitly or implicitly, on a delegation of powers by the political authority. Central banks are to be credible and trustworthy. In a regime of fiduciary money, the sound operation of the fiscal authority is a necessary condition for guaranteeing the value of the currency. The central bank can achieve the aims assigned to it, by law and by the state, by freely maneuvering the items of its balance sheet. The central bank derives the effectiveness of its action from being part of the financial system; however, it must also be enabled, by banking and financial legislation, to control certain operations of banks and financial markets. The juridical status of central banks, with special reference to their role and powers, is sometimes not clearly defined in the institutional framework of modern industrial economies.

A central bank has to be accountable for its actions and policy. Whether it is accountable to public opinion, to parliament, or to the executive power is a constitutional problem to be solved on the basis of political, social, and juridical analysis. Economic analysis provides some indications and minimum requirements to be observed for the correct and effective performance of the central bank's role.

Bibliography

Crawford, M.H., *La moneta in Grecia e a Roma* (Bari, Laterza, 1982).

Forzoni, A., *La moneta nella storia,* Vol. 1, in the original reform of Caracalla (214 A.D.) (Bari, Cacucci, 1989).

Friedman, M., *An Independent Central Bank: In Search of a Monetary Constitution* (Cambridge, Massachusetts: Harvard University Press, 1962).

———, and A. Jacobson Schwartz, *A Monetary History of the United States 1867–1960,* National Bureau of Economic Research (Princeton: Princeton University Press, 1963).

Hart, Albert L.G., "The Chicago Plan of Banking Reform," Part I, "A Proposal for Making Monetary Management Effective in the United States," in *Review of Economic Studies* (London), Vol. 2 (1934–35), pp. 104–116.

Hawtrey, R.G., *The Art of Central Banking* (London: Longmans, Green, 1932).

Keynes, J.M., *A Treatise on Money* (London: Macmillan, 1930).

———, *The General Theory of Employment Interest and Money* (London: Macmillan, 1936).

League of Nations, *International Currency Experience* (Geneva, 1944).

Modigliani, F., "Liquidity Preference and the Theory of Interest and Money," *Econometrica* (1944).

———, "The Monetary Mechanism and Its Interaction with Real Phenomena," *Review of Economics and Statistics* (Cambridge, Massachusetts), Vol. 45 (February, 1963) pp. 79–107.

Patinkin, D., *Money, Interest, and Prices: An Integration of Monetary and Value Theory* (New York: Harper & Row, 1965).

Simons, H.C., *A Positive Program for Laissez Faire: Some Proposals for a Liberal Economic Policy* (Chicago: Chicago University Press, 1934).

Spufford, P., *Money and Its Use in Medieval Europe* (Cambridge: Cambridge University Press, 1988).

Timberlake, Richard H., Jr., *The Origins of Central Banking in the United States* (Cambridge, Massachusetts: Harvard University Press, 1978).

9

Central Bank Independence in New Zealand

R. LINDSAY KNIGHT*

Since the commencement of New Zealand's new central banking legislation, on February 1, 1990, the Government that created it has been voted out of office, but not because of the legislation—although the prolonged drive toward lower inflation has undoubtedly been politically costly. The change of government is not likely to have a significant effect on the legislation itself because both main political parties supported its introduction—a very unusual circumstance deriving partly from the widely perceived misuse of the previous legislation by the so-called conservative National Government in the early 1980s.

Origins

The relevant part of the old legislation (Reserve Bank Act of 1964) provided for the Reserve Bank to provide advice to the government on monetary policy and to carry out the monetary policy of the government. There was also a mixed bag of objectives for monetary policy, which included the maintenance and promotion of social welfare; the promotion of trade, production, and full employment; and the maintenance of a stable internal price level. At times the relative importance of the objectives was changed according to political whim or current political pressures. Hence, the Bank had great difficulty in giving consistent advice to the government in terms of the legislation. Not only were there inherent conflicts between these objectives but also absolute power in decision making was in the hands of the minis-

*The author is Deputy Governor of the Reserve Bank of New Zealand. This paper is a summary of the presentation given by Mr. Knight at the seminar.

ter of finance—a set of circumstances that led to a disastrous outcome for the New Zealand economy in the early 1980s.

New Zealand's Economic Scene in 1982–84

Advice given by the Reserve Bank and the treasury on monetary policy was rejected by the Government. Large fiscal deficits arose—financed by a mix of Reserve Bank credit, compulsory government stock purchases by financial institutions, and foreign borrowing. After a prolonged period of high inflation, a price and wage freeze was imposed in an attempt to suppress inflation. Control of all interest rates and of the lending activity of institutions was widespread. No effective monetary policy was being applied; the fixed exchange rate was overvalued; large external deficits were present; external debt was growing; and, last, but not least, was a maze of controls on every aspect of the financial system.

Following my return to New Zealand in 1982, I was given the task of planning the eventual liberalization of the financial system. I became chairman of an informal high level committee of senior Reserve Bank and treasury officials. The committee examined the whole framework of the New Zealand financial system in detail and prepared a series of policy papers embodying proposals for eventual deregulation of the system.

A new (Labour) government was elected in July 1984 in the middle of a financial crisis. For a period of one month, the Reserve Bank faced the knowledge of an impending change of government and the promise of a significant devaluation of the currency. This expectation naturally placed enormous pressure on the foreign exchange market. We learned then just how ineffectual exchange controls can be: there was a massive outflow of foreign exchange in a very short period financed by large, short-term borrowings by the Reserve Bank of New Zealand and the New Zealand Treasury.

The new Government promptly took a number of new steps. The exchange rate was immediately devalued by 20 percent. Interest rate and other financial controls were quickly removed. The fiscal deficit was fully funded by the sale of government paper through the domestic capital market. Exchange controls were removed at the end of 1984, and the exchange rate was floated in March 1985. Orthodox monetary policy was restored, with low inflation the declared objective. The whole financial system was thus remodeled in a remarkably short time, perhaps illustrating that you do not have to have a crisis to bring about major economic reform, but it certainly helps.

The Reserve Bank Changes

The procedure for determining monetary policy and the Bank's relationship with the government had been drastically changed in 1984, but with no change in the existing Reserve Bank Act. A new finance minister, Roger Douglas, came to the Reserve Bank in 1985 and suggested that the Bank explore ways for it to achieve more formal autonomy in the conduct of monetary policy. The main aim was to prevent a reversion to the kind of policy followed by former Finance Minister Muldoon and to protect the new framework by setting up procedures having transparency and clarity. Reserve Bank reform was also seen as a logical part of the general reform taking place within the New Zealand public sector. So a search for a new central bank statute began.

A range of central banking models was examined by Reserve Bank officials. The natural focus was on those with a high level of autonomy—Germany, the United States, and Switzerland. The eventual model chosen was probably more like that of Canada but with some unique features. The Reserve Bank staff team worked carefully through the technical issues, in close consultation with the treasury. Then it took another year for the legislative process to be completed before the new Act was passed in December 1989 and became effective from February 1, 1990.

The Framework

The framework of the Act was that price stability is the single basic objective of monetary policy, with some acknowledgement of the need for concern about the efficiency and soundness of the financial system. Public transparency was made a key feature; hence, there is provision for a Policy Targets Agreement to be signed by the minister of finance and the governor of the Reserve Bank. There is also provision for a six-monthly public statement by the Reserve Bank explaining the policy. The effect of the Act is to provide a trade-off between more policy autonomy for the bank and greater accountability—both in policy and financial terms—to the Government and the public.

There has been some argument about the single objective of price stability but generally support has been quite broad. It is interesting to note that manufacturers and farmers have taken different views of the new policy: farmers support it; manufacturers oppose it. The objective of inflation spelled out in the initial target agreement (0–2 percent by the end of 1992) has attracted much more criticism. The National Government elected on November 20, 1990 has proposed moving the target date to December 1993. The specific target arose primarily from a desire for clarity as to the meaning of price stability; some people would view it as being unduly precise.

There are four specific caveats within the target agreement allowing for the inflation target to be varied. These relate to a change in indirect taxes; a material change in the terms of trade (e.g., the current oil shock); a major domestic crisis; and a significant change in the consumer price index (CPI) arising from changes in house prices or mortgage interest rates. (This provision relates to Reserve Bank disagreement about the way the CPI is calculated.) The targets may be renegotiated if any one of these occurs.

Main Legislative Provisions

The key clauses of the new Act provide that the Bank formulate and implement monetary policy with the economic objective of achieving and maintaining stability in the general level of prices; that the minister, before appointing any person as governor, fix in agreement with that person policy targets for the Bank during that person's term of office; that the Bank when formulating and implementing monetary policy have regard to the efficiency and soundness of the financial system and consult with and give advice to the government and others to achieve and maintain its economic objective; that the Government may direct the Bank to pursue an economic objective for monetary policy other than price stability for a period of not more than twelve months, with provision for extension; that the Bank publish statements at least every six months explaining its policies and objectives for the target period and reviewing its past performance; and that the governor be removed from office for, among other things, inadequate performance in relation to the policy targets. There is also provision for a five-year Funding Agreement to be signed by the minister and the governor, specifying the maximum allowable expenditure by the Bank over that period.[1]

Board of Directors

The principal role of the Board of Directors is to monitor the governor's performance. The new Act provides for a maximum of ten directors, up to seven of whom will be outside directors. They have the power to recommend the governor's dismissal (in extremis) but do not participate in policy formation; hence, they do not have advance

[1]See Clauses 8–10, 12, 15, and 49 of the Reserve Bank Act of New Zealand of 1989.

access to market-sensitive information. The governor is chairman of the board (which will include two deputy governors in future—one of whom will be deputy chairman of the board). Governors are appointed for five-year terms and other directors for three-year terms.

Functions of the Reserve Bank

Normal central bank functions will continue under the new Act. These include note and coin issue; foreign reserves management; bank licensing and supervision; and conduct of a stock registry (a commercial function for which a tax obligation will accrue). It is perhaps useful for me to comment on two specific functions: prudential supervision and bank licensing.

Prudential Supervision

Prudential supervision was first introduced in the 1986 Amendment Act operative from April 1987. The announced aim of the prudential supervision powers was to ensure the maintenance of public confidence in the financial system as a whole. It is important to note that there was no specific provision for either protection of depositors or the protection of individual financial institutions. This was made quite explicit.

As background, it is worth noting that there has been no history in New Zealand of deposit insurance or explicit depositor protection—one institution (Securitibank) was allowed to fail in 1977 and, more recently, the case of the Development Finance Corporation of New Zealand (DFC) in which the Government and the Reserve Bank played an important role in assisting a settlement with creditors involved use of the Bank's statutory management powers under the Act.

The supervision initially covered licensed foreign exchange dealers, commercial banks (there were only four at the time), and any other nonbank financial institution specified by the Reserve Bank as being important enough to warrant supervision. The main practical aim was to provide a mechanism for collecting information on the main financial players and to maintain oversight of developments in the system.

The 1986 Act included extensive provisions for failure management, that is, preventing the failure of one institution from spilling over into a generalized loss of confidence in the financial system. There was a wish to avoid explicit regulatory controls; this was understandable in light of New Zealand's previous negative experience with financial controls. Later, the capital adequacy proposals of the Basle Committee were adopted. Increasing attention was also given to specific supervisory matters, such as large exposure rules. The basic approach (i.e., financial system concern rather than depositor protection), nonetheless, remains in place. Coverage now extends to banks only, and banks are in future to be directly charged for 75 percent of the cost of supervision.

Bank Licensing

For many years the four major commercial banks in New Zealand (three overseas-owned, one government-owned) operated on comfortable margins with little real competition. The decision to open up the foreign exchange market was taken in 1983; some basic qualifying criteria were devised and the market was opened to new applicants. Soon there were about twenty players and foreign exchange margins were greatly reduced. In 1986, the banking market was opened, again with some basic qualifying criteria (e.g., minimum capital of $15 million) but with no specification by the authorities as to how many banks there should be. This was left for the market to determine. There was no headlong rush by new applicants. Initially, eight new banks (mainly overseas-owned) were licensed. Today, there are about twenty-two banks. One or two have come and gone, and there have been several mergers and takeovers. The banking system remains open and competitive. Some banks, notably the government-owned Bank of New Zealand, have had problems following the 1987 share-market crash, but there have been no serious concerns about the system as whole.

Appraisal of Progress

Inflation has come down to 5 percent (year to September 1990) after years of inflation at 10–20 percent. The 0–2 percent inflation target is still seen as achievable but will be very difficult. The new Government proposes to extend the target date to December 1993. The old built-in public inflation expectations of high inflation have made the job of getting inflation down difficult and have added to the social and economic cost of that process. Unemployment is now close to 8 percent and is much higher among the Maori population; Maoris comprise some 10–15 percent of the total population.

Political agreement is strained within both main parties; there are some outstanding dissentients (including former Finance Minister Muldoon) but they do not seem too important at this stage. The new finance minister, Ruth Richardson, is a tough and resolute inflation fighter. The framework of the Reserve Bank Act does not appear to be under any real threat.

The pre-election accord between the Government and the combined trade unions was an interesting exercise. The unions agreed to deliver a 2 percent wage round (plus some allowance for productivity) in return for government action on the fiscal deficit and the promise of a neutral monetary policy. The accord is clearly at risk with the new government in office.

Since February 1990, there has been some government criticism of Reserve Bank monetary policy actions in the financial markets. The imminence of the elections lay behind that criticism; it was a new experience that made everyone aware of the new world of central banking in New Zealand.

In summary, there have been some costs for the Reserve Bank in moving to the new legal framework, but there have also been considerable gains both for the policy role of the institution and, more important, for the future of monetary policy. The likelihood that New Zealand will maintain a stable financial environment in the future has probably been greatly enhanced.

10

Central Bank Operations and Independence in a Monetary Union: BCEAO and BEAC

E. SACERDOTI*

The Banque Centrale des Etats de l'Afrique de l'Ouest (BCEAO) and the Banque des Etats de l'Afrique Centrale (BEAC) are the central banks of two regional groupings of countries in Western Africa and Central Africa that have adopted a common currency. The BCEAO is the central bank of the seven member countries of the West African Monetary Union (WAMU), with headquarters in Dakar, Senegal. The WAMU comprises the states of Benin, Burkina Faso, Côte d'Ivoire, Mali, Niger, Senegal, and Togo; the common currency is the *franc de la Communauté Financière Africaine* (CFA). The BEAC is the central bank for the six countries that are members of the Central African Monetary Area (CAMA). The members are Cameroon, the Central African Republic, Chad, the Congo, Equatorial Guinea, and Gabon; their currency is the *franc de la Coopération Financière en Afrique Centrale.* Together, these groups form the CFA currency area.

The CFA currency area was established at the end of 1945, at which time it covered a somewhat wider geographic area than at present. With the accession of the francophone countries of Western and Central Africa to independence, monetary agreements were established between France and the member countries of the zone. The West African Monetary Union was formally established in 1962. At the same time, the francophone countries in Central Africa entered into a mon-

*The author is Advisor in the African Department of the International Monetary Fund.

etary agreement between themselves, and with France.[1] The two central banks were established in 1962, but their statutes were revamped in 1972–73 in order to devolve more responsibilities to the member countries; as part of the new agreements, the headquarters of the two banks were transferred from Paris to Dakar (BCEAO) and Yaoundé (BEAC). Although the institutional arrangements were modified, the main characteristics of the two monetary areas remain unchanged. These can be summarized as (1) a single currency having legal tender throughout the union; (2) monetary integration through the pooling of external reserves in an account with the French Treasury, called the Operations Account, which also functions as an overdraft facility; (3) external convertibility of the currency of the two monetary areas, guaranteed by France, effected through the Operations Account, and observance of restrictions on capital movements with other members of the franc zone; and (4) a fixed exchange rate with the French franc, at CFAF 1 = F 0.02, unchanged since October 1948.

The main motivation of the two monetary unions is a political commitment to financial stability and regional solidarity, rather than strong intraregional trade and factor mobility—the elements generally considered in the literature as a primary justification for currency areas. In the two monetary areas, intraregional trade is limited, as the countries mainly export primary commodities to industrial countries; intraregional labor mobility is not particularly encouraged, and labor markets remain segmented, despite a large inflow of workers to Côte d'Ivoire from some neighboring countries.

The participation of the member countries in the common monetary area rests on the advantage of having a common currency, which is convertible, as a medium of exchange and a store of value, and on the benefits for small open developing economies of maintaining a fixed exchange regime, which provides a nominal anchor for macroeconomic policies. The political will to achieve gradual economic and political integration has also contributed to the solidity of the two monetary unions.

Trade liberalization, in the framework of the trade associations in the two areas,[2] and common features of the fiscal system (particularly in the context of the UDEAC) are also elements underlying the design of gradual economic integration of the countries belonging to the two monetary unions. Coordination of fiscal policy has been limited in

[1]Mali left the WAMU in 1962 and rejoined in 1984. Equatorial Guinea joined the CAMA in 1985. Mauritania, an original member of WAMU, resigned its membership in 1973.

[2]Communauté Economique des Etats de l'Afrique de l'Ouest (CEDEAO) in the WAMU area and Union Douanière et Economique de l'Afrique Centrale (UDEAC) in the CAMA area.

both, despite strict limits on central bank government financing, as governments have been able to finance deficits by borrowing from multilateral organizations or in the international capital markets. The absence of developed capital markets, which for the developed countries are the vehicle through which inconsistent fiscal policies spill over to other countries, has reduced the need to harmonize fiscal policies.

The convertibility of the CFA franc is an important advantage from which the members of the two unions benefit, unlike many other developing countries. The pegging of the exchange rate provides a useful nominal anchor for macroeconomic policies, if the currency to which the exchange rate is pegged achieves financial stability. In the case of the CFA franc, the peg to the French franc has not been altered since 1948. This pegging imposes strict constraints on the conduct of monetary policy, as net foreign assets positions have to be maintained at a sustainable level and domestic rates of inflation of member countries have to remain aligned with that of France. Accordingly, both the treaties establishing the monetary unions and the statutes of the central banks highlight the need to safeguard the common currency with appropriate policies.

The statutes recognize the need for the central banks to adequately support economic growth and development. To that end, the structures of the central banks include, in addition to centralized organs, national credit committees and national agencies established in each member state, which are responsible for making the credit system responsive to the specific situation of member countries.

Safeguards of Convertibility

The guarantee of convertibility provided by France implies that the Operations Account with the French Treasury, in which a minimum of 65 percent of the foreign reserves must be deposited, can be overdrawn. To protect the reserve position and to avoid requiring the French Treasury to extend support for more than transitory periods, a number of safeguards are built into the rules of operations of the two central banks.

First, their statutes include a limit on the financing of the government, which cannot exceed 20 percent of the ordinary budgetary revenues in the previous year. Second, if the ratio of the foreign assets of each central bank to its sight liabilities falls below 20 percent for a period of three months, the boards of directors must convene to adopt corrective measures. The statute of the BEAC specifies that these measures be a reduction of the refinancing ceilings and an increase in the discount rate. The BCEAO statute provides that in these circumstances the decisions regarding credit have to be taken by a unanimous vote. The statute of the BEAC also prescribes a reduction of the refinancing ceilings by 10 percent if the holdings in the Operations Account pertaining to a country fall below the threshold of 15 percent of the currency in circulation; if the Operations Account shifts into a negative position, the refinancing ceiling is curtailed by 20 percent.[3]

In addition to tightening monetary policy, should the balance of payments weaken and the position of the Operations Account deteriorate, member countries are encouraged to increase their recourse to foreign financing and, in particular, to enter into arrangements with the International Monetary Fund (IMF) and seek assistance from other multilateral organizations. This is explicitly stated in the *convention de compte d'opérations* signed with France, which provides that when the assets of each monetary union fall below a certain level, the central banks will replenish the accounts by using their other external assets and by urging their members to convert their SDR holdings into French francs and to utilize the facilities of the IMF.

In practice, the Operations Account of the BCEAO, which had always been in a positive position until 1979, shifted into large negative positions in the period 1980–84; after a return to a positive position, negative positions were again recorded in 1988 and 1989. The ratio of external assets to sight liabilities fell below the 20 percent threshold in 1980, rose to 18.5 percent in 1986, and declined again in the period 1987–89; at the end of 1989, the ratio stood at 8 percent. In the BEAC, the Operations Account recorded negative positions in 1987–89, which prompted immediate tightening of refinancing ceilings and an increase in the discount rate; by mid-1990, the Operations Account returned to a positive position. The external assets-to-sight liabilities ratio was below the threshold in 1986 and 1987 but rose above it again in 1988.

Institutional Arrangements

The present organization and operational arrangements of the WAMU and the BCEAO were institutionalized in 1973 with the revision of the original 1962 treaty establishing the WAMU and of the statutes of the BCEAO, which modified the original 1962 arrangements. The WAMU has two policymaking organs: the Council of Heads of States

[3]Separate monetary accounts, including foreign assets, are established for each member country of the two monetary unions. The currency put in circulation in each country by the agency of the central bank is identified by a separate code (in the WAMU), or by different bank notes (CAMA area).

and the Council of Ministers; the latter has responsibilities in the monetary policy area as specified in the central bank's statutes. The arrangements with France are embodied in a cooperation agreement between France and the WAMU members and in an Operations Account convention. Similarly, in the Central African area, the BEAC statutes were modified in 1972. The cooperation between the BEAC member countries is specified in a convention of monetary cooperation between the Central African states, and the cooperation convention between France and the member states of the BEAC.

The organs of the BCEAO and the BEAC are somewhat different inasmuch as those of the BCEAO include—in addition to the governor, board of directors, and the national credit committees—a council of ministers, which has responsibilities with regard to the appointment of the governor, changes in the exchange rate parity, the conventions with new members, and the broad orientation of the union's monetary and credit policy. The two boards of directors are charged with the overall management of monetary and credit policy in the two central banks. The BCEAO board comprises sixteen members, two from each country and two from France; the BEAC board comprises four members of the largest country, Cameroon, two from Gabon, one each from the other four countries, and three from France. The boards of directors specify the terms and conditions of the central banks' refinancing policies, and the global amount of central bank refinancing available to the government and the deposit money banks and other financial institutions. The governor is the chairman of the board (in the BCEAO but not in the BEAC), is in charge of carrying out the decisions of the council of ministers and of the board of directors, and is in charge of the day-to-day management of the bank. In the BEAC, the governor only attends the board with a consultative voice; the chairman is one of the ministers of finance. An additional BEAC organ is the committee of three comptrollers (one each for Cameroon, Gabon, and France) who attend both the board of directors and the national committees with a consultative vote.

At the country levels, the national committees propose the amount of refinancing that can be granted to banks and financial institutions and the financing that is available to the government; they also establish limits on rediscountable credits to individual enterprises, authorize credits, which are subject to prior approval because of their amount, and adopt measures of credit control, such as credit ceilings. The national committees can delegate their responsibility to the national directors.

Thus, the national committees and the national directors have a significant role in the allocation of refinancing facilities between individual banks, as well as in the determination of the amount of credit extended to individual enterprises. In the BEAC, the national committees exercise substantial initiative in proposing the global refinancing limits for each country, which are then submitted to the board of directors for approval. With the deterioration in the external situation of the CAMA, the BEAC board reduced the rediscount ceilings in each country in early 1988 and kept them unchanged thereafter.

In the BCEAO, the national committees have the important macroeconomic role of proposing monetary and credit targets in the framework of an annual exercise that involves the council of ministers, the headquarters of the bank, and the committees themselves and that aims at establishing the refinancing ceilings for the BCEAO as a whole and for each country. Once country ceilings are established, the allocation of the global amount of refinancing in each country among the banks is left to the national committees and the national central bank agencies. To eliminate the presumption of a right to rediscount, the commercial banks are not informed of the decisions of the national committees. In order to limit the exposure of the central bank, it cannot refinance more than 35 percent of a commercial bank's portfolio of ordinary credit (i.e., credit other than for crop financing).[4] Until 1989, selective credit ratios were established in many WAMU countries, requiring commercial banks to allocate a minimum share of their resources to preferential sectors; however, they were not always respected.

As evidenced by the institutional arrangements and the operational procedures, the commitment of the two central banks to protect the external position and safeguard the common currency does not derive from a status of independence from political authorities, but rather from the institutional responsibility enshrined in the monetary union treaty and in the statutes of the central bank. A certain degree of independence from the national governments comes from the fact that the political authorities control the central bank in a collegial manner.

In practice, as discussed below, the central banks responded with a gradualistic policy with regard to the deterioration in the balance of payments and the Operations Account positions in the early 1980s. Credit to the economy was not squeezed, nor were interest rates brought to levels that could have hampered economic activity; however, in 1989–90, the tight refinancing policy of the BCEAO contrib-

[4]Until a reform in October 1, 1989, the refinancing of crop credit was maintained outside the global ceiling.

uted to a liquidity squeeze in Côte d'Ivoire, in the context of a growing portfolio of nonperforming loans.

Operations and Instruments of Monetary and Credit Policy

The operations of the two central banks concentrate on granting credit to the government and providing rediscounts to the commercial banks.

Operations

In the absence of a domestic market for government paper, there are no open market operations. A money market operates in the WAMU countries with intermediation by the BCEAO. Credit to the governments takes the form of overdrafts, advances to banks secured by government securities, purchases from commercial banks of government securities with a remaining maturity of one year or less, and discount or rediscount of public securities with a maturity of ten years or less to finance development projects, including infrastructure. The total of these credits cannot exceed 20 percent of the government's fiscal receipts in the preceding budgetary year. This limit is adjusted downward by the amount of government debt held by commercial banks availing themselves of central bank refinancing and upward for the treasury deposits at the central bank. Refinancing of commercial bank credit to the nongovernment sector takes the form of rediscounting of short-, medium-, and long-term credit (remaining maturity of less than ten years), classified as eligible for rediscounting. The total amount of refinancing to each country is subject to a ceiling, both in the BCEAO and the BEAC. Until recently, the refinancing of crop credit was maintained outside the ceiling and carried a preferential interest rate; however, abuses led the BCEAO to bring such credit under the global refinancing ceiling in 1989 and to unify the discount rates. The BEAC took a similar decision in October 1990.

Instruments of Monetary Policy

The main instruments of credit policy both in the WAMU and the CAMA are limits on central bank refinancing. The BCEAO also relies on credit ceilings, while in the CAMA national credit ceilings are established in the framework of adjustment programs with the IMF, but are not a normal instrument of control of the central bank. The interest rate is changed infrequently, although more often since 1988.

As indicated above, for each main country, the BCEAO establishes refinancing and credit ceilings in the framework of macroeconomic projections of the main real, monetary, and credit aggregates. The exercise starts each September, with the council of ministers formulating the objective for the external position of each country for the coming year, in line with the overall external situation of the union. Thereafter, the national agencies and committees have the responsibility for preparing the projections of real and nominal GDP for the year ahead and of the money demand associated with these projections. The supply of credit consistent with these projections is allocated between the government and the rest of the economy, by estimating the change in the government's net credit position toward the banking system and obtaining credit to the economy as a residual. A main component of the net position of the government toward the banking system is the use of the statutory advance from the central bank; the possible use by the government of its deposits at the central bank and the commercial banks must also be estimated. Finally, in order to determine the amount of central bank refinancing compatible with the credit projection, the reserves held by the commercial bank at the central bank have to be estimated, together with the split of the net foreign asset position between central and commercial banks. To derive the refinancing available to the financial institutions, central bank credit available to the government is deducted from the overall ceiling on central bank financing. In October and November, all projections are reviewed in consultation between headquarters and the national agencies.

In December, the board of directors of the BCEAO reviews the credit objectives and ceilings for central bank refinancing proposed by each committee and submits them to the council of ministers for endorsement. Until 1989, crop financing had been excluded from the refinancing ceilings. The liberal concession of such a refinancing by the central bank, in the context of a decline in commodity prices and of losses of the marketing boards, resulted, however, in financial woes for the commercial banks. Since 1990, crop financing is subject to a subceiling. Ceilings on the total credit expansion in each country are also established, with a subceiling for credit to government, and are communicated to the national credit committees. The national credit committees, in turn, establish credit ceilings bank by bank, together with rediscount ceilings. While crop credit was traditionally excluded from the ceilings, the practice was terminated in 1990 to introduce more discipline in the concession of this credit.

In the BEAC, no comprehensive monetary programming is formulated. Refinancing limits are the main instruments of control. Two different ceilings are applied for short-term credit: one for crop credit, which is refinanced in full, and one on short-term credit, which is limited to 80 percent of the primary credit. A separate refinancing ceiling applies to medium-term credit. Refinancing limits are proposed by the national monetary committees, on the basis of projections of sources and uses of funds for each banking institution and are submitted for approval to the board. Until 1988, a large unused margin existed under the refinancing limits, which, therefore, were not binding. The refinancing limits were tightened across the area in 1988 and 1989 because of the negative net foreign asset position.

Sectoral credit controls have been implemented in both monetary areas with a variety of instruments, but lately, a shift away from these controls has occurred. In the WAMU, an important instrument of selective control has been the *prior approval system*, under which commercial banks are required to submit to the central bank, for prior approval, credits that raise total outstanding loans to any given borrower above a certain amount, in the range of CFAF 30–100 million ($120,000–400,000), depending on the country. This system was abolished on October 1, 1990 and replaced by a general classification of primary borrowers to determine their eligibility for central bank refinancing. A system of ratios requiring commercial banks to allocate a portion of their resources to preferential sectors has not been implemented effectively and has recently been repealed.

Prudential ratios are imposed by both central banks. The BEAC imposes several, the values of which are set by the national monetary committees. These ratios include a minimum liquidity ratio; a solvency ratio, currently set at 5 percent; and a ratio of deposits to nonrediscountable credits, which limits nonrediscountable credit to a maximum of the sum of 25 percent of demand deposit liabilities and 50 percent of time deposit liabilities. In the WAMU, the BCEAO imposes a minimum liquidity ratio and two solvency ratios, a risk distribution ratio, which is the maximum ratio of unsecured loans to any single borrower to the bank's own funds—currently one to one—and a capital/risk ratio, currently set at 6 percent.

Interest Rate Policy and the Money Market

Until recently, interest rate policy was used only sparingly as a policy instrument. In the WAMU, the discount rate serves as a reference for the whole structure of lending and deposit rates, which is uniform in the area. In the CAMA, national monetary committees have the authority to establish the structure of deposits and lending rates, which have, therefore, been somewhat different across countries. Until recently, in addition to a normal discount rate, the two central banks also maintained a preferential rate for operations in favor of crop financing, small and medium-sized enterprises, and individual housing. The preferential rates were eliminated in October 1989 (BCEAO) and in October 1990 (BEAC). In the WAMU, the normal and preferential discount rates, and consequently the lending and deposit rates, were adjusted only three times between 1975 and 1985; they were adjusted four times between 1986 and 1989; even less frequent adjustments have been made by the BEAC (Chart 1).

The rate of the money market in the WAMU is fixed by the central bank but adjusted more frequently. The money market had been established in 1975 with a view to recycling the excess liquidity of deposit money banks within the union, and thus curbing capital outflows. Until recently, access to money market funds was limited to deposit money banks. The money market is managed by the BCEAO. Surplus funds are deposited in the central bank, which grants advances to banks in need of liquid funds; these advances are guaranteed by rediscountable papers deposited in the central bank. The money market rate has been modified 5 to 7 times a year, on average; a small spread exists between the rate on advances and on deposits. These rates are identical throughout the union and are kept above the Paris market rates to prevent capital flight. Since October 1989, all BCEAO credits to commercial banks are extended through the money market, except for occasional debit balances and for consolidated credits.

Operationally, the market works as follows. In the morning, in each WAMU country, each commercial bank advises the national agency of the BCEAO of the amount they want to borrow or deposit on the market. By the end of the morning, each national agency communicates to the BCEAO headquarters in Dakar the net situation of its money market; the position of each country is consolidated, and the funds available in the surplus countries are allocated to the national agencies of the deficit countries, through transfers in their accounts with the BCEAO headquarters. If necessary, each national agency provides the market out of its own resources with the funds needed to balance the offer and demand of funds. Interest rates on advances are applicable only to the extent that the corresponding funds are provided by commercial banks in the WAMU; interest rates for funds provided by the BCEAO out of its own resources are computed on the basis of the discount rate. Since October 1989, the discount rate has been higher than the money market rate by 0.5 percentage points. This method results in a higher cost of funds for banks in deficit areas;

Chart 1. CFA Franc Zone: Interest Rates, 1980–89
(In percent)

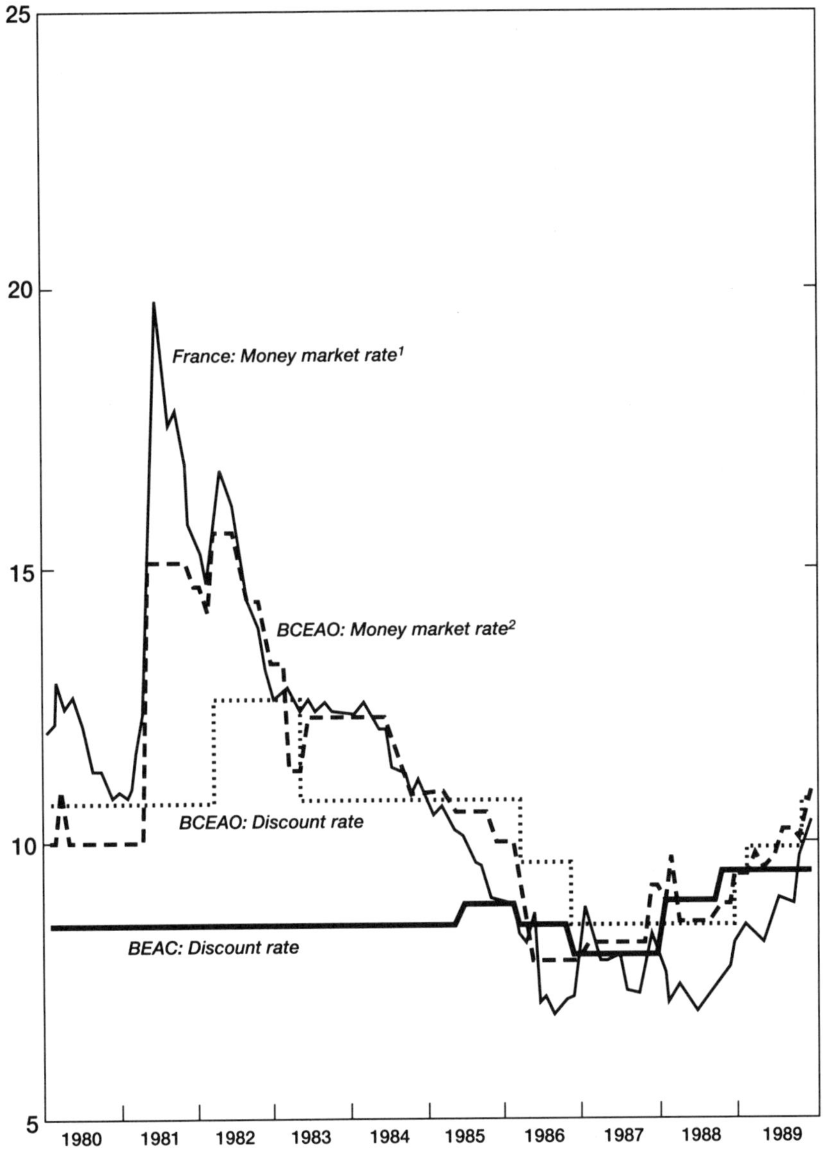

Sources: International Monetary Fund, *International Financial Statistics*; and Fund staff estimates.
[1]Overnight rate.
[2]Rate paid on overnight interbank advances.

however, the difference is modest, given the small differential between money market and discount rate.

The development of the money market has important implications for the future of monetary policy in the WAMU. Refinancing ceilings, which traditionally have been the main credit and monetary instrument of the BCEAO, are losing some of their relevance, because in many countries (Mali, Niger, Togo, Burkina Faso) the offer of funds by local banks exceeds the demand. In this context, the BCEAO may sterilize excess liquidity in some countries with a system of reserve requirements, but there may be a reluctance to set the reserve requirement too high. Bank credit ceilings are an alternative system of control, which the BCEAO envisages to strengthen, by giving a more active role in their establishment to the central bank's headquarters. Moreover, given the drawbacks that the allocation of individual ceilings to banks represent for the efficiency of the banking system, the BCEAO recognizes that a policy of indirect credit control will have to be developed, relying on a further development of the money market, for instance through issues of central bank bills and secondary market operations. A policy of indirect credit control could have the effect of increasing interest rates in countries with a liquidity shortage, and ultimately, through liquid funds flowing from surplus to deficit areas by interbank transactions, of raising interest rates throughout the zone.

Restructuring the Banking System

In recent years, the two central banks have had to address the serious deterioration of the banking system, which requires comprehensive restructuring. In the two areas, a number of banks have become burdened by a large amount of nonperforming loans, as a result of inadequate management, extension of credit without proper collateral, accumulation of arrears by governments, and the deficits of crop-marketing boards, which have prevented the repayment of crop credits. The consequence was increased demand for central bank refinancing, which could not ultimately be accommodated. These burdens were particularly acute in Cameroon and Côte d'Ivoire, where a liquidity crisis occurred in 1989. In these circumstances, governments had to intervene to recapitalize the troubled banks, partly through external assistance on concessional terms. At the same time, the two central banks agreed to consolidate a large part of their outstanding credit to the restructured banks. The amount of credits consolidated by the BCEAO has been substantial, accounting at the end of 1988 for about one third of total outstanding claims on commercial banks. The number of troubled banks is evidence of a weakness in the system of bank supervision—a responsibility that had been left to the national authorities. To tighten bank supervision, two new supranational banking commissions were established in 1990, which are under the oversight of the two central banks.

Economic Performance

This section includes a short presentation of the main aspects of the domestic and external financial performance of the countries of the region, as they relate to the policies of the central banks.

Domestic Financial Performance

The central banks have, in general, succeeded in containing credit growth within limits consistent with a containment in the rate of inflation. Before 1983, domestic credit expanded rapidly in the BCEAO area, contributing to a decline in the net foreign asset position. After 1983, credit expansion stabilized, and the external position improved. In the CAMA, credit expansion was relatively rapid up to 1986, but was reduced thereafter (Chart 2). The rapid growth of credit in the economy was associated with a strong investment expansion spurred by high oil revenues in three oil producing countries of the region. Reflecting the growth of credit, in the period 1980–85, monetary expansion in the CAMA was sustained, close to 20 percent a year. The rates of inflation declined in both areas after 1982 and have been close to those prevailing in France.

While monetary policy in the two CFA franc areas has been successful in preventing inflationary growth in domestic credit, it has not prevented the emergence of large public sector financial imbalances, which were financed by an accumulation of external debt and domestic and external payments arrears. In the early 1980s, most countries in the WAMU and the CAMA pursued expansionary fiscal policies related to ambitious investment programs. In the CAMA, oil revenues were substantial, so that overall deficits did not exceed 2 percent of gross domestic product (GDP). In the WAMU, total government financing needs were on average 11 percent of GDP in the 1980–83 period (Chart 3). Domestic financing averaged 3 percent of GDP, and external grants 2.3 percent, so that external financing excluding grants was very large, leading to a further buildup of external debt; fiscal adjustment was made difficult during the 1980s by declines in the non-oil revenue/GDP ratios, while current expenditure was difficult to contain. Contractual interest payments due on the external

Chart 2. CFA Franc Zone: Counterparts of Money Supply, 1980–89

(In billions of CFA francs; end of period)

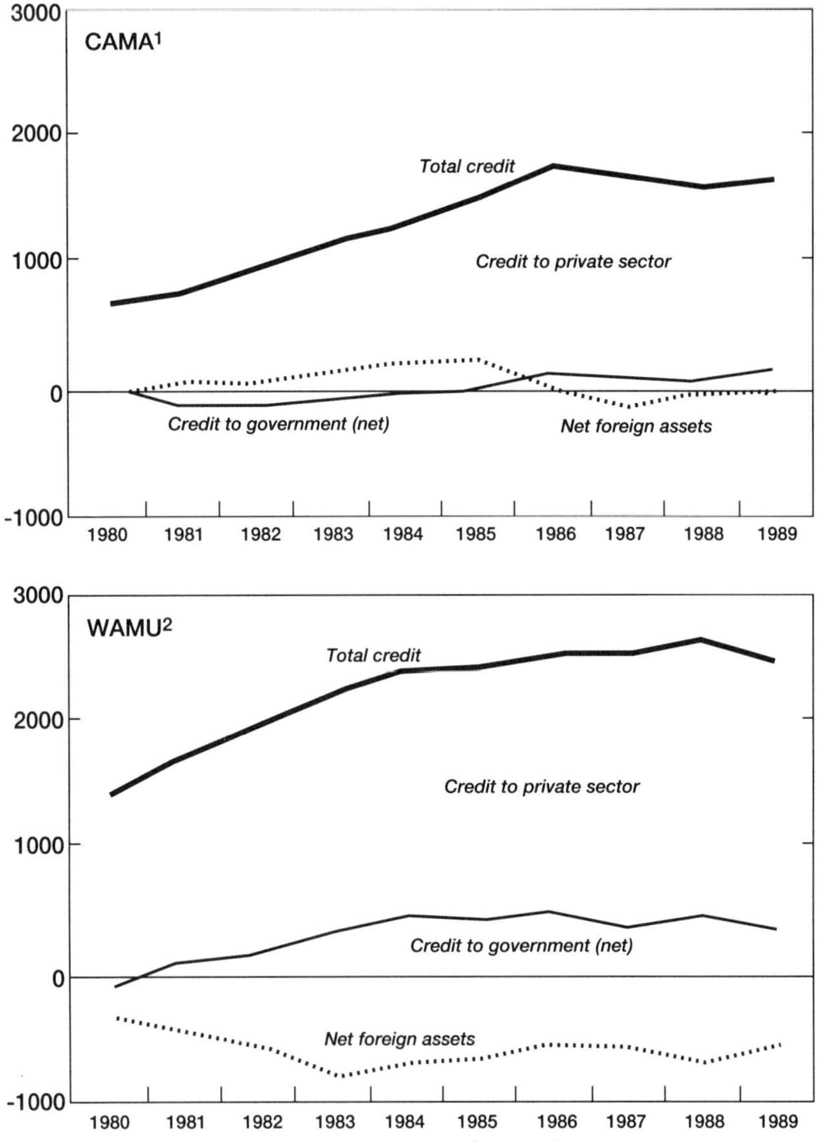

Sources: Date provided by Banque des Etats de l'Afrique Centrale and Banque Centrale des Etats de l'Afrique de l'Ouest.

[1]Excluding Equatorial Guinea.

[2]Excluding Mali before 1984.

Chart 3. CFA Franc Zone: Financing of Government Operations, 1980–89
(In percent of GDP)

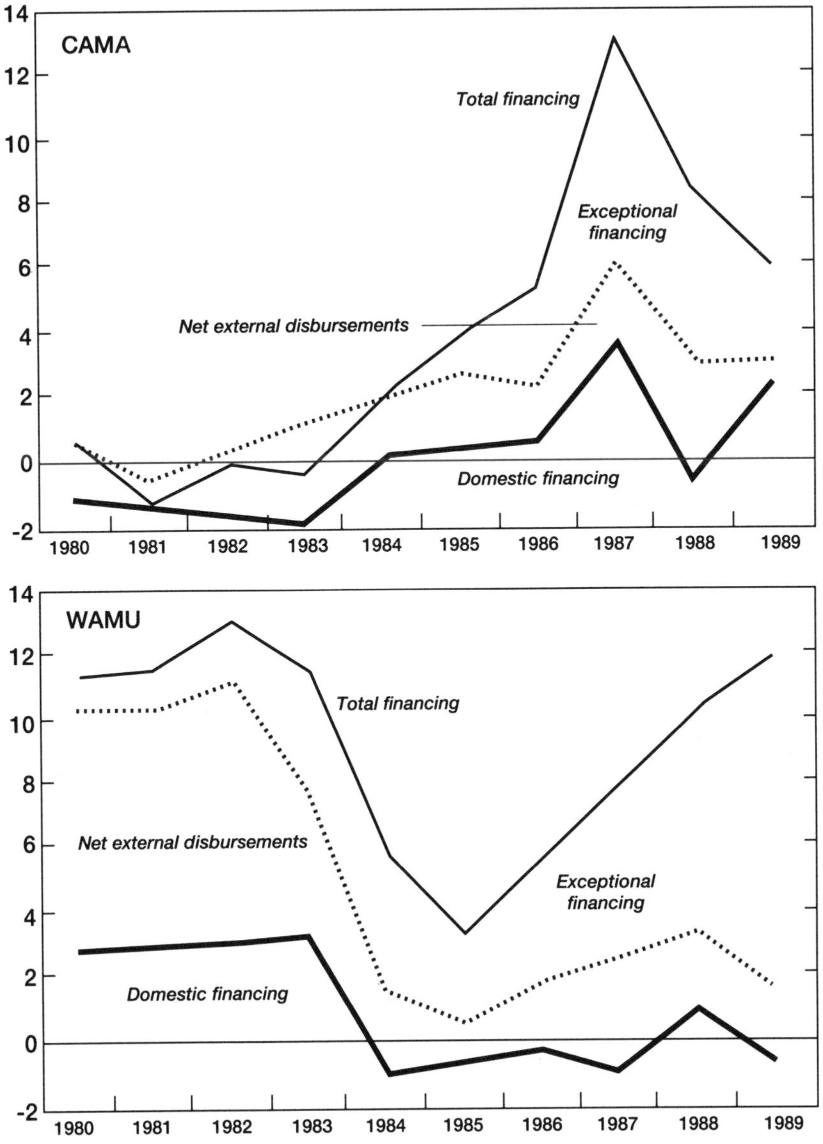

Sources: Data provided by the authorities; and Fund staff estimates.
Note: CAMA = Central African Monetary Area; WAMU = West African Monetary Union.

debt roughly doubled between 1980 and 1989 both in the WAMU and the CAMA. The external debt burden proved unsustainable for most countries of the WAMU by 1983–84, so that the governments had to resort to debt rescheduling.

In the CAMA, the three oil exporters (Cameroon, Gabon, and the Congo) enjoyed growing oil revenues up to 1985, so that the overall fiscal position of the region was relatively strong; however, with the decline of oil revenues in 1986–87, fiscal deficits widened substantially, exceeding 10 percent of GDP; because of lags in curtailing investment outlays, all the countries of the area had to have recourse to debt rescheduling; they also accumulated large domestic payments arrears.

Thus, while the fiscal situation has not affected the stance of monetary and credit policy differently than in many other developing countries, the inadequate fiscal discipline in the CFA franc countries has led to serious financial difficulty and a buildup of external debt and payments arrears.

The Balance of Payments and the Foreign Reserve Position

As mentioned, the credit policy of the two central banks has been formulated in a framework that gives weight to the need to maintain a strong reserve position. In practice, however, the central banks could do little to reverse the sharp deterioration, in the late 1970s, in the current account and in the overall balance. The current account deficit (including official transfers) of the CFA franc zone averaged 8 percent of GDP in the period 1978–82; following a decline in the deficit in 1984–85 owing to favorable developments in Côte d'Ivoire and in the oil producing countries, it widened again in 1986–88, to an average of 8.5 percent of GDP (Chart 4). The deterioration in the early 1980s stemmed from a number of factors, such as declines in the prices of the main export commodities of the drought-stricken Sahelian countries and the sharp increase in international interest rates. The terms of trade deterioration worsened after 1985, as export prices of the main commodities plummeted.

As a result of these factors, the net foreign position of the BCEAO became sharply negative in 1980 and reached a trough in 1983 (Chart 5). Thereafter, the position improved somewhat, owing to the mobilization of external assistance, including debt rescheduling, by member countries, but it remained substantially negative. Extensive use of IMF resources attenuated the impact on the BCEAO's Operations Account with the French Treasury, which was in a negative position between 1980 and 1984 but became positive in 1985–87; after

Chart 4. CFA Countries: Current Account Balances, 1980–89[1]
(As percent of GDP)

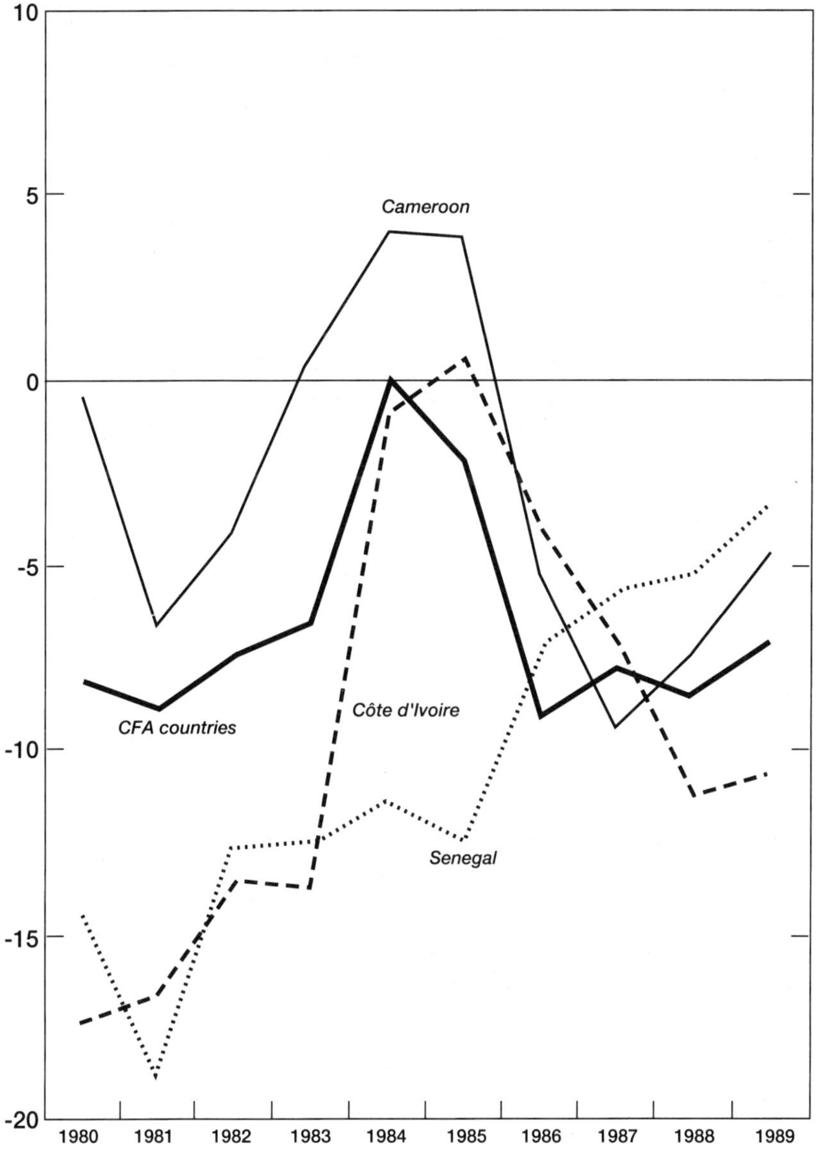

Source: International Monetary Fund, *World Economic Outlook: A Survey by the Staff of the International Monetary Fund,* World Economic and Financial Surveys (Washington, October 1990).
[1]Including transfers.

Chart 5. CFA Franc Zone: Central Bank Net Foreign Assets, 1980–89
(In billions of CFA francs; end of period)

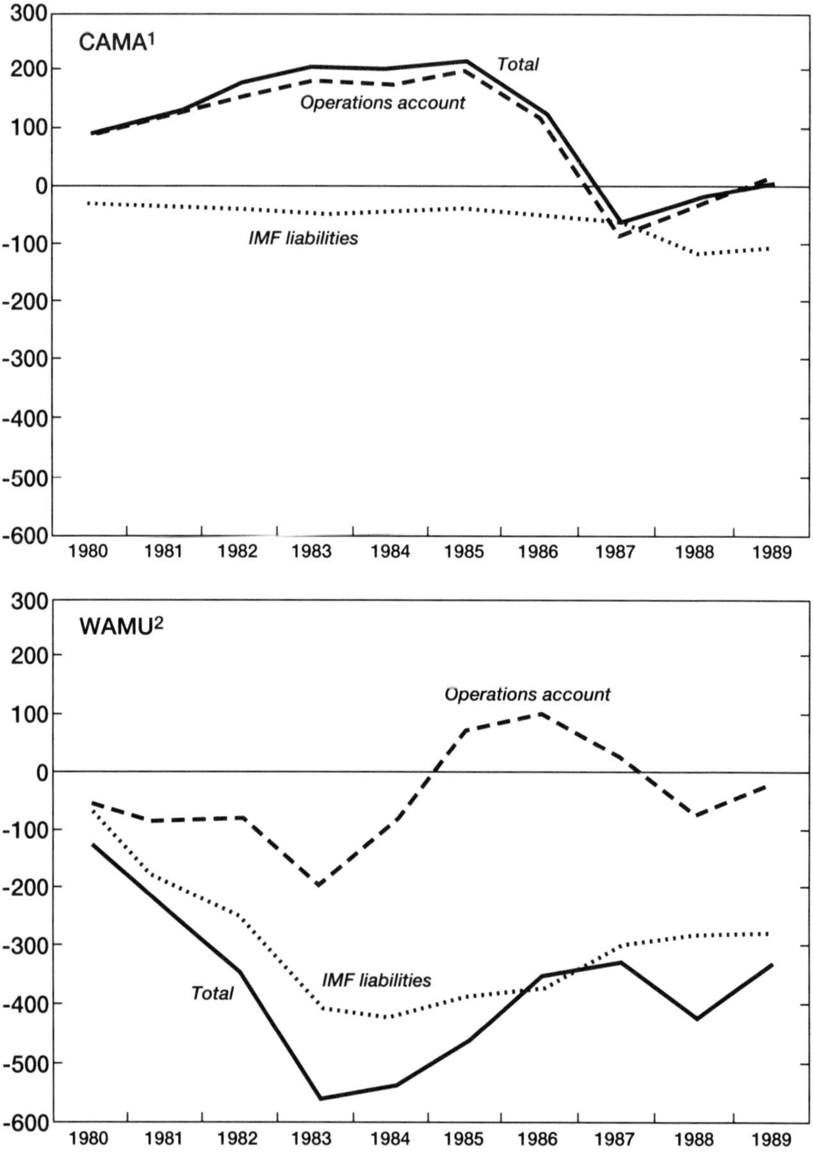

Sources: Date provided by Banque des Etats de l'Afrique Centrale, Banque Centrale des Etats de l'Afrique de l'Ouest; and Fund staff estimates.

[1]Excluding Equatorial Guinea.

[2]Excluding Mali before 1984.

deteriorating in 1988–89, the account was again positive in 1990. Credit policy was generally not able to deter the deterioration of the balance of payments. In fact, the convertibility of the currency also facilitated capital outflow, which was prompted on some occasions by political uncertainty in the member countries; the modest interest rate differential with France was not an effective disincentive.

During this period of balance of payments difficulty, the stability and convertibility of the exchange rate has provided the benefit of moderating inflation and avoiding the emergence of parallel exchange rate markets. At the same time, there is some evidence of loss of competitiveness, and the diversification of these economies has not been very rapid.

Concluding Remarks

The two supranational central banks in Western and Central Africa represent a successful example of two institutions managing a monetary union among sovereign states. Their institutional features and their operating procedures present a balance between independence and responsiveness to the economic situation of the member countries. The independence in the conduct of overall monetary credit policy has benefitted from the existence of a fixed exchange rate rule and from the associated constraints in the expansion of credit to government and in overall credit that are firmly established in the statutes of the two central banks. Thus, monetary policy has generally followed a steady course; the national authorities, which control the decision-making process of the two central banks, have had to abide by the predetermined rules of operations; however, the strict limits on credit to the government have not resulted in overall government financial discipline, as individual governments have had large recourse to external assistance, including exceptional assistance in the form of debt rescheduling. While preserving monetary stability, the two central banks have not been able to stop the emergence of serious imbalances in the balance of payments during the last decade, a fact that reflects to a large extent exogenous factors, but also the inability of the member countries to diversify rapidly their economies.

Two major challenges that confront the two central banks are the restructuring of the banking systems, which in recent years have been affected by a sharp deterioration of the loan portfolio, and the improvement in the instruments of monetary control, to attenuate the reliance on quantitative ceilings. Stronger bank supervision is being put in place, accompanied by a consolidation and recapitalization of the banks in difficulty.

With regard to monetary controls, the development of money markets and of the intervention of the central banks in these markets are under consideration. To the extent that this would imply more intense flows of funds through each of the two areas, it would require an acceptance by the political authorities of a larger degree of financial integration among the member countries' economies.

11

Central Bank Independence in Austria

MARIA SCHAUMAYER*

I would like to discuss the evolution of central bank independence in Austria and how it functions today. I shall first give a short history as background and then describe the present state of the central bank. This will be followed by a description of the aims of the central bank's independence.

A Short History

Maria Theresa, the great empress who reigned over Austria from 1740 to 1780, was considering the foundation of a central bank. In 1761, a draft was drawn up to set up a bank according to the model of the Bank of England, but it did not occur until half a century later, in 1816, after the Napoleonic wars. Napoleon had been warring with Europe, and his forces had been occupying Austria. During that occupation, French troops distributed a lot of counterfeit money. To stop the use of this money was an immediate objective of the newly founded Austrian National Bank. Austria was much bigger then than now, so it was not from Vienna that Emperor Franz I signed the edict for the foundation of the Austrian National Bank, but from Milano; already, the first central bank of Austria was given independence from the state. The prohibition to grant loans and credits to the state followed later.

History brought many changes to the country, the economy, the currency, and, of course, to the central bank. In 1878, after the agreement between Austria and Hungary, the "Privileged Austrian National Bank" changed its name to the "Austrian-Hungarian Bank"; its inde-

*The author is Governor of the National Bank of Austria.

pendence remained unaffected. After World War I, the Austrian-Hungarian Bank had to be liquidated in 1919, according to the peace treaties. After the end of the war and postwar inflation, which brought about a grave devaluation of the currency, the Austrian National Bank resumed its activities in 1923. The year after, the currency was changed by law from the crown to the schilling. In 1938, another deep inroad was made in the history of Austria. The schilling was abolished by German occupation authorities and the reichsmark was imposed forcefully at the rate of 3:2. A decree to liquidate the Austrian National Bank was issued, but this liquidation was not finished until the war ended.

Austria regained its independence in April 1945, and the Austrian National Bank resumed its activities. Another law was passed, and the statutes of the Austrian National Bank were adjusted to the extraordinary circumstances of the immediate postwar times. The most important task of the Austrian National Bank in 1945 was to prepare the reintroduction of the schilling currency and to reduce the money circulation, which was much higher than production. The first Austrian parliament passed a law in November 1945 that changed reichsmark into schilling at a rate of 1:1, but one could get only a maximum of 150 schillings per person in cash, whereas remaining assets were credited to accounts, which one could not dispose of without permission. The currency reform of 1947 got rid of the surplus money in circulation, and from 1947 to 1951 there were five price income contracts. By these contracts, which started the successful "*Sozialpartnerschaft*" (Social Partnership), the danger of inflation could be restricted.

The Austrian currency was stabilized in 1952 by a number of budgetary, fiscal, and monetary measures, which provided the foundation for the further economic development of Austria. In the 1950s, a gradual liberalization and the National Bank Act of 1955, passed after the State Treaty had been signed, set up a new legal frame for the Austrian National Bank. This law of 1955 contained also the necessary modern instruments for monetary policy to enable the Austrian National Bank to function from then on not only as guardian of the currency but also as lender of last resort. The Bank Act of 1984 contained and repromulgated all the amendments that had been passed since 1955.

The Present Situation

The general provisions of the National Bank Act of 1984 stipulate that the Austrian National Bank is a joint stock company, that it has the function of regulating the circulation of money in Austria and of attending to the settlement of payments with foreign countries. It has to ensure with all the means at its disposal that the value of the Austrian currency is maintained with regard both to its domestic purchasing power and to its relationship with stable foreign currencies. The general provisions also stipulate that the Austrian National Bank is under obligation to ensure within the framework of its credit policy that the credits it places at the disposal of the economy are distributed with due regard to the country's economic needs.

The Austrian National Bank is free to participate as an organization and financially in international institutions that are concerned with cooperation between central banks or which otherwise aim and promote international cooperation in the field of monetary and credit policy. The Bank, in its own name and on its own account, may also take part in any measures or operations undertaken by such institutions in which a participating interest is held by it or by the Republic of Austria.

Article 4 of the Act reads as follows:

> In determining the general lines of monetary and credit policy to be followed by the Austrian National Bank in this field for the purpose of performing the functions incumbent upon it, due regard shall be paid to the economic policy of the Federal Government.

This Article 4 in connection with Article 21, which entrusts the Governing Board with outlining the general directives of monetary and credit policy, safeguards the independence of the Bank. If the Governing Board feels impeded by the Government's supervision or if there is an infringement of any of the prohibitions for the Federal Republic "Länder," and local authorities, the Governing Board as a whole or any individual member of the Board may appeal to an Arbitration Tribunal, which has to give a final decision within three days. According to Article 40(4) the Arbitration Tribunal shall be composed of the President of the Supreme Court, who shall preside, and four members, two of whom shall be appointed by the Federal Government and two by the bank.

As said before, the Austrian National Bank is a joint stock company, though sui generis. Half of its capital according to Article 9 is subscribed by the Federal Republic, and the Federal Government has to decide what persons and enterprises are permitted to subscribe the remaining capital of the bank. In fact, these "private" or rather non-state shareholders represent the main economic factors and institutions, such as industry, trade and commerce, the employers' chamber, trade unions; in short, they are representative of Austrian *Sozialpartnerschaft*.

Let me dwell a little on this *Sozialpartnerschaft*, which has become a trademark of Austria. At first, it might sound like a deviation from market economy: representatives of the Employers' and the Employees' Association, together with representatives of the Chamber of Agriculture, form an extraparliamentarian body and sit down to discuss macroeconomic problems. What is the essence? It is not more, but also not less, than shared information about objective economic and social facts. What is the result of such equal, although not always undisputed, information? I am tempted to answer that it is a convergence of policy re prices and wages and therefore it is stability instead of fights, the prey of which are usually the weak ones. Let me say, as an aside that the price of this Austrian kind of stabilization has been a slower restructuring and modernization of the economy. Let us hope that countries envisaging the introduction of market economy may hear the message and be able to combine the best of both experiences.

Capital ownership is also reflected in the Governing Board, which consists of the governor, two deputy governors and eleven other members; six are elected by the Bank's General Meeting; the other five are appointed by the Federal Government. Not more than four active bankers are permitted on the Governing Board; there are no civil servants or members of government and legislative bodies. The governor is appointed by the President of the Federal Republic, the two deputy governors by the Federal Government. The term of office is five years for all; no dismissal is possible, except when the requirements for the appointment are no longer met or the member is prevented for more than a year to perform his or her duties. Five years is the maximum term for officers in joint stock companies in Austria—a sensible period that gives enough leeway to make the appointment successful and should it be inappropriate, the end of the term is in sight. It should also be understood that the governor, as the way of appointment signifies, should feel responsible to the general public. The governor is independent, but accountable, not to Parliament, not to the Government, but to the general public who also, according to the Austrian Constitution, elects the President of the Federal Republic. I am sure the delicate balance between independence and accountability will concern also the authorities who are entrusted with finding viable solutions for European monetary union and a European central banking system.

The Governing Board is charged with the supreme direction of the Bank, not only with the supervision of the Board of Executive Directors, a maximum of six persons, who are responsible for the overall running of the Bank in accordance with the law and the directives issued by the Governing Board.

Another provision of the Act that allows central bank independence is Article 42. The article expressly states, that no transaction may involve the granting of any loan or credit by the bank to the Federal Republic. Nothing of that kind must happen, not even in disguise. All these provisions are safeguards for the Austrian National Bank's independence.

Aims of Independence

What are the aims of independence? Clearly, stabilization is the principal aim of the Bank's independence and also, of course, its principal concern. Primary responsibility of the central bank is the maintaining of the value and purchasing power of the Austrian currency. This task dominates other economic goals as for example full employment or economic growth. When Article 4 of the National Bank Act says that the Austrian National Bank has to pay due regard to the economic policy of the Federal Government, this quite clearly expresses that the Government's economic policy should not be counteracted. But it also implies that the Austrian National Bank may participate when economic policy is formulated. Laws concerning economic matters have to be appraised by the Austrian National Bank. I would also like to emphasize that the Austrian National Bank has always made it quite clear that a consistent budget and wage policy in line with the exchange rate strategy is vital. Of course, the Austrian National Bank has a vital interest in full employment, in economic growth, in international compatibility, and in competitiveness of the Austrian economy. It has no direct instruments to pursue such real economic goals, but its policy aim is to create stable and predictable conditions for the economy and for the business community.

But human beings are not purely rational, they have hopes and fears, and their economic behavior reflects their experiences. Since the last century Austrians have experienced wars, the collapse of the Austro-Hungarian Empire, several runaway inflations, occupations, and loss of currency and state. History has taught my people to save, after World War II, perhaps not so much in order to get rich, but to provide for times of need. Saving in Austria is now nearly four times as high as the federal budget.

This would not have happened without the deep belief of the society that stability makes it worthwhile to work hard, to save, and to spend reasonably. The confidence in a policy of stability, a hard and well-funded currency that the man on the street realizes and cherishes when traveling abroad, lends strength also to the Austrian National

Bank, which is seen as an independent guarantor of the strong schilling with beneficial effects for all.

Conclusion

Let me turn now to the final remarks. What are the instruments to achieve the goals of stability? You all know that the Austrian National Bank stabilizes the Austrian schilling exchange rate by pegging it to the deutsche mark. Switzerland and Germany have flexible exchange rates with monetary aggregates as their nominal anchor. Price stabilization in those two countries is achieved by monetary growth rules. Let me be quite frank, Austria's foreign trade would go to, say, the United States or the United Kingdom to the same extent as it goes to Germany, and were the currencies of the United States and United Kingdom as stable as the deutsche mark, Austria would have pegged to the U.S. dollar or the British pound. The deutsche mark was chosen purely in conformity with trade relations and stability—an example followed by various European countries for similar reasons.

By the mechanism chosen, it is not possible to control the monetary supply over a longer period. The Austrian National Bank determines the proportion of domestic and foreign assets serving as cover for the money in circulation by expanding the domestic source component by more or less than the increase in the demand for money. This means that official reserves are controlled via the domestic source component. This way stability is imported, given the anchor's stability. The policy taken also provides that nominal wage settlements are moderate. Together this helps fight inflation. This is even more important as the European countries in the European Community (EC) try to create a zone of stability in Europe. Austria is taking part in this stabilization program and also in its success without being a member of the EC so far.

The published goals of Austrian monetary policy have remained unchanged in the past few years. Since the 1970s, monetary policy decisions in Austria have focused on holding the exchange rate of the schilling stable against the deutsche mark. This leads to optimal macroeconomic stabilization effects, as well as to a high degree of stabilization of positive expectations.

We continue to regard exchange rate policy as the optimum monetary policy approach for Austria. This also holds true in view of the alternatives that are likely to be discussed within the framework of European integration. The liberalization of financial markets, however, calls for far-reaching harmonization of the legal framework. A new stock exchange law took effect in Austria in 1990. The "Capital

Market Law" is in preparation. It will create a new legal basis for the public offering of securities and other financial investment instruments. The Banking Supervision Law and the Banking Law will have to be adjusted in line with EC developments. The central bank's tasks will increasingly focus on ensuring efficient financial markets as well as on monitoring and control functions, in particular with a view to minimizing risks associated with the system of highly integrated financial markets.

The outline of the future European monetary system points to radical changes in the role of the Austrian central bank should Austria join the EC. The Austrian economy, however, will hardly be affected by this "change in paradigms," because it will benefit from the exchange rate strategy which Austria has been pursuing for a number of years. The extension of the optimum currency area will even facilitate economic decision making. Whether international economic policy can be better harmonized and exchange rate expectations further stabilized will depend on the methods of economic policy coordination.

Considering the present situation, it can be said that Austria is further downstage than most members of the exchange rate mechanism (ERM): minute fluctuations of the schilling against the deutsche mark, concurrence of fundamentals, and liberalization of capital movements.

The Austrian central bank cannot pursue direct money supply targets because it has chosen the exchange rate as an intermediate monetary policy goal (and because of the need for intervention this choice entails). Changes in the central bank money stock are determined by the demand for money. In principle, it would be possible to publish a subordinate, adaptive money supply target announced in the form of a band definition along with the exchange rate target; however, this could dilute the predictability of central bank policy. We base our reasoning on the concept of a "reverse causality" of money resulting from the endogenous determination of the money supply. This concept consists of influencing the source of money creation (domestic or foreign source component); the objective for the Austrian National Bank's foreign exchange balance is to conform with the objective of the exchange rate strategy. Clear guidelines govern the application of the domestic and foreign source components; in essence, these guidelines are determined by the actual and expected developments on the foreign exchange market (use of the domestic source component of central bank money creation only if the size of our change in the foreign exchange balance permits, use of the foreign source component otherwise).

This money supply concept would not require any changes in the event that Austria formally participates in the European Monetary

System, provided the exchange rate goal continues to be used as a policy base and as long as there is no obligation to announce a national money supply target. Since the Austrian National Bank also regularly ascertains the internationally common monetary indicators, the "concurrent" announcement of an aggregate like the money supply target would not represent a problem in principle, if such a procedure should be compulsory within the framework of international monetary cooperation. Many facts seem to indicate, however, that within the framework of an exchange rate link, such as the one between the schilling and the deutsche mark, the money supply developments of the key currency country are for all practical purposes imported, especially insofar as (under the condition that payment habits are comparable) the money supply of the "key currency country" should be in line with the demand for money in the other economies of the exchange rate zone, as a result of the required harmony between the fundamentals of the countries orienting their exchange rate toward the deutsche mark and Germany.

Interest rate policy is hardly independent, not only because of the exchange rate goal but also because of the liberalization and globalization of financial markets. The process does not operate in a purely mechanical fashion; institutional and structural peculiarities may result in temporary deviations (e.g., Austrian overnight money rates will fluctuate more than comparable rates in Germany because the Austrian market is thinner than the German one). Nor does the international connection imply that there is only one equilibrium interest rate in each case or that the system converges toward this rate; even if the market for a specific financial service can be determined precisely, an interest rate structure can and will develop on account of the regional differences of economic variables and their effects on the demand for capital and on account of the differences in how well developed financial markets are, what the extent of an economy's savings formation is, and whether a country is a net importer or an exporter of capital.

Against this background, the Austrian National Bank pursues an exchange rate policy without explicitly formulating a concrete exchange rate target; rather, it pursues an implicit target aimed at minimizing exchange rate fluctuations. What is important—with a view to both short-term reactions by exchange dealers and long-term developments on capital markets—is that market participants' expectations are stabilized. "Exchange market intervention" is pursued beyond the scope of its conventional meaning, as it includes all measures designed to minimize fluctuations of the schilling-deutsche mark exchange rate (which also encompasses measures under the heading of capital import policy, such as the timing of the Federal Government's capital imports). According to this concept, the money market rate is to be considered an intermediate objective controlled by means of direct interest rate policy measures (key interest rates, open market interest rates), liquidity policy measures (use of the domestic or foreign source components of money supply creation), or by forgoing such measures. A logical consequence of the concept is that general interest rate policy measures (in particular the central bank's key interest rates) are in line with steps taken internationally, especially in Germany. In practice the technical instruments differ slightly from those used abroad. Unlike Germany, Austria does not resort to a tender procedure for banks' basic refinancing: Austria has a limited special open market refinancing facility, swap instruments are used more frequently, and the minimum reserve obligation is not identical with that abroad.

Specific macroeconomic factors represent important framework conditions for this exchange rate policy. In this connection, the central bank monitors particularly the development of relative labor costs compared with those of trade partners, price indices, structural changes in the current account, and the Federal Government's budget management. Recently, other factors have come to the fore, especially because capital transactions and financial services have been liberalized: the international competitiveness of banks, insurance companies and the stock market, efficient financial markets, effective and internationally coordinated supervisory structures.

Reserves of the Bank have grown in the last years. Interest rates are linked to the deutsche mark. By fine-tuning the interest rate differential, the Austrian National Bank is able to influence the official reserve position. Inflation in the country was around 3.2 percent in August 1990. Full employment is achieved if one takes into account that an unemployment rate of roughly 5 percent is also the balance of more than 100,000 immigrants that have come within the last year from Eastern European countries.

Monetary policy is ultimately a government responsibility. In Austria, the Parliament entrusted the Austrian National Bank with the power to conduct monetary policy. Stability is the aim and the result; independence and accountability to the public are the necessary means to conduct this policy.

12

The Role of an Independent Central Bank in Europe

HANS TIETMEYER*

A central bank independent of government influence is essential for a successful monetary policy. This is the rule that one arrives at when looking at the experiences of those countries that perform the role of the central bank in maintaining price stability. There is the rare exception: France appears to be the most obvious example; in recent years, it has achieved relative price stability without its central bank being independent of the government. It is often said that "the exception proves the rule." And the rule is that countries with an independent central bank show a better record on inflation than those without. Indeed, a fairly close correlation between inflation performance and the degree of independence of the central bank seems evident.

The Case for Central Bank Independence

The issue of central bank independence can be treated as a matter of high principle or of common sense and practical experience. The current British debate provides a lively illustration of the argument over high principle versus actual experience. On one side are those who insist that the elected parliament and government should hold unlimited power over monetary policy, as they do over other policy areas; on the other side are those arguing for an independent central bank on the basis of past and current experience—but also perhaps based on economic reasoning.

In many countries, particularly after World War II, the central banks' money printing powers were needed to finance the deficit

*The author is a member of the Executive Board of the Deutsche Bundesbank.

spending policies that gave priority to full employment and high growth. Monetary policy had virtually no role to play, except that money had to be cheap. "Money does not matter," was part of the accepted economic doctrine, especially in the Anglo-Saxon countries. In any case, monetary policy was not to impede full employment policy.

In the United Kingdom, the "Radcliffe Report," published in 1959, affirmed the view that the government's economic policy had to include monetary policy as an integral part of a consistent whole; fiscal and monetary policies could not be allowed to be pulling at different ends. In many other countries, too, monetary policy was fully subjected to the requirements of an activist fiscal policy aimed at full employment and high growth. The victims were usually the balance of payments and price stability. The treatment applied included balance of payments restrictions and exchange rate adjustment, and price controls and incomes policy.

Recourse to restrictions on trade and current payments was made subject to closely monitored rules and international codes of good behavior; the experience of the 1930s had shown that they were undesirable and counterproductive. Restrictions on capital transactions, by contrast, were considered acceptable; the Articles of Agreement of the International Monetary Fund (IMF) gave express permission to use them. Exchange rate adjustments were frequent even though under the IMF's Articles they were only permitted in case of "fundamental disequilibrium," a concept that was left somewhat vague and open to interpretation.

Price controls supported by subsidies were widely applied. Incomes policy became popular in the 1960s in some countries as a formula designed to arrive at a more favorable trade-off between inflation and unemployment, or a shift of the Philipps curve to the left. The results were disappointing. Price controls and incomes policy provided no substitute for an anti-inflationary monetary policy. Likewise, trade and payments restrictions or devaluations proved ineffectual for fundamental economic imbalances rooted in wrong policy mixes, with the central bank forced to assist the government's growth and full employment policies.

The notion of independence for a country's central bank has to be based on a very different understanding of the role of monetary policy. It has to start from recognition of the fundamental truth that inflation is essentially a monetary phenomenon. Other factors may play a role at times. But as Gottfried Haberler wrote in the 1950s, ". . . there is no record in the economic history of the whole world, anywhere or at any time, of a serious and prolonged inflation which has not been accompanied and made possible, if not caused, by a large increase in the quantity of money."[1] This holds true even if one makes allowance for changes in the velocity of money circulation, which follow cyclical patterns and react to shocks of various kinds. In fact, as Haberler himself pointed out,

> . . . except in periods of hyperinflation (which could not develop without a sharp and sustained rise in the quantity of money) a rise in velocity by itself has never caused or substantially intensified serious inflationary trouble.[2]

If, as history tells us (I quote Haberler, page 20, again), ". . . in every inflation, money is a causal factor, either active or permissive, . . . ," then price stability obviously calls for a monetary policy that will not allow monetary expansion to exceed that needed to accommodate noninflationary economic growth. If experience, furthermore, tells us that monetary policy is a powerful instrument to keep inflation in check, but is much less powerful to stimulate economic growth and employment, then there seems to be a strong argument in favor of monetary policy being committed to pursue price stability as its primary objective. If price stability is, moreover, seen to provide the most solid basis for sustained economic growth and high employment, whereas inflation is recognized to be its worst enemy, if only because it will over time undermine a country's social fabric, then the case for an independent central bank committed to price stability would seem to become overwhelmingly strong.

Acceptance of the central bank's independence by parliament will be tantamount to political recognition of the need for safeguards against the misuse of the potentially unlimited financing powers of the government through resort to the printing press. Individuals are warned strongly against resort to illicit issuing of money, for very obvious reasons; the state has clearly reserved that power for itself. Those like Professor Hayek favoring monetary arrangements based on currency competition between private issuers would reverse that situation, by depriving the state of its money printing monopoly and allowing private citizens to issue bank notes instead. There are strong arguments against that concept, and it would hardly be practicable.

Limiting the state's recourse to the printing press by entrusting responsibility for monetary policy to an independent central bank with clearly defined powers and objectives can be shown to be in the

[1]Gottfried Haberler, "Internal Factors Causing and Propagating Inflation," Chapter 2 in *Inflation*, proceedings of a conference held by the International Economic Association in 1959, ed. by D.C. Hague (London: Macmillan and Co., 1962), page 19.

[2]Ibid., page 20.

public interest. It may even be in the interest of the government itself, because the temptation to use the powers of the printing press will always be present; the consequences of yielding to such temptation are not always self-evident and, all too often, are left to succeeding governments to deal with.

For all these reasons, independence from the government would seem to be a necessary constitutional element for a central bank if it is to achieve its primary objective, price stability. This view has not always been accepted generally. But it has gained acceptance in the years of high inflation in the 1970s and after.

The success of the Deutsche Bundesbank with the independence bestowed upon it by the Bundesbank Act (which was adopted in 1957) has helped to make this viewpoint more generally attractive to many other countries as recent examples of new central bank legislation show.

The Independence of the Bundesbank

The Bundesbank is committed by law to the task "of safeguarding the currency."[3] In pursuing this objective, it is often regarded as the central bank with "a relative maximum of independence." As the expression indicates, the Bundesbank's independence is not total, but it is relatively high in relation to the government and compared with that of other central banks. When discussing central bank independence, different aspects should be distinguished, of which the institutional, functional, and personal independence aspects are probably the most important.

Institutional Independence

In exercising its powers, the Bundesbank as an institution is independent of instructions from the government, the parliament, or any other government institution. Needless to say, it is also free from interference by other bodies. Most important, the exertion of direct influence on the conduct of monetary policy by the Government is thereby ruled out. In its policy, the Bundesbank is guided by the mandate

[3]Article 3 of Deutsche Bundesbank Act (*Gesetz über die Deutsche Bundesbank*) of 1957, according to an unofficial English translation. See Deutsche Bundesbank, *The Deutsche Bundesbank: Its Monetary Policy Instruments and Functions*, Special Series No. 7 (Frankfurt, 3rd ed., 1989), pp. 110–35.

given to it under the law. But institutional independence alone is not sufficient.

To be assured of full control over monetary policy the central bank also needs to be functionally independent. The Bundesbank has the sole and unrestricted authority to use the traditional instruments of monetary policy, namely, rediscount policy, minimum reserve policy, and open market policy in order to pursue its functions. It disposes of the full array of monetary policy instruments and is not inhibited from using them by interest rate ceilings or other limitations. Public authorities have no recourse to borrowing from the Bundesbank, except within very limited short-term overdraft credit lines. With fully functioning money markets such access has of course become less relevant to the financial operations of public entities, though most of them still make regular use of the overdrafts for convenience. Recourse to them was particularly attractive so long as access was at below-market interest rates; only recently has this been changed.

The functional independence of the Bundesbank is not complete. The Federal Government has the right to decide on the exchange rate regime and to determine the parities, or central rates for the deutsche mark, in a system of fixed exchange rates. It is generally recognized that obligations to intervene in the foreign exchange market to defend a particular parity may conflict with monetary policy, even though the central bank may be able to offset all or part of the immediate liquidity effects on the banks through other operations. At times this proved difficult or impossible, and serious conflicts arose between the Bundesbank and the Federal Government over external monetary policy, especially under the old fixed parity regime with the U.S. dollar at its center. To avoid such conflicts as much as possible in the future, it was agreed between the Federal Government and the Bundesbank in 1978, prior to the creation of the European Monetary System, that should a fundamental conflict arise for monetary policy as a consequence of the obligation to defend a particular exchange rate the Bundesbank would have the option to suspend its intervention obligation in the exchange rate mechanism ("opting out").

The Bundesbank's functional independence is also somewhat limited in other ways. Members of the Government may attend and propose motions at meetings of the Central Bank Council. They even have the right to ask Council decisions to be delayed for up to two weeks. But this has, so far, never led to any serious problem regarding the conduct of monetary policy. The "veto right" has actually never been used to date. And, as said, it can only be used to delay action by the Central Bank Council, not to block it.

Personal Independence

With regard to the aspect of personal independence, the members of the Central Bank Council are appointed upon nomination by the Federal and the Länder (state) Governments. Their terms are for a relatively long period (maximum eight years), during which they cannot be removed from office. They are not subject to any specific mandate other than that enscribed in the Bundesbank Act. In particular, the Länder central bank presidents are not expected to pursue any special interests of their Länder or to receive instructions from them. The Länder central banks are integral parts of the Bundesbank; they are not shareholders of the system, nor are the Länder. The Federal Government holds the capital of the Bundesbank and receives any profits, but it too does not derive any further rights from this fact. The Bundesbank's financial structure thus does not impair its autonomous status.

One other factor of independence may be worth mentioning and that is the geographical distance between the site of the Federal Government (Bonn) and the site of the Bundesbank (Frankfurt). This, too, may have helped to prevent too strong informal channels of influence being established. The Federal Parliament has just passed legislation providing for the Bundesbank's seat to remain in Frankfurt even if the government should move to Berlin. Here again, the independence of the central bank is duly recognized. The Bundesbank Act contains a provision which stipulates that "[w]ithout prejudice to the performance of its functions, the Deutsche Bundesbank is required to support the general economic policy of the Federal Government."[4] This is understood to mean that in case of conflict, where supporting the Government's policies would impair the Bundesbank's ability to pursue its primary objective, the commitment to price stability would carry the day.

The recent debate about the Bundesbank's role in regard to German economic and monetary union and to European economic and monetary union prompts me to add the following: the Bundesbank is required by law to give advice to the Federal Government on matters that are relevant to monetary policy. The Government can seek the Bundesbank's advice, or the Bundesbank can offer it. But the Government is also free to accept it, or not to accept it. In any case, the Government may have to accept the consequences, if the Bundesbank sees a need to act in the pursuit of price stability.

[4]Article 12 of Bundesbank Act, according to an unofficial English translation. See Deutsche Bundesbank, *The Deutsche Bundesbank: Its Monetary Policy Instruments, and Functions*, Special Series No. 7 (Frankfurt, 3rd ed., 1989), pages 110–35.

As far as German economic and monetary union is concerned, the Bundesbank's well-publicized advice was clearly based on economic and monetary considerations, not political considerations. The Bundesbank initially saw merit in a step-by-step approach, like most economic experts; this was based on the assumption of two German states remaining in separate existence. The rapid train of events made full economic and monetary union imperative, giving political considerations precedence over economic and monetary concerns. The Bundesbank's advice of a 2:1 conversion rate both for stock and flow variables (i.e., savings accounts, outstanding liabilities of companies, wages and salaries, etc.) was not followed "to the letter," but the Government's decision on this issue came out close enough to that of the Bundesbank, if translated into a weighted average, to invalidate the existence of major disagreement. Above all, the Bundesbank's advice on organizational matters relating to its own involvement in the transition to economic, monetary, and social union was fully accepted, and this has contributed substantially to the successful conclusion of the union of Germany.

On European economic and monetary union (EMU), there can be no question of the political nature of the decision if and when to enter into EMU, or into its various stages. This is not a matter for the Bundesbank to decide. But the Bundesbank has been closely involved at every stage of the debate and has made its views known to the Government and to the public. In a recent statement on the issues involved, it set out the conditions that in its view need to be met if further steps are to be taken, and it reaffirmed the basic requirements of a future European central bank system. Needless to say, the institutional requirements and safeguards, including the political independence of a future European central bank, will not by themselves guarantee success of the EMU. Other conditions have to be met for full success. I shall come back to these questions in a moment.

The reasons for the success of German monetary policy in defending price stability are in part historical. The experience gained twice with hyperinflation in the first half of this century has helped to develop a special sensitivity to inflation and has caused the wider public to believe in the critical importance of monetary stability in Germany. For this reason, the strong position of the Bundesbank is widely accepted by the general public—questioning its independence even seems to be a national taboo. This social consensus has yielded strong support for the policy of the Bundesbank. I have already mentioned that no government has ever used its right to "veto" a decision of the Central Bank Council. No government has ever seriously considered modifying the Bundesbank Act as a means to deal with cases of conflict, although it could have done so with a simple majority of the Parliament.

Historical experience in Germany testifies to the success of the concept of an independent central bank. Inflation rates have remained far below the average rates of most other industrial countries. Stable prices have contributed to a fairly stable social climate, which is felt to have favored growth of the German economy; this has strengthened its role in the world economy. The German currency, the deutsche mark, has become a major reserve currency in the world and the "anchor currency" in the European Monetary System, and it enjoys a high standing. The former British Chancellor of the Exchequer, John Major, said in his address to the Annual Meetings of the IMF and World Bank in October 1990 in Washington with reference to the ERM: "Increasingly it has functioned like a modern day gold standard with the deutsche mark as the anchor."[5]

In the light of the success of the Bundesbank, it is only natural that the German public will expect any successor, which could take its place at the European level, should be at least as well equipped as the Bundesbank to defend price stability. The Governor of the Bank of England, Robin Leigh-Pemberton, said only a week ago in Berlin that

> [t]he Bundesbank has acquired its reputation as an inflation fighter after a long period of skillful monetary management, and it is this that gives the Bundesbank its credibility and legitimacy. A new institution would begin with no such inherent credibility or legitimacy.[6]

Independence of a European Central Bank System

Progress in economic and political integration induced the Heads of State and Government of the EC member states to decide on the early establishment of a European economic and monetary union (EMU). An Intergovernmental Conference has been convened in Rome to discuss and work out the contractual basis for this union. How much time this conference will take to arrive at full agreement, which according to treaty rules calls for unanimity, is difficult to say. A monetary union rests on the irrevocable fixing of exchange rates between the currencies concerned, with the possible—or likely—introduction of a single currency. This implies, at the same time, the need to relinquish sovereignty over national domestic and external monetary policies, and to transfer the responsibility for such policies

[5]International Monetary Fund, *Summary Proceedings* (Washington, 1990), page 85.

[6]Robin Leigh-Pemberton, "Approaches to Monetary Integration in Europe," *Auszüge aus Presseartikeln*, No. 83, Deutsche Bundesbank, (Frankfurt, 1990), page 3.

to a Community institution that could be named the European Central Bank System (ECBS).

The construction of an ECBS is a step on virgin soil. European national authorities will, for the first time, have to give up their powers in an important field of public policy, namely monetary policy. A monetary union will be an irrevocably sworn fraternity, in which the participating economies will be linked inextricably. At the present state of the discussions, there is a wide measure of agreement on certain basic characteristics of a future European central bank system.

First of all, an ECBS must be committed to price stability as its primary objective. This must be its special area of responsibility and its "token of success." For this purpose, it is essential that its position within the constitutional order of the Community, its internal organizational structure, and its instruments enable it to pursue this objective. The ECBS will be expected to support the general economic policy of the Community, but only to the extent that this does not interfere with its prime objective of price stability.

Second, it is indispensable that the ECBS be independent in institutional, functional, and personal terms. Not only has the German experience shown that monetary stability can best be realized in a system that is independent of political interference, but the European environment may also add a further dimension to the issue. It cannot be excluded that in the EC there will be a tendency for compromises to be sought to deal with arising difficulties; this could be at the expense of price stability. It is therefore crucial for the ECBS that, in the performance of their duties, the members of its governing bodies are not subject to instructions from other national or Community authorities.

Third, the ECBS can only be successful, if it retains full control over the instruments that are necessary for conducting monetary policy. These include instruments not only for domestic monetary policy, but also for external monetary policy. Hence, the ECBS must also be given sole responsibility for exchange market intervention against currencies outside the system. Decisions on the exchange rate regime, including the fixing of parities or central rates and their change, will have to remain in the hands of the political authorities. In all other decisions affecting external monetary policy, especially in the event of exchange rate policy decisions, the ECBS should be involved in good time and on a basis of co-responsibility.

Fourth, and as a matter of course, the ECBS should not be allowed to extend credit to public authorities in the Community or in member states.

Fifth, too many tasks assigned to the European central bank could complicate the conduct of monetary policy. The ECBS should be free, therefore, from responsibilities other than those for monetary policy. In particular, banking supervision should not be assigned to the ECBS but left with national authorities, if only to prevent the ECBS from being forced into a "lender of last resort" function that would not be compatible with its task of safeguarding the currency. There are different views on this issue, but it seems clear to me from our own experience and that of some other countries that a successful monetary policy does not require that the central bank itself be given full control over the banking system and thus for banking supervision; indeed, this could even reduce the effectiveness of monetary policy. Experience also shows that central banks that are not charged with such additional responsibilities enjoy a higher degree of de facto independence.

Sixth, the national central banks must be integral parts of the European central bank. A uniform monetary policy cannot result from decisions of separate independent institutions. Monetary policy by its nature is indivisible. Coherence of monetary policy requires central decision making and uniform rules for the implementation of monetary policy decisions. National central banks will still have a role in the implementation of the decisions of the ECBS. But this will only be possible if they have previously been given the same degree of independence within their states as the ECBS enjoys at Community level, and if monetary policy instruments have been duly harmonized among the member countries. At present, the central banks of a number of member countries are in some respects only executors of instructions from their respective governments. Especially in some of our major partner countries, France, Italy, Britain, and Spain, monetary policy is still under government control. It will probably be necessary to give national central banks a sufficient amount of time to practice their new autonomy before the ECBS is implemented.

To guarantee the uniformity of monetary policy, on the one hand, and to take account of the federate structure of the Community, on the other, the ECBS should have a management structure comprising two governing bodies: a Council and an Executive Board. While the Council should be responsible for the setting of monetary policy targets and for certain other key policy decisions, the Executive Board should be empowered to control their implementation. For this purpose, the Executive Board will need some discretionary latitude to respond flexibly to developments in the markets.

The Council should be composed of the governors of the national central banks and the members of the Executive Board. A sufficiently long term of office without possibility of dismissal (except for serious cause) and an effectively independent status must be guaranteed to all members of the Council. It is of the highest importance that its members do not regard themselves as representatives of national interest. For that reason, it is necessary that all national central banks be made independent from their governments before the foundation of the ECBS.

The Executive Board members would be appointed by the European Council by virtue of their experience and ability. As the ECBS has to act in line with its goals and not in the pursuit of national interest, all members of the Council should have equal voting rights. Weighted voting would give undue emphasis to regional or national interests in decision making, which would be in conflict with the need for a single monetary policy geared to price stability in the Community as a whole.

The Committee of Governors of the EC central banks submitted a draft ECBS statute to the Intergovernmental Conference, which largely meets the criteria listed above. The final discussions in the Governors' Committee will take place in the coming weeks.

There can be no doubt that the creation of a successful European Monetary Union will promote economic integration. It will eliminate uncertainty regarding exchange rates between the member countries and hence reduce transaction costs for international business. For these and other reasons, some of them of a more emotional nature, the concept of European economic and monetary union with a European central bank system as its center has widespread appeal. But the economic good expected of EMU has to be weighed against the risks associated with the setting up of the EMU. These risks are likely to be seen differently from the standpoint of the various countries. As stated in a recent Commission study entitled "One Market, One Money,"[7] a major risk lies in the elimination of the exchange rate as an adjustment tool. If exchange rate changes are ruled out, authorities lose an important instrument to deal with regional imbalances within the Community. These imbalances still exist in Europe, and it is not clear that they will be eliminated in the near future. Lack of exchange rate flexibility will also deprive countries with greater price stability of a means to reduce the risk of imported inflation.

At present, economic, fiscal, and monetary policies and performance in the EC are still marked by great differences between some of the member states. It is true that some member states have made substantial progress toward greater convergence in the field of anti-inflation policy, owing in part to the European Monetary System. Throughout the whole EC, however, deep-seated divergences still

---

[7] *European Economy*, No. 44 (October 1990), pp. 3–347.

remain, and in some areas are actually widening again. These divergences are reflected, in particular, in inflationary cost and price trends, excessive budget deficits in some countries, and large external imbalances. These "convergence deficits" are especially pronounced in Greece and Portugal—neither are yet participating in the ERM; in the United Kingdom, which has joined the mechanism just recently, and, in Italy and Spain, they are unmistakable. They are in some cases not only transitory but are rooted in considerable differences in institutional structures, economic fundamentals, and the attitudes of management and labor.

It is not clear that convergence has already proceeded far enough to allow the EMS to dispense with exchange rate correction as a means to facilitate external adjustment inside the Community. In any case, it may be wise to retain the possibility of exchange rate adjustment as an "ultima ratio" for as long as there may be a need for it. The fact that realignments in the ERM have been rare in recent years should not mislead us into believing that there will be no need for exchange rate adjustment in the future.

In monetary union, unsustainable fiscal policies or excessive wage demands would have serious consequences for the respective regions and for the Community as a whole. That is why in an economic and monetary union binding rules for limiting fiscal deficits and their financing are likely to be necessary; market discipline is not likely to be sufficient. A framework providing for advance consultations, surveillance of budget outcomes, and possibly also sanctions would seem to be the minimum required before the ECBS can start to take up responsibility for monetary policy. From the viewpoint of a stability minded public in Germany an early irrevocable fixing of exchange rates and the transfer of monetary policy powers to a Community institution would involve considerable risks to monetary stability, given these prospects and the actual economic and economic policy situation in the Community. Further progress toward stability in various partner countries is clearly needed before one should think of implementing monetary union.

One other point deserves attention. Even if it were possible to agree on a system that fulfills the necessary legal conditions for an independent stability-oriented monetary policy, the factual success of that system would also depend on other circumstances. The Governor of the Bank of England, Robin Leigh-Pemberton, alluded to this recently when he said:

> However independent a central bank is in principle, it cannot be impervious to the pressures of public opinion or indifferent to public support.

> It must rely for its legitimacy on the public's aversion to inflation and to the public's trust that potentially unpopular short-term measures of restraint will be justified by longer-term benefits.[8]

To sum up, the essential steps to be undertaken before the establishment of the ECBS seem to be the following. First, the single-market program should have been implemented in full. After all, economic union comprising a common economic area without internal borders is the basis for monetary union. At present, there are still some major deficiencies in decision making and implementation. Unless they are overcome, the elimination of border controls, which is envisaged for 1992, will jeopardized. This applies particularly to the harmonization of indirect taxes, which is regarded as an essential precondition for lifting border controls. Without the full implementation of the single market, a monetary union lacks the necessary counterpart in the real sphere.

Second, adequate economic convergence must be achieved. This means that price differences have been virtually stamped out and that inflation has been largely eliminated. Furthermore, budget deficits in the participating countries will have to be reduced to a manageable level in terms of anti-inflation policy. And the durability of this convergence must be reflected in the markets' verdict, that is, in virtual harmonization of capital market interest rates. To satisfy these conditions, all countries willing to join the ECBS should previously have been full members of the EMS for a sufficiently long period. Experience in the 1980s has shown that full membership in the EMS has contributed significantly to price stability in the participating countries.

Third, significant convergence in the statutes of the central banks of the Community toward independence is indispensable. Otherwise, these central banks cannot be expected to be integral parts of the ECBS. As I argued before, such harmonization also includes an adequate harmonization of monetary policy instruments.

Finally, there have to be guarantees that the stability-oriented policy of the union cannot be counteracted by unsustainable budget policies. For that reason, contractual arrangements for ensuring budgetary discipline must be adopted at Community level. I hope that the Intergovernmental Conference will arrive at full agreement on these points without delay. The heads of state and government agreed at the end of October 1990 to an ambitious timetable. Whether it can be adhered to

---

[8]Robin Leigh-Pemberton, "Approaches to Monetary Integration in Europe," in *Auszüge aus Presseartikeln*, No. 83, Deutsche Bundesbank (Frankfurt, 1990), page 3.

or not will depend decisively on the ability to find a consensus among the participating governments and on the determination of member states tc adapt their policies quickly to the requirements of EMU. The coming years will demonstrate whether they are able and willing to do so.

Part III

Role of the Central Bank in Financial Crises

13

Role of the Central Bank in Banking Crisis: An Overview

ANDREW SHENG*

In recent years, bank failure has become a growth industry. Banking crisis around the world has become so pervasive that many central bankers are likely to have some personal experience of one financial crisis or other in the last five years. As banks around the world begin to feel the onset of recession, with rising loan losses arising from property and share price falls in Japan, the United States, and the United Kingdom, and as banks in highly indebted countries still suffer the effects of major structural adjustment programs, an unprecedented global shake-up in the financial sector is likely to occur in the early 1990s. If so, central bankers must be prepared to deal with banking crises as they arise, or better still prevent crises from happening. This paper looks specifically at the role of the central bank in domestic banking crises.[1]

The decade of the 1980s has taught central bankers around the world quite a lot about banking crises, although controversy still exists about the exact causes and cures. The landmark bank failures of the 1970s, Herstatt and Franklin National, appear today small-fry compared with the losses of the savings and loan debacle in the United States, and the banking crises in Spain, Latin America, Africa, and Asia in the 1980s. A number of these cases have become fairly well

---

*The author is a Senior Financial Specialist, Financial Policy and Systems Division, World Bank, on leave from his position as Advisor, Bank Regulation, Bank Negara Malaysia. All views and opinions expressed in this paper are entirely those of the author and do not represent those of the World Bank or Bank Negara Malaysia.

[1]The subject of dealing with international financial crises is outside the scope of this paper, although many international crises have national origins. For a survey of the issues involved in international banking crisis, see Krugman (1989).

documented in the International Monetary Fund and the World Bank. This paper attempts to synthesize broadly the practical lessons drawn from these cases, based upon a research project in the Bank on bank restructuring in developing countries. It begins with the definitions of banking crises, then looks at the contractual nature of banking and the macroeconomic and microeconomic origins of crises. Various country cases are then grouped into various types of crises and the methodology of crisis resolution is then examined. Finally, a case study is presented on the management of banking crisis from the vantage point of the central bank, based upon the experience of the Malaysian banking crisis of 1985–87.

Definitions

In this paper, the terms banking crisis and financial crisis are interchangeable. Most definitions of a financial crisis would be close to that offered by Goldsmith (1982):

> a sharp, brief, ultra-cyclical deterioration of all or most of a group of financial indicators—short-term interest rates, asset prices (stock, real estate, land prices), commercial insolvencies and failures of financial institutions.

In the narrow sense, the actual crisis (such as a large bank failure that sparks off a large run that spreads to a number of banks) is a decisive event that marks the turning point in the business cycle. However, real and financial conditions deteriorate—managements behave speculatively, structures become fragile, supervision becomes lax, depositors become nervous—over a fairly long time horizon. Moreover, the resolution of a banking crisis, particularly where the root causes are structural, takes not less than three to five years. The U.S. thrift crisis took about a decade to unfold: from the first technical insolvencies caused by high interest rates in the beginning of the 1980s to government action in 1989 to restructure the regulatory, supervisory, and liquidation agencies to handle the large number of thrift failures.

Banking crises typically occur when financial distress prevails. Distress is defined as the condition when the banking system as a whole has negative capital and current profits are insufficient to cover losses to such an extent that the banking system is unable to generate internally positive capital (Hinds (1988)). There are, however, different degrees of severity of crises. Mr. Corrigan (1989/90), of the Federal Reserve Bank of New York, has recently differentiated between "financial disruptions" and "financial crises," the latter being episodes that cause clear and significant damage to the real economy. Under this definition, major bank failures or market crashes in the postwar period would certainly count only as "disruptions." For example, stock and land prices fell sharply in Taiwan Province of China and Japan in 1990, but these factors do not appear to have caused significant changes in real economic growth, changes in the balance of payments, or foreign exchange reserves—factors common in a number of financial crises. In strong economies, some banks may be hurt and peripheral financial institutions may fail, but real economic activity need not be severely affected.

This definition of financial disruption is similar to what Anna Schwartz (1985) calls pseudofinancial crises, that is, declines in asset prices of equity stock, real estate, commodities; depreciation of the exchange rate; financial distress of large firms, financial industry or sovereign debtors. In her view, real financial crises occur when the stability of the banking system is threatened.

Nature and Origins of Banking Crises

There are a number of schools of thought on the causes of banking crises. Schwartz and others in the monetarist school consider that financial crises are not triggered by financial distress but by the failure of authorities to respond correctly to financial distress and that they are aggravated by the private sector's uncertainty about the correct policy responses. On the other hand, the Minsky and Kindleberger school has evolved a theory of financial fragility, which is defined broadly as a long period of economic growth that leads to euphoric behavior by economic entities. The financial fragility of players (governments, enterprises, banks, and households) increases over the growth cycle as capital cushions deteriorate, leverage increases, and the economy becomes more vulnerable to economic shocks. Political events, external shocks, local or sectoral problems all create doubts over the sustainability of such euphoria, and the speculative bubble bursts when asset prices fall. The forced debt liquidation accentuates declining asset values, tightening liquidity, and precipitating insolvencies of debtors, thus triggering bank failures.[2]

Controversy also exists over whether banking crises have macroeconomic or microeconomic origins. The macroeconomic school blames structural imbalances, inappropriate economic policies and external shocks, or a combination of such factors. Typical factors

[2]Excellent surveys of the literature on financial crises are found in Bordo (1985) and Sundararajan (1988).

include large fiscal and balance of payments deficits, overvalued exchange rates, negative real interest rates, high external debt, inflation, and fundamentally inefficient domestic industries. These factors, plus flaws in the financial structure, make the economy (and hence the banking system) highly vulnerable to external shocks, sudden relative price changes, or major policy shifts.

Changes in the macroeconomic environment are not the only factors accounting for ailing banks. Many financial systems have not been designed to withstand shocks. The monetary sector of the financial system is usually highly regulated and protected by the central bank, but other components, such as rural savings institutions, deposit-taking cooperatives, stock markets, and informal curb markets are usually self-regulated or very loosely regulated. These secondary or fringe financial institutions do not have lender of last resort facilities, nor effective supervision to ensure that public savings with them are adequately protected from fraud and management abuses. Failure in these unregulated subsectors often spill over to the monetary sector. In addition, the duplication of supervision or gaps in supervision (particularly where there are lacunae in the law) do not allow the authorities to act flexibly and quickly in response to problems in any particular sector.

Macroeconomic and structural issues aside, experienced bank supervisors invariably have no hesitation in pinpointing microeconomic roots in bank failures—bad bank management, supervisory inadequacies, poor accounting standards, and weak legal framework (U.S. Treasury (1988) and Sinkey (1979)). Aristobulo de Juan's dictum (1987) on how good bankers become bad bankers through the stages of technical mismanagement, cosmetic mismanagement, desperate management, and, finally, fraudulent management is now well-known. Temptations to steal in banking are so large that elements of fraud or conflict of interests are found in almost all cases of bank failure. In Malaysia, there is a saying that "you don't let monkeys look after bananas." Strong and effective bank supervision can play a major role to detect bank problems, but as can be seen later, cannot wholly prevent bank failure.

In practice, there is often a macro-micro negative feedback mechanism. Macroeconomic maladjustments, such as an overvalued exchange rate, large fiscal deficits, heavily protected industries, corruption, and excessive domestic speculation lead ultimately to losses incurred by borrowers. These losses show up as nonperforming loans in the banking system. Banks initially may be able to absorb such losses, so long as nonperforming loans remain a small proportion of their total loan portfolio. The costs of loan-loss provisions are usually absorbed through higher spreads, such costs being borne by depositors and performing borrowers. If loan-losses persist, however, and erode the banks' solvency, the management may seek to hide their losses through cosmetic accounting, or through "evergreening" loans to keep large borrowers alive, bidding up deposit rates to maintain their liquidity. Perverse incentives occur. Distressed borrowers have no hesitation in paying excessive real interest rates to have access to new credit in order to maintain the illusion of solvency. On the other hand, distressed asset sales drive down asset prices and erode further the collateral base of the banks. Faced with uncertainty and large losses, banks contract credit and raise real interest rates, thus dampening investment and growth.

At this point, doubts over the soundness of a particular financial institution, whether true or unfounded, could lead to a bank run, inducing flight to quality, or in more serious cases of contagion, a flight to currency. If the contagion is not stopped quickly, nervousness about the soundness of the banking system would create capital flight. As experience shows, central bank lending to banks during capital flight only adds fuel to the fire and is self-defeating, as it entails immediate loss in foreign exchange reserves. The resultant depreciation of the exchange rate could cause more panic. Raising interest rates to stem capital flight would contract economic activity further, sending the economy into a deflationary spiral. Consequently, few central banks dare to treat potential problems of banks lightly. Because of the constant threat of contagion, it is impossible to tell ex ante whether a bank problem is a financial disruption, or what ex post turns out to be a full blown financial crisis. It is the fear of systemic risks (discussed later) that drives central bank intervention in problem banking situations.

The role of the central bank at this stage is crucial. The central bank is required fundamentally to maintain financial stability. This involves not only maintaining the internal and external value of the currency, but also the stability of the banking system. But, what does "maintenance of the stability of the banking system" mean in practical terms? Providing liquidity to a solvent banking system to ease sporadic shortage of funds and maintaining integrity of the payments mechanism is generally accepted doctrine. The provision of central bank funds to an insolvent financial system to maintain stability, however, has quasi-fiscal implications and is much more controversial and less well understood.

Is a central bank obliged as guardian of the system to provide not only liquidity but also to safeguard system solvency? Indeed, under conditions of crisis and uncertainty, it is extremely difficult to distinguish between a liquidity need and a solvency need. My personal experience is that when bankers come to the central bank for liquidity help (after they are not able to obtain help from other institutions), it is no longer liquidity assistance, but a question of solvency. This dilemma was considered by Bagehot (1978), whose view of the proper role of the lender of last resort was succinctly restated by Summers (1989) as central banks should adopt, announce, and follow a policy of lending freely and aggressively but at a penalty rate to all sound but no unsound borrowers in time of crisis.

There are three good reasons behind this advice. First, provision of liquidity to good borrowers would assure the smooth and stable functioning of the payments system, thus heading off problems of confidence in the ability of even good borrowers to meet their commitments. Second, by lending only at penalty rates against good security, the central bank deters moral hazard behavior of distressed borrowers and protects its own solvency at the same time. Third, in a crisis, the central bank may be the only available buyer of good securities. Its presence in the market could check the free fall of the price of bonds or quality commercial paper, the forced debt liquidation of which may make even normally sound borrowers insolvent.

Central bank intervention in banking crisis has wide monetary and fiscal implications. Central bank lending to problem banks is expansionary on money supply. Central bank's losses through measures to subsidize ailing banks, assumption of foreign exchange losses of banks or enterprises, or takeover of bad assets of insolvent banks are all quasi-fiscal deficits in nature. If these losses are monetized, the result could be higher inflation. In an open economy, there is always the danger that if the public perceives that the central bank is itself "insolvent" by absorbing too much loss, then capital flight would ensue. At the worst stage, a central bank with net foreign exchange liabilities would be caught in a downward spiral in which it tries to buy foreign exchange to service its debt only at higher and higher rates, thus losing monetary control and depreciating at the same time. The devaluation worsens the foreign exchange losses of the central bank, and the central bank itself becomes the source of monetary inflation.

There are tempting reasons for governments to use central banks not only as the lender of last resort but also as equity provider of last resort to help rescue banks. Central banks are, after all, institutionally created to act quickly to deal with financial crises. It may not be possible for the government to appropriate funds from the budget quickly enough to help stem a crisis. In times of crises, when there is a shortage of risk capital in both the private and public sectors, there may be no alternative to the central bank putting its funds at risk;

however, the central bank can do this if, and only if, the losses on the assets it acquires are less than its income from other assets, otherwise the central bank's own solvency is affected. As the case studies described later will show, experience suggests that it would be perilous for governments to tinker with a central bank's solvency, since that damages the public's confidence in the stability of the domestic currency. The capacity of a central bank to absorb losses of the banking system is a theme to which I shall return.

The Contractual Nature of Banking

The periodic instability of financial systems has its roots in the contractual nature of banking. As financial intermediaries, banks essentially straddle two sets of contracts in the economy, a bundle of deposit contracts with savers and various loan contracts with borrowers. Bank failure is fundamentally the breakdown of contractual obligations between banks and their borrowers to the point that banks have to break their contracts with depositors. All markets, other than barter markets, are markets in contracts. Economic entities (principals and agents) trade products, or rather contractual obligations, under a written or unwritten set of regulations that protect and enforce the property rights of the market participants. All markets operate under conditions of uncertainty and risk. Implicitly, the Basle Committee on Banking Supervision (1990) in its recent work on credit concentrations has conceptually acknowledged the contractual nature of banking by categorizing banking risks into two broad categories: counterparty risks (credit risks, sectoral concentration exposures) and market risks (foreign exchange, interest rate, equity, and asset price fluctuation risks).

All financial products are by definition different forms of contracts that allocate risks and obligations between the various parties involved. Holders of obligations can only eliminate counterparty risks (such as credit risk) by final settlement in cash. In the meantime, both parties are subject to market risks, such as changes in interest rates, exchange rates, prices, or general market conditions that may affect the liquidity or solvency of the counterparty to deliver on the due date. What is not normally understood is that while contracts protect rights and obligations when both parties are solvent, the minute one party becomes insolvent, the holders of the insolvent party's obligations immediately assume losses. In other words, rational self-preservation behavior calls for an insolvent institution to borrow as much as possible, since contractually it passes losses to all holders of its obligations. Eventually, it reaches the stage of "too big to fail" and the creditors are obliged to bail out that institution in their own self-interest. Hence, the fundamental truth of the anecdote that if you owe the bank $1,000, you are in trouble; if you owe the bank $100 million, the bank is in trouble.

In a world of volatile prices, no transparency in accounting disclosure, and general uncertainty, holders of contracts are never sure when the counterparty becomes insolvent or engages in cheating behavior, such as reneging on the contract. Market participants deal with each other on the basis of past experience or reputation. Confidence is generated through repeated successful conclusion of contracts. When a contract fails, confidence is eroded. Thus, banks are able to generate public confidence through their ability to meet deposit withdrawals on demand. Banks are therefore also subject to reputational risks. Contagion occurs when the public perceives, rightly or wrongly, that banks (or their subsidiaries or affiliates) may not be able to meet their obligations. Reputational risks occur when creditors (including depositors) associate problems of one economic entity with another related entity. The withdrawal of credit from one entity to entities of the same group typically creates a liquidity crisis for the group as a whole. Hence, bank supervisors tend to supervise financial institutions on a group or consolidated basis. Experience suggests that reputational risks can quickly destroy large groups of companies, particularly where these have been weakened by connected lending and excessive reliance on funding from associated financial institutions.

Systemic risks are in a sense an extension of reputational risks from individual institutions or groups to the financial system as a whole. A closer examination of systemic risks suggests that such risks occur mainly at the payment system level. Failure of one participant in the payment system triggers a chain reaction in nonpayment by other participants, particularly when the affected parties are unable to raise liquidity themselves in time to fulfil their own contractual obligations. The inability of (reputationally) first-rate institutions to meet their obligations creates uncertainty and can lead to panic self-protective measures by depositors, such as a run. Consequently, the central bank as lender of last resort has to step in quickly before problems spread throughout the system.

One can extend this argument to the economy as a whole. All financial contracts are measured and based on the currency contract, money being the measure and store of value, as well as the means of final settlement. When the central bank, as the issuer of domestic currency, is unable to maintain the stability of the value of the currency internally and externally, depositor and borrower behavior changes, and the crisis is worsened by inflation and currency flight. The reputation of the central bank is destroyed, as its credibility to defend the currency or the stability of the financial system itself is questioned. At that point, perhaps the worst type of financial crisis, the central bank may itself be a party to the crisis of confidence.

In sum, financial crises arise when real losses in the economy occur. These real losses ultimately are reflected in the banking system, through the breakdown of borrower and depositor contracts. A crisis occurs when the existing financial system (the institutions as well as the legal and regulatory framework) is unable to withstand external shocks to the system through sudden relative price changes or through internal corrosion, such as fraud and mismanagement (or a combination of both). A liquidity crisis when solvency is not at stake is a financial disruption. A solvency crisis, in which large parts of the financial system are insolvent, is a genuine financial crisis. The central bank may be able to address short-run crises of confidence through the temporary provision of liquidity, but ultimately it must also address the questions of insolvency of financial institutions and loss allocation. If depositors are to be protected from losses, then the losses are borne ultimately by other sectors of the economy, through inflation, taxation, or levies on the banking system. All these are in the realm of political economy, as the following case studies show.

Types of Financial Crises

Before proceeding to a survey of the different types of banking crises encountered in recent years, it may be useful to make a general observation about banking developments in the 1980s. The catch-phrases globalization, securitization, innovation, and deregulation that arose from the "big bang" are an appropriate starting point.[3] The world is becoming one big financial market through liberalization of exchange controls, freeing of exchange rates, and improvements in telecommunications and bank processing technology. In their search for profits and through competition, banks have introduced a number of innovations, particularly new financial products (contracts), such as swaps, options, securitized paper, and off-balance sheet obligations, for which the risks and regulatory framework are by no means clear. National governments have helped the process of innovation and

[3]The "big bang" is the term usually applied to the liberalization of the U.K. securities markets in 1986 and is generally extended to the financial liberalization efforts of the 1980s.

competition through deregulation, although the process of deregulation varies considerably from country to country.

On the other hand, periodic financial disruptions, such as the problems of Continental Illinois or Johnson Matthey, have evolved an illusion of a banking safety net that the central banks will always step in to protect banks that are too big to fail, or whose failure would disrupt the payments or market-clearing mechanisms. This was justified on the basis that the direct costs of rescuing a bank would be lower than the social costs of disruptions to the payments system and the confidence in the banking system as a whole. Implicitly through central bank action or explicitly through deposit insurance schemes, governments around the world have de facto if not de jure guaranteed the nominal value of the liability side of the banking system's balance sheet, while having relatively little control over the asset side.

Indeed, through innovation, deregulation, and greater volatility of prices, interest rates, and exchange rates, the asset side of banking systems around the world has become much more vulnerable to shocks, at a time when competition and the search for profits have tended to erode the banking system's capital base. The Basle Committee's work has helped considerably to stem this erosion, but in a world where share prices can rise and fall 15 percent in one day, and when banks are heavily exposed to property and highly indebted countries well in excess of their capital base, it is not surprising that the public is concerned over the safety and soundness of the banking system. The size of these asset losses are not always transparent to the public, due to the poor state of accounting standards in many countries, inadequate bank supervision, and general unwillingness in a number of countries to deal with such complex problems. These issues become more evident from the following brief survey of country experiences.[4]

Recent experience of financial crises can be grouped broadly into four country groups: the developed economies with advanced financial systems and reasonably strong supervision; the small, open-market-oriented developing economies that suffered shocks and bank fraud or mismanagement; the centrally planned economies with de facto nationalized banking systems; and finally, the hyperinflation economies that are still undergoing various stages of financial crises and structural adjustment.

The classification of these case studies remains fundamentally qualitative and judgmental, as the quantitative research and analysis is still

---

[4]This brief survey cannot do full justice to the complex origins and factors involved in each case. For detailed discussions of cases mentioned, please refer to references cited.

going on.[5] The basis for classification is intuitively simple: solvent authorities (including central banks under this category), defined as those with large reserves, low debt, or the capacity to borrow or tax without affecting significantly monetary and price stability, have generally been able to solve banking crises with relative ease. At the other extreme, governments with large fiscal deficits and heavy external debt may themselves be the fundamental cause of financial crises, and inappropriate measures to deal with crises without maintaining fiscal and monetary discipline only worsen the situation.

Developed Country Experience

Financial disruptions in the advanced economies have so far proved to be relatively easy to solve, because of their sophisticated financial structure—sound contracts, good legal systems, established laws and enforcement agencies, availability of bank management skills, relatively high standards of bank ethics, and reasonably adequate bank supervision that could respond fairly quickly to detect and solve problems. Problems in these economies came mainly from either macroeconomic policy mistakes or flaws in the banking structure that were not corrected in time.

For example, the problems of the U.S. thrifts originated in their flawed funding structure. Their portfolio of long-term fixed interest housing loans were funded from short-term deposits, and many thrifts became technically insolvent when tight monetary policy in 1980–81 raised domestic interest rates. Instead of addressing the capital shortfall directly, the authorities made a number of policy errors: they allowed the thrifts to try to outgrow their problems by liberalizing their asset portfolio (without corresponding improvement in supervision), and they allowed the thrifts to finance the asset expansion through a raised limit ($100,000) on the deposit insurance scheme. Over the last decade, inadequate supervision, plus the moral hazard raised by the high deposit insurance scheme, allowed thrift management to incur large losses in junk bonds, real estate, and other areas where they had traditionally no expertise (Silverberg (1989)). The U.S. savings and loans saga, plus the present problems in the banking industry, came partly from the structural flaws of highly segmented banking markets, regulatory constraints on nation-wide branch banking, and difficulties of coordinating supervision. The saga is still unfolding.

---

[5]An excellent analysis of seven cases—Argentina, Chile, Uruguay, Thailand, the Philippines, Spain and Malaysia—was presented in Sundararajan (1988). For short summaries of individual cases, see Sheng (1990).

The English secondary banking crisis of 1973–75 was mainly the result of overborrowing on the part of real estate and securities firms that suffered from the collapse of property and share prices following tight monetary policy in the wake of the 1973 oil crisis. While the large clearing banks were not affected, the smaller secondary banks, which were highly exposed to real estate and securities sectors, became both illiquid and insolvent, creating a situation of instability at a time when the economy was adjusting from a balance of payments crisis. The decisive action by the Bank of England to organize a "lifeboat fund" amounting to £1.2 billion (equivalent to 40 percent of the capital base of the English and Scottish clearing banks) jointly with the strong clearing banks, contained the problem. Twenty-six deposit-taking institutions received help from the fund, and eight were eventually liquidated (Bank of England (1978)).

The Spanish banking crisis of 1978–83 was partly the result of structural adjustment in the economy following the oil crisis of 1973 and 1979 and too many new banks as a consequence of financial liberalization. Fifty-one banks out of 110 were affected, involving nearly 20 percent of total deposits. Nearly 90 percent of the problem banks were relatively new institutions (Larrain and Montes-Negret (1986)) and bank mismanagement and fraud was much to blame (de Juan (1985)). Again, decisive action by the Bank of Spain to establish the Spanish Guarantee Fund (jointly with the banks) helped to stem the crisis. The Spanish Guarantee Fund was a model for bank restructuring in a number of other countries.

An interesting case of bank crisis in a largely self-regulated and free market banking environment was the failure of a number of smaller banks in Hong Kong in 1985–86, caused mainly by fraud and mismanagement and lack of effective supervision. The failures were exposed in the wake of the decline in share and property prices following uncertainty over the political future of Hong Kong during negotiations between China and the United Kingdom in 1983–84. In the absence of a central bank, the Hong Kong Government used reserves from the Exchange Fund to finance the liquidity as well as share acquisition support for the affected banks. The Hong Kong case suggests that even in a much vaunted free market environment, financial markets are not very efficient in self-regulation and some effective government supervision is necessary to check fraud and mismanagement.

Developing Country Experience

The second group of small-to-middle-income developing countries that experienced financial crises or distress of relative degrees that are so far documented include Thailand, Malaysia, the Philippines, Colombia, Ghana, and Guinea. These economies with mixed (large public sector banks, operating with private, as well as foreign banks) banking systems suffered a variety of problems, ranging from the effects of structural adjustments in the economy; commingled with extensive fraud and mismanagement, brought about partly because of inadequate supervision, inadequate legal powers to deal with bank problems, and, in some cases, political interference.

The "purest" case of bank failure that could be attributed almost exclusively to fraud and mismanagement without any apparent macroeconomic origins is the case of Guinea-Conakry (Tenconi (1989)). The authorities closed down six state-owned banks, which accounted for 95 percent of the assets of the banking system, after it was found that fictitious assets and accounts accounted for 76 percent of total assets. The Government bore the brunt of its losses from the budget.

For the middle-income countries of Thailand, the Philippines, Malaysia, and Colombia, banking problems demonstrated partly the vulnerability of small economies dependent on a narrow range of export commodities. Overexuberant lending at the height of a commodity boom, followed by strong measures to tackle macroeconomic imbalances in the wake of a sharp decline in commodity prices, had the usual effects of deflation that affected overborrowed enterprises. In Colombia, problems also came from overseas branches of domestic banks, which were used to bypass domestic credit restrictions (Montes-Negret (1990)). In the Philippines, political interference in the government-owned banks' credit process was a major cause of losses for the two largest banks (Lamberte (1989)). In all these countries, losses were evident in banks that had loan concentrations to large groups, or specific economic sectors, such as real estate. For Thailand and Malaysia, strong corrective measures on the macroeconomic front and tighter bank supervision helped to overcome the distress, and the banking systems recovered rapidly, as these economies enjoyed high growth rates in the last three years. In both cases, the central banks played critical roles in dealing with the crisis, with liquidity or financial support coming mainly from the central banks.

The Malaysian case had remarkable similarities with the Norwegian banking crisis (Solheim (1990)) and the U.S. Texas banking problems, all three economies being oil producers with a high degree of commodity concentration. The Malaysian economy suffered a classic case of Dutch disease in the second half of the 1970s, as high oil income on top of rising commodity prices generated an economic boom, and led to an overvaluation of the currency. This caused a large shift towards nontradables, particularly speculation in real estate. Large fiscal and external account imbalances emerged by 1981–82, with a fiscal deficit as high as 18 percent of gross domestic product (GDP) and a current account deficit of 14 percent of GDP in 1982. With a collapse of oil prices coming on top of the slide in commodity prices in the early 1980s, the authorities cut back on fiscal expenditure, and the resulting deflation brought about massive collapse of share and property prices. The central bank had to step in to resolve 35 deposit-taking cooperatives that failed, 4 badly affected banks, and a number of small finance companies.

Generally, the lessons from this group of case studies appear to be that those countries that successfully tackled their macroeconomic imbalances managed to resolve their banking crises, but not before major restructuring of their financial systems by changing laws, tightening supervision, and improving bank management.

State-Owned Financial Systems

Centrally planned economies with almost wholly nationalized or state-owned banking systems are perhaps the most interesting group of case studies. Theoretically, there should be no runs against state-owned banks, since the banking system carries a blanket state guarantee; however, crises in the financial systems of centrally planned economies emerge as currency flights and monetary overhangs that threaten to explode into hyperinflations. State-owned banking systems have a large capacity to hide losses, because of price distortions in the economy, directed and subsidized credit to loss-making and inefficient enterprises or borrowers, or weak and inefficient bank management. Soviet-style accounting used widely by enterprises and banks in those economies, from China to Eastern Europe, is designed to report compliance with central plan targets and not the viability and solvency of borrowers or banks. In other words, the real losses or inefficiency of borrowers are hidden largely in the books of the banking system, and since the system is a monopoly on public savings (with a state guarantee), such losses can be carried for a long time without erupting into periodic financial crises.

On the other hand, state-owned banks operating in environments with limited private sector enterprises also tend to suffer from fraud and corruption as lowly paid bureaucrats and bank managers can easily succumb to bribes to give loans to enterprises, since all loan losses are borne by the state. Central banks in these environments have great difficulty in supervising state-owned banks because their management are either bureaucrats of the same or equivalent rank or, in many cases, are politically appointed and not accountable to the central bank.

Banking crises in centrally planned economies have a special feature in that all losses of the banking system are effectively quasi-fiscal deficits.[6] The typical monobank or recently divested two-tier state-owned banking system carries on its liability side a large deposit liability, partly denominated in foreign currency and the external debt, against which there is very little hard currency reserves. On the asset side, the banking system carries large loans to state-owned enterprises or public sector investments, many of which would not be viable under international prices. Where the currency has undergone devaluation in recent years, it is often not surprising to see large revaluation losses on the asset side of the balance sheet. Where the external debt is vested in the books of the central bank, the central bank suffers large revaluation losses when the domestic currency is devalued. Usually, the cost of financing these losses and servicing the external debt is so large that the central bank loses monetary control. In the Yugoslav case, 80 percent of the National Bank's revenues at one stage was used to finance interest payments on foreign debt (Gaspari (1989)). The capital losses were as large as 11.8 percent of social product in 1986. When the central bank is called upon to refinance loss-making enterprises on top of monetization of its own revaluation losses, stabilization of the economy through monetary policy is almost impossible.

Given the shortage of convertible currency, some banking systems in these economies allowed banks to accept foreign currency deposits from residents, and the proceeds were surrendered to the central bank in exchange for domestic currency. This placed a large internal debt, denominated in foreign currency, on the central bank. The large net foreign currency liability to residents was a source of monetary instability in Yugoslavia and a number of other Eastern European countries, as residents could quickly shift in and out of domestic currency as a hedge against inflation or impending devaluation. This structural flaw, found in a number of centrally planned economies and other economies, threatens to break out periodically as capital flight whenever political crises occur, thus exacerbating the fragility of the economic system.

High-Inflation Economies

The last group of case studies comprises the economies that suffered extremely severe financial distress, and some are still going

[6]By definition, when there is an implicit or explicit government guarantee on bank deposits of a banking system, and the government would not allow any bank to fail, all losses of the banking system (after deducting capital and reserves) are quasi-fiscal deficits.

through various stages of crises. The most severe case recorded is that of Argentina, which had two bouts of hyperinflation in as many years and appears in the last decade or so to be in a prolonged state of financial crisis. The overhang of excessive external debt and large fiscal deficits were primary causes of financial instability. With external funding shut off as a result of the international debt crisis, attempts to correct the balance of payments deficit through devaluation caused large foreign exchange losses in enterprises, which were transferred to the central bank under an exchange rate guarantee scheme. Large fiscal deficits, caused partly by loans to loss-making state enterprises, were funded through central bank rediscounts, which were in turn financed through high reserve requirements and forced investments on the banking system. Central bank monetization of the large fiscal and quasi-fiscal deficits was a major cause of the hyperinflation. The system was subject to disintermediation from the banking system and periodic bouts of capital flight, held back only by excessively high real interest rates. Bouts of crises were arrested by drastic austerity measures and attempts to curb the fiscal deficit, which were eroded over time by public pressure to increase nominal wages and subsidies to loss-making public enterprises.

These types of crises demonstrate the complexity and extremity of distress when central bank financing of large fiscal (and quasi-fiscal) deficits are at the root of the crisis. The inequities caused by the breakage of the currency contract create complex political problems, which make the financial crises more difficult to solve. Rich savers have the knowledge and skill to benefit from speculative behavior during high inflation and to avoid direct taxation or even the inflation tax through capital flight. The small saver is forced to hold currency for basic transactionary purposes and therefore bears the brunt of the inflation tax.

Probably the most successful case of a turnaround in the banking crises in a high inflation economy was the Chilean banking crisis of 1981–83. Problem banks that were liquidated or intervened by the Government represented 60 percent of the banking system's portfolio (Larrain and Montes-Negret (1986)). The immediate causes of bank failure were the macroeconomic adjustments to control inflation and correction of balance of payments and fiscal deficits, which sent the economy into a recession and caused extensive borrower defaults. This came, however, on top of a weakened banking structure after the extensive denationalization of the banks in the early 1970s, when the abolishment of legislation against concentration of ownership meant that banking became controlled by large private groups with interlocking interests in industry, commerce, and banking. The Chileans used two major techniques: an across-the-board debt rescheduling for borrowers and coverage against foreign exchange losses and a "carve-out" of bad loans from the banks by the central bank in exchange for central bank promissory notes, to be repurchased over time. Once the macroeconomic situation was stabilized and inflation brought under control, the banking system gradually returned to profitability.

Crisis Resolution

The exact techniques of crisis resolution are dealt with in Chapter 14, by Brian Quinn. This section will deal with the four key stages of resolution of banking crisis, namely, diagnostics, damage control, loss allocation, and rebuilding profitability.

The diagnostic stage in crisis resolution is critical to the identification of the problems and central bank understanding of the depth and scope of the crisis. De Juan calls this "getting out of the dark." A timely, accurate, and reliable central bank off-site surveillance reporting system, plus other information sources, such as market talk, consumer feedback, research studies, industry surveys, and bank consultations all help to piece together a reliable composite picture of market performance. Having good bank-accounting standards, particularly loan classification and income accrual standards, are critical to an appreciation of the extent of nonperforming loans and to assess whether an ailing institution is only illiquid or in reality insolvent. The reporting system should be able to detect potential problem areas, such as loan concentrations, connected lending, high exposures to market risks, noncompliance with prudential regulations, and any unusual behavior. The off-site surveillance system should be complemented by a team of on-site bank inspectors or external auditors, which can move quickly to assess first-hand the extent of the damage, when a financial institution begins to display signs of failing. Moreover, an alert supervisor would be able to detect structural flaws in the system, which call for major legal and institutional reforms.

Two lessons from experience deserve mentioning in the diagnostic stage: the-sooner-the-better and the-problems-are-always-worse-than-expected. The first dictum requires prompt action—hesitation and procrastination in dealing with a crisis situation have inevitably proved costly. This advice is closely related to the second dictum: bankers have a tendency to sit on a problem until it becomes too big to handle. De Juan relates how the Spanish experience suggested that loan-loss provisions by external auditors tend to be double those made by bank management. Bank examiners would double the provisions made by the auditors, and in a liquidation situation, loan losses would turn out to be double those estimated by the bank examiners. Once a bank moves into negative capital, the losses are effectively passed either to the depositors or de facto to the central bank or deposit insurance fund. As lenders of last resort, central banks would bear the ultimate risks unless such loans are fully secured.

The next stage of damage control (sometimes conducted almost simultaneously with diagnostics) is to stop or minimize losses. This involves an immediate change in management of the problem institutions, if incompetence or fraud is suspected, or at least the placement of competent advisers who can institute effective internal controls and measures to prevent further losses from speculation, continued lending to bad borrowers, and wasteful expenditure. On the part of the central bank, an effective monitoring system has to be established quickly to ensure that the losses and financial condition of the ailing institutions are monitored and reported constantly. Where existing tax measures, regulations, and bad practices have been causes of bank losses, remedies should be taken as soon as possible. On the whole, bank supervision and examination staff should be strengthened, and power for the central bank to act promptly should be provided.

The loss-allocation process is in practice the most difficult stage of crisis resolution, as loss allocation is not always defined in the law, and may have to be done arbitrarily. There are numerous interest groups in the loss-allocation process: the borrowers, bank shareholders, employees, other creditors, depositors, the central bank, and the government. According to present Western convention, defined partly in company and banking law, the bank losses should be borne first by the borrowers, then the shareholders, then other creditors, including employees, and thereafter by the depositors or the government through the deposit insurance fund. In practice, the process of loss allocation depends on the power of individual interest groups. For example, in a number of Latin American cases, foreign exchange losses of the enterprises and borrowers were passed to the central bank. In one African case, the powerful shareholders of failed banks received some compensation from the government. Bank unions can also ask for large compensations. Part of the reason why governments favor deposit insurance funds as liquidators of banks is the sheer complicated process of unwinding thousands of deposit and loan contracts, on top of employment contracts of failed banks, which can easily be disrupted by legal suits.

Thus, more often than not, it becomes politically expedient to absorb bank losses directly into the budget or off-budget in the books of the central bank. The point to remember is that losses absorbed by either the government or the central bank is a fiscal or quasi-fiscal deficit that has to be financed by taxation, borrowing, sale of government assets, or through inflationary financing. Periods of financial crises and structural adjustments are not always the appropriate time to raise taxes. Hence, it is always tempting to political decision makers to request the central bank to absorb the losses. When the central bank has large reserves relative to the size of losses, the problems can be resolved; however, when the degree of losses exceeds even the capital and reserves of the central bank, then the net losses of the central bank tend to become monetized and the loss burden is distributed in the economy through the inflation tax.

Consequently, a critical issue of banking crisis is how the losses are ultimately distributed or borne in the economy. Since the central bank is part of the government, the government may initially take responsibility for the losses, but it is eventually passed on to the population in the form of higher taxes, borrowing, or through the inflation tax. Experience shows that measures that affect the solvency of the central bank is self-defeating and may prove highly costly in the long run. The government has to deal with the loss directly through the budget, and become the "equity provider of last resort." How the bank losses are ultimately distributed to the system would depend on the combination of techniques adopted.

For example, the government need not bear the full brunt of the losses. In a number of cases, losses were borne partly by the depositors. In Malaysia, the depositors of the failed deposit-taking cooperatives received 50 percent of their deposits in the form of equity in a licensed finance company that took over the assets of the failed cooperatives, while the balance of 50 percent was repaid over a three-year period at a low rate of interest. In Thailand, depositors of failed finance companies received only the principal portion of their deposits in ten equal installments over ten years, interest free. This represented roughly a 50 percent loss in real terms when deposit rates were around 10 percent a year. This technique of cofinancing by depositors was also recently adopted in an Australian failed building society. Another way to recover costs is through ex post levies on the banking system, which would pass the costs back to the consumer through higher bank spreads.

Finally, the root cause of bank losses must be addressed. Often these can be found either in distortions in the enterprise sector, fiscal imbalances, or structural imbalances in the economy that require major policy changes. In addition to laying down a sound and competitive framework for banks to operate in, under which they can rebuild profitability, it is essential that a sound and stable macroeconomic environment is built for the real sector, with appropriate policies that encourage competition and efficiency. Dealing with bank crisis without tackling real sector distortions will invite a repeat crisis in the near future.

Crisis Management by Central Banks

Much has been written about banking crises, but relatively little about how one manages institutionally during the crisis. References on how to handle a financial crisis are few. The only helpful practical advice remains variations on Bagehot's dictum for the central bank to lend liberally in a financial crisis against good security. The academic literature has been sparse on the practicalities of dealing with crises.

How one deals with crises depends on the circumstances of each case, such as the legal framework, institutional structure, and often the capabilities of the crisis management team. Since central banks are directly responsible for the stability of the financial system, it is often assumed that central bank management knows how to handle crises. The case study of Malaysia illustrates this point. The Central Bank of Malaysia's capacity to deal with bank problems was shaped by its early history. Following runs on a large domestic bank in the mid-1960s, the Malaysian central bank, Bank Negara, began to build up its bank supervision and examination capacity. It developed, early on, teams of inspectors with the capacity to identify quickly bank problems, especially in the credit portfolio, and to assess the quality of bank management. At the same time, an off-site surveillance system was installed with a comprehensive bank data base. In the early 1980s, as banks began to "herd" into lending to finance the property sector, the Bank put into place close monitors on lending to property and shares.

The Bank also led the way in installing a sophisticated dealing room with good telecommunications to help develop the domestic money and foreign exchange markets. Under a flexible exchange rate regime since 1973, the Bank soon built up its own skills in managing the interbank money and foreign exchange markets and relied heavily on the dealing room to monitor market trends.

In 1983–84, the Bank was closely involved with the Ministry of Finance and the Economic Planning Unit of the Prime Minister's Department to address the large twin deficits in the budget and the balance of payments. It realized that the self-imposed structural adjustment program, calling for very large budgetary cutbacks in the face of declining commodity prices, would have a massive deflationary impact on the economy, and hence on the banking system. Early signs of the impending recession came when the stock market crashed first in 1983, recovered for a short while, and then crashed again in December 1985, when the Kuala Lumpur stock exchange was closed for a few days.

In preparation for potential banking problems, the banking law was changed to allow the Bank to acquire shares in ailing banks. No deposit insurance scheme was envisaged as the stronger banks were not willing to finance the failure of weaker institutions. By coincidence, emergency legislation was drafted as a contingency plan to deal with illegal deposit-taking corporations that sprung up during the period of tight liquidity. This piece of legislation was a powerful tool for the Bank in dealing with the collapse of 24 cooperatives, involving more than half a million depositors in July and August 1986. The suspension of payments by the cooperatives (not supervised by the Bank) caused immediate runs against a number of the weaker licensed finance companies, which the Bank had to deal with.

A clear issue in dealing with financial crises was which agency should deal with the day-to-day problems, and how could the problems be managed from an issue and policy point of view. How could that agency, for example, be accountable for financial and other decisions that have budgetary and political implications? These issues fortunately were spelt out in the Malaysian emergency legislation. The central bank was vested with the responsibility and power to deal with the crisis. It could not, however, carry out its wide powers, such as investigate or "freeze" bank accounts of cooperatives or bank management suspected of fraud, without clearing it through an advisory panel, comprising the governor as chairman, the secretary-general of the treasury, the attorney general, the chairman of the Association of Banks and a private sector member. This panel de facto became the policy-making body that oversaw the handling of the crisis, summoning as and when needed advice from the Cooperative Department, police, or other government departments. The secretariat of the panel was vested in the Bank Regulation Department of the Bank, which prepared regular position and policy papers for decision by the panel. The panel met sometimes daily but at least once a week to decide on important issues. Administrative costs for managing the crisis were borne by the central bank.

To manage the 17 firms of auditors plus numerous teams of bank examiners that had to investigate the 600 odd branches of the cooperatives, the Bank established an Operations Room, continually manned to monitor, coordinate, and direct operations. This served as the center in which all information sources were concentrated and digested. For example, reports came in from newspaper articles, public tip-offs, calls from banks or finance companies, examiners returning from onsite inspections, and other sources about the occurrence of bank runs or any incidence affecting the banks, finance companies, or licensed finance companies. When a bank run occurred, the Operations Room would be able to register the incident, determine the cash requirements, obtain authority from the head office of the branch concerned to provide the Bank with collateral or funding, and promptly authorize the nearest central bank branch to issue cash against such collateral. The Bank used the opportunity to obtain from the bank or finance company management or shareholders maximum cooperation for assistance. In a number of instances, the Bank was able to effect required changes in management or commitments to increase capital, before additional funding was approved. The policy of the Bank in bank runs was to supply as much cash as required to meet the deposit withdrawal, until depositors realized that it was pointless to run against a bank or finance company behind which the central bank stood as lender of last resort. Prompt press releases were made to give assurances to the public that the central bank was providing liquidity support. Hesitation in meeting deposit withdrawals always worsened bank runs.

The Operations Room was critical as an information and decision center. It had current information on the financial conditions of each licensed institution and was able to refer quickly to senior staff for decisions. It coordinated information received from all sources, including the dealing room, which monitored behavior in the money and foreign exchange markets. Information gaps and monitoring deficiencies were quickly corrected. For example, the Bank's information on bank exposure to shares prior to 1986 was subject to considerable lag. This was quickly corrected, since it became apparent that a number of smaller finance companies had been lending considerably to finance shares and were vulnerable to further declines in share prices. By the October 1987 stock-market crash, the Bank had current information on the exposure of each bank to each stockbroker. The Operations Room was a useful adaptation of a military innovation that helped to deal with immediate problems without losing sight of the overall strategic directions. It played a key role to keep the central bank management, other government departments, and the political decision makers constantly informed of developments, policy issues, implications, and options for decisions. Once decisions were made, the Operations Room implemented the decisions, issued necessary press releases to keep the public informed to allay problems of public uncertainty, and maintained the pace of reforms and measures necessary to deal with the crisis.

The lesson of the Malaysian banking crisis of 1986–88 in the management aspect is perhaps that it was critical to have political backing and intragovernmental consensus and cooperation to deal with the crisis. Once it was decided that the central bank should be the lead organization to handle the crisis, an administrative decision-making mechanism and structure was quickly built to cope with the crisis as it unfolded. Timely, reliable, and accurate information was critical, and the Bank used external auditors to supplement its own examination teams to verify the information. The information received was quickly digested and analyzed, and policy recommendations evolved from the advisory panel decision. Having the legal powers to act quickly and effectively under the emergency legislation was important. Keeping the public informed and winning the confidence of the public in the tough action taken against bank mismanagement and fraud was equally critical. It was quite clear, however, that without the correction of the macroimbalances, specifically cutting the fiscal deficit and turning around the balance of payments current account to a surplus, the banking crisis could not have been solved so quickly.

Conclusions

In sum, the nature of financial crisis is complex, with economic, political, institutional, and legal implications. There are immense difficulties and complex conditions under which different central banks work in dealing with financial crises. Each central bank has to work with different resource constraints, financial as well as manpower, under disparate cultural, national, political, and bureaucratic environments.

It is too easy to say that prevention is better than the cure. Certainly, the avoidance of macroeconomic imbalances, the existence of efficient and competitive banking systems under strictly enforced bank supervision to prevent fraud and mismanagement, and an underlying strong real sector all help to prevent crises, or at worst the minimization of financial disruptions.

Central bankers have to deal, however, with the real world, where such imbalances and crises exist. Central bankers have an institutional role to maintain the integrity of the currency contract—that is, the stability of the internal and external value of the currency. This implies above all financial discipline on banks, enterprises, and governments, particularly fiscal discipline. It is when the currency contract is broken, when the public loses confidence, when the banking system and ultimately the government will not protect their savings that crises break out. The solvency of the central bank, that is, its net capital and reserves, only helps to bolster that confidence. In the last analysis, it is the professional competence, integrity, and independent judgement of the central banks that can steer policy in the right way or the wrong way. Without financial discipline, banking crises are historical inevitabilities.

Bibliography

Bagehot, Walter, "Lombard Street, 1873," in *The Collected Works of Walter Bagehot*, Vol. 9, ed. by Norman St. John-Nevas (London: *The Economist*, 1978).

Baliño, Tomas J. T., "The Argentine Banking Crisis of 1980," IMF Working Paper, No. 87/77 (unpublished, Washington: International Monetary Fund, 1987).

Bank of England, "The Secondary Banking Crisis and the Bank of England's Support Operations," *Quarterly Bulletin*, Bank of England (April 1978).

Basle Committee on Banking Supervision, "Measuring and Controlling Large Credit Exposures" (unpublished, Basle, March 1990).

Bordo, Michael D., "Some Historical Evidence 1870–1933 on the Impact and International Transmission of Financial Crises," NBER Working Paper, No. 1606 (Cambridge, Massachusetts: National Bureau of Economic Research, April 1985).

Corrigan, E. Gerald, "A Perspective on Recent Financial Disruptions," *Quarterly Review*, Federal Reserve Bank of New York (Winter 1989/90).

de Juan, Aristobulo, "Dealing with Problem Banks: The Case of Spain," paper presented at the third Central Banking Seminar, International Monetary Fund, July 1985, Washington.

———, "From Good Bankers to Bad Bankers: Ineffective Supervision as Major Elements in Banking Crises" (unpublished, Washington: World Bank, 1987).

Gaspari, Mitja, "Balance of Payments Adjustment and Financial Crisis in Yugoslavia," in *Financial Reform in Socialist Economies*, ed. by Christine Kessides, Timothy King, Mario Nuti, and Catherine Sokil (Washington: World Bank, 1989), 214–29.

Goldsmith, Raymond, "Comment" in *Financial Crises: Theory, History, and Policy*, ed. by Charles P. Kindleberger and Jean-Pierre Laffargue (Cambridge; New York: Cambridge University Press, 1982), pp. 41–43.

Hinds, Manuel, "Economic Effects of Financial Crises," Policy, Planning, and Research Working Paper, No. 104 (Washington: World Bank, October 1988).

Krugman, Paul, "International Financial Crises," paper presented at an NBER conference on Reducing the Risk of Economic Crises (Cambridge, Massachusetts: National Bureau of Economic Research, October 1989).

Lamberte, Mario, "Assessment of the Problems of the Financial System: The Philippines Case" (unpublished, Washington: World Bank, August 1989).

Larrain, Mauricio, and Fernando Montes-Negret, "The Spanish Guarantee Fund" (unpublished, Washington: World Bank, 1986).

Montes-Negret, Fernando, "An Overview of Colombia's Banking Crisis, 1982–1988" (unpublished, Washington: World Bank, 1990).

Schwartz, Anna J., "Real and Pseudo-Financial Crises," in *Financial Crises and the World Banking System*, ed. by Forrest Capie and Geoffrey E. Wood (New York: St. Martin's Press, 1985), pp. 11–31.

Sheng, Andrew, "The Art of Bank Restructuring: Issues and Techniques," paper presented at an Economic Development Institute senior policy seminar on Financial Systems and Development in Africa, Nairobi, January 29–February 1, 1990 (mimeo, Washington: World Bank, January 1990).

Silverberg, Stanley, "The Savings and Loan Problem in the United States," Policy, Research, and External Affairs Working Paper, No. 351 (Washington: World Bank, 1989).

Sinkey, Joseph F., Jr., *Problem and Failed Institutions in the Commercial Banking Industry* (Greenwich, Connecticut: JAI Press, 1979).

Solheim, Jon A., "The Banking Crisis in Norway," paper presented at an Economic Development Institute Seminar on Financial Sector Liberalization and Regulation, Cambridge, June 10–15, 1990 (unpublished, Washington: World Bank, 1990).

Summers, Laurence H., "Planning for the Next Financial Crisis," paper presented at an NBER conference on Reducing the Risk of Economic Crises (Cambridge, Massachusetts: National Bureau On Economic Research, October 1989).

Sundararajan, V., "Banking Crisis and Adjustment: Recent Experience, paper presented at an IMF seminar on Central Banking in Washington, November 28–December 9, 1988 (unpublished, Washington: International Monetary Fund, 1988).

Tenconi, Roland, "Restructuring of the Banking System in Guinea" (unpublished, Washington: World Bank, December 1989).

U.S. Treasury, Office of the Comptroller of the Currency, *Bank Failure: An Evaluation of the Factors Contributing to the Failure of National Banks* (Washington, June 1988).

14

Techniques For Dealing With Problem Banks

BRIAN QUINN*

I hope you will not mind if I interpret the title I have been given rather widely: I intend to address three broad areas. First, some background to the issues that confront regulators and central bankers in dealing with problem banks, and then, going beyond the techniques, I will look at public policy issues. Last, I intend to look at the role of the central bank itself.

In a number of ways, the environment for banks is becoming increasingly hostile. At the root is a problem of excess capacity; banks' markets are shrinking, at the same time, a growing number of competing institutions and products and inexorably rising costs are adding to the pressure. Also, a growing secular pressure on banks' profits and capital exists, amid political professions of adherence to the free-market model. At the same time, consumer expectations are becoming higher, with the media taking up the role of self-appointed protectors of depositors—effectively rejecting, or at least compromising, a central principle of market efficiency: the readiness to accept failure and loss to depositors.

Deregulation does not just increase competition; it also leads to changes in the financial system itself and to the role of the banks in it. Structures are becoming more complex, and banks are increasingly becoming or aiming to become members of *groups*, the companies within which are linked by joint demand for products and services and by common ownership. Hence, the financial system is no longer a collection of largely separate components but is becoming ever more closely related. These developments raise new issues—for the market

---

*The author is Executive Director at the Bank of England.

and for regulators. As profitability of the sub-units are linked, risks are also.

The job and the risks are still further complicated by the increasingly close links between the financial services industries in different countries. The industry, and the problems for the regulators, now have a global scope, and the implications of a bank failure are correspondingly far-reaching.

There are doubts that markets are efficient in analyzing these changes, or in assessing the risks involved in new groupings. But my focus today will be on the implications these changes have for regulators, central banks, and governments in addressing the question of what to do when a bank is facing the prospect of failure.

Authorities' Response to Bank Failures

It is important that we do not concentrate solely on the moment of crisis. Stating a truism, each crisis has a before and after: before, it is the authorities' task to promote a sufficiently risk-averse approach by bankers to ensure that some balance is achieved between the risk of failure and a vigorous and independently managed banking sector; after, adequate arrangements for depositor protection must be in place if a failure does occur. Both supervision and deposit protection arrangements are public territory in the sense that the responsible authorities operate within a known framework of principles and policy that go beyond purely commercial considerations. The involvement of the authorities in the crisis or failure itself, however, must be determined by the set of circumstances pertaining at that precise moment. There can be no certainty that they will act, for this brings with it the moral hazard of, in effect, subsidizing the bank's risk taking. But equally, there can be no presumption that the authorities will not step in, because there may always be wider, systemic risks resulting from the failure of an individual bank.

The "package" of institutional arrangements in place can be broken down, more or less in order of their applicability, into supervision, intervention (including closed and open banks), and deposit insurance. The balance between them will vary from country to country; so, the following comments are general in nature.

Supervision

Supervision might be described as the effort to limit failures; it is concerned with the safety and soundness both of individual institutions and—especially for central banks—of the financial system. The nature of supervision in many countries has changed significantly in the last few decades. Banks themselves have become more sophisticated in the instruments and markets in which they deal; they have developed a wider range of business interests and operate increasingly within complex group structures and in areas not normally associated with banking—such as estate agency or travel services; and their international operations have drawn ever tighter the web of connections between banks and banking systems across the world. They, and their regulators, are thus exposed to a range of new risks and new responsibilities.

In recent years, supervisors have been meeting in international groups in which they exchange information about the banks that are their mutual responsibility and seek to develop ways in which to avoid the emergence of problems among international banks. Out of these discussions came, in 1975 and 1983, the Basle Concordats, which sought to define where responsibility lay for the supervision of banks and banking groups and how it should be shared between the supervisors involved. The Concordats drew attention to some important desiderata for supervision.

Capital Adequacy

At the heart of safety and soundness is, of course, capital adequacy. International standards of capital adequacy for banks were agreed by the Group of Ten countries two years ago and have been adopted by a large number of others. The European Community's (EC) own requirements for the capital adequacy of banks are similar to the Group of Ten standard. This gradual convergence of regulatory standards has emphatically not been a case of finding the lowest common denominator. This, I think, has been clearly demonstrated in recent months as, first, American and then Japanese banks have been the subject of critical attention in the markets regarding their ability to meet the standard of the Bank for International Settlements (BIS). The work on capital adequacy, in both the Group of Ten and EC forums, is now going beyond the credit risks addressed in the 1988 standard, to focus on a range of other risks inherent in a bank's business, including interest rate risk, foreign exchange risk, and the risks arising from large individual exposures.

Liquidity

A second fundamental focus of supervision must be the liquidity of banks. This is a very complicated area, and one in which it has so far proved much more difficult to reach agreed international methodologies, let alone standards. It is also an area that may sit less easily with the principle of home country control, which lies at the heart, for instance, of much of the EC's work. As the Basle Concordats recognized, while capital adequacy is best measured on a whole-institution basis, the liquidity, or cash flow, of individual units within the whole, particularly national branches, may also be very important. It may therefore be that banks active in several markets are seeking to meet very different supervisory measures of liquidity. This is clearly an area where much work remains to be done.

Management

Turning away from statistical measures, supervisors must also take a close interest in the management of companies under their care. This needs to be at the heart of any supervisory system, for the comfort to be drawn from the statistical measures discussed above is entirely dependent on the banks being properly and prudently run, with proper systems and controls over risk taking. There are of course many ways of assessing the adequacy of management, ranging from formal checks or inspections to informal discussions; but it is a principle of most supervisory systems that prudent management must be demonstrated in order that a bank may be authorized to do business.

Payment Systems

My final desideratum ranges wider than the banking supervisor's role to that of the central bank: this is the maintenance of, and possibly supervision of, stable payments and settlements systems. It is an area that is increasingly becoming the focus of attention, but one for which at the moment, there are more questions than answers. Nonetheless, the first steps are being taken, and the Group of Ten central banks in a committee chaired by Professor Lamfalussy have recently put a considerable amount of work into developing a report on, and recommending minimum standards for, netting systems.[1] Payments systems are fundamental to the operation of our national and international financial systems, and we need to understand a great deal more of the risks that may be involved.

Indeed, it is a valuable discipline on the market to bring home to operators in it that they run genuine risks in their business, and per-

[1]Bank for International Settlements, *Report of the Committee on Interbank Netting Schemes of the Central Banks of the Group of Ten Countries* (Basle, November 1990).

haps even more valuable to allow the consequences of failure to be demonstrated. It will always be difficult to bring those in the market to look closely at the less obvious counterparty risks without an example that forcefully focuses attention on them. For instance, the Herstatt crisis provided clear—and very damaging—evidence of the risks involved in settlement of foreign exchange transactions, a form of risk that even now, a decade and half later, has not been definitively dealt with.

In this area, as in all the others I have mentioned, it is vital that coordination of supervision continues and grows. This will be both on an international level, between banking supervisors, and on an inter-functional level, between supervisors of different financial services. In the United Kingdom, we have developed a system of colleges of supervisors designed to ensure that all supervisors with an interest in a financial group should be adequately informed of all its activities. At an international level too, contact between different financial supervisors has become more regular and more practically orientated. In particular, the work I mentioned earlier on position risk is being taken forward jointly by Group of Ten bank supervisors and by representatives of the International Organization of Securities Commissions (IOSCO) grouping of securities supervisors.

The Object of Supervision

But in developing closer contacts and more closely approximating systems for supervision, supervisors need to address some important policy issues. Fundamentally, they need to be clear about the object of supervision. Is it to prevent failure? To limit damage to the system? To protect depositors?

Speaking for myself, and I know that some of my fellow supervisors may have doubts about this, I do not believe that we supervisors should ever set ourselves the aim of preventing the failure of banks. High standards of capital adequacy offer banks some protection against difficulties that may arise, but there will always be problems that exceed an individual bank's ability to cope. Such situations will be exceptional, and supervisors must recognize the tension between profitability and safety. To set ever higher standards in the hope of protecting against such circumstances would make banks unprofitable and uncompetitive, and could still not guarantee that they would not fail. International cooperation does not resolve this tension; but the Basle capital accord delivers a common minimum standard that may help reduce it.

Intervention

In any system from which risk has not been eliminated—and this, as I have said, is not an attainable objective—the supervisor is faced with the possibility of a failed bank. Should this possibility crystallize, action can be taken by the authorities in advance, to head off the crisis, or afterwards, to head off its worst effects. In many countries, deposit insurance organizations have the ability to make funds available to support an institution before it fails; in some of these there will be collaboration with the central bank, and in countries where the insurance organization does not have such powers, the role—acknowledged or not—falls to the central bank alone.

Costs and Benefits: The Issues for Policymakers

Whoever performs the function, the underlying principle that must characterize all such decisions is the need to judge where the net benefit to the community lies. This encompasses, but is not confined to, financial calculations. Some estimate has to be made of the alternative costs of the dedication of public funds to maintaining the liquidity or solvency of the bank, on the one hand, and the costs of compensating depositors and, where relevant, investors on the other.

In some countries this is institutionalized in the arrangements for making support available. In the United States, the Federal Deposit Insurance Act empowers the Federal Deposit Insurance Corporation (FDIC) to offer direct assistance to any insured bank that is closed or is in danger of closing, for systemic reasons, or to take direct action to reduce or avert a threatened loss to itself. In Belgium, there is an Intervention Fund Committee, comprising only representatives of the banks, which, unless it is satisfied that offering support would be less costly than reimbursing depositors following a winding up, or that there is an overriding systemic concern, can prevent the Intervention Fund itself from acting.

Other considerations of costs and benefits must, however, also be made by the authorities. This is where the difficult judgments lie, and they usually override considerations of a strictly financial nature.

Solvency or Liquidity Crisis? . . .

Other things being equal, it is a more legitimate use of public funds to meet liquidity problems. But this is easier to say than to carry out in practice. First of all, it is not always clear what the nature of the problem is. Furthermore, liquidity problems can conceal more deep-seated difficulties. Also assets can change value by the very fact of public knowledge that an institution faces problems or is in need of official support. But solvency support need not be ruled out: getting value sometimes proves more feasible for an official lender that can be more patient than a party from the private sector.

Beneficiaries? . . .

But who receives the benefit of the official support? In dealing with a single unit—a bank—it is a fairly straightforward matter to ensure that the support from the authorities is for the direct and indirect benefit of the nonbank depositors and not the shareholders. The matter is more complicated in a conglomerate. Assistance provided to the bank may be crucial in preserving value for the shareholders in the wider group, directly or indirectly. This is not normally an object of public policy: shareholders provide risk capital and should not look to the authorities to compensate them or to support the value of their investment.

Contagion . . .

At a different level, what is the probability of contagion and a more generalized loss of confidence? There can be two dimensions to this issue. Difficulties in a solo bank can be communicated to other banks, most notably via the interbank or foreign exchange markets. This could become a problem for the whole banking sector or for banks that were thought to have the same risk profile, for example, sovereign risk or property exposure. This judgment is always difficult, particularly in circumstances of market nervousness. The question of contagion takes on a more far-reaching aspect when looking at a failing bank that is part of a financial services group. The other side of the coin that carries the designation "synergy" is that the fortunes, literally and metaphorically, of each part of the group are closely linked, and those links go beyond each of the entities into their own respective sectors.

At the International Level . . .

International considerations may also play a part. Since 1974 and the Herstatt affair, it has been clear that failures in one financial center can quickly be communicated to another. Since then the number of banks conducting international activities has grown, and the markets have become even more closely interrelated. This was illustrated by the serious effect of the stock market crash in October 1987. International financial centers cannot neglect such repercussions; nor can sizable national centers. The authorities of a bank cannot dismiss the possible effect on confidence in its banks in other financial centers should one of them default on an obligation expressed in another currency.

Depositor Protection Arrangements . . .

The arrangements for protection of depositors may also be a factor. A generous deposit insurance or protection scheme obviously softens the impact of a bank failure on the depositing public, with the welcome side effect that pressure from the media and body politic is reduced. Conversely, schemes that compensate only in part, particularly those where the upper limit of relief is also low, run a risk of damaging or destroying depositor confidence in the banking system. If the bank is part of a larger financial group, complications could be considerable and delays in the administration of deposit insurance arrangements could create pressure for a rescue operation.

Moral Hazard . . .

The deposit protection arrangements are closely related to the question of moral hazard and public subsidy. This is the most difficult judgment of all. Striking the balance between maintaining confidence in the banking and financial system, on the one hand, and discouraging imprudent behavior among owners, managers, and depositors, on the other, can be judged only in the particular circumstances applying. That judgment will be informed by all of the other factors mentioned above and particularly by whether the banking and financial systems at the time are in robust or fragile health. There are a number of problems in striking a balance—not least is the need to act, usually at very short notice.

Too Big to Fail . . .

There are, too, considerations of equitable treatment among troubled institutions and the resulting treatment of bank creditors of all classes. Some bank failures are necessary to drive home the fundamental point that regulation or supervision does not and should not aim to prevent all bank failures. Losses to shareholders and depositors must be allowed to happen often enough to make the threat of failure real. It is difficult to determine in advance how this perception can be achieved and the charge is frequently made that the authorities show the resolve necessary to allow failure only when smaller banks are involved.

Until one of our larger banks runs into serious difficulties the proposition remains untested. But size is not the only criterion by which we should judge. There may be banks that play an important role in particular markets but are not in themselves large. For instance, Johnson Matthey Bankers played an important role in the London bullion market, and in 1984 the Bank of England took the view that it was too-important to be allowed to fail. There can be, in my view, a rational defense of a "too-important-to-fail" doctrine, which could be offered in support of a rescue exercise for a large commercial bank.

These banks are at the center of industrial and commercial life in our countries. Their assets and commitments to lend represent the working capital of much of the economy. A breakdown in their ability to provide a store of value for individual savings could shake confidence in the entire banking and financial systems. Their central role in the payments system places them in a position in which failure to meet their obligations could set off profound and damaging reverberations in the economy. Overseas, as well as domestic, financial institutions could be affected. Hence, there may be some grounds for considering that the prospect of failure in a bank at the center of the system would command financial support from the authorities. But that is not invariably or inevitably true. It is vital to assess what I have called the nonfinancial costs and benefits. There may also be other avenues available that do not require the provision of official financial assistance.

Even if support were given, this does not necessarily mean that a significant increase in moral hazard is a certain result. The authorities can exact penalties for imprudent behavior by demanding the replacement of senior management, a change of ownership and a write-off of investment. These penalties can be, and have been, applied ahead of failure. Too important to fail, perhaps; too big to suffer, no.

Institutional Implications

Here then are several policy issues that virtually all central authorities would agree are at the core of any decision to offer financial support to a failing institution. We have looked at whether it may be done; let us turn to how it might be done.

The spectrum of approaches to offering support reflects in part national characteristics. There is differing emphasis on the law or on traditional practice, on requirements for specific predetermined triggers or criteria to be fulfilled, on the one hand, or on the judgment of some relevant body, on the other. Indeed, there is a variety of relevant bodies, and a variety of available powers, from the purely financial to those ranging rather wider. The variety of institutional arrangements can perhaps be best demonstrated by looking at some specific examples. If I start with the FDIC, it is partly because the arrangements are well-known, and a series of options, clearly specified in law, is available.

A *purchase and assumption transaction* will often be the first route tried, sometimes taking only a day or two, and involving the FDIC acquiring the problem assets while passing the clean assets to another bank, which assumes those liabilities and assets. In order to arrange such a transaction, it may be necessary to create a *bridge bank* (officially a deposit insurance national bank), to which will be transferred the insured deposits of the failed bank for a limited period. Alternatively, the FDIC may give *direct assistance* to an insured bank that has closed or is in danger of closing, for systemic reasons. This may involve making loans, purchasing assets, or depositing funds in the bank. A further alternative is an *arranged merger* under Section 13 of the Federal Deposit Insurance Act, with similar funding or purchasing arrangements applying; this route may be followed if the financial assistance provided in arranging such mergers to date is judged to be less than would have been required using another route. Finally, the most recently devised alternative (in 1982) allows the FDIC to make periodic *purchases of net worth certificates* where institutions are significantly involved in residential mortgage lending, are incurring losses, and have low net worth. Absent the satisfaction of the market disruption test, the use of any of these options must meet a legal requirement to be cost effective.

By contrast, the U.K. Deposit Protection Fund cannot provide anything except insurance against losses. Any other support must come from the monetary authorities rather than the fund; here, the decision is governed by custom and practice rather than by law, though the options may in practice come to something similar to those used in the United States. Elsewhere, in Belgium, the arrangements allow for the provision of financial support but not for the Intervention Fund to acquire the troubled company. In Germany, wide-ranging discretionary powers are available, and in the Iberian countries preventative support operations even for banks with *solvency* problems are explicitly allowed, to the extent of subscribing equity—going beyond the liquidity assistance usually envisaged in financial support arrangements.

It is clear from the above that there are no generally applied approaches. Historical experience in each country is clearly crucial to the range of powers, and to the legal, customary, or constitutional underpinnings. One factor common to most countries, however, is that the essential support arrangements are closely allied to deposit insurance or protection schemes. They provide the final element in the package, and their terms often influence the decision on the use of intervention powers.

Deposit Insurance Schemes

If anything, variety between deposit insurance schemes is still greater. First, such schemes, though common, are by no means universal, even now. Where there are schemes, some work on a legal basis and some are informal arrangements; within both groups, there may be voluntary, as well as effectively compulsory, membership. Within the EC, for instance, the U.K. scheme has both a base in statute and effectively compulsory membership; those in Germany have neither. The French scheme, while compulsory, is nonstatutory; and in Spain it is based on statute, but membership is voluntary.

The scheme may be administered officially, as for instance in the United States and Japan, or privately, as in Germany or France. It may offer insurance only, as in the United Kingdom, or broader support, as in the United States. It may maintain a standing fund, as in the United Kingdom or Germany, or operate on an ad hoc levy, as in France, or on commitments from members, as in Italy. Contributions may come from the private sector only, as in the United States or United Kingdom, or also from the official sector, as in Spain and Portugal; and schemes may also have borrowing powers to supplement the levy arrangements, as do the U.S. and U.K. funds.

In addition to this great variety of bases for the schemes, their scope can be radically different. Looking simply at the amount of each depositor's money that is protected, we can see that schemes range from the United Kingdom, where deposits up to £20,000 are covered, through the United States, where it is $100,000, to that in Italy, where maximum coverage is over $2 million equivalent. These differences are increased when one considers that the U.K. scheme covers only 75 percent of the eligible deposit, while in the United States 100 percent is covered and in Italy there is a sliding scale from 100 percent to 80 percent. The U.K. scheme offers per *depositor* cover; the U.S. scheme per *deposit* coverage. Furthermore, while the U.K. scheme covers only sterling deposits in the United Kingdom, the German scheme, at the other end of the scale, covers deposits in any currency, whether in Germany itself or with foreign branches of German banks.

Their Purpose

This variation, of course, reflects different perceptions of the purpose of deposit protection. Perhaps I can offer three general propositions as to what its purpose might be. First, it offers a level of protection to the small depositor or investor, who is perceived to lack the capacity to evaluate the soundness of banks (though views on the level at which that capacity is attained vary considerably, as we have seen). Second, it underpins systemic confidence, providing a buffer against possible runs on banks as a group. Third, where depositors' money is not fully covered, it may act as a form of market discipline, imposing on banks the necessity of recognizing a duty of care to depositors.

The evidence for this last proposition is far from clear. But however limited the role of deposit insurance may be as a market discipline, it must be allowed to play its part in the balance of all three elements—supervision, intervention, and deposit insurance—which go to make up the risk equation for banks, central banks, and creditors.

Role of the Central Bank

Crucial to this package or equation is where the central bank features in it. Sometimes, of course, it does not feature at all in a formal way, as for instance in Germany where supervisory functions are located in a separate entity, while deposit insurance and intervention powers rest with the administrators of the private sector owned fund. In other countries, such as the United Kingdom, the central bank provides supervisory and deposit protection arrangements (though the fund is legally separate) and has also been provider of financial support. Nonetheless, all central banks have a distinctive position in relation to their respective financial systems. As conductor of monetary policy, the central bank requires a stable financial system, and this interest usually gives the central bank an overview of the interconnections between financial markets. So, for instance, in October 1987, it was through the central bank network that communication between the various financial markets and national systems was effected. Within the United Kingdom, the Bank of England monitored the markets continually, and held regular meetings with other financial market regulators and with representatives of the exchanges, despite the lack of a formal role in respect of these markets. Perhaps more interestingly, in Germany where supervision of the markets is managed in a separate institution, the Bundesbank maintains a continuing interest in banks and financial markets based on its monetary policy role.

It will, therefore, be interesting to watch developments both in Eastern Europe and in the EC over the coming years. In the former, banking systems will be evolving and the authorities, including central banks, will need to determine for themselves how they handle the package I mentioned earlier— the balance between supervision, intervention powers, and deposit insurance. In the EC, the situation is rather different: rather than establishing a commercial banking system around an existing central bank, thought is being given to the creation of a new European central bank to take on certain central banking tasks in the context of economic and monetary union. There are difficult issues here, including how much of traditional central banking—perhaps including supervision—can continue to be carried out at a national level within the unified market and how much needs to be centralized. Even within the single-market program, new issues concerning all three elements of the package may arise. We certainly cannot say that, since the main role of any future European central bank would be the running of European monetary policy, it need have no regard for issues of supervision or systemic stability; as we have seen earlier a central bank cannot disregard the stability of the financial system within which it seeks to operate policy.

No doubt, in both cases, there will also be conflict between the demands of the three separate elements, as there may be in longer established systems, but as other systems show, those conflicts can be managed, if not ultimately resolved.

15

Resolving Troubled Thrift Institutions and Bad Banks: Lessons for Central Banks in Developing Countries

HENRY N. SCHIFFMAN*

When depository institutions are in difficulty because of an inordinate volume of nonperforming loans, public policymakers may attempt to adopt a strategy to correct the situation; of the advice taken, that of the central bank should be among the most important. In the case of state-owned institutions, the government will play a decisive role, and even with privately owned institutions, the bank supervisory authority can influence remedial measures that could be taken. In countries with deposit insurance, like the United States, where a deposit insurance agency becomes the owner of assets of insolvent institutions, the government plays a leading role in resolving insolvent depository institutions. This paper analyzes the initiatives in the United States in recent years of both privately owned commercial banks and of the government agency that was created to resolve insolvent thrift institutions; the initiatives illustrate techniques and policies that can be utilized in developing countries for restructuring troubled financial institutions.

A basic technique that has been employed in the United States, and which has a few leading examples in the restructuring of troubled private commercial banks, is the segregation of nonperforming assets in a separate banking organization.[1] Some of the objectives to be

*The author is a Consultant in the Central Banking Department of the International Monetary Fund.

[1]In the United States, a banking organization has been used because of the securities laws. In other countries, a nonbank company could be utilized to dispose of former bank assets.

realized by privately owned banks in separating nonperforming assets are also realized in the case of public institutions, including those which acquire assets of insolvent financial institutions by virtue of being taken over by a deposit insurance agency. In this analysis of troubled private institutions, the objectives to be realized by a depository institution that wishes to survive its crisis caused by excessive nonperforming loans will be emphasized. By removing bad assets, the remaining healthy institution will have improved its credit standing and, consequently, will have reduced its high cost of funding, which was caused by a large volume of nonperforming assets. Equally important, by allowing management of the now healthy institution to concentrate on basic commercial banking for the future, rather than on the problems of the past, the prospects for conducting future profitable business are enhanced. These factors should also improve the price of the stock of banks that are publicly owned and thus the prospects for raising additional equity capital are improved.

The segregation of nonperforming assets into a separate entity also improves the chances for achieving greater values for such assets than might otherwise be realized had they remained in the bank. This is because such separate entities should become specialists in collecting or liquidating nonperforming loans and should be more effective than commercial banks, particularly if the same commercial banker who was responsible for extending the loan is responsible for its collection. When a bank seeks to collect its loan, it is often reluctant to undertake stringent measures in relation to a company that maintains a banking relationship with that institution. Commercial banks would normally be more lenient toward recalcitrant borrowers than an independent entity whose sole business is the realization of nonperforming assets. Liquidation specialists are often more conscious of the time value of money and of the importance of collecting sooner a lesser sum than that which is owed rather than hoping to collect payment in full over longer time frame.

Financial Structure and Conditions

A key question in the possible establishment of a separate entity to collect nonperforming loans is the funding of such a vehicle. For a solvent institution in an economy where asset-based financing is customary, financing may be obtained from the capital markets. The tradition of asset-based financing in the United States made possible the financing of the assets of Grant Street Bank, a "bad bank," by the holding company of Mellon Bank to liquidate Mellon.Bank's nonperforming assets in 1988. This bank was known as a "bad bank" as distinguished from the now healthy Mellon Bank, which was the "good bank." Mellon Bank transferred assets that had an original book value of $1.35 billion and were valued at $640 million when transferred. Based on this asset value, the bad bank was able to place $513 million of high-yield, three- and five-year notes to fund most of its assets. The public investors had confidence that upon liquidating its assets, the bad bank would be able to pay its obligations.

In countries that may not have capital markets that can appraise the quality of assets of an entity that borrows to fund the purchase of nonperforming assets, credit enhancement techniques may be used to accomplish the same purpose, albeit at a slightly higher cost to compensate the party that provides credit enhancement. For example, a well-known financial institution in the country that can appraise the value of the asset portfolio could issue its guarantee on debt obligations issued by the entity that owns the nonperforming assets. Such a guarantor could even be a government agency in a country in which such a liquidation entity were an important part of financial public policy.[2]

When the government assists in the disposition of nonperforming assets as part of the restructuring of a financial institution and wishes to encourage the private sector to acquire nonperforming assets of financial institutions, either from going concerns or assets of liquidated institutions, it has several techniques that can be employed to induce the private sector to acquire nonperforming assets. The government could provide cash or debt obligations that yield a market rate of interest to fund the acquisition of assets. It could also provide tax relief to entities that acquire nonperforming assets, for example, to allow tax loss carry forwards that exceed the normal period, or allow the losses of an entity that acquires nonperforming loans to offset gains from activities of affiliated profitable companies. Certain contractual provisions that enhance the attractiveness of acquiring nonperforming assets can also be used. The government could agree to take back certain assets for a certain period of time ("asset puts"), if the purchasing entity is unable to liquidate those assets in a certain time frame at such prices as it anticipates are required. The government could also provide that the acquiring entity would have guaranteed income at a certain level which will induce it to acquire the nonperforming assets. In such cases, the government would hope that

[2]It was recently estimated that in the United States, a dozen banking companies and at least one securities firm have issued $40 billion of commercial paper for special purpose companies to finance assets ranging from trade and credit card receivables to business loans, and some of this commercial paper has been guaranteed by letters of credit from major banks.

the private sector would be able to adequately dispose of nonperforming assets; however, if, because of unanticipated adverse circumstances that is not possible, the ability to put assets to the government or an income guaranty could make the difference between the government indirectly disposing of assets and being saddled with assets without an appropriate means for their disposition.

Other Financial Feasibility Issues

In order to assess whether the establishment of a separate institution to administer nonperforming loans is feasible, two basic questions must be asked: (1) who bears the cost; and (2) what is the cost. As experience in the United States with private commercial banks has shown, the bank itself can bear the cost if capital is sufficient. When nonperforming assets are written down or written off before the establishment of the separate institution, these write-downs and write-offs are made against the income or net worth of the transferring institution. Thus, if the net worth of an institution is sufficient, the cost will be borne by the capital of that institution. For government-owned institutions with insufficient capital to bear the cost, the government would, of course, bear the cost by realizing a loss in the capital accounts or income of the transferring institution and also perhaps in funding the separate institution. For a privately owned institution with insufficient capital to bear the cost, if the burden of nonperforming assets might cause its failure with an attendant cost to the government, either because public policy would require the government to pay depositors of the failed institution or because of an obligation of the government under a deposit insurance scheme, the government may wish to fund the cost of disposing of that institution's nonperforming assets as a projected lower-cost alternative to letting it fail.

While the transfer of nonperforming assets to a separate institution does not necessarily require immediate cash payment by that institution to the transferring bank, the financial impact on the transferring bank will of course be reduced if the separate institution compensates the transferring bank for the transfer of assets. The cost of compensation, in the case of the Mellon bad-bank structure used recently in the United States, was borne by bond holders who were satisfied that the value of the transferred assets was sufficient to enable the separate institution to pay off the bonds. The separate institution could issue notes to the transferring institution as compensation, which could be interest-bearing to provide income. The separate institution could also simply have a balance sheet with equity represented by the transferred assets and, as assets, the transferred assets with equity owned by the bank transferring the assets.

Let us consider the total cost of establishing a separate institution to manage nonperforming assets. The most easily calculable cost is the cost of assets that have been identified as worthless: loans that have no chance of repayment and for which there is no collateral to dispose of. Where the transferring bank injects some equity capital into the separate institution as a means to attract third-party financing, a second cost would be the opportunity cost of this allocation of capital. When the transferred assets are exchanged for notes that bear an interest rate somewhat below the yield that may have been obtainable on other assets, another cost is incurred: the differential between the payment on the notes of the separate institution and the yield obtainable on alternative investments. Yet another cost, and what may be the largest cost (although if the assets are particularly troubled the write-offs may be the largest cost), is the difference between the book value of the assets and any accrued interest and the amount that will be ultimately recovered in the collection process. Another significant cost is the maintenance of assets like developed real estate or transportation equipment. A final cost is the management costs of the separate institution. This could be considerable, especially in an environment where the costs of legal process to recover assets are high. Thus, against all these prospective costs must be calculated the projected benefits that are to be achieved by the survival of a viable financial institution.

Examples of Asset Disposition Institutions

It is instructive to consider more closely some examples of the use of private sector debt collection entities in the United States to see how they have been structured and what some of the difficulties have been.

Let us consider first Grant Street Bank, Mellon Bank's bad bank. To emphasize the asset-based financing nature of this transaction, one significant legal aspect is that title to Grant Street's assets and the proceeds from collections were pledged to a trustee to secure repayment of the notes that were issued to finance the acquisition of the assets from Mellon Bank. Thus, bond holders had some additional confidence that they were purchasing the assets and not the business prospects in a more general sense of Grant Street Bank. Some flexibility in financing was another feature. Both classes of notes had provisions whereby the stated maturity dates could be extended for one year, in which case there would be higher interest payments of 0.5 percent and a premium paid on the principal of from approximately 1 percent to 3 percent, depending upon the maturity date. Thus, there was some flexibility to the financing, although such built-in rescheduling may not be acceptable to some prospective investors.

The liquidation of Grant Street Bank's assets is administered by a specially established subsidiary of the Mellon Bank Corporation, the holding company of Mellon Bank. This creates the potential for certain conflicts of interest, since Mellon Bank still maintains relationships with some of the obligors on the assets that are held by Grant Street Bank. The company that administers the liquidation is compensated by receiving 3 percent of the net cash flow that results from its activities. Net cash flow is defined by the excess of receipts from asset sales over operating expenses related to asset management. The separate liquidation company was chosen because it was felt that it would have a better focus and incentive to sell assets as soon as possible taking into account the time value of money. As mentioned earlier, the traditional loan workout approach of commercial bankers was considered to be ultimately more costly since they generally sought to collect full payment in a longer-term time frame.

The process of the liquidation of assets has several aspects. It includes restructuring certain loans, negotiating with banks that originated loans with respect to which Mellon Bank had loan participations, foreclosing on loans, selling collateral, participating in insolvency proceedings of borrowers, and managing and improving real estate. Again, the basic objectives of asset disposition are to produce proceeds from sales of assets in a time frame that permits payment of principal and interest on the notes and to maximize the net sales proceeds on a present-value basis.

The economics of the Mellon Bank transactions were projected to have been very good. Detailed forecasts of cash flows had indicated that after three years, the net cash available would have been $515 million, after five years, $770 million, and after 10 years, $964 million, which left an ample margin for debt service on the $513 million in three- and five-year notes. In fact, in the first year of operation, Grant Street had realized $334 million from asset sales, or more than half of the initial book value of the asset portfolio.

Another example in the United States of the use of a separate institution to dispose of assets of troubled banks is the reorganization of the First City Bancorporation of Texas, Inc., in 1988. Here, it appeared that a regional bank-holding company with assets of approximately $13 billion as of 1986 would fail because of a growing lack of confidence in its future by the money markets, and the Federal Deposit Insurance Corporation (FDIC) was faced with the possibility of a significant loss to the deposit insurance fund in the repayment to depositors upon liquidation of the subsidiary banks of the bank holding company.

A reorganization plan was devised by the FDIC, a New York investment bank, and a prominent American banker and presented to the First City Bancorporation board of directors and its shareholders on a "take it or leave it" basis; a prominent feature of the reorganization was the establishment of a so-called collecting bank, which would dispose of the nonperforming assets of the subsidiary banks of the holding company. As Chart 1 indicates, in this transaction the holding company's subsidiary banks transferred assets with a book value of $1.8 billion to the collecting bank, which were written down to approximately $1 billion. The FDIC issued a note to the subsidiary banks for $970 million, and the FDIC received in turn $100 million in subordinated notes of the collecting bank and preferred stock in the collecting bank, which would only have value if the collecting bank did extraordinarily well. It was estimated at the inception of the transaction that the ultimate cost to the FDIC would be approximately $700 million.

Removing the bad assets from the subsidiary banks was the key to enable the restructuring of the First City Bancorporation to proceed, and that was based upon an injection of new equity capital from sophisticated investors and a line of credit from institutional investors. The collecting bank issued a note for $764 million to the subsidiary banks, which constituted a critical component of their assets. That the collecting banks' assets were written down to approximately $1 billion and that the subsidiary banks also injected $230 million in equity in the collecting bank made the $764 million note a credible asset. The shareholding interest of the existing investors in First City Bancorporation was diluted to approximately 2.5 percent by the interest obtained by the new equity investors.

The Resolution Trust Corporation

The recent experience of the U.S. Government in taking over, managing, and selling or liquidating thrift institutions provides useful information on certain policies and procedures to be followed, which can be adapted to developing countries that are restructuring financial institutions. Because of the dimension of the work of the Resolution Trust Corporation (RTC), considerable effort has been put into resolving these troubled financial institutions at the least cost to the government; therefore, this experience, while very recent, is illuminating. An example of the dimension of this effort is that as of July 31, 1990, the RTC had in conservatorship 258 institutions with total assets

Chart 1. First City Bancorporation Reorganization

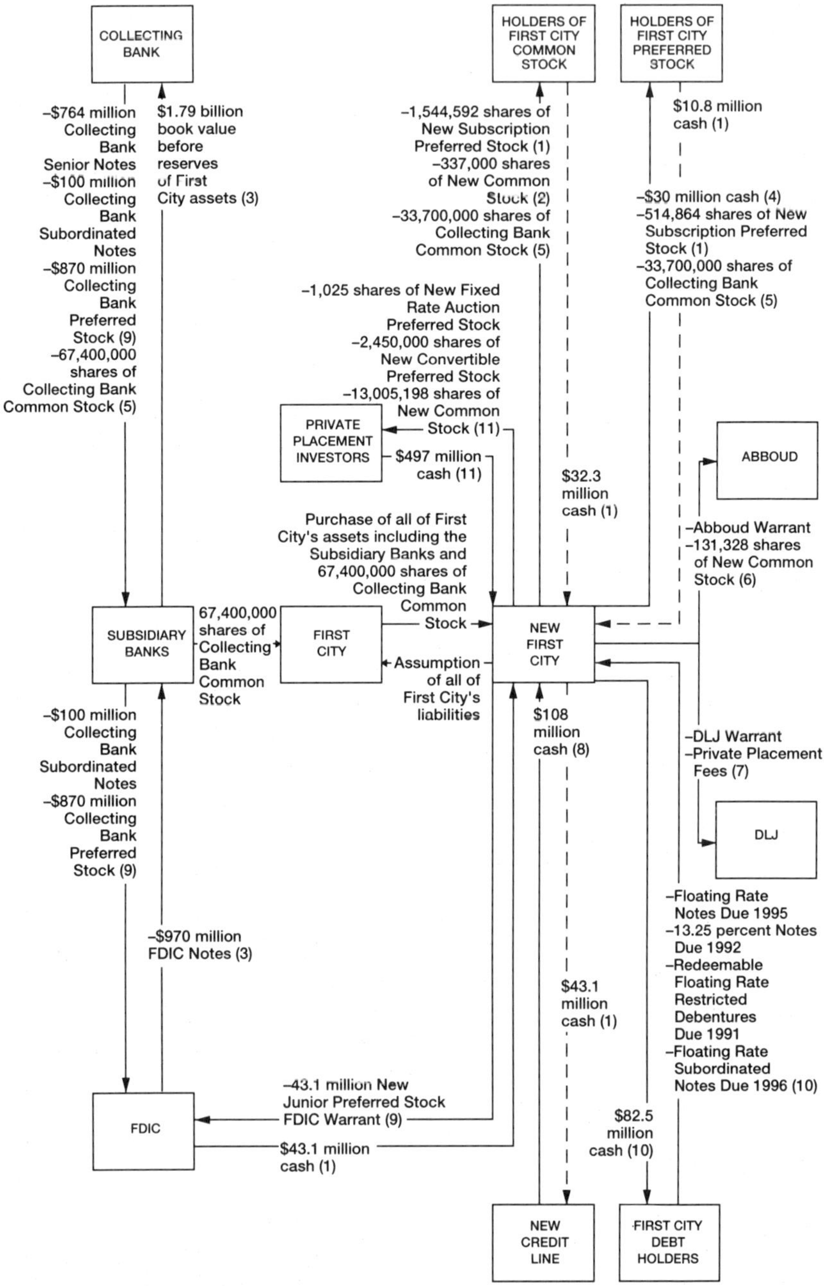

of $124 billion; it also had in receivership 211 institutions with total assets of $40 billion. Institutions in conservatorship are ongoing businesses intended to be sold in whole or in part to another institution or rehabilitated; those in receivership are generally those that are to be liquidated piecemeal (a "liquidation receivership") and to be transformed for conservatorship (a "pass-through receivership"). It is interesting to note that as of that date, of the total assets under RTC management, some 24 percent was in cash and securities and some 46 percent was in performing loans, for the most part residential mortgage loans, and thus 70 percent of its assets were good assets. However, in the highly leveraged business that is depository institutions, bad assets in excess of a low level of capital are sufficient to terminate the viability of an institution, and that is the case with the institutions under RTC management. In such institutions, some 10 percent of total assets are in nonperforming loans and approximately 11 percent of assets are real estate assets that have been foreclosed upon. It might be useful to briefly consider the reasons why the U.S. Government has the enormous task of resolving troubled thrift institutions. The immediate reasons for the deterioration of the industry over approximately ten years were their inability to cope with economic adversity and fundamental changes in financial markets; broadened banking powers; insufficient supervision by regulators; capital requirements, which required too little owners' stake in the business; problems in real estate and high-yield bond markets; and mismanagement and misconduct. In a broader sense, the problem reflects the policy toward competition and licensing of financial institutions in the United States, whereby the criteria for chartering new institutions are more lenient than they could have been and too many thrifts found themselves being managed by people who were unable to cope with fundamental changes in circumstances.

The basic objectives of the RTC are to manage and resolve institutions and to dispose of assets in a manner that maximizes returns and minimizes losses and minimizes the impact on local real estate and financial markets. In pursuit of these objectives, which would appear to be valid for any country embarking upon a program of restructuring financial institutions, the RTC has adopted policies in four main areas: case resolution, asset disposition, conflicts of interest and ethical standards, and relations with the public, which appear to have been well-founded.

With respect to case resolution or the management of institutions in conservatorship, a policy that has been adopted is that while institutions are in conservatorship, the RTC takes action to reduce its risk exposure from such institutions, to reduce their operating losses, and pay down their high-rate liabilities. To the extent feasible and cost-effective, the asset side of the balance sheet is reduced through the packaging and securitization and sale of financial assets. The RTC attempts to reduce the liabilities of thrifts so that the only liabilities remaining are deposits that have significant franchise value, that is, core deposits that could be sold at a meaningful premium to another depository institution. Those institutions that the RTC identifies as having significant franchise value because of their deposit base are permitted to maintain their asset levels. For those institutions with insignificant franchise value, the RTC has adopted procedures to begin shrinking such institutions' balance sheets in a coordinated and orderly manner. Thus, procedures have been adopted such that loan origination ceases, and the cash flow from payments of principal and interest is used to repay high-cost deposits and secured borrowings. An exception to this rule would be when additional lending would reduce losses on existing loans.

With respect to the policy as to priorities in resolving institutions, those with the highest losses (both in absolute terms and relative to the expected cost of the resolution) and the greatest erosion in franchise value are given the first priority in order to save the RTC those additional losses. Similarly, the ongoing risk exposure to the RTC resulting from institutions with large interest rate or credit risk-exposure is considered.

With respect to alternative methods of resolution, which generally take the form of either liquidations or assisted acquisitions, the policy is to adopt the least-cost alternative. In an assisted acquisition, the acquiring institution assumes some portion of the assets and liabilities of the failed institution. The RTC provides sufficient cash to the acquiring institution to offset the difference between the amount of liabilities assumed and the market value of assets acquired from the failed institution, net of any premium paid by the acquiring institution for the franchise value. While the RTC would prefer to sell a troubled institution as a whole, often an acquiring institution acquires only the good assets (e.g., cash, securities, and performing loans) and the transaction is termed a "clean thrift" purchase (of assets) and assumption (of liabilities).

With regard to the forms of financial assistance that the RTC may provide and the consideration that the RTC seeks for such assistance, the financial assistance can include cash, notes, yield-maintenance agreements, capital loss coverage, asset puts, and regulatory forbearances. One policy is that the period of financial assistance involving a financial contingency (asset puts, asset guarantees, or capital loss coverage) for the RTC should, in general, not be longer than six months and should cover only the period required by the acquiror to complete its due diligence on the acquired assets. By taking an ownership in resolved institutions, the RTC can protect its financial interest when, at the time of the resolution, there is uncertainty regarding the value of the resolved institution, and, therefore, the appropriate level of assistance. This uncertainty creates the potential for large upside gains for the acquiror. Equity participation, such as common stock, gives the RTC a direct ownership position in a thrift and allows the RTC to share an upside gain. Equity participation, however, may create a conflict if the RTC assumes a controlling position and, thereby, becomes a competitor with other financial institutions. Therefore, the RTC prefers to use warrants, which are a passive equity instrument that allows the RTC to share in the profits of the resolved institution, but avoids the control issue.

With respect to bidding procedures, the RTC believes that a significant way to reduce the cost of resolution is to encourage active participation in the resolution process by all qualified bidders. This can best be achieved, according to the RTC, by having an open and widely publicized bidding process and a broad dissemination of information regarding institutions being marketed and the terms of previous transactions. This is to assure that the RTC receives the best offer from prospective purchasers of institutions or assets.

With respect to the management of the resolution process and the use of the private sector, the RTC uses the services of private persons and firms if such services are available, and it determines that the utilization of such services is practical and efficient. Such services include managing institutions or performing due diligence for the RTC.

With respect to the disposition of assets acquired by the RTC, these assets fall into three categories: cash and readily marketable loans, servicing rights, and securities; high-risk or other undesirable, but performing, loans; and real estate owned and nonperforming loans, including loans in foreclosure.

One important policy decision was to dispose of assets as soon as possible and avoid deferring the marketing of properties. It was felt that holding properties off the market for an extended period of time would increase the ultimate cost of asset disposition because of the expenses associated with managing and financing property while it was under the RTC and the risk of deterioration. Holding property off the market may also be contrary to the interest of the local community because of the uncertainty arising from not knowing when the property may be placed in the market for sale.

In the disposition of assets, the RTC also must use the private sector for the management and disposition of assets, subject to RTC policies and audit. The RTC attempts to use appropriate incentives for contractors as a means of ensuring that the government receives the maximum net present value return on its assets. For example, contractors receive as compensation a percentage of the proceeds net of expenses, with the percentage increasing as proceeds increase relative to the estimated market value of assets. In other cases, the RTC enters into contracts that have the RTC and the contractor sharing in better-than-expected returns, as well as sharing the risk that net proceeds will fall short of expectations (i.e., yielding the contractor less than the market rate of return). The RTC has attempted to dispose of assets in large, wholesale transactions as being the most efficient method of disposing of assets; however, in some instances, such as the sale of single family homes or rural homes in distressed areas, adverse market effects of such wholesale transactions may dictate another course of disposition. For example, in areas where the RTC is a large holder of similar properties, disposition can be made according to a pre-advertised multi-month marketing schedule rather than disposing of a large number of properties in a single day.

With respect to the RTC's continuing involvement with assets, the policy is to generally avoid retaining long-term equity interests in assets under its jurisdiction; however, it does considers ways in which it can participate through passive equity interests in an extraordinary gain that may be realized by the acquiror of an asset. The RTC will sometimes invest in capital improvements (i.e., buildups of incomplete properties and rehabilitation of completed structures) prior to marketing. There may be cases in which the net present value of properties will be enhanced by capital improvements prior to sale, but in most instances, properties are sold in an "as is" condition. The RTC has decided to finance asset sales sparingly and only when necessary to complete real estate transactions that maximize the present value of return to the RTC, net of the value of any concessions provided in the financing. The general policy is that only real estate is eligible for RTC financing; the buyer of the asset should make a significant equity contribution (i.e., at least 25 percent) and pledge the asset as collateral; RTC-provided financing should be senior to that of other creditors; concessionary terms on the financing should be minimized and always recovered through a higher sales price; and all loans made by the RTC should be sold, to the maximum extent feasible.

With respect to the basic objective of minimizing the impact on local real estate markets of its asset dispositions, the RTC has adopted a special policy for distressed areas. It should not sell at less than a specified minimum disposition price, which is 95 percent of market value, except when sales at prices below 95 percent would save interest expense and the holding period for properties and transactions costs sufficient to offset any shortfall fall below the 95 percent figure. Of course, the term "market value" can be subjective. The RTC has recognized that appraisals are an appropriate tool for estimating market value for many RTC assets; the lack of qualified appraisers, however, is not an obstacle that stalls the process of asset disposition. A firm policy is that the RTC should not attempt to outguess the market by speculating on future developments not reflected in the current market values of properties.

In the area of conflicts of interest and ethical standards, the RTC has issued rules and regulations that apply to independent contractors regarding conflicts of interest, ethical responsibilities, and the use of confidential information. Other rules apply to officers and employees of the RTC and govern the avoidance of conflict of interest, ethical responsibilities, and postemployment restrictions. Specific, written guidelines concern the avoidance of political favoritism and undue influence upon awarding contracts and decision making.

With respect to relations with the public, the RTC has decided that maintaining open communications with the public regarding the RTC's policies and procedures for the sale or disposition of real estate is critical for the success of its efforts. As a result, considerable effort is undertaken to keep the public informed as to past actions of the RTC, its current policies, and ways in which the private sector can work with the RTC, including through the purchase of institutions or assets.

Supervisory Conversions

Another experience in the United States involving troubled thrift institutions that may have relevance for developing countries, for commercial banks as well as for thrift institutions, is the process of supervisory conversions of mutual thrift institutions. This occurred during the 1980s when more than one hundred mutual savings institutions were converted to stock form of ownership. These institutions were converted by the thrift supervisory agency to be able to sell capital stock to the public and were compelled to raise new capital largely as a result of asset and liability interest rate mismatches and consequent losses, which eroded capital. Many now survive as financially sound institutions. In approving the conversions, the supervisory authority approved a new business plan and often new management; this was an inducement to investors as it indicated that the troubled institution would be rehabilitated. Financial assistance was not provided in these cases.

This experience may be illustrative for countries that have government-owned institutions that the government may wish to privatize in whole or in part. Often government-owned institutions must be converted to a corporate form of organization so they can sell equity interests to private parties. The government would have to provide financial assistance to the ailing institution that pretends to sell equity interests to the public, in many cases, as a matter of fairness, so that the public would be investing in a solvent institution with reasonable prospects for future success. In the United States, the former mutually owned institutions had substantial success in selling stock because sales were often to existing customers and to others in the local community that had come to look favorably upon these institutions as desirable community thrifts and were interested in seeing the institutions survive. This may also be true in some developing countries. In others, a troubled institution may have a negative image in the mind of the public and a better solution may be to liquidate the existing institution and attempt to sell stock in a de novo institution, which perhaps could purchase good assets and assume certain deposits of the former institution, as in a pass-through receivership.

Lessons for Developing Countries

The corporate structures, financing techniques, and policies and procedures for the disposition of assets that were described above and that are based on the recent experience of private banking organizations and the U.S. Government's RTC can be adapted in many circumstances to developing countries that are restructuring troubled financial institutions.

The facets of rehabilitating or liquidating financial institutions that were discussed will not be repeated here, but certain basic points will be emphasized. The first is that it is desirable to address the problems of financial institutions that are caused by nonperforming loans at an early rather than a late stage, to reduce the ultimate cost of restructuring. At an early stage, there may still be value in selling an institution stripped of its bad assets or an institution may be rehabilitated. Over time, the situation may deteriorate to the point where liabilities are at a higher cost, new loans are higher risk, and the cost of paying off depositors will be much greater.

A second point is that the segregation of bad assets in an institution that specializes in loan collection and asset dispositions may well result in higher recoveries than if nonperforming assets are left for collection by a depository institution. The use of liquidation specialists, bulk sales techniques, incentive compensation for asset brokers, and emphasis on net present value recoveries are all factors that are often lacking in a financial institution that originated a loan when it comes to loan collection or liquidation of collateral. A third point is that in countries where the government must bear the ultimate cost of failed financial institutions, governments should take bold steps to resolve failed institutions, including the provision of financial assistance for the purchase of financial institutions and financing of asset purchases.

It should also be noted that as a matter of policy, in almost all cases in situations involving a conservatorship and generally when any financial assistance is being extended by the government, as in the case of a bad bank like that of First City Bancorporation, the upper echelons of management of a troubled financial institution who presided over the unhappy state of affairs should be replaced. This includes officers as well as inside and outside directors. Discipline is an important part of financial restructuring and those who contributed importantly to or who had legal responsibility for an institution that was managed in an unsafe or unsound manner should be held accountable.

For countries contemplating restructuring financial institutions using some of the techniques discussed above, it is important that there be an adequate legal foundation. Thus, laws that allow the financial institution's supervisor to intervene and place an institution in conservatorship or receivership are required. In addition, to increase the prospect of recoveries on nonperforming loans, there should be a basis to execute upon assets of borrowers who are in default on their loans. Finally, it should be emphasized that it is crucial that governments establish sound bank supervision laws, regulations, and practices to assure that the problems that led to the need for major financial institutions restructuring will not arise again, or if they do, they will be more manageable.

Part IV

Role of the Central Bank in Economic Transition and Reform

16

Financial Sector Reform and Central Banking in Centrally Planned Economies

V. SUNDARARAJAN*

In centrally planned economies, economic reforms refer to measures aimed at decentralizing decision making on prices and quantities, and giving market forces a more active role. The objective of such reforms is to effect a more efficient allocation of resources and a better balance between supply and demand. Since the mid-1980s, financial sector reforms have become important components of this overall process of economic liberalization, and the accompanying stabilization programs.

The accelerating pace of financial sector reforms reflects the consideration that such reforms not only foster broader structural reforms of the nonfinancial sector but also provide the necessary support for macroeconomic stabilization, which is essential for the success of all structural reforms. For example, the development of commercial banks and other financial institutions that are autonomous, sound, competitive, and profit-oriented would facilitate decentralized decisions on credit allocation and enterprise restructuring in the face of major changes in relative profitability of firms that accompany price liberalization and stabilization policies. At the same time, the development of central banking in centrally planned economies introduces monetary policy as a new dimension of macroeconomic regulation, the rate of interest and the exchange rate as key instruments of stabilization policy and as components of pricing reforms, and prudential regulation as a new approach in fostering sound decisions on credit allocation and managing risk exposure.

*The author is Assistant Director in the Central Banking Department of the International Monetary Fund.

A typical initial step of recent financial reforms in these economies has been the shift from a monobank system to a two-tier banking system. This has been followed by different degrees of effort—depending on the country—to develop a more efficient framework for monetary management, to provide greater autonomy to central banks in macrostabilization efforts, to strengthen competition in the banking system, to build up a banking supervision system, to foster money and securities markets, and to streamline the payment system. While such efforts are found in the financial sector reforms of all developing countries, the particular structural features of centrally planned economies at the outset of reforms have posed special challenges in designing the specifics of reform measures and in the sequencing of these measures in coordination with other structural and stabilization policies.

This paper outlines some key aspects of recent financial sector reforms in centrally planned economies, based mainly on the experiences of four countries: Hungary, Poland, Czechoslovakia, and China. The experience of Yugoslavia is also covered in view of the broad similarities in issues relating to financial sector reforms. The paper is organized in seven sections. The first outlines as background the typical financial structure and policies of these economies prior to the reforms. The second describes issues in the transformation from a monobank to a two-tier banking system, and the role of central banks (and commercial banks) that emerged following such transformation. The third describes the issues in the design of a new monetary control system after the banking reform. The fourth describes the efforts to develop money and securities markets. The fifth outlines the status of reforms in banking supervision. The sixth considers the issues in reforming the payment system. And the last section offers some concluding remarks.

Typical Prereform Financial Structure and Policies

In a typical centrally planned economy, a state bank usually has a significant monopoly over banking and credit.[1] Under this "monotype system" there is no significant secondary credit expansion, but the monobank has unlimited capacity to create bank deposits. For exam-

[1]In contrast, the pre-reform banking system in Yugoslavia consisted of a large number of banks owned "socially"; that is, associations of workers in nonfinancial enterprises joined together to form each bank. In effect, banks were "owned" by enterprises. The state bank—the National Bank of Yugoslavia, and the national banks of the regions—was a major partner in extending credit to enterprises in selected sectors in the form of cofinancing (so-called refinancing) with individual commercial banks.

ple, the Soviet monetary system—emulated by many other centrally planned economies—has been a classic case of managed fiat money whose magnitude is determined directly by the state authority and effectively insulated from outside influences by a state monopoly over foreign exchange transactions. In addition, specialized financial institutions provide banking services to particular sectors but essentially channel credit to enterprises in these sectors in line with the directives specified by the central authorities.

There are two distinct and separate financial circuits in traditional centrally planned economies. One serves the household sector, which receives personal incomes in cash and effects payments for consumption in cash. The other serves enterprises that receive credit from banks and make payments to other enterprises and budget entities through current bank accounts, while paying wages and salaries in cash. Households can deposit funds (mainly in saving accounts) with the bank or banks serving the household sector, which also extend credit to the household sector. Private citizens, however, cannot invest in, or directly lend to state enterprises, or buy whatever is designated production input from these enterprises. Enterprises cannot acquire anything in retail outlets, with trivial exceptions. Banks (or other entities) serving households do not engage in transactions with state enterprises and vice versa, thus resulting in little competition for funds.[2]

The role of the monetary system is to finance the production plan; in essence the physical plan dictates a financial plan, decomposed into a budget, a credit plan, and a cash plan. Monetary policy is exercised through controlling the volume of credit to state enterprises and budget entities and making available the growth of cash in line with the planned gap between monetary receipts and outlays of the household sector. The state bank has little autonomy but is charged with monitoring the observance of the central plan by guaranteeing the enterprises the loans needed to carry out planned transactions and by seeing that these loans, and the enterprises' own deposits, are used only for those transactions. Every transaction of any importance, such as enterprise withdrawals of cash for wage purposes, must be effected through the drawing of a check on the state bank.

Given the reliance placed on the direct allocation of credit in a centrally planned economy, interest rates and the exchange rate have

[2]This was the case in Poland, Czechoslovakia, and Hungary until recently. In China and Yugoslavia, all banks—other than the state bank—were allowed to offer household deposits and limited types of loans to households. In all five countries, the payment system was segmented between households and enterprises by type of payment instruments and settlement arrangements.

virtually no allocative role. Credit is usually extended to enterprises at low fixed interest rates, with no tailoring of interest rate levels to repayment risks and maturities of particular loans. Also, interest rates offered on financial assets held by enterprises have been kept at relatively low levels and in many cases surplus funds have been siphoned off usually by ad hoc agreements with the government, and in some instances by high tax rates. As a result, there has been a strong tendency for enterprises to accumulate real assets (inventories, plant, and equipment) as opposed to acquiring financial assets.

Just as the cash plan and credit plan are companions to the physical input and output plans, so too are the foreign exchange and external borrowing and import plans. It is through these plans and attendant administrative controls that the economy is linked to the international economy. The exchange rate was mainly an accounting device to enable conversions between foreign and domestic prices to be made consistently.[3]

The dominance of state enterprises as borrowers from the banking system obscured issues of risk. Bankruptcy was not a relevant event and the ultimate owner of both enterprises and banks was the government. In China, this was the concept of "eating out of one big iron rice bowl." Any surplus of receipts over expenditures in the banking system was transferred to the government. Similarly, large transfers, including those of depreciation funds, were made by enterprises to the treasury, and the state budget was the predominant source of investment funds. Thus, financial policies and the absence of risk and accountability appear to have contributed to the "investment mania" of state enterprises in many centrally planned economies, which has co-existed with a relatively undeveloped network of financial institutions.

The Emergence of a New Banking Structure

The first important step in financial sector reforms is the transformation of an essentially monobank system to a two-tier banking system. In setting up a two-tier banking system, the state or national bank assumes the traditional central banking functions, focusing on regulating overall credit and interest rates, and divesting itself of deposit and loan transactions with households and enterprises, which are transferred to newly established banks (with existing specialized banks being granted greater autonomy). Examples of the recent creation of a

[3]The commercial exchange rate often did not suffice to translate foreign prices into domestic prices. Therefore, price equalization schemes were used to adjust transactions (border) prices to domestic prices.

two-tier banking system include China in 1984,[4] Hungary in 1987, the U.S.S.R. in 1988, Poland in 1989, and Czechoslovakia in 1990.

Yugoslavia has also been establishing a new banking system since early 1990, based on new central banking and banking laws that were enacted in mid-1989. The main motivation for the banking reform in Yugoslavia has been to strengthen the autonomy of the central bank, and to change the ownership structure and recapitalize the banking system, which carries a large portfolio of nonperforming loans estimated at 15 percent of gross social product.

The creation of a two-tier banking system called for the resolution of a host of legal and structural issues, many of which are still being decided. In formulating the new central banking and banking legislation, authorities had to decide on permissible banking functions (ranging from specialized to universal) permissible types of ownership structure for new banks, rules governing entry and exit of banks, the degree to which a central bank should retain autonomy over monetary policy and exercise supervisory functions, and the range of monetary policy instruments and prudential regulations.[5] Even prior to making these decisions, technical questions had to be answered on the number of new banks to be created, their size and regional distribution, the level and sources of capital for new banks, the distribution of weak loans among new banks, the redeployment of erstwhile state bank staff among new banks and their branches, the changes needed in the accounting and payments system arrangements, etc. In preparation for these decisions, most countries began maintaining separate accounts for commercial activities, note issue, and other central banking activities of the monobank for some years prior to the reforms. In Poland, a computer simulation was used, based on three variables (volume of transactions, volume of credits, and number of accounts) to decide on the number of banks and the number and location of branches of each bank, to be formed by regrouping the existing branches of the National Bank of Poland (NBP). In Hungary, enterprises in similar industries were assigned to the same bank, and this led to markedly different credit-to-deposit ratios among banks; some banks received a disproportionate share of doubtful loans. In China, the specialized banks were given a monopoly position with different

[4]Separate specialized banks were established in China in 1979/80, but the transformation of the People's Bank of China (PBC) into a separate central bank did not occur until 1984 when new legislation delineating the functions of the PBC and specialized banks was enacted.

[5]Many of these decisions have implied a reduction in the traditional dominance of the budget and planning authorities. The emergence of a new central bank and its assumption of the macroeconomic regulating functions has usually meant a redistribution of power, which has not always been easy.

groups of clients, which limited competition among the banks. In Czechoslovakia, two credit banks were created, one in each republic; while some of the long-term credits of the State Bank were shifted to the Investment Bank, which had only very limited credit activity prior to the reform.

The newly formed central banks assumed most of the traditional central banking functions, but certain differences among countries remained, reflecting both historical factors and the authorities' preferences. The National Bank of Hungary (NBH) initially retained both commercial and official transactions in foreign exchange, while the National Bank of Poland had only a limited role in such transactions, which were handled by a separate state-owned bank, Bank Handlowy.[6] In China, one of the specialized banks (the Bank of China) has continued to play the dominant role in external debt management and foreign exchange transactions. The banking supervision functions were assumed by the central banks in Poland, Czechoslovakia, Yugoslavia, and China, and by the Ministry of Finance in Hungary. The payments processing and settlement functions have been traditionally handled by the central banks in Poland, Czechoslovakia, and Hungary, but a separate institution has continued to perform this function in Yugoslavia.[7] The central banks continue to act as government debt managers and fiscal agents in Hungary, China, and Yugoslavia; while in Poland and Czechoslovakia the central bank is not involved so far in the management of domestic or external debt.[8]

In recent years, significant efforts have been made to strengthen the autonomy of the central banks in Hungary, Yugoslavia, Czechoslovakia, and Poland; related legal issues have been debated in China.[9] The National Bank of Yugoslavia was given significant additional powers to set monetary policy and exercise firm supervision of banks under the

[6]The NBH began to decentralize commercial foreign exchange transactions in late 1989. The NBP still maintains a sizable volume of foreign exchange deposits of individuals, but it did not provide commercial payment and collection services related to foreign trade, as in Hungary.

[7]This feature is being re-examined in Yugoslavia. In China, the clearing and settlement system is based on the exchange of payment orders between bank offices at clearinghouses organized at different geographic levels. The PBC monitors the clearinghouses but does not handle the paperwork itself.

[8]In Poland, a newly resuscitated state bank—the Bank for National Economy—which is chaired by the Minister of Finance, managed some initial issues of government domestic debt. The NBP is expected to take on a more active role in domestic debt management in due course. External debt in Poland is managed by a separate Foreign Debt-Servicing Fund (FOZZ), with Bank Handlowy as executing agent for service payments abroad.

[9]The powers of the PBC in regulating the specialized banks remain weak or ambiguous under the current banking legislation, which covers both the People's Bank and other specialized banks. The PBC has drafted extensive revisions to the regulations with the aim of strengthening the role of the central bank.

new legislation enacted in mid-1989. In Hungary, a new law, still under consideration strives to strengthen the appointment procedures for the board of management of the NBH, set limits on central bank credit to the government, and make it directly accountable to the Parliament. In Poland, following the political changes in mid-1989, major legal reforms were implemented, inter alia, to limit central bank credit to the government, reduce the scope of the credit plan, modify the statutory objectives of the NBP, and strengthen the NBP's powers in using indirect instruments of monetary control. In Czechoslovakia, the initial legislation that governed the creation of the two-tier banking system did not provide adequate autonomy to the central bank in setting interest rate policy; the devolution of powers between the center and the republics in various areas—particularly licensing, supervision and representation on the central bank board—remained to be further developed; and powers of banking supervision and monetary management were inadequate. New legislation under consideration addresses these issues.

Modernization of various functions of the newly formed central banks and the assumption of new functions, such as banking supervision and expanded role in foreign exchange operations,[10] necessarily implied a need for reorganization of the various departments, with attendant shifts in staff deployment, administrative arrangements, and information flows. The development of a new organizational structure that will ensure adequate vertical and horizontal communication from an earlier structure that was highly hierarchical has been a challenge that is currently being addressed in all countries. Another key issue in organizational reform related to the role of central bank branches, which has become a difficult issue in some countries (Czechoslovakia and China) owing to the attempts to exercise newly granted autonomy by local and republican governments.

As regards the activities of the newly established commercial banks,[11] their ability to compete for deposits and loans of nonbank entities were somewhat circumscribed owing to the large concentration of the banking industry that emerged, and various regulatory impediments which are being removed only gradually. The large concentration in the banking industry structure reflected mainly the dominance of many specialized banks that existed prior to the reform (Poland, China, Czechoslovakia, and Hungary) and an insufficient

[10]For example, in Poland and Czechoslovakia changes in exchange rate arrangements imply a greater role for the central bank in fostering and managing foreign exchange markets, and in managing international reserves.

[11]Including old banks re-established under a new legal and regulatory framework.

number of banks that were formed following the reform (Hungary and Czechoslovakia).[12] The restriction that an enterprise maintain only one basic account with a specified bank was also a factor limiting competition in the early stages of the reform in some countries. This restriction was eliminated in Poland in July 1989, and in Hungary in 1987.

While the system of specialized banks has continued, based on traditions and management inertia, the regulatory environment has been freed to permit freedom in lending, undertake a wide range of investments and services, and to foster a new range of financial institutions;[13] however, some of the regulated specializations were continued for a transitional period in Hungary. For example, the National Savings Bank, which specialized in household deposits and housing loans, was initially insulated from competition from newly established banks so as to ensure that the Savings Bank would have sufficient funds to continue making housing loans at low and fixed interest rates and to contain the interest subsidies for housing. The competition for household deposits was opened to all banks in 1989, following the transfer of low-interest housing loans to a separate agency. In contrast, the State Savings Bank in Poland and the savings banks in Czechoslovakia had to face competition immediately from other newly established banks for household deposits. The ability of others to compete has been limited by the vast network of branches and the dominant size of the savings banks. Also, the bank-specific ceilings on credit—which were used while new instruments were being developed—proved to be a disincentive to competition, both in Czechoslovakia and Poland.

In Yugoslavia, the domination of individual banks by enterprise groups, the regional concentration of banks in each associated group, and cartel arrangements until 1989, together limited competition for deposits and loans. Since early 1989, banks have been free to set interest rates, cartel arrangements have been eliminated, and the banking system is being restructured to promote better prudential safeguards and more effective competition.[14]

The newly established commercial banks in the centrally planned economies were technically autonomous in their loan and management decisions and were expected to pursue profits—instead of other nonpecuniary social objectives. Nevertheless, many factors—in addi-

[12]The share of the two largest banks in total assets of all commercial banks was 63 percent in Hungary, 76 percent in China and Poland, and 50 percent in Czechoslovakia.

[13]The specialized banks in China are not allowed to deal in securities, but can act as brokers.

[14]The number of banks was reduced by half from about 190 in mid-1989 to about 93 in mid-1990, through a process of mergers and bank closures.

tion to the highly concentrated banking structure—continue to hamper the autonomy and competitiveness of commercial banks: the large dependence of banks on central bank funds; the extensive reliance on interest subsidies from the budget or from preferential refinance; the large share of low-interest loans, particularly for housing; problem loans to state enterprises; the dominance of large state enterprises in the loan and deposit portfolio; and finally, the state ownership of most banks.[15] Of course, the relative importance of the above factors differs from country to country. Solutions to partially alleviate these problems are in various stages of formulation and implementation in many countries. The banking industry structure is, however, undergoing rapid transformation in many countries, notably Poland. Reflecting the liberal licensing policies, the number of licensed commercial banks has increased from 17 in mid-1989 to over 70 in late 1990.

Reforms of Monetary Management

The banking reform has been associated with major changes in the monetary policy framework and in the mix of instruments for monetary control. Significant efforts have been undertaken to strengthen the independence of central banks in formulating and implementing monetary policy in many centrally planned economies, with attendant implications for the power of the budgetary and planning authorities. The detailed credit plan and the cash plan are being replaced by various intermediate and operating targets of monetary policy, supported by appropriate monetary programming techniques. Currently, the instrument mix consists primarily of central bank refinancing quotas and bank-specific credit ceilings, supplemented as needed by reserve requirements, special deposits with the central bank, and issues of treasury or central bank securities. Also, interest rate policies have been given a greater role to influence financial savings and to induce more efficient use of capital. In addition, policies have been implemented in Poland and Hungary to replace the system of automatic provision of central bank credit to government (often at zero interest) by a strengthened strategy for domestic debt management. Monetary control has been complicated by the uneven structure of the banking system, the growing role of foreign currency deposits in some centrally planned economies, and the interest-inelastic loan de-

[15]Under state ownership, the longer-term goals of building a stronger capital base and strengthening the institutional life of banks may lack operational meaning, unless the state-owned bank is given significant autonomy and is held accountable for clearly specified commercial objectives. Such "corporatization" of state economic activities could be seen as a desirable transition phase before full privatization.

mand.[16] Moreover, the effectiveness of interest rate policy in inducing efficiency has been constrained in the initial stages by weak financial discipline of enterprises, and by major distortions in relative prices owing to incomplete price reforms.

The design of monetary policy instruments has been influenced by the structure of the banking industry following institutional reforms in Czechoslovakia, Poland, and Hungary, a structure characterized by an uneven distribution of deposits and credits. This uneven distribution resulted in a large dependence on central bank refinance for many banks,[17] particularly the new ones and for the system as a whole, large variations among banks in the share of refinance to total liabilities, and the co-existence of a limited number of large surplus banks. The large dependence of the newly created banks on central bank refinance reflected in the first instance the surplus of credits over deposits transferred from the monobank; however, this circumstance derives, in the final analysis, from the lack of well-developed interbank markets, the role of the central bank in recycling surplus funds of some banks, and in some cases, simply the excessive creation of credits by the erstwhile monobank.

These institutional features have implications for the design of monetary policy instruments. Given the structural and uneven dependence on refinance, the refinance policies—the interest rates on refinance, and the method of distributing aggregate refinance among the banks—had a far-reaching impact not only on the effectiveness of monetary control but also on the structure of the banking industry, and on the evolution of the interbank and money markets.[18] In Yugoslavia, Hungary, and Poland, refinance policies have emerged as the major instrument to influence market-determined deposit and lending rates and the growth in monetary aggregates. Indeed, incor-

[16]Interest-inelastic loan demand in centrally planned economies in the past reflects the continuation of a soft budget constraint that condones financial undiscipline by firms that cannot go bankrupt. Also, in the absence of realistic exchange and interest rates, burgeoning foreign liabilities and foreign currency deposits of residents create large solvency risks for banks, which are realized when a more appropriate exchange rate policy is adopted.

[17]In 1989, claims of the central bank on the deposit money banks formed 39 percent of total credit in Poland, 28 percent in China, and 24 percent in Hungary. For the newly created banks, the share is much higher in all countries. The share of central bank credit to banks was only 11 percent of total bank credit in Czechoslovakia, but this was because the gap between loans and deposits of the newly created banks was closed in part by arranging large interbank deposits from savings banks, with a matching reduction in savings banks' deposits at the central bank. Such interbank deposits constituted 28 percent of total credit of all banks.

[18]The highly uneven distribution of deposits and credits also influenced the design and operations of reserve requirements and open market-type operations. In particular, it became difficult to adopt a uniform reserve requirement ratio, to adjust the ratio flexibly, and to develop competitive auction markets among banks alone.

rect settings of the refinance volume—often based on the projected gap between deposits and credits instead of appropriate reserve money programming—fueled inflationary pressures in the period following the banking reform in Hungary and Poland.

Also, the design of refinance policy, and in particular the procedures for the allocation of refinance among banks, has posed difficult questions in part because of weaknesses in interbank markets and other structural factors, as explained below.[19]

In Hungary, the aggregate refinance quota was distributed to individual banks in two tranches as a multiple of capital, and this allocation did not match the initial gap between deposits and credits of individual banks following the reform. As a result, there were significant pressures to extend special liquidity credits from the central bank, which further weakened monetary control in the initial stages of the reform. The first tranche ("overdrafts") of the short-term refinance quota was accessible automatically at a basic refinance rate, while the size of the second tranche ("supplementary facility") was adjusted from time to time for monetary policy purposes and was available at higher rates. In addition, special "liquidity" loans were introduced in February 1988 to meet structural dependence on refinance. Subsequently, however, active long-term interbank markets and loan syndications emerged, and competition for deposits became intense at times as refinance limits were progressively reduced in 1988. Since early 1989, the second tranche of refinance has been eliminated and consideration is now being given to allocation based on auctions.

In Poland, where the dependence on refinance is much larger than in Hungary, an application of uniform criteria (such as capital or deposits) for allocating refinance quotas (or market-based allocation such as auctions) proved difficult to implement because the needed redistribution of funds through the interbank market was regarded as too large for the nascent money market to handle. As a result, the authorities initially relied on bank-specific agreements to distribute refinance according to projected needs. Subsequently, refinance limits for individual banks were reduced on a case-by-case basis in response to availability of bank reserves from external surpluses. In addition, a payment credit facility was introduced to deal with shortfalls in the clearing accounts of banks, and banks have been offered a bill rediscount facility to encourage a bill market, and a medium-term refinance facility to meet structural needs.

[19]The discussion below refers to refinance facilities operated by the central bank for monetary policy purposes and excludes the selective refinance facilities and facilities to on-lend funds borrowed abroad.

In Yugoslavia, the allocation was based on refinance proportions applied to specific categories of loans, and this served to support regional development but did not provide adequate control over the total volume of refinance. A reform of this system was introduced in 1990 based on bank-specific refinance quotas (allocated based on historical use) within which applicable refinance proportions could be utilized. Further reforms of this system are under consideration.

In Czechoslovakia, the initial refinance credit—arising from the need to close the gap between deposits (both customer deposits and interbank deposits) and loans of newly created banks—was structured as a long-term loan. However, reserve requirements were imposed at a high enough level to force commercial banks to borrow to meet the reserve requirements. It is planned to meet this borrowing requirement by a short-term refinance facility and a bill rediscount facility.

While interest rates have been liberalized in Yugoslavia and Poland, significant controls remain in China, Czechoslovakia, and Hungary. As is to be expected, the refinance rate became the key interest rate influencing or guiding the deposit and lending rates in Hungary, Poland, Czechoslovakia, and Yugoslavia. As part of stabilization measures, real interest rates were increased substantially, and in some countries to positive real levels. The scope for active management of interest rates, and the effectiveness of such management is constrained by both structural and policy factors. First, the level and structure of interest rates has been influenced by the high degree of concentration of the banking structure, by the large share of loans at low and fixed interest rates in most countries, and by the massive volume of nonperforming loans in Yugoslavia. Second, the allocative effects of interest rate policy are weakened by the lack of interest sensitivity of nonbanks (and hence banks' derived demand for refinance) in all countries reflecting financial undiscipline, incomplete price reforms, and slow progress in restructuring enterprises and establishing accountability for profits. Finally, flexible management of interest rates has proved difficult in the absence of market-based instruments of monetary control, which are being developed despite the presence of the above structural constraints.

Many of these constraints are being addressed as part of the ongoing program of structural reforms. In particular, the authorities are either implementing or considering various methods to deal with the large volume of loans at low and fixed interest rates in major financial institutions, which has weakened interest rate policy and stabilization efforts. Similar but more complex problems arise with regard to the large volume of nonperforming loans in all countries, particularly Yugoslavia.[20]

In both Poland and Hungary, the large stock of housing loans of long maturity (30–40 years) at low and fixed nominal rates (1–6 percent) on the books of the savings banks has complicated monetary management and stabilization efforts. The recent increases in nominal interest rates on deposits for stabilization purposes resulted in either a large increase in budgetary outlays for interest subsidy or a significant distortion of interest rates on deposits and general loans of the largest banks (with a dominant share in the deposit market) that have carried the low-interest housing loan portfolio. A solution to this problem of "old" credits at fixed rates therefore became urgent. For this reason, on January 1, 1989, the Hungarian authorities formed a separate Housing Fund to which the "old" housing credit portfolio has been transferred, relieving the banking system of the burden of such credits and replacing such credits with government-guaranteed securities (issued by the Housing Fund) at negotiated rates.[21]

In Poland, new interest rates were applied to the old credits,[22] but only a part of the interest payments was serviced by the end-users of credit. The remainder was partly met by budgetary subsidies to end-users, and partly by mandated capitalization of interest. This approach served to freeze the sectoral distribution of bank credit, particularly when nominal interest rates were high.

The sharp growth in foreign currency deposits of households (and also enterprises in some countries) in the domestic banking system has posed special challenges to the implementation of monetary policy in Poland and Yugoslavia. A major problem has been the significant short-run shifts in the demand for domestic currency assets and in the national currency money multiplier, owing to changes in exchange rate expectations and the consequent substitution between domestic and foreign currency deposits. Also, the sizable foreign currency exposure of the banking system has led to large losses or reduced profits, and at the same time, currency depreciations have

---

[20]In Yugoslavia, a separate federal government agency has been created to take over and manage problem loans of banks, following detailed portfolio audits of banks.

[21]The deficit of the Housing Fund is to be covered by the budget. The issue of how to finance the losses of the Housing Fund has to be resolved. Various tax-based solutions with the incidence of the tax targeted to fall primarily on the beneficiaries of housing loans were under consideration. Simultaneously, all banks were freed to compete for household deposits, but ceilings on household deposit rates were imposed to contain the budgetary impact of interest subsidy on new housing loans. While new housing loans carry market-related rates, a part of the debt service is met through budgetary subsidies.

[22]This required a change in the laws on credit relationships so as to modify the fixed-rate contracts on the old credits to preferential sectors.

also resulted in large valuation losses, which have the potential to lead to massive monetary expansion. Various approaches to dealing with these problems have figured prominently in the debate on financial sector reforms.[23] A lasting solution to these problems requires financial policies that must ensure that local currency deposits yield more than foreign currency ones on a sustained basis. The approaches to dealing with prudential aspects of the problem have included the replacement of accumulated foreign exchange losses by income-earning securities issued by the government (e.g., Yugoslavia), a strengthening of prudential regulations pertaining to foreign exchange transactions and the imposition of foreign exchange exposure limits.

Money and Securities Markets

While unregulated markets in inter-enterprise credits have been a source of disintermediation and prudential risks in most centrally planned economies (and Yugoslavia's), attempts to evolve a regulatory framework for short-term money markets have been quite recent. Indeed, until recently, money and securities markets were discouraged in the these economies owing to concerns that such markets would interfere with the credit plan. Some preliminary measures to stimulate money and interbank markets have been implemented in Poland, Hungary, and Yugoslavia. Treasury bills were introduced in Hungary in 1988, and in Poland in late 1989. Since mid-1990, the National Bank of Poland has begun issuing its own bills on an auction basis for monetary policy purposes. A new law adopted in 1985 created a basis for the issue and trading of commercial bills in Hungary. In Poland, the Bill of Exchange Act was revived and the bill as a credit instrument has been introduced since December 1, 1989, after a hiatus of nearly forty years. The rediscounting of specified bills of exchange is being used both in Hungary and Poland as a means to stimulate the use of this instrument. In Yugoslavia, the negotiable bills of exchange with bank guarantees have been discontinued owing to major defaults experienced recently, and a completely new legal and institutional framework has been introduced since November 1989. The new framework combines a centralized money market that provides brokerage services with decentralized over-the-counter transactions and allows for the future development of new money market instruments and institutional practices. In China, interbank and money markets

[23]These problems are not unique to centrally planned economies. Similar problems have been addressed in Ghana, Venezuela, and Egypt as part of stabilization and structural reforms.

are not well developed;[24] new laws to regulate securities markets are being formulated.

The money and interbank markets in most centrally planned economies remain thin, illiquid, and highly segmented. The volume of long-term interbank loans (three months and above) rose rapidly in Hungary, mainly to fund customer loans in the face of an allocation criteria for refinance that did not match the loan-deposit gap of each bank. The recent growth of interbank transactions in Poland reflected a tightening of refinance policies, while some banks were building up excess reserves. In China, interbank markets have been impeded in part by local political interference to interregional mobility of funds. The interbank markets in Yugoslavia are highly segmented, based mainly on transactions between banks within each republic. The volume of interbank transactions has been thin owing to the automatic and liberal access to refinance windows of the National Bank of Yugoslavia. In all these countries, short-term and liquid money and interbank markets have not yet evolved, reflecting uncertainties in the settlement system for payments, lack of high quality paper for trading among money market participants of diverse credit standing, and the absence of active liquidity management by the central banks. Many of these issues are being addressed.

The legal framework for bond markets has been strengthened in all countries in recent years, and varying degrees of progress have been achieved in promoting enterprise and government bond issues. Enterprise bond issues were liberalized in Hungary during 1985–87, and secondary market arrangements were also established, although such markets have become fairly thin since 1987 owing to insufficient adjustments in bond prices to reflect increases in market interest rates. In China, government bonds have been sold since 1981 at uncompetitive rates on the basis of administrative allocation primarily to households and to enterprises; also, in recent years, enterprise bonds with a profit-sharing feature and bank bonds have grown rapidly. Since 1989, a secondary market has emerged in long-term government securities held by households. Long-term bond markets have not yet developed in Poland and Yugoslavia, where outstanding issues are fairly small. In 1990, the Polish Government sold limited amounts of special medium-term, indexed bonds that are convertible into shares of newly privatized companies. A significant growth in the

[24]In China, in addition to interbank deposits, bankers' acceptances and commercial papers are also traded in the money markets. For example, the Short-Term Funds Adjustment Centers sponsored by the PBC facilitate such trades, while most money market transactions occur over the telephone.

Polish bill and bond markets is expected from treasury issues in 1991. In Czechoslovakia, newly established commercial banks have issued medium-term bonds mainly to test the market.

As regards the equity market, the legal framework and the institutional arrangements are still in the preparatory stages in many centrally planned economies (with the exception of Hungary and Yugoslavia) and further progress will depend mainly on the legal clarification of permissible forms of ownership, and the speed with which privatization and diversification of state enterprises can proceed.

Banking Supervision—Slow Progress

The introduction of effective banking supervision has not kept pace with the rapid developments in the banking system. This reflected weaknesses in the legislation (China, and Yugoslavia until recently), protracted debates on the appropriate role and structure of banking supervision (Poland until mid-1989, and Czechoslovakia more recently), and limited resources devoted to the supervision function (Hungary). The need to adapt the traditional accounting concepts to the needs of a market-oriented economy, and difficulty in building up staff with the requisite training also slowed the development of supervisory systems.

Following the banking reform, supervisory functions have consisted primarily of specifying some prudential regulations, off-site monitoring of compliance with regulations based on periodic reports, and audit requirements in some centrally planned economies.[25] Comprehensive and regular on-site examinations have not been developed, and examination of asset quality and financial analysis of banks remain to be developed in most of these economies. In Hungary, the State Bank Supervision Department of the Ministry of Finance has built up an off-site monitoring system, based on a set of prudential regulations covering capital adequacy, liquidity, loans to large customers, and profitability. Based on additional supervisory powers granted by the new legislation, the National Bank of Yugoslavia has also set up regulations on risk exposure, capital adequacy, investment limits, liquidity, and licensing, and has begun to strengthen banking supervision within the National Bank. In Poland, banking supervision was assigned to a separate body within the National Bank—General Inspectorate of Banks—that reports directly to the President of the

[25]The People's Bank of China is legally required to audit all financial institutions. In Yugoslavia, the Social Accounting Service audits and monitors liquidity of both financial and nonfinancial enterprises and reports to the central bank. Poland and Czechoslovakia have no specific audit requirements.

NBP. Its initial tasks included the development of a new chart of accounts for the commercial banks, establishment of new prudential regulations and reporting systems for banks, and the setting up of financial analysis procedures. Skills in on-site inspection are being developed concurrently. In Czechoslovakia, some prudential regulations have been issued, a new chart of accounts for banks is under preparation, and a banking supervision department is being established and staffed. The role of the People's Bank of China in the prudential supervision of specialized banks has been fairly limited. The specialized banks have to provide the People's Bank of China with information, to set aside reserves for bad debts as determined by the People's Bank, and are required to be audited by them to ensure compliance with financial policy regulations.

The implementation of prudential supervision has been complicated by many structural factors, some purely technical. The difficult macroeconomic decisions on how to absorb the losses due to bad loans and foreign exchange exposure, and the inadequacies of loan recovery and bankruptcy laws all complicate prudential controls in many centrally planned economies. The large share of nonperforming loans in total assets of Yugoslav banks has made it difficult to implement prudential rules until the banks and their customers are rehabilitated and recapitalized, as needed, and the concept of ownership has been clarified in the law. Other technical factors that have complicated the application of prudential norms include: the dominance of large loan or deposit customers in many countries, the limited scope for raising capital in most centrally planned economies—other than through budgetary appropriations for state-owned banks—and the absence of reliable accounting standards and loan monitoring systems in commercial banks.

Payment System Reforms

The settlement systems for payments are usually on a gross (item-by-item) basis, with no netting or subclearing arrangements. Even when subclearing takes place at regional or provincial levels, the systems as operated are in effect on a gross basis, reflecting the practice of checking the legality of each payment, and could be characterized as continuous settlement systems with no third-party guarantees. The payment system is governed by detailed regulations on the use of cash, on the use of payment orders or settlement checks, and on the priorities in payments if an agent has insufficient funds to meet all payments issued by him. The settlement systems in Yugoslavia and Czechoslovakia are technologically sophisticated, involving paperless electronic transfers of payment instructions. Hungary has only recently introduced automation in processing payments; however, both China and Poland still rely mainly on postal or telegraphic services to transmit payment lists. In all countries, except Yugoslavia, the banking reform itself has called for changes in settlement arrangements to reflect the new reserve maintenance rules established for the new banking system, to make further distinctions between inter- and intra-bank transactions, and to handle the increased volume of payment traffic due to greater mobility of funds.

The lack of clearing arrangements, the delays in transmitting information, and the preoccupation of the system with the legality of payments more than the speed of delivery of good funds have created large uncertainties (float) in the amount of banks' clearing account balances, and have distorted monetary statistics, and prudential returns. The issue of designing new and more efficient clearing systems, for example, with national and regional clearinghouses, and of upgrading technology to speed up payments and to meet new business requirements are being implemented in Poland, Czechoslovakia, and China. The delineation of the precise role of the central bank in the new payments system, given the traditional dominance of the erstwhile monobank on all aspects of the system (clearing, accounting, and technology), has posed complex technical and institutional issues.

Concluding Remarks

The banking and monetary policy reforms in the centrally planned economies have promoted greater interest rate flexibility and have assigned a more important role to financial policies in macrostabilization efforts. The initial experiences with these reforms have been generally favorable in fostering greater competition in the banking system and improving the efficiency of banking services. Nevertheless, significant impediments to competition still remain. Efforts to strengthen the autonomy of central banks in monetary policy formulation and implementation have also gained momentum in many of these economies. While much progress has been made to adapt the new monetary control instruments to the structure of the banking industry, considerable scope remains to develop market-oriented instruments of monetary policy based on active money markets and an efficient settlement system. The development of money and interbank markets and of an efficient settlement system should remain high on the agenda of financial sector reforms, owing to their impact on the effectiveness of monetary policies. The prudential supervision of banks is still in its infancy in most centrally planned economies. The appropriate strategy to develop further this function, including the appropriate balance between supervisory controls and competitive freedom, is still to be resolved. There is, however, an increasing recognition that key prudential accounting standards can contribute to an effective implementation of adjustment and structural reform policies by fostering sound lending practices and expediting enterprise restructuring.

Financial sector reforms are being implemented in a period of significant instability in the macroeconomic environment, weakness in balance of payments, and major distortions in relative prices and investment allocation. The need to implement stabilization policies, financial sector reforms, and other structural reforms raises complex questions regarding the appropriate sequencing of financial sector reforms in coordination with macroeconomic adjustment, price, exchange rate, and enterprise reform policies.

The interactions among policy measures are close. On the one hand, it would seem that since financial sector reforms are intended, among other things, to create conditions for more effective monetary control and more efficient credit allocation, they should be implemented expeditiously. On the other hand, the achievement of macroeconomic stability supported by parallel reforms in other sectors is essential for the effectiveness of financial sector reforms, particularly for the effectiveness of interest rate policies. For example, a restructuring of weak enterprises—initially at least the major loss makers—would be necessary to ensure that the demand for credit is sufficiently sensitive to interest rates and that interest rate policies prove effective in promoting stability and growth. An efficient restructuring of enterprises, based on decentralized decision making by banks and their customers, requires reasonable stability in the macro environment and a realistic structure of relative prices and interest rates. In the course of bringing about stability and relative price adjustments, the banking system gets exposed to much greater risks than would be the case in a more stable environment. Therefore, proper supervision of banks and continued strengthening of their financial condition are needed to preserve the soundness of banking operations and to prevent crises.

In view of such close interaction between financial sector reforms, other structural reforms, and adjustment policies, the design of growth-oriented stabilization programs should incorporate a package of structural components right at the outset. This package should include, among other things, a minimal program of enterprise restructuring, price (including the exchange rate) reform, and specific reforms in monetary management, money market development, and banking supervision, all to be put in motion right at the beginning of the stabilization program. The stage would then be set for effective stabilization and would facilitate further structural reforms.

Following the initial implementation of such a package, more comprehensive restructuring of banks and enterprises, and further financial system reforms can proceed more effectively. The losses associated with past bad debts, undue risk, and exposure do exist and must be removed. Ultimately, the costs will be born by the general population—the key is to share the burden of the major losses. How to do so is best addressed by developing appropriate institutional arrangements and financial policies to recapitalize banks and deal with problem loans and enterprises. Such arrangements should be designed to make the magnitude of the problems transparent, avoid shifting the losses to the central bank, and promote effective loan recovery and industrial restructuring. Such considerations apply to all countries facing macroeconomic instability and significant structural distortions. What distinguishes the case of most centrally planned economies is the large one-time adjustments of relative prices, institutional arrangements, and consequential changes in economic values that are being pursued in order to correct the past misallocations sustained through long-term isolation from the international economy.

17

The Evolving Role of the Central Bank in China

TOMÁS J.T. BALIÑO*

The role of the central bank in China has undergone major changes since 1979. These changes were part of the reform process that introduced a significant number of market elements in the functioning of China's economy. The reform has been gradual and has involved a lot of experimentation. In the financial sector, including the People's Bank of China (PBC), the process of reform has had similar characteristics.

This paper presents a brief review of the broad economic reforms that have taken place in China and then focuses on the evolution of the financial sector and the role of the PBC. In this context, it discusses key issues that had to be addressed, such as the importance of financial reform in the economic reform process, the degree of independence of the central bank, the choice of monetary targets and instruments, and the need to reform bank supervision.

Broad Economic Reforms

In 1979, China started an economic reform process that endeavored to increase economic efficiency by allowing market forces to become a major determinant of resource allocation and consequently reduce the role of the central plan. Various forms of property ownership, including private ownership, were allowed, but public ownership

*The author is Division Chief in the Central Banking Department of the International Monetary Fund. This paper was prepared while he was a member of the Asian Department. The author wishes to thank Ms. Linda M. Koenig and Messrs. Martin J. Fetherston and Michael W. Bell for their comments and assistance.

remained dominant; the role of economic incentives was stressed, thus transferring a much greater degree of influence to the price mechanism. The economy was opened to the rest of the world.

Reform covered enterprise management, rural and industrial development, financial intermediation, and public finance. Starting in agriculture, and spreading to urban industry, production units have been granted more autonomy, including in price setting. A "two-track" system of price determination has evolved, under which one set of prices is negotiated with the state and another, for production in excess of quota, is market determined. For the past four years, a dual exchange market has been in place. It includes an official segment at a fixed exchange rate and a segment with somewhat freer access in which the rate is allowed to vary.

Greater decentralization of government functions has accompanied the reform process; local and provincial authorities have been allowed to play a larger role in economic decision making than before the reform.

Financial Institutions and Monetary Policy Before the Reform

Before the reform, the main task of financial institutions and monetary policy was to ensure the fulfillment of the production targets embodied in the central plan. The banking system was centralized in the PBC, a monobank that combined the functions of the central and commercial banks. All specialized banks were part of the PBC, except for the Bank of China, which was responsible for foreign exchange operations.

As in other prereform centrally planned economies, monetary policy was entirely passive or accommodative and relied on two planning frameworks: the credit plan and the cash plan. The *credit plan* was the financial counterpart of the production plan, determining the amount of credit to be allocated to each enterprise. Enterprises were obliged to remit all surplus funds to the central government. All investment was financed through the budget. Thus, bank credit to enterprises financed working capital requirements only. The PBC also provided credit to the budget on several occasions. Credit to enterprises was viewed as noninflationary (because it was backed by commodity flows), while credit to the budget was viewed as inflationary. This distinction was reflected in the fact that only the former was included in the credit plan.

The *cash plan* was determined by the planning authorities and was designed to supply the amount of currency needed for wages and for agricultural procurement by the state. The plan reflected the separate circuits that existed for enterprises, on the one hand, and for households and agricultural producers, on the other. Enterprises had to carry out most of their transactions through bank transfers. They could use their bank deposits to settle only transactions authorized by the production plan. Moreover, their use of currency was strictly regulated. Households could hold cash and savings deposits only; they could not have checking accounts and had no access to credit. Therefore, currency was the only asset that provided freely usable purchasing power, which made its control through the cash plan so important.

The arrangements outlined above provided for a very limited role for monetary policy—and hence for an independent central bank—in economic management. The PBC thus participated in the formulation of the credit plan and was responsible for its implementation but did not set its own monetary targets. Moreover, with regard to the cash plan, it could only monitor its execution and provide warnings when deviations occurred, since it had no control over the transactions that led to the creation and absorption of currency.

Financial Reform in the 1980s

China carried out substantial financial reform over the past decade. Commercial banking functions were gradually separated from the PBC, which became a full-fledged central bank in 1984. Four specialized banks—Industrial and Commercial Bank of China (ICBC), Agricultural Bank of China (ABC), People's Construction Bank of China (PCBC), and the Bank of China (BOC), for handling foreign exchange transactions—were established to deal with different economic sectors, although some degree of competition among them was increasingly permitted. Over time, additional financial institutions came into operation: two universal banks at the national level, local commercial banks, nonbank financial institutions, development banks, urban credit cooperatives (a network of rural credit cooperatives has existed since the prereform period), and finance companies.

The PBC After the Reform

The functions and responsibilities of the PBC have come to resemble more closely those of a central bank in market economies. It formulates financial policy, determines interest rates, issues currency, and formulates and implements credit policy. It supervises bank and nonbank financial institutions. It acts as banker to the government by managing the state treasury. It is the custodian of the official foreign currency reserves. And last but not least, it acts as banker to banks by extending advances, rediscounting and refinancing to the specialized banks, and providing banking services such as clearance.

The degree of development of these functions varies: some, like currency issue, are fully developed; others, such as prudential bank supervision, have not began as yet. In addition to the foregoing functions, the PBC has occasionally been called on to perform others that would not normally be associated with a central bank, such as direct lending to selected projects.

While China has not passed yet a central bank law,[1] the PBC's position within the state institutions is defined in the "Provisional Regulations of the People's Republic of China on the Control of Banks," promulgated in 1986, whose Article 5 reads: "The People's Bank of China is the State organ through which the State Council leads and controls the fiscal affairs of the nation, and is the central bank of the State . . ." Thus, final authority on major financial decisions rests with the State Council rather than the PBC.

The PBC has a large number of branches, which have been subject to "dual leadership": the head office of the PBC and the provincial authorities. The shift of commercial banking responsibilities from the PBC to other banks has resulted in a reduction in the number of its branches and staff: in 1979 it had 15,000 branches and subbranches and a staff of over a quarter of a million; by the late 1980s it had reduced its branches to about 2,500 and reduced its staff by about two thirds. Despite this reduction, the number of branches and, more important, their powers to act independently from head office have exceeded what is typical in market economies.

Issues Faced by the PBC

The reform process transformed the responsibilities of the PBC from providing passive financing for plan transactions to playing a key role in macroeconomic management. This posed several major issues for the PBC: On what monetary targets should it focus? What techniques and instruments should it use to attain those targets? What should be the relationships between the PBC's head office and its branches, and between them and the rest of the financial system? What should be the roles of the market and of the PBC (or the Plan) in

[1]This reflects the authorities' desire to gain experience in the workings of the financial system after the reform before drafting final legislation.

allocating credit across sectors? And how should the PBC supervise the banking system?

Monetary Policy and Instruments

The economic reform process, by decentralizing decision making among economic agents, has made the economy more responsive to changes in the monetary policy stance. Therefore, the variability in growth of monetary aggregates that was observed in the postreform period had significant effects on growth, inflation, and the balance of payments. Some of that variability reflected periodic changes in the priority that the State Council assigned to various economic objectives, which limited the PBC's ability to focus on macroeconomic stability, and some reflected the challenge of reforming monetary policy instruments. The reform, by increasing the financial autonomy of enterprises, made currency targeting increasingly less relevant and targeting broader aggregates (such as broad money and domestic credit) more important.

The annual credit plan and the cash plan have nevertheless remained the central elements in the formulation of monetary policy. But whereas formerly the credit plan was driven almost exclusively by the financial needs of the physical plan, now the PBC incorporates macroeconomic criteria (objectives for growth, inflation, and balance of payments overall position) in determining the permissible credit expansion. Moreover, while the cash plan still exists, the PBC no longer focuses its attention exclusively on currency but also on broader monetary aggregates. To supplement the credit plan, a general financial program was introduced in 1989. It consolidates the lending carried out by all financial institutions and also covers credits for budget financing.

The PBC relied on both direct and indirect *monetary instruments* to carry out monetary policy after the reform. *Credit ceilings* have been the main direct monetary instrument. The credit plan establishes such ceilings for each specialized bank, which in turn sets a ceiling for each of its branches. The intensity with which these ceilings have been enforced has varied, depending largely on the overall monetary policy stance. While these ceilings have been effective in targeting credit aggregates, they introduce distortions in the financial system. As of March 1989, the credit plan was extended to all financial institutions, except financial leasing companies. The PBC has also created some *indirect monetary instrument*, which have gained in importance over time. Three of them are discussed below.

Reserve requirements. Banks must redeposit with the PBC a certain fraction of their deposits. Until 1985, the ratios were relatively high and differed substantially according to the type of bank. They were then unified and lowered substantially: set at 10 percent in 1985, they have been gradually raised to stand at 14 percent in 1990. While rural and urban credit cooperatives must observe the same reserve requirement as banks, their reserve balances must be maintained with the ABC and ICBC and other banks, respectively. In addition, in 1989 the PBC required financial institutions to keep excess reserves at a minimum of 5 to 7 percent of deposits.

Interest rates. Until 1988, adjustments were infrequent despite changing economic circumstances (especially inflation rates). Recently, interest rates have been moved relatively frequently and the yield on long-term savings deposits is now guaranteed to be at least equal to inflation. Institutions have been given somewhat greater latitude in determining their own rates.

PBC lending to specialized banks. This lending finances about one third of specialized banks' loans. While potentially a most important tool of monetary targeting, the existence of credit ceilings has limited its usefulness.

Relationship Between the Head Office and Branches of the PBC

The relationship between the PBC head office and its branches has been a major issue in the adaptation of the PBC's structure to the postreform situation. The "dual leadership" concept and the powers vested in the branches created some difficulties. In particular, the fact that PBC branches could extend credit on their own to the corresponding branches of specialized banks weakened the PBC's grasp on the supply of credit. In 1988, two important steps were taken to increase the control of the PBC's head office over its branches. First, the power of the branches to extend credit on their own was sharply curtailed. Second, the PBC's head office was empowered to appoint the managers of its branches.

Sectoral Credit Allocation

The Chinese authorities have been balancing two objectives in credit allocation: ensuring that "priority" sectors and projects get financing, and allowing financial institutions greater freedom in credit allocation. These objectives have conflicted in many instances, which has resulted in changes in regulations and practices. The PBC has been involved in the sectoral credit allocation, including at times through direct lending to specific projects.

Bank Supervision

The "Provisional Regulations of the People's Republic of China on the Control of Banks," mentioned above, vest in the PBC the power to supervise, regulate, and inspect financial institutions. The PBC has delegated some supervisory powers with regard to rural and urban credit cooperatives on the ABC and ICBC, respectively. The focus of regulations so far has been on compliance with financial regulations, rather than on prudential supervision.

Some Lessons from the PBC Experience

While financial reform in China has not been completed yet, the experience accumulated so far makes it possible to show some important lessons: (1) Market-oriented reform entails decentralization of decision making in the economy. At the same time, preserving macroeconomic stability in this context requires strong central institutions and instruments of macroeconomic management. (2) The central bank should have full powers, at the head-office level, to adopt the monetary policy decisions that are required to attain the broader economic goals of the government. (3) Monetary targets and instruments may need to be changed or reformulated in order to be effective under the new circumstances. For instance in China's case, targeting a broad monetary aggregate became much more important after the reform than before the reform. (4) In order to reap the benefits of the economic reform, the central bank should replace direct controls with indirect monetary instruments that increase the efficiency of the financial system while allowing the attainment of the monetary targets. (5) There is likely to be a conflict between credit allocation according to plan priorities and credit allocation according to market criteria. Resolving the conflict in an efficient way may require adopting decisions in areas (such as pricing) that go beyond financial sector policies. (6) Bank supervision needs to be broadened to include prudential supervision, in addition to checking compliance with financial regulations. This becomes more urgent to preserve the soundness of a two-tier banking system as enterprise reform makes progress and enterprises are allowed to fail.

18

The National Bank of Poland: A Central Bank in Transition

ANDRZEJ OLECHOWSKI*

In September 1989, a government took office in Poland that was determined to move the economy as quickly as possible to a market base. The economic program launched in January 1990 was unprecedented among centrally planned economies in scope and speed. It aimed simultaneously at stabilizing the economy and setting in motion market-oriented reforms. The program assumed quite radical changes in the conduct of monetary policy and the commercial orientation of the banking system.

For two years now, it has been my privilege to be involved in this economic reform, particularly as it concerns the transformation and modernization of the National Bank of Poland. I consider it a great honor to have been invited to share with you some experiences of a central bank in transition.

My remarks are organized in three sections: the past, the present, and the future of the National Bank.

The Past

The relevant past for the purposes of these remarks starts in the late 1940s and early 1950s, when the financial system of Poland was modeled after the socialist prototype of the U.S.S.R. The outcome was a strikingly simple financial system. Despite four specialized banks, it was effectively a monobanking system dominated by the National

*The author was First Deputy President of the National Bank of Poland at the time he gave this address to the Central Banking Seminar. He is currently State Secretary in the Ministry for Foreign Trade.

Bank of Poland. In 1987, the National Bank operated 732 bank branches out of a country-wide total of 808 (not counting some 1,160 cooperative banks). A savings bank department in the National Bank monopolized the collection of household deposits. Money and capital markets did not exist, and the only financial instruments available were currency and deposits.

This simple structure served to facilitate the National Bank's main function, which was to help implement the central economic plan. The National Bank was clearly subordinated to the Government, as reflected in the official title of its President, which was Deputy Minister of Finance. The National Bank extended credit as needed to enterprises to enable them to fulfill their assigned production targets. To guard against plan deviations, it monitored closely all financial transactions through the one bank account each enterprise was permitted.

The banking reform began in 1982. At that time, legislation was passed separating the National Bank from the Government. It also expanded Parliament's influence over economic policy, giving it the right to establish a ceiling on foreign borrowing and to discuss monetary policy objectives. The new legislation further laid the basis for the two-tier banking system by introducing the possibility of establishing new banks. A council of banks, convening all bank presidents under the chairmanship of the President of the National Bank, was created as a voice for the principle of an independent banking sector. Important also was the adoption of a Bankruptcy Law, intended to strengthen the banks' hands with their clients in enforcing credit contracts.

The first concrete change occurred in 1986 when the Export Development Bank was created, followed in 1987 by the conversion of the National Bank's savings department into a savings bank. The most important step came in February 1989 when the monobanking system was effectively converted into a two-tier banking system. The National Bank, at that time, shifted all its dealings with enterprises, that is, credits and deposits, to nine new independent credit banks created out of the National Bank's branch network. Retaining only the Warsaw head office plus 49 district branches, the National Bank henceforth concentrated on traditional central banking functions.

The special and independent status of the National Bank as central bank was codified in a constitutional amendment, passed in 1989, dealing with the appointment procedure for its President. Henceforth, its President was to be appointed by Parliament upon nomination by the State President, analogous to the appointment procedure for the Prime Minister. Although responsible to the State President and Parliament, and not the Government, the President of the

National Bank attends cabinet sessions. As some ten other guests, he may participate in the deliberation, but he may not vote.

The coming to power of a Solidarity-led government, in the fall of 1989, gave an enormous boost to the economic reform process. For the National Bank, it presented an opportunity to plead for more independence. Drastically revised already in early 1989 to allow for the creation of the credit banks, the National Bank Act was revised again as of January 1, 1990. The National Bank was given broad powers to execute monetary policy and was protected against pressures to lend to the Government by a strict limit on such lending, equal to 2 percent of budgeted expenditures (excluding so-called central investment projects, which are eligible for special National Bank refinancing).

The Present

Turning now to the present, I would describe the National Bank as a central bank in transition. On the one hand, it has acquired all the authority normally invested in a central bank, notably for monetary policy, bank supervision, and reserve management. Indeed, it has already had to assert its monetary policy authority in order to suppress the hyperinflation that had come to prevail toward the end of 1989. On the other hand, it is also still involved in many activities that are normally the responsibility of commercial banks, such as their internal account administration. All of the National Bank's traditional central banking functions urgently need to be modernized to meet the demands placed on them by a competitive, market-oriented financial system.

A brief description of its various current functions serves to illustrate the point about its transitional nature. Being a core central bank function, currency issue is obviously the charge of the National Bank, both notes and coins. Not obvious in a two-tier banking system is that the National Bank should also continue to be responsible for all the logistics of the currency distribution. Neither is it obvious that the National Bank should be responsible for supplying foreign currency cash to the banks and foreign exchange counters, as it does at present.

Reserve requirements are at the moment a key instrument of monetary policy. To combat the excess reserves in the banking system, deriving from a large balance of payments surplus among other factors, the National Bank raised the requirements almost to their legal limit of 30 percent of deposit liabilities. In addition, it has been trying to restrict access to its refinance facilities. A novel instrument to absorb excess bank reserves is the auctioning of bills, which the National Bank began to do in July 1990. These indirect monetary instruments, however, are not yet adequate to restrain the highly inelastic demand for credit on the part of loss-making state enterprises. They have been supplemented, therefore, temporarily by limits on credit growth for the major banks. Aside from a minimum rate for current accounts and some moral suasion from the National Bank as to the desirable prime lending rate, interest rates are free. The refinance rate is being adjusted on a monthly basis in line with the desired monetary policy stance.

A fixed exchange rate with the U.S. dollar has been one of the nominal anchors of the stabilization program. Formally, exchange rate policy is determined by the President of the National Bank in consultation with the Minister of Finance and the Minister of Foreign Trade. In practice, the President of the National Bank has been playing the lead role. In support of this function, the National Bank's President has taken over from the foreign trade bank the task of managing the country's foreign reserves. In addition, it is delegated partial control of foreign exchange, namely, the issuance of individual foreign exchange permits for transactions not covered by the general permit issued by the Minister of Finance. The general permit, it should be noted, is so broad as to cover most current account transactions.

The bank supervision function in the National Bank had to be built up more or less from the ground, starting with the introduction of a modern accounting system in the banks. Prudential guidelines are copied from the European Community (EC). In the National Bank's head office an off-site inspection capability will be developed, while for regular on-site inspections it will have to rely on specialized staff in its branches.

Given the still underdeveloped state of the financial system, the National Bank attempts to actively promote commercial banking. For that reason, it applies a fairly liberal bank-licensing policy, requiring only a $2 million capital base ($6 million for foreign-owned banks), a business plan, and managers with a sound reputation. As a result, some 60 licenses (three for foreign banks) were issued in 1990. Most new banks are privately owned. Although, perhaps, undesirable from a bank supervision viewpoint, the liberal licensing policy was adopted because of the great public dissatisfaction with the shortage of banking services. Poland currently has more than four times the number of potential customers per bank branch than do Western European countries.

A legacy from the monobanking system is that the National Bank continues to do the account administration for the banks that once were part of it. While everyone agrees that this would be better done by the banks themselves, precisely how and how fast the National Bank should cease to offer these services remains to be decided. For the same historical reason, it provides miscellaneous other services to the banks, such as the maintenance of office equipment and alarm systems, intrabank payments, and, as was noted before, currency transportation.

When the nine credit banks were created, the National Bank did not rid itself of all operations with the nonbank public. It continued to maintain some 650,000 foreign exchange accounts for nonbanks, mostly households, as well as zloty accounts for selected enterprises. Here, too, it is only a matter of time before these functions will be shifted to the commercial banks.

Besides banking services (within the above-mentioned lending limit), the services to the Government extended by the National Bank include the compilation of the balance of payments and the maintenance of contacts with international financial institutions.

In modernizing its various functions, it is receiving a great deal of assistance from half a dozen central banks, organized and coordinated by the Central Banking Department of the International Monetary Fund. Specifically, the National Bank of Austria is assisting with central bank accounting and internal auditing; the Bank of France, with bank supervision; the Deutsche Bundesbank, with foreign exchange operations; the Netherlands Bank, with monetary and balance of payments research and analysis; the Bank of England, with monetary operations and money market development; and the U.S. Federal Reserve, with the payments system.

The Future

The challenge of the future for the National Bank will be to bring the current transition to a successful completion. I see an agenda with four main points.

First, the National Bank must disengage itself from activities that either harbor a potential conflict with its prime tasks as central bank or that simply present too great a burden and threaten to distract it from its prime tasks. Among the "conflict" category, I would include the services currently provided to nonbank customers and the involvement in on-lending loans obtained from abroad, such as those from the World Bank. Activities that overburden the National Bank include commercial bank account administration and intrabank payments clearing, providing cash and banking services to local governments, and keeping detailed accounts for the Central Government.

The second point on the agenda should be a further strengthening of the National Bank's independence. This would involve, among other things, completing its separation from the commercial banks, creating a supervisory body to control its President and lend more authority to the institution, and defining in the National Bank Act a sufficiently long tenure for its President—there is none at the moment.

The National Bank will further need to continue to work on financial market development. Already it is issuing its own bills, and treasury bills are soon to follow, as are other financial instruments. A market for foreign exchange does not yet exist but is a prerequisite for a more flexible exchange rate policy in the future.

Finally, it will need to improve its own performance. This will mean that sufficient attention must be paid to issues of organization and staff development, including salary structure.

19

Financial Reform, Financial Policy, and Bank Regulation

JACQUES GAUTIER*

Financial reform will be discussed in this paper in relation to bank regulation, or, better still, banking supervision. First, I shall define the subject. The purpose of financial policy is to stipulate conditions for the highest economic growth, lowest inflation, and lowest unemployment through the most efficient allocation of financial resources. In view of this, the purpose of financial reform is to enable the financial sector to operate along the lines described in cases where it does not. Liberalization is the key word.

Banking regulation—or supervision—is to be seen here from its prudential aspect, that is, rules and techniques that aim to protect the depositors through the protection of the soundness of the financial sector, or what is generally described as its solvency, liquidity, and profitability. Why do we associate the question of financial reforms (liberalization) with the idea of protection of depositors? We do so because banking supervision does not deal only with protection of depositors; more widely, it relates to the well functioning of the financial system and the well functioning of the financial system is indispensable to the success of financial reforms.

I would like to present the subject from the point of view of a bank supervisor, which is what I am, that is, from a pragmatic point of view. We have observed a great number of financial reforms (the transition from credit policy to more indirect tools) in various developing and industrial countries. The reforms have not always been successful and have often ended with inflation, bank crisis, or both. I shall break the

* The author is an Advisor in the Central Banking Department of the International Monetary Fund.

subject into two parts: the lack of proper banking supervision, which, in many a case, was at the root of the lack of success, or at least one of the reasons, and a review of how to boost banking supervision to support financial reform, especially in the transition from a centrally planned economy to a market-oriented economy.

Financial Reform

The main objective of financial reform is to enhance intermediation. It should attract more deposits and remove excessive regulation on interest rates (often coupled with unduly heavy taxation) so as to offer positive interest rates to depositors; savers rely on unproductive assets or capital flight if no asset is available that can be expected to retain its value over time. It should also let lending institutions themselves select those to whom they lend, using the criterion of the highest return (taking into account the degree of riskiness attached to any lending operations). This means removal of credit ceilings and priority sectors—subsidies, if any, to be granted from budgetary resources—as well as liberalization of lending rates, plus increased competition.

In short, the object of financial reform is the removal of what is called financial repression. Financial repression is defined as policies that distort domestic capital markets through a variety of measures; consequently, the development of the financial system, savings, and investment suffer generally.

Comparison Across Countries

Among the many countries that implemented financial liberalization policies during the 1970s and 1980s, several were unable to achieve their goals; instead liberalization left them with a sharp increase in real interest rates, an outburst of inflation, a drop in output owing to bankrupt firms (both financial and nonfinancial), and a widened external imbalance. Argentina, Chile, the Philippines, Turkey, and Uruguay are the countries mentioned in this regard; whereas Korea, Malaysia, and Sri Lanka had successful reforms.

The pace at which reforms were introduced, despite economic instability or inadequate bank supervision at the time, affected each country's achievement. Argentina, Chile, and Uruguay had severe macroeconomic imbalances when interest rate reform and financial liberalization policies were implemented. Ratios of growth of output, savings, and investment were all low; inflation rates were high; and the external current account deficits were large in relation to national income. The strategy in these three countries involved the entire and *abrupt* removal of interest rate ceilings and credit controls, and the relaxation of government supervision over the banking system, combined with virtually free deposit insurance, explicit or implicit. This combined strategy is regarded as especially important.

Much of the same pattern of events occurred within a relatively short time in the Philippines, Turkey, and Malaysia. In Malaysia, however, where the macroeconomic environment was stable and banking supervision was adequate, the reform took place successfully.

The reforms were also a success in countries where they were implemented more progressively, for example, in Korea (1981) and Sri Lanka (1977). In these countries, positive real interest rates were achieved and maintained through credible macroeconomic policies that successfully reduced inflation to low levels. At the same time, the efficiency of banking supervision was improved, while incremental adjustments were made in regulated nominal interest rates in order to maintain a positive real level. Positive rates stimulated deposits that, in turn, increased the amount of credit available to productive firms. Full liberalization of interest rates was implemented only when economic stability was firmly established and a permanently effective system of banking supervision was in place and enforced.

Implementing reforms over time is not sufficient if, during the period, the economy is not stabilized and banking supervision is not maintained at the required level of efficiency. For example, in Indonesia, complete liberalization of interest rates was achieved, although the measures implemented to stabilize the economy had not reached their goal; the result was inflationary pressure and destabilizing capital flows, which ended in volatile interest rates and an unstable banking system.

From the above, it appears that two components are needed for a financial reform to succeed: macroeconomic stability and effective banking regulation and supervision. In cases where one or both of these conditions are not met, there is need to improve the situation before the reform is implemented, but this cannot be done overnight, hence the need for progressive implementation. I will not elaborate on the macroeconomic aspect, which is discussed in other papers and illustrated by specific country cases. I will concentrate on the question of banking supervision. I will first explain why the lack of proper supervision may result in a failure of the financial reforms.

Link Between Lack of Proper Supervision and Failure of the Financial Reforms

Why does the lack of proper banking regulation and supervision impede the successful achievement of financial reforms?

What has generally been noticed as a reaction to the liberalization of interest rates is an increase in the lending rates coupled with a widening of bank margins. This is normal and expected, as controlled lending rates were usually set too low. However, it is normally expected that the trend toward an increase will be limited by (1) increased competition, which is generally favored as part of the reform, and (2) a reduction in reserve requirements, which is also often part of the financial reform. It has, nevertheless, occurred that the increase in lending rates reaches—in real terms—high levels, that is, levels that by themselves trigger the problem.

At this stage, a short theoretical explanation is necessary. When lending interest rates have been liberalized, banks, as they are looking for the highest return, will be induced to increase their lending rate up to the point where supply and demand for loans will meet. This point may be defined as the market-clearing equilibrium interest rate. This is the point at which the maximum number of potential borrowers can be satisfied. If lending rates were increased beyond this point, the number of applicant borrowers would decline. On the contrary, if lending rates were reduced below the market-clearing level, there would be potential borrowers who are prepared to pay more and who are not accommodated (as was the case prior to the liberalization).

Well-managed banks will not behave in this way. Wise bankers will realize that, beyond a certain level that is lower than the market-clearing level, any increase in the lending rate is counterproductive. It is counterproductive for two reasons: (1) the most creditworthy borrowers are discouraged and are likely to drop out of the market, and (2) other borrowers, those who are less creditworthy, are induced to choose the projects that are associated with the highest expected profits in order to compensate for the high level of interest they have to pay, but these projects are also the riskiest ones, that is, those that give rise to the highest probability of default.

In short, because wise bankers take into account the degree of riskiness of loans, that is, the repayment probability, they apply a lending interest rate at which the demand for credit is greater than the supply. This means that bankers are in a position to screen the applications for loans so as to retain those which appear the less risky. As a result, the losses on loans at this interest rate are expected to be limited, which means that the final return will be higher than the return obtained at the market-clearing level once the losses are deducted from the profits.

Several conclusions can be drawn from the preceding discussion. First, as the risk of default on losses increases when macroeconomic instability is a problem, one may expect that well-managed banks will fix their lending rate at a level lower than that during economic stability. Second, not all bankers are wise and prudent bankers. There is a risk that banks do not realize that fixing lending rates at the market-clearing level does not produce the highest return. This means that there is a risk that banks fix their lending rate at a level that will increase the likelihood of loan defaults; this risk is especially high if the macroeconomic environment is unstable.

Finally, from the experience of several countries, it would also appear that this risk is particularly high if bank deposits are guaranteed by a system of deposit insurance (be it implicit or explicit). Simply put, banks' managements are not averse to making risky loans or investments if they think there is no risk to their depositors. I prefer a more elaborate explanation. Depositors are generally not aware of the respective degree of soundness of individual banks. Even if they are informed, they are not induced to shift their funds from one bank to another if they feel that the deposit insurance scheme provides them with adequate protection. As a result, management does not feel any pressure to limit the riskiness of their loan portfolio for fear of a drain on liquidity caused by withdrawals of deposits. This is what is called banks' moral hazard, that is, the tendency to provide risky loans at high interest rates in the expectation that large losses will be covered by deposit insurance. Moral hazard is even higher when not only depositors but also shareholders are guaranteed against any loss.

When unwise bank management is coupled with moral hazard, especially in an unstable macroeconomic environment, a sharp increase in interest rates is likely, further to a sudden liberalization of these rates. The sharp increase may, in turn, make the demand for credit inelastic. This means that more and more firms are unable to pay the interest on their borrowings. Banks are forced to capitalize interest; the additional facilities themselves are charged the high level of interest that is in effect; many firms exhaust their capacity to borrow and nonperforming loans carried by banks begin to grow rapidly. The financial reform has been a failure.

Let us now turn to the role of banking supervision. In this context, we have said that not all bankers are prudent and wise. This is true. That they behave in a prudent fashion is due to an effective system of prudential supervision. Especially important in this regard is what pertains to loans classification and provisioning, interest in suspense, concentration of loans and advances, and connected lending. Countries in which financial reform was a failure have had an inadequate system of banking supervision in addition to moral hazard and an unstable economy. Banking supervision was often confined to mere control of compliance with credit policy and foreign exchange regulations; it had little to do with real prudential supervision. It is true that in Argentina and Chile, banking regulation was strengthened during the reform, but some critical rules were not included in the additions that were made and, more important, implementation of the regulation was weak. It is reported that, in Argentina, for instance, the frequency of on-site inspections declined following the reforms.

If it is now understandable why lack of proper supervision can prevent the success of financial reforms, the case is even much clearer in a situation where a sizable fraction of financial institutions are technically insolvent (sometimes these institutions have lost their capital several times over). This is present in both public and private banks, but more common in public ones. Undue concentration of risks, pressure from the government, and connected lending have been common features. This has two major policy implications: (1) By rolling over the loans made to weak firms, banks are unable to shift lending priorities to new activities and investments; and (2) Higher interest rates on deposits will impede cash flow, as interest on loans is just rolled over. In this case, the reform reveals the real situation of the banking system, as it hastens the emergence of a liquidity crisis and it transforms a bank in distress (an institution technically insolvent that goes on operating as if everything were in order) into an element of a real banking crisis.

Boosting Banking Supervision to Support Financial Reform

From the above, it would appear that before finalizing financial sector reform, especially before freeing interest rates completely, there is a need to enhance the efficiency of the prudential banking supervision system, if there is one, or to set up such a system, if there is none. This may not be sufficient for the financial reform to be a success; however, it appears to be a prerequisite.

Let us suppose that the Central Banking Department of the International Monetary Fund has been requested to provide advice on how to implement enhanced banking supervision. This may pertain either to a developing country or an Eastern European country that plans to shift from a centrally planned economy to a market-oriented one.

The first step would be to assess the present supervisory capability of the country and to get at least an impression of what the banking system comprises. From one country to another, the picture can be completely different. Here, I will discuss mainly the case of centrally planned economies shifting to a market-oriented economy, that is, a situation where banks are often in distress, or possibly where there are no real commercial banks at all, and practically no banking supervision.

Now, if we assign experts or consultants to advise the authorities, what do we expect from them? At this stage, the next step would be for them, and for the authorities, to acquire a clearer knowledge of the situation of the banking system. Prudential supervision is not a simple set of rules and regulations that can be applied everywhere and at all times in the same fashion. There are permanent principles and constant features, but they have to be adapted to the existing context. It is of the utmost importance to take into account (1) the major features of the legal framework (company law, rules—and practice—regarding collateral, bankruptcy, etc.); (2) the quality of the communication network; (3) the actual nature of the operations carried out by the banks; (4) the nature and the degree of stability of banks resources and the apparent value of their assets; needless to say, the latter is critical; (5) the accounting organization and techniques, including a detailed review of the balance sheets and profit-and-loss accounts; and (6) the organization chart of banks, their staffing, including information on how well trained is the staff.

The review must be conducted mainly through numerous meetings and discussions held with bank representatives of various levels. These meetings should preferably be held on the banks' premises, where it is possible to consult their books and files in order to acquire a concrete understanding of their organization and methods.

The review will frequently reveal—or simply confirm—a situation where one or several banks are in distress; a bank in distress usually keeps its real position hidden. If a significant share of the banking system is in distress, no monetary policy can be carried out. Banks in distress are unable to react to market signals and will need injections of liquidity that may be contrary to what the central bank is trying to achieve through its monetary policy. It is also an impossible task to set up an interbank money market in a situation where banks are not prepared to lend money to each other because they are aware of their respective weaknesses.

The task of consultants of the Central Banking Department at this stage is to draw the authorities' attention to three important facts that are often ignored—not always in good faith—(1) prudential supervision cannot resuscitate a dead body and it is useless for banks in distress; (2) someone will have to foot the bill (central bank, depositors, taxpayers); the question is to decide who will bear the cost; and (3) the later the decision is made the higher the bill (high amount of interest paid versus little interest received, prospects for collection of debt vanish as time elapses). It is essential that a thorough audit of problem banks be conducted as soon as possible by a competent accounting firm if the situation is not clear, and it is essential that steps are taken in order to remove the bad assets—those that do not appear collectible—from the banks' balance sheets. This will lead to mergers, divisions, liquidations, recapitalization, in short what is usually called "restructuring" or "rehabilitation" of the banking system. The remaining banks will be the viable ones. Needless to say, this is said more easily than done. The whole process generally requires several years. The major difficulty is to properly assess the value of a loan portfolio and to make an estimate of what will be recovered. Not surprisingly, in most cases the first assessments were too optimistic. Nonetheless, the rehabilitation process should be started as soon as possible and completed as quickly as possible. Any monetary policy instruments that are being developed at this stage should be used to absorb excess liquidity generated by the recapitalization measures.

Prudential supervisors should deal with the remaining banks, which are regarded as viable and which are expected to react to monetary policy decisions in the manner desired by the authorities. These are the banks that will permit an increased financial intermediation following the financial liberalization process.

At the end of the initial review, central bank staff and experts from the Central Banking Department have acquired an overall knowledge of the banks' operations and of the existing reporting system (if any). Keeping in mind the nature of the information with which supervisors should be provided in order for them to carry out their supervisory function, their next step is to design a set of reporting forms through which this information will be collected. In practice, the forms may consist of a statement of assets and liabilities completed by a certain number of appendices. These periodic reports are designed to enable central bank staff to monitor the development of banks' activities, mainly in order to discover as soon as possible any unfavorable trend that would require corrective action. In due course, as soon as various types of rules and regulations are introduced, the reports will also be used to monitor the compliance with the said rules and regulations.

The reporting forms need not be very sophisticated; they have to be adapted to the actual nature of bank operations and will be developed to include more and more detailed information when banks' operations and the types of risks incurred become more diversified. Another possibility is to require a certain number of data, but to allow some flexibility, during a transition period, for those banks that are not yet in a position to produce the said data.

As it is important that all banks submit their data to the authorities in a similar way for comparison, a common accounting plan for banks is useful. Such a plan may be designed, if this is technically feasible, before the reporting forms. In this case, forms are based on the accounting plan. As the latter defines in detail how to enter the various operations in the books, it is easy to obtain forms that are transparent. Depending on local circumstances, the design of an accounting plan may require a long time; two years would not be exceptional; in addition banks must have time to adapt their internal organization to the common plan. Consequently, a common accounting plan is sometimes not to be regarded as a prerequisite for the design of the reporting forms. In the absence of a common plan of accounts, the authorities will have to describe precisely and in detail how to fill out the forms. It is true that the accuracy of the returns will not be foolproof, but it is also true that this is never achieved. Experience worldwide shows that—with or without a common accounting plan—errors in reporting forms, sometimes significant ones, are common. What is most important is that supervisors be vigilant for accuracy, so as to ascertain that banks are improving the quality of the returns when there is a need to do so.

In truth of fact, it must also be recognized that banks require some time (generally several months) to adapt their internal organization to the common plan. What creates difficulty is when banks must break down the balance of some of their accounts in order to comply with the plan of accounts (or the return forms). Then, it is often difficult not to tolerate some delay in the complete implementation of the plan. In the meantime, banks should be authorized to either leave the line blank or base the reported information on a statistical approach or on pure estimates. As a result, whether or not the accounting plan is implemented very rapidly (after a few months) or only after two or three years does not make a great difference.

It is indispensable for supervisors to be closely involved in the design of the accounting plan so that the various risks faced by banks can be easily identified and quantified in the books. This should be regarded as indispensable not only for proper prudential supervision but also for proper management. The information recorded in the books and reported on the returns should normally include the following, which is generally not available in developing and Eastern European countries before the implementation of the reform:

(1) Classification of loans and advances, depending on the repayment probability; interest in suspense; provisions for bad debts. In countries that do not have sound experience in banking supervision, it is regarded as preferable to decide on the degree of riskiness of loans and advances, not on a case-by-case basis, but in view of objective criteria, for instance, on the length of time a payment has been in arrears.

(2) Off-balance sheet items, which are designed to record all the commitments underwritten by a bank in the form of a promise to lend, extension of guarantees, and other obligations. Such commitments involve a risk for the bank in spite of the fact that no disbursement has yet been made. Guarantees and commitments extended by other parties in favor of the bank also have to be recorded.

(3) Regularization accounts, which attach incomes and expenses paid in advance or to be paid at a later stage to the year to which they are related, whatever the date of the actual payment.

(4) Detailed recording of income and expenses, in order to permit a precise analysis of the profitability of a bank.

(5) Assets and liabilities, as well as off-balance sheet items, in foreign currency to be accounted for in a way that enables banks to determine their profit and loss in foreign currencies, as often as they want, and to know at all times the extent of their foreign exchange risk. The concept is clear but its implementation requires some technical adjustments in accounting procedures, especially in electronic data processing, which may need some time.

(6) The same remark applies to the breakdown of major assets and liabilities on the basis of their remaining life in order to permit the computation of a bank's liquidity position.

At the same time as new reporting forms are designed, a set of prudential rules needs to be introduced or the existing set revised, if one exists. These two different tasks should be done concurrently and within the framework of the same approach, that is, (1) taking into account the actual situation of banks and the overall economic, legal, and psychological environment and (2) being in close contact with the banks' representatives. Knowing that prudential rules are rules that any wise banker would adopt spontaneously, unlike credit policy or foreign control regulations, better compliance may be expected if banks are convinced that the proposed regulation is not against them but in their favor.

At this early stage, and especially for countries that have no experience at all in prudential supervision, this is not a complete and sophisticated set of regulations that can be envisaged. The various parties involved need to become familiar with new practices, step by step. It must be verified that some rudimentary rules are (1) applicable and (2) by and large correctly applied, before issuing rules that would be more detailed and more demanding.

The first step, which is of utmost importance, is to remind banks of some basic principles recognized universally in the banking industry but which are not yet familiar in the country. This should include the requirement to conduct a formal appraisal of credit applications and to make the board of directors of each institution define who has the responsibility to make decisions on such applications, depending on the size of the loans. It is also essential to define rules that will prevent excessive concentration of loans as well as connected lending. Another indispensable requirement is the careful monitoring of loans and advances (in particular overdrawn current accounts). Any arrears in the repayment of a loan or in the payment of interest should be recorded immediately so that the decisions to set aside provisions for bad debts and to keep interests in suspense (instead of including them in the income) are made in due time and with a realistic view of the probability of repayment. In addition, it is essential to convince the fiscal authorities that provisions for bad debts should be deducted from the profit before tax.

It is also necessary to require at this early stage that banks set up proper internal control measures and internal audit policies. Their attention must be drawn to the importance of having the capacity to discover errors made by their staff before they become a catastrophe. Banks should be given some time to develop a minimum level of control before entire liberalization is decided.

There is nothing against introducing a capital adequacy ratio and, for instance, a liquidity ratio, but these should be provisional ratios, introduced on a tentative basis, and the design should be as simple as possible. A capital adequacy ratio at this stage may complement stabilization policies by limiting the expansion of assets by banks. This may be useful in the framework of financial liberalization, as experience shows that the response of credit growth is generally more rapid than the response of deposit growth. Only at a later stage will it be possible to introduce a risk-weighted capital ratio. This will be possible only when the exact situation of banks is well known and when banks are technically able to carry out the computation of a sophisticated ratio. One of the requirements that should be formulated from the outset is the fact that, for the computation of any capital adequacy ratio, the shortfall in provisions for bad debts, if any, must be deducted from the amount of capital as it appears in the books. This is indispensable if a realistic view of the situation of a bank is to be had; my personal experience has shown me that this is often forgotten and that this may lead to very damaging consequences.

As far as the surveillance of liquidity is concerned, it will generally be impossible for banks to compute from the outset a ratio based on the comparison of the remaining life of assets and liabilities. This will be impossible for technical reasons. As a result, if a liquidity ratio is introduced at this stage, it should be a ratio following what is called the "stock approach," that is, comparison of liquid or easily liquefiable assets compared with the global amount of liabilities or only with some types of liability. Needless to say, however, banks should be free to choose the type of liquid assets that they want to keep. In this regard, a liquidity ratio designed for prudential purposes is different from a rule that would prescribe a minimum investment in a particular type of asset, for example, treasury bills.

Limits on foreign exchange exposures may also be issued but, here again, only once the actual position of banks is well known. Issuing a regulation that would be inapplicable would be counterproductive. It must also be kept in mind that foreign exchange control will remain in effect for some time and this tends to limit the magnitude of the foreign exchange risk of banks (at least on the asset side).

The same applies to interest rate risk. The quantification of the interest rate risks—if one wants to take the overall aspect of this risk into consideration—involves such a degree of technicality and sophistication that it cannot be envisaged in the first step of prudential supervision. A bank's management must be warned, however, of the existence of a risk it faces in receiving as income low, fixed rates on long-term loans, that is, for an expanded period of time, while it has to remunerate the deposits at rates that will be variable, and probably much higher.

For this reason, both foreign exchange risk and interest rate risk should be considered from the outset when assessing whether banks have to be rehabilitated or not. These two risks cannot be ignored. If the size is huge, necessary steps should be taken within the framework of the rehabilitation process.

Enhanced competition is one piece of regulation that must be defined and applied as soon as possible, and, especially, freedom of entrance. The doors should be open to new banks, both national and foreign, providing that (1) they have a strong capital base and that major shareholders have the capability to support the bank if need be in the future (capital to be subscribed by those who have money to invest, not by those who have money to borrow); and (2) management is experienced. In this regard, the feasibility study that is often required in the regulation governing entrance of new banks must be regarded less for its own merit than as evidence of management's expertise. Enhanced competition is essential to prevent the dramatic increase in lending rates that would crowd out good borrowers and trigger a failure of the financial reform.

At the early stage of implementation, banking supervision, although it is indispensable, as already said, cannot be organized as per the textbook. Shortage of skilled staff and lack of experience limit the scope and frequency of off- and on-site supervision. The staff is still in the process of training, both theoretically and practically. In this regard, short spot checks limited to specific areas may be a useful approach to on-site inspection, keeping in mind that full-fledged examinations will not be carried out before several years. In terms of organization, it is also useful not to distinguish between those who carry out off- and on-site supervision. On the contrary, as it is the most efficient way, it is advisable to set up a structural organization where the same individual is in charge of supervising a few banks, looking at the returns as soon as they are received, and conducting on-site visits from time to time with the assistance of junior staff members. This can be complemented, at least in the early stage, and as long as permitted by the overall number of banks, by regular contacts between high level management of the central bank and commercial bank managers, in addition to the contact that will necessarily take place between these managers and the supervisors.

The main purpose of banking supervision in the early stage of a shift to a market-oriented economy is to draw the attention of those who are in charge of banks to the dangers they may face and to their responsibility. Banking supervision cannot prevent all banks from failure (this is verified everywhere, even in the most advanced countries). Its purpose should be to prevent the emergence of a general banking crisis. I believe that this is something that can be achieved. Let us repeat, however, that if prudential supervision is an indispensable element of the reform, it alone is not sufficient. This means that, in the framework of a financial reform, the liberalization process will need to be delayed if the economic situation is not stabilized.

20

Sequencing Financial Reform

R. BARRY JOHNSTON*

The idea of sequencing is that certain measures are better taken before others in achieving policy goals and minimizing the various risks and uncertainties associated with reforming the financial system. Fundamental to the approach is the view that financial markets cannot be left to manage themselves, particularly during periods of significant structural change. We have a good knowledge of what are the major components of financial reform and what elements are important, even essential, in reducing the risks. The precise sequence for financial reforms that will maximize economic welfare will depend on the initial conditions of the economy and the financial system and progress in broader economic liberalization and stabilization. Nevertheless, it is possible to derive from country experiences some general rules of thumb that can guide the sequencing of financial sector reform.

This paper largely focuses on case studies of countries that have implemented such reform. The case studies provide useful insights into what specific components of the reforms are best implemented at different stages in the financial reform and stabilization process. They also illustrate the major risks that can arise and provide important lessons for managing and sequencing a successful reform. Before examining these experiences, let me first discuss some broader questions about the reasons for financial sector reform and the approaches adopted.

*The author is a Senior Economist in the Central Banking Department of the International Monetary Fund.

Background on Financial Reform

Reasons for Financial Reform

What I have in mind when we speak of financial reform might more appropriately be called "financial liberalization." The reforms normally cover measures aimed at making the financial system more responsive to market forces and more competitive. The major elements are (1) reforms of the interest rate regime supported by market-based monetary control procedures and the development of money markets; (2) reforms of prudential regulations and the supervisory system; (3) recapitalization and restructuring of weak financial institutions; (4) measures to strengthen competition among banks (relaxation of entry restrictions, unification of portfolio regulations, granting of autonomy to state banks, disclosure of information, etc.); (5) reform of selective credit regulations; and (6) development of long-term capital markets.

The most important reasons for reform are to ensure efficient allocation of resources and to promote savings. Reflecting the view that satisfactory growth and national welfare depends on the efficiency of markets, financial sector reforms aim at a greater freedom for market processes and increased competition. Moreover, developing financial institutions and markets, and an appropriate structure of interest rates, helps reduce the savings investment gap and, therefore, achieves more rapid and sustainable economic growth.

The advantages of a liberal financial system are only now becoming widely appreciated. For many years, the financial system received little attention in economic analysis, and economic policy was generally interventionist in the financial system with the objectives of supporting real sector development. For example, in many developing countries, authorities intervened both through selective credit policies, interest rate controls, and high reserve and liquid asset ratios. In centrally planned economies credit has been allocated in support of production plans, with no role for market processes. Financial reform often involves a completely new role for interest rates, financial institutions, and markets in allocating credit in these countries. Even in many industrial economies, the trend toward financial sector liberalization is relatively recent. Financial reform in these countries may be less dramatic, associated with the breakdown in the segmentation of activities between different financial institutions and markets, both domestic and foreign. Even so, such reform generally improves welfare, as it increases the range of financial instruments available to borrowers and depositors and reduces financial transaction costs.

The Broad Context of Financial Reform

Financial reform is often an integral part of broader economic liberalization that involves a shift from allocating resources through directives, controls, and subsidies toward market processes. In this broader context, the academic literature has attempted to describe a logical sequence of economic reforms. The general conclusion is that macroeconomic stabilization is a prerequisite to successful structural adjustments and that fiscal adjustment should be completed before embarking on financial sector reforms. It is also viewed as better to liberalize domestic financial markets before removing controls on international capital flows. Trade liberalization and real sector adjustments should also precede financial sector and capital account liberalization.

This approach would serve to place financial sector reform relatively late in the overall sequencing of reforms. There are some good reasons for this. For example, for interest rates to have the appropriate impact on resource allocation, lenders and borrowers have to be responsive to market prices, and the price structure itself needs to reflect underlying conditions of supply and demand. Nevertheless, several comments are relevant in deciding the appropriate timing of financial reform.

First, certain structural reforms might be necessary to support the effectiveness of stabilization policies. Here, I have in mind, for example, the need to develop indirect monetary instruments, because direct controls tend to become ineffective over time, and the importance of strengthening financial institutions in order to avoid financial crisis.

Second, from a practical policy point of view, there is often an urgency for reform in countries facing critical economic conditions. In these countries, the option of a drawn-out approach to economic and financial reform may not appear appropriate, or perhaps desirable, because the welfare costs from delaying the reforms may outweigh the potentially greater risks of a rapid liberalization.

Third, to achieve economic and structural change in countries with rudimentary market processes and attitudes, there is often a need for an initial critical mass of reforms involving many sectors simultaneously. By drawing on an analogy from high school physics, we can liken these economies to bodies in stable, if low-level, equilibrium. A small displacement changes nothing fundamentally; a large displacement is necessary to change the bodies' equilibrium. Once a body is displaced, complex processes are set in train. For those familiar with Walt Disney's *Fantasia*, an analogy with the sorcerer's apprentice is perhaps now the more appropriate one. The challenge for policy-makers is to design the initial disturbance and to manage the subsequent adjustment.

Perhaps the most dramatic examples of rapid change are the sweeping monetary and banking reforms currently under way in many centrally planned economies—or what are known as emerging market economies—and which play a leading role in the reform process.[1] Reforms in indirect monetary instruments and money markets have developed early as these have been viewed as important in macroeconomic stabilization and the development of the financial system.[2] At the other extreme, a small group of relatively high savings and high growth economies have followed a very gradual approach to financial reform. I would include in this group Japan and Germany. Reforms in these countries have tended to emphasize the development of the longer-term capital market in advance of liberalization of the banking system and the development of the money and short-term markets. Between these extremes are a large number of countries that are reforming their financial systems. It is mainly on a sample of these countries that I will focus, although examples close to both extremes are included.

Countries' Experiences with Sequencing Reforms

A study prepared in the Central Banking Department examines experiences with financial sector reform in five countries: Argentina (1976–81), Chile (1974–80), Indonesia (1983–88), Korea (1980–88), and the Philippines (1980–84).[3] Conditions prior to embarking on economic and financial reforms ranged from severe financial repression, distortion in prices, and economic imbalances (for example, in Argentina) to a more progressive financial sector and smaller economic and structural distortions (for example, in some Asian economies).

In all the sample countries, activities of financial institutions were tightly controlled prior to financial reforms with a high degree of policy-induced segmentation between different types of financial

---

[1]The earliest stages of reform in these countries has often focused on (1) restructuring the credit plan by giving national banks control over aggregate credit expansion and reducing detailed credit allocation; and (2) establishing a commercial banking system by splitting up the national banks.

[2]For a fuller discussion, see Anton A.T. Op de Beke "Issues in the Transition to Market-Based Monetary Control in Former Centrally Planned Economies" (unpublished, Washington: International Monetary Fund, 1990).

[3]"Issues in Managing and Sequencing Financial Sector Reforms" by Amer Bisat, R. Barry Johnston, and V. Sundararajan (unpublished, Washington: International Monetary Fund, 1990).

institutions. Interest rates and credit were subject to official administration and a substantial proportion of total credit was subsidized and directed. Interest rates and market mechanisms played a relatively small role in the allocation of credit. As a result of the financial repression, financial sector competition, savings mobilization, and the efficiency of the allocation of investment were all weak. Overall economic performance was deteriorating with slowing real growth, expanding fiscal imbalances, increasing inflation, and a widening balance of payments deficit. Financial sector reform was undertaken in each country as part of a broader economic stabilization package.

Reform followed no unique sequencing in the countries examined and the time frame for implementation varied substantially. The success of countries' economic policies reflected a broad policy mix, including exchange rate, fiscal, and monetary policies. I will return later to the question of the consistency of these policies with the sequencing of financial reform. In all countries, financial reform was followed by financial deepening as measured by the development in various financial aggregates and the growth of new financial institutions.

A deregulation of interest rates and credit controls occurred early on in the reforms in Argentina, Chile, and the Philippines. These countries experienced significant financial deepening but also faced problems of a loss of monetary control following their financial reforms. Indonesia liberalized its interest rates but, along with Korea, maintained significant administered control over bank credit. Indirect instruments of monetary control were introduced relatively early in all the countries, except Korea, which continued to rely on administered interest rate and credit controls. Generally, however, indirect instruments had to be strengthened and refined later in the reform process and were not implemented in a sufficiently timely and effective manner to avoid the loss of monetary control.

Policies to increase financial sector competition, including the breakdown in segmentation between different types of financial institutions and the lowering of entry barriers for new institutions, were initiated early in the reform process in most countries. The extent and effectiveness of these policies in promoting competition, however, varied substantially. The reforms had limited impact on financial sector competition in Argentina and, initially, in Chile, despite an increase in the number of financial institutions, as there was increasing concentration of ownership. Korea followed a more gradual approach; because of the large number of already existing privately owned financial institutions competition improved relatively rapidly. The liberal entry policies for new financial institutions in the Philippines and

Indonesia increased competition significantly but also created a vulnerable component of the banking system. In the Philippines, the increase in competition was unsustainable.

As regards the liberalization of the capital account in the sequencing of reforms, exchange controls had been liberalized prior to the financial reforms in Indonesia and the Philippines. This had both benefits and costs for their financial systems. It increased competition and the need to develop indirect monetary instruments as the principal monetary instruments and therefore accelerated the reforms. Larger capital flows, however, may have added to instability in liquidity and therefore made monetary management more difficult. Argentina and Chile gradually relaxed their exchange controls as part of their financial reforms, but remaining controls continued to protect their domestic financial systems, which, as a result, were less competitive. Both countries faced substantial capital outflows because of uncertainty in their exchange rates, which became significantly overvalued. In these circumstances, capital controls were generally ineffective in preventing the outflows and thus in supporting domestic interest rate policies. Korea maintained tight exchange controls until relatively late in its financial reform.

Korea was the only country that actively promoted its capital market as part of its financial reform. Capital market development played little part in the reforms in Argentina and the Philippines, and Indonesia developed its capital market only in the later phase of reform. A capital market boom accompanied the Chilean reforms, but this was mainly related to temporary financial conditions, and the boom and subsequent stock market collapse accentuated financial instability following the reforms.

The critical need for effective prudential supervision was identified only late in the reform process in many countries, as was the need to reform deposit insurance as a means of increasing discipline on financial institutions. New prudential regulations were introduced in the initial stage of the reforms in Argentina and Chile; the effectiveness of the new regulations, however, was weak. Indonesia did not strengthen prudential regulations as part of its initial reforms, and the Philippines had relaxed prudential regulations in the years before financial reform. Korea changed the emphasis of bank supervision as part of the reforms, with a greater emphasis on on-site inspections.

In three countries—Argentina, Chile, and the Philippines—financial liberalization was followed by a financial crisis that disrupted the financial sector and was accompanied by a sharp contraction in gross domestic product (GDP) and a reversal of the financial deepening that initially followed the financial reforms. It is important to stress that the countries' experiences need to be seen in the context of the success of their stabilization policies as well as the approach to financial reform. In Argentina, the fiscal deficit was not contained; the real exchange rate appreciated sharply; and the substantial capital outflows reflected a general lack of confidence in the economy. In Chile, the fiscal deficit was reversed; the real exchange rate, however, appreciated to unsustainable levels, resulting in speculation against the peso. The authorities did not believe the subsequent liquidity shortages; the result was very high real interest rates that impaired the value of the banks' assets. The banking crisis in the Philippines was preceded by a crisis in the balance of payments and a moratorium on external debt payments that seriously damaged investor confidence. In contrast, Korea had a successful real sector adjustment that included exchange rate depreciation and fiscal correction; this resulted in a substantial strengthening of the balance of payments and capital inflows. In Indonesia, the fiscal deficit was reduced and the authorities were active in managing financial sector liquidity and avoiding sharp fluctuations in interest rates in the face of speculative flows of capital.

Lessons for Managing and Sequencing Financial Sector Reforms

Let me now attempt to draw out what are the major lessons for managing and sequencing financial sector reforms from these countries' experiences.

Dynamics of Money and Credit

In all countries, financial sector reform had a major impact on the behavior of the key monetary and credit aggregates, which need to be taken into account in setting monetary targets in the postreform period. In all countries, except Korea, financial liberalization was followed by a period in which credit growth exceeded the growth of deposits, and in most of these countries the gap between the growth of credit and the growth of deposits widened following the reforms. In other words, the financial reforms were immediately followed by a widening in the gap between private expenditure and savings and increased pressure on resources.

The initial tendency for credit to grow more rapidly than deposits is not perhaps surprising where credit growth was previously constrained by direct controls with an excess demand for credit. Once the direct controls are removed, financial institutions respond by meeting the excess demand and credit expands rapidly. In the prereform period, deposits were not limited by direct controls and so a similar excess demand did not exist. With reform, deposit growth, therefore, responds more slowly as a portfolio response to the new liberal financial situation.

The countries' experiences also suggest, however, that the tendency for credit to grow more rapidly than deposits is only a temporary phenomenon when countries maintain positive real interest rates. Following the initial stock adjustment—reflecting the initial excess demand—credit growth slows down. Deposit growth continues, nonetheless, in response to the ongoing financial deepening. After some time, the growth of deposits and credit converge, allowing for balanced growth with a higher level of overall resource mobilization, as well as improved efficiency in resource allocation. In countries that did not maintain positive real interest rates in the postreform period, credit growth continued to be more rapid than deposit growth; this underlines the increased importance of interest rate policy in monetary management on the postreform period.[4]

Unless carefully managed, the initial tendency of credit to grow more rapidly than deposits in the postreform period can increase resource pressures and can thus add inflation and put pressure on the balance of payments. First, the authorities would need to have available effective indirect instruments of monetary control to replace the direct controls and to manage interest rates. Hence, a reform of monetary control procedures should occur very early in the reform process. Indirect instruments do not rely on discriminatory controls but only on the capacity of the central bank to control its own balance sheet, particularly central bank finance of government and refinance policy. Moreover, the use of instruments such as treasury bill auctions and reform of the discount window can be catalysts in the development of money markets and can promote financial sector competition. Thus, these instruments are consistent with the broad objectives of financial reform—savings mobilization, efficiency in investment allocation, and stabilization.[5]

Second, to the extent that the initial credit growth reflects a one-time adjustment to a new equilibrium position,[6] an attempt to constrain credit demand solely through interest rates could result in very

[4]This subject is examined in detail, ibid.

[5]See R. Barry Johnston and Anton A.F. Op de Beke, "Monetary Control Procedures and Financial Reform: Approaches, Issues, and Recent Experiences in Developing Countries," IMF Working Paper, No. 89/48 (unpublished, Washington: International Monetary Fund, June 1989).

[6]Or reflects low or perverse interest elasticity of credit demand on account of distress borrowing and loans to related interests.

high real interest rates. This would carry attendant risks for the real economic growth, the maintenance of an appropriate exchange rate, and thus external adjustment and stability of the financial sector. Chile's experience in 1981 illustrates these risks. Therefore, special transitional arrangements may be needed.

The need to rely on tight monetary policy to maintain macroeconomic balance, which is the cause of the upward pressure on the interest rates, would be reduced by a larger fiscal adjustment or an increase in foreign resources, or both. The fiscal adjustment would help reduce overall resource pressure and, therefore, the need to raise interest rates—the private sector would be allowed to "crowd out" the public sector. Success in attracting foreign resources to help finance the resource imbalance may depend on (1) the development of the domestic money and capital market; (2) the maintenance of positive real rates of returns, and an appropriate exchange rate and exchange control policy to encourage voluntary capital inflows; and (3) a comprehensive macroeconomic adjustment program that is supported by overseas creditors.

Another transitional option would be to support indirect monetary instruments through temporary continuation of direct credit controls. The postliberalization adjustment in credit probably cannot be avoided, but it could be phased using direct controls more closely aligned with the otherwise lagging growth of bank deposits. A phased approach was followed in Korea and Indonesia and succeeded in reducing private resource imbalances. Credit ceilings that allow banks to increase credit only in response to increases in deposits might achieve the desired phasing, while reducing disincentives to deposit mobilization. These ceilings would have to be supported by positive real interest rates and an adjustment in the indirect instruments of monetary policy. A postliberalization growth in credit that is the result of structural weaknesses in credit allocation would have to be addressed by restructuring bank portfolios and strengthening prudential controls.

Interest Rate Management

Let me turn now to the related question of interest rate management. The experiences of the five countries suggest that the impact of financial liberalization on the cost of funds to borrowers also needs careful management. Not only did real interest rates rise with financial reform, but the reforms tended to widen initially banks' gross lending margins. These margins reflected a number of influences. The removal of interest rate controls allowed banks to price credits and risks more appropriately, and this may have acted to raise margins, since controlled lending rates were usually set too low. Against this, reserve requirements were normally lowered as part of the reforms that reduced the cost wedge between deposit and lending rates. In addition, financial sector competition was increased through the reduction of barriers to entry and segmentation between different types of financial institutions.

To prevent average lending spreads from widening, authorities must reduce more rapidly the costs to financial institutions of reserve and liquid asset requirements, for example, by lowering reserve requirements and paying market rates of interest. This would also require that instruments of indirect monetary control to manage the cash reserves of the banking system be in place. Moreover, liberalizing interest rates and removing direct credit controls is likely to provide an environment most conducive to an increase in financial sector competition and innovation.

Nevertheless, the speed and nature of interest rate liberalization—and the phasing in of various prudential regulations—may have to be adjusted, taking into account the financial structure of nonfinancial firms and the pace with which problem banks and their debtors can be restructured. If nonfinancial firms are highly leveraged, any sharp increase in real interest rates could further weaken the repayment capacity of these firms and the condition of banks. The preferable option would be to recapitalize the banks and restructure their portfolios. This may require budgetary transfers and, therefore, a larger fiscal adjustment in support of the financial reforms. Without such transfers, the ability to control interest rates may become a critical issue. It may be desirable to liberalize bank interest rates only gradually, while pushing ahead with industrial sector restructuring and the recapitalization of banks.

Maintaining Financial Sector Stability

This brings me to the third area in managing financial sector reform: the critical need to strengthen the banking system both to avoid the serious disruption that would follow a financial sector crisis and in support of a more efficient allocation of financial resources.

The connection between financial sector reforms and financial crises is complex, and I have already drawn attention to the importance of the broader stabilization policy. The case studies show that the timing and intensity of the crisis and the timing and scope of the reforms differed considerably. The major common elements were the unsound liability structures of nonfinancial firms prior to reform (owing to subsidized credit, and following reform owing to insider loans, etc.); changes in relative prices that influence the viability of borrowers; weaknesses in the institutional structure of banking that facilitated risk taking; and weak prudential regulation and banking supervision that condoned excessive risk taking.

Certain characteristics of the reform may have contributed to the crises. First, the very rapid growth of bank credit following the liberalization may have strained the credit approval process and resulted in an increase in lending to more risky projects. This was a particular problem because of extensive lending to interrelated entities, and the lack of regulation of loan classification, provisioning, and interest capitalization. Second, the abruptness of the financial liberalization may not have given the private financial institutions time to develop the necessary internal monitoring and credit appraisal processes or for the public sector banks to develop a more commercial approach. Third, information systems—accounting, financial disclosure rules, company analysis, credit-rating systems, etc.—that are necessary for efficient allocation of resources were not developed. Hence, there was no adequate signal of the riskiness of different financial institutions. At the same time, public supervision was not developed, and, because of explicit or implicit deposit guarantees, depositors were safeguarded against loss and were thus largely indifferent to bank credit risks. Hence, insolvent banks were able to attract deposits and to disguise their true financial positions by continuing to pay interest and dividends out of deposit receipts.

A proper sequencing of financial sector reforms—including early and timely attention to developing vigilant bank supervision and well-designed prudential regulations—could have helped detect and contain the buildup of financial fragility. Concomitantly, addressing the problems of bank portfolios and preventing the growth of banking distress through recapitalization and reorganization, including timely closures and mergers supported by sound financial policies (fiscal, relative price and exchange rate adjustments, and maintenance of real interest rates), would have helped to reduce the vulnerability of the financial system.

In some countries, financial reform was, in fact, accompanied by a strengthening in prudential regulations; however, implementation of the regulations was weak and some critical regulations—for example, restrictions on lending to interrelated entities, on loan classification and provisions, and on accounting rules on interest accruals—did not exist and others were rescinded because of inability to implement them. This underlines the importance of not only having adequate regulations but also the capacity to implement them. Such a capacity is in part technical, but also requires the absence of political interference. The achievement of such a capacity takes time and often involves the strengthening of key public institutions, particularly the central bank, as part of the process of financial reform.

Summary and Conclusion

I began by emphasizing the importance of pragmatism and taking account of countries' particular circumstances. I will end by setting out some simple rules of thumb in the sequencing of financial sector reforms.

First, a minimal system of prudential regulation is necessary before embarking on financial sector reforms. Moreover, enforcing these regulations and recapitalizing the banking system are desirable at the beginning of the reforms in order to support efficient credit allocation and to safeguard against a financial crisis that could undermine monetary control and macroeconomic adjustment.

Second, key monetary control reforms must be initiated early in the reform process. This reflects the critical importance of maintaining macroeconomic control during the reform period while simultaneously allowing for the removal of the various discriminatory controls on interest rates, credit, and financial institutions' portfolios that is essential in the development of a market-oriented financial system.

Third, the speed of the liberalization of interest rates and credit controls should take account of the extent to which fiscal and external policies are available to support monetary policy in achieving overall macroeconomic balance. Fiscal and external policies need to support the initial increases in resource pressure that can follow financial liberalization. The larger is the contribution of fiscal and external adjustment the faster will be the optimal liberalization of interest rates and credit controls.

21

The Transition from Direct to Indirect Instruments of Monetary Policy

CARL-JOHAN LINDGREN*

The transition from direct to indirect control of monetary policy is a part of the general move toward increased reliance on market forces, economic liberalization, and deregulation, and away from directives, controls, and subsidies. It is also frequently a part of macroeconomic stabilization and adjustment of relative prices. These issues and the sequencing of financial sector reform in a broader context have been covered by other speakers. Financial sector liberalization includes a broad range of structural reforms aimed at improving the efficiency of resource allocation and financial intermediation. It has been widely recognized that financial resources are better allocated by the market than by administrative fiat.

I will not here go into the pros and cons of direct and indirect instruments but will assume that the case has been made in favor of indirect ones; the appendix to this paper provides some further thoughts on this matter. Before I get to the transition process, let me give a brief background and talk about objectives and targets, define the concept of direct and indirect instruments, and make some comments on the role of fiscal policy in monetary management.

*The author is an Advisor in the Central Banking Department of the International Monetary Fund.

Background

Objectives and Targets

Optimal resource allocation is the objective of financial sector reform. This means an institutional, regulatory, and policy environment that promotes savings, efficient financial intermediation, and efficient credit allocation. Macroeconomic stability and especially a sound fiscal policy should be considered basic preconditions for successful financial sector reform. The principal objectives for monetary policy should be to achieve domestic price stability and a certain level of international reserves. Monetary policy formulation would convert these objectives or ultimate targets of monetary policy into intermediate and operational targets.

The objective of monetary policy instruments should be to achieve their operational target efficiently; that is, they should be flexible and effective. Flexibility means that the instruments could be changed as needed, frequently or infrequently, in small or large increments. The central bank should be able to reverse them at any time—even the same day. They could be implemented quietly, or openly and well publicized. Flexibility means that the access or use of an instrument should be at the initiative of the central bank as much as possible rather than at the initiative of the banks or others. Flexibility also means that the central bank should be given the freedom to act quickly, that is, allowed to make decisions independently or within predetermined monetary policy parameters. A need for government decisions or a broader political debate on monetary policy could slow the decision-making process.

Effectiveness means that the instruments should transmit the policy effect and signals quickly and effectively throughout the financial system and the economy and help achieve the central bank's operational target. Effective instruments should be designed so as not to distort the financial intermediation process, not create inefficient market segmentation, nor an unsound credit allocation. Effective instruments should therefore normally support increased competition and domestic money and capital market development.

Direct and Indirect Instruments

The concepts of direct and indirect policy instruments should be defined. Direct monetary control instruments seek to control the amount of money and credit or the level of interest rates directly. The typical direct instruments are credit ceilings and administratively determined deposit or lending rates. Indirect instruments, on the other hand, seek to control interest rates and banks' capacity to attract deposits and extend credit indirectly by influencing liquidity conditions and interest rates more generally. The distinction between direct and indirect instruments is not always so clear in practice. If narrowly defined, direct instruments become more similar to selective controls than monetary controls, while at certain extreme levels indirect controls may become quite similar to direct controls.

One could view any type of instrument that affects liquidity conditions as an indirect instrument, for example, many prudential regulations and selective credit controls or incentives. Here, I will only consider those instruments that are principally used for monetary and macroeconomic management. Many central banks consider statutory liquid asset requirements a monetary instrument. I would regard that as either a prudential regulation, if allowing a wide range of market-priced liquid instruments, or a selective credit instrument, if used to channel credit to the government or other priority sectors. I should add that I do not view selective credit allocation as a role for a central bank; this is a budget function and should be handled as such.

Traditional indirect instruments include reserve requirements, rediscount facilities, and open market operations in government securities. Other indirect instruments are special deposits in the central bank, operations in government deposits, operations in central bank securities, and even foreign exchange intervention. One could consider virtually all the assets and liabilities of a central bank with the exception of the currency issue as potential indirect instruments of monetary intervention. (Credit to the government also could be beyond the central bank's control.)

A more important distinction than direct or indirect may be whether an instrument is statutory or market based. Most statutory indirect instruments involve a reallocation of costs and therefore involve some element of distortion. A basic criterion for a market-based one is that it is voluntarily held at a certain price. But the concept of a market-based instrument is not that clear-cut either. What constitutes a proper market? In the presence of substantial statutory controls the market may be rigged and distorted and resultant interest rates may not be very representative. Extreme examples are interbank rates in a situation where all banks are subject to credit ceilings and have excess liquidity or rates for government securities that need to be held statutorily—in both cases, any yield higher than zero may be an acceptable market rate for banks.

The Role of Fiscal Policy

The precondition for any monetary reform is prudent fiscal policy. For sound monetary policy, there must be sound fiscal policy and control of the government's deficit. Excessive fiscal imbalances are likely to limit structural changes and any move toward market-determined interest rates. Monetary policy can offset fiscal imbalances but only up to a point. If the government demands more credit than the system can accommodate, there is little room for effective monetary policy.

Ideally, the choice of whether or not to hold claims on the government should be a decision of the central bank and should take the form of deciding whether or not to buy government securities. This decision should be made for monetary—rather than fiscal—reasons. However, too many central banks are required to provide automatic credit to the government, often at no interest or at interest rates below those in the private market.

It would be unrealistic, and impossible, in many countries to stop central bank lending to the government, no matter how desirable. Market-based funding is often not feasible simply because neither the market nor the instruments exist. But a number of measures should be taken in order to subject the government to financial discipline and prepare the way for eventual market funding of the government's financing needs.

All government bills or securities should carry market yields. This would give a major impetus to market determination of interest rates and market development. Market pricing can be expected to be resisted by the government, whose objective is to fund its deficit at the lowest possible cost. Government policy may thus conflict substantially with the interest rate policy that the central bank wishes to pursue. It should be recognized that government funding from the central bank at below market yield is a cost to the government anyway either in the form of reduced profit distributions from the central bank or an accumulation of quasi-fiscal losses that will require a recapitalization of the central bank at some later point.

The Transition Process

Strategy

There are no perfect models for how to move from direct to indirect instruments of control. A transition would need to follow the pace of other developments, such as the emergence of a money market and even a strengthening of the capabilities of the human resources in the central bank. Each country would start its transition from a different point with different financial traditions, with banking systems and money markets at different stages of evolution, and with financial institutions of different degrees of soundness. Some countries may start from disequilibria and distortions that make rapid and substantial changes necessary, others may be able to move slowly and cautiously. The macroeconomic environment and the pace of reforms in other sectors will also be of importance. Legal limitations may slow or complicate the process. But be it as it may, there are some general considerations that should be kept in mind.

It would seem to be important to have a clear view, a "blueprint," of the result expected to be achieved at the end of the transition process. This should include (1) the type of instruments to be used, (2) the type of changes that will be needed in the process of formulating monetary policy, (3) the type of market that can be realistically envisaged, and (4) the legal institutional, administrative, operational, and human changes that would be needed to make it all happen.

Once the final objectives are defined, a program for the transition process has to be determined. Such a program has to fix realistic and internally consistent intermediate goals for the process. Direct and indirect instruments may coexist, and probably should do so, until it is clear that the indirect instruments work; loss of monetary control cannot be risked. It should be understood, however, that unless the two systems are perfectly harmonized only one of the sets of instruments will be effective at any one time. The strategy should be to place primary reliance on the indirect instruments as soon as possible and gradually make the direct controls redundant.

Before credit ceilings are removed, it is essential to sterilize any existing excess liquidity with indirect instruments. Such excess liquidity is a common feature under credit ceilings. Sterilization would assure that the removal of credit ceilings will not lead to a sharp credit expansion. If the amount of excess liquidity to be sterilized is large, it is most likely not going to be possible to use market-based instruments. Instead, statutory measures, such as an increase in reserve requirements, or perhaps the use of moral suasion to force banks to buy some sort of medium- or long-term securities, would be necessary. Until a market has developed, excessive reliance cannot be placed strictly on market-based instruments.

How Are Indirect Instruments Expected to Work?

Indirect instruments absorb or sterilize in the central bank liquidity from the banking system and through the banking system from the rest of the financial system and the economy as a whole. When liquidity is absorbed, banks' capacity to lend is reduced and money market rates rise, deposit and lending rates tend to rise, financial savings tend to increase, and credit demand tends to taper off. When liquidity is injected, the reverse happens. Banks' capacity to lend is increased, interest rates tend to fall, deposits to taper off, and credit demand to increase.

Indirect instruments should aim at controlling banks' reserves, and in particularly their excess reserves, and thus their capacity to expand credit, and also at controlling interest rates so as to strike a balance between the supply and demand for money and credit in the economy. The aim of indirect policy instruments should be to keep banks fully invested, that is, to make sure that their liquidity is invested in such a way that they have as little excess reserves as possible with which to expand credit. Excess reserves are the most volatile and potentially most expansionary element of banks' liquidity.

Banks can be expected to keep a certain amount of excess reserves as precautionary balances. How much is an empirical question—but one could expect such balances to decline as the money market develops and other dependable sources of liquidity emerge. The intervention policy should aim at keeping excess reserves close to their precautionary levels.

The indirect instruments used could be either statutory ones or market-based ones. Statutory instruments would sterilize the liquidity more effectively but would tend to distort interest rates, while market-based instruments would result in representative interest rates but would be more volatile and uncertain.

The Design of Instruments

As I have mentioned before, almost any of the asset or liability items in the central bank's balance sheet can be used as a policy instrument, as long as they can be used to absorb or inject liquidity and affect banks' reserves. Although it makes little difference, in principle, whether a central bank uses changes in reserve requirements, rediscount facilities, or open market operations to achieve an initial volume impact, the different instruments can be expected to have substantially different cost implications.

In the design of instruments, the key issue is to get the interest rate right. One should seek, therefore, to make sure that the distortive effects of any instrument on intermediation costs be as small as possible. This would also make the instruments more readily interchangeable and would increase the central bank's flexibility to manage its own balance sheet. A central bank could redesign each instrument in isolation, but there clearly are advantages of doing the redesign as part of a broader strategy that would assure internal consistency between instruments. The following considerations may be useful for the redesign of the principal instruments.

Reserve Requirements

Legal reserve requirements should be uniform for all institutions and all categories of liabilities. If so applied, there would be no segmentation. There is no monetary justification for different requirements based on categories of deposits or maturities. Compliance should be measured and tested for average holding periods, typically for weekly periods, to give banks some flexibility to manage their liquidity and thus promote money market development. Shortfalls should be subject to strict penalties, be expressed as penalty interest rates, and be applied to the average shortfall during the entire holding period. The penalty rates for such shortfalls should be the highest interest rates in the system. The central bank should have the power to prescribe how the requirement is calculated, which liabilities and institutions it applies to, etc.

Unremunerated reserve requirements imply a tax on banks. They increase their effective cost of funds, their spreads, and thus affect final deposit and lending rates. If non-interest-bearing reserve requirements are very high, they will have many of the same distortive effects as direct controls, and especially so if they do not apply equally to all institutions. Reserve requirements should therefore be reduced as other instruments come on stream and be kept as low as possible. Considerations should also be given to remunerating them in full or in part above a certain level, say in the range of 5–15 percent.

Reserve requirements can always be easily lowered, but they are not that easy to increase, as they may require substantial portfolio adjustments for individual banks. They are therefore not very flexible. But they are very effective and should be part of any central bank's arsenal.

Rediscount and Refinance Facilities

Central banks often start the reform process with all types of refinance facilities, including long-term facilities for special projects or subsectors. There are often as many different refinance rates as there are facilities. Refinance rates are seldom linked to market rates and are often subsidized. Such refinance facilities are mainly used as selective credit instruments rather than monetary instruments—although they have, in aggregate, a direct monetary impact. They often involve the central bank in micromanagement decisions and may not even apply equally to all banks. They are often open-ended facilities, and their use is hard for the central bank to control. As monetary instruments they are therefore inflexible and almost entirely at the initiative of banks.

The multitude of facilities and refinance rates should be merged to one general facility at one rediscount rate. There is normally a need for a general rediscount facility to provide liquidity to the market and prevent excessive fluctuations in short-term interest rates, particularly interbank rates. Such a facility should be uniform for all banks with automatic access subject to certain pre-established access rules and limits. Access limits could be linked to banks' capital or to certain collateral.

There should be a set maximum maturity. This maturity should be kept as short as possible for all credit, in order to allow the central bank to change the access rules at its own initiative when needed. Some central banks do not allow maturities longer than a few days. This would not mean that banks could rely on the central bank funding for longer periods than the maturity of central bank credit but that they would have to do so by rolling over short-term credit at changing terms rather than having access to long-term central bank credit. This should also be the case for cyclical or seasonal financing.

What is important is the ready and reliable access to liquidity at a price, not the possible end-use of such credit (which is a nonoperational concept anyway, as money is fungible). Central banks that start the transition with substantial outstanding long-term credit to banks should introduce a program for their gradual phasing out. In cases where the central bank functions as a development bank, this function should be separated from the central bank and given to an independent institution that is separately funded through the government budget.

The key policy variable for a rediscount facility is the rediscount rate. In the absence of a developed money market or reliable market signals, it would need to be set administratively. Some central banks auction access to central bank credit to determine a price. The rule of thumb should be to always keep the rediscount at a level higher than deposit rates to give banks incentives to raise deposits first and rely on central bank credit last. As soon as feasible, the rediscount rate should be determined as a margin over a money market reference rate. The size of the margin, that is, the cost of liquidating assets, should be considered a policy instrument.

In addition to a liquidity facility, most central banks need to play the role of lender of last resort. I will not get into the special features of such a facility, which is a major topic in itself. Nevertheless, one feature should be that the bank supervisory authorities always and immediately be alerted. The use of a lender of last resort facility may inject substantial liquidity into the market, which may have to be offset by a tightening of other instruments.

Central Bank Term Deposits

Some central banks have successfully used term deposits to sterilize excess liquidity. If such deposits cannot be withdrawn prior to maturity, their effect is similar to that of a reserve requirement except that they are voluntary. In order for banks to invest their liquidity in such deposits they need to have attractive maturities and interest rates. They would therefore not involve major distortions. If such deposits have relatively long maturities, cannot be withdrawn prior to maturity, and are nontransferable, they could be a relatively efficient instrument for sterilization of liquidity.

The problem with this instrument is how to determine the yield, which would need to be set administratively with due regard to other market rates. Another problem is banks' preference for very short maturities, which makes the sterilization vulnerable. Furthermore, once the yield and maturity have been set by the central bank, the initiative lies entirely with the banks. Some central banks have used this instrument as a step in the development of a money market. The next step would be to make such deposits negotiable certificates of deposit (CDs).

Open Market Operations

Traditional open market operations require relatively deep secondary markets. For such operations to work, both the central bank and banks or other market participants would need to hold or be prepared to hold government or other securities that can be traded—and at low risk. By buying and selling securities out of its own portfolio or conducting repurchase operations and similar transactions, the central bank could influence liquidity conditions and interest rates in the market. This is clearly the most flexible and market-based instrument for monetary control. But it is also one that is beyond most countries' reach—even in the medium term—because few countries can expect to have money markets that are deep enough for such transactions on a major scale.

Open Market-Type Operations

The fact that there is no deep money market does not mean that one cannot conduct transactions with similar effects as those of open market operations. One can approximate the effects of such operations by developing and conducting transactions in the primary market for short-term bills. Such operations could be called open market-type operations. The idea would be to use the primary issuing process as the mechanism for selling bills at market prices. Such bills could be issued either by the central bank itself or by the government.

There is always a question whether it is better to issue government or central bank bills. It would clearly be preferable to use government bills with interest paid by the government. The central bank could act as its agent and issue government bills according to monetary criteria, including, in particular, market interest rates. But if such issuing is done for monetary control purposes, the government should be prepared to deposit any excess over its programmed financing needs in the central bank. If the government were to spend the excess, it would not be sterilized and therefore would not have the desired monetary effect. These conditions may not be met. There could be legal impediments, or the government could be unwilling to sterilize the proceeds and would rather spend them. It may, therefore, be necessary for the central bank to issue its own securities. This could take the form of certificates of deposit or bills.

A better way would be for the central bank to use its own portfolio of government assets (advances, bills, or securities). This might require that advances be securitized and that nontransferable securities be replaced by negotiable ones. The yields and maturities of these assets may be unattractive and need to be renegotiated. However, as long as the central bank holds securities that it can negotiate freely, it can always do short-term repurchase operations. And it is important to note that the central bank can set a market price regardless of the yield and maturity of the underlying security.

Regardless of the security used, the idea of open market-type operations is to sell securities regularly in the primary market at a negotiated price. At the beginning, securities would need to have short maturities, say three months. Many central banks issue bills on "tap"—but this requires a predetermined administered price. In my view, the preferred arrangement would be to use an auction or tender system, which would give the central bank market signals. In a tender, those bidding the highest price (lowest yield) would receive bills. By conducting regular tenders, say once or twice a week, the central bank could absorb (inject) liquidity by selling more (less) bills than those maturing. To sell more, would probably require an increase in the yield—to sell less might require a decline in the yield.

The key issue as always would be the pricing. In a tender the central bank would need to determine a price based on the amount of intervention needed to bring bank reserves to the program path indicated by its monetary program. (I will return to the programming framework below.) The central bank would also need to assure reasonable interest rate stability should it wish to promote the emergence of market makers and secondary trading. The central bank would therefore need to determine a cut-off price in any tender. Clearly, such a system would have major deficiencies. It would be a market managed by the central bank. But if it is managed with proper integrity it would produce yields that would be transparent and perceived as market-based yields. This is important. A credible market rate could be used as a reference rate to which other administered rates, such as the refinance rate and the rate on government securities, could be linked.

Interest Rates

With the exception of pure open market operations, all the instruments mentioned above would involve some central bank interference in the determination of interest rates. But this would be indirect intervention and not direct control of deposit and lending rates. In its policy intervention a central bank at all times should seek to foster market determination of rates as much as possible. It should be recognized and accepted that if the market is to be important and play a greater role, the central bank has to play less of a role, be less involved, to stand back from the market. This point—although obvious—should be stressed as it is crucial for free interest rate determination and especially for operating a tender of the type mentioned before.

The fact that the central bank is to play less of a role does not mean that it should not intervene if it so chooses. A reduced role for the central bank does not mean that it will not continue to influence interest rates. Of course it will do so—that is the role of a central bank—but it should not be seen as totally dominating the market. It would influence interest rates through its intervention with various indirect instruments, especially its rediscount rate and its cut-off price in tenders. In addition, the central bank should seek to develop a proper structure of interest rates by setting its refinance rate properly in relation to market rates, possibly introducing a yield curve for rediscounting, etc.

Foreign Exchange Operations

All market intervention involving foreign exchange could be considered monetary intervention because it directly affects bank reserves. A central bank normally has little control over spot transactions in foreign exchange, but it may be able to influence the timing of external borrowing, both public and private (if the latter requires approval), and the repatriation of export receipts of government entities. Other instruments would be forward operations and, particularly, swaps.

Monetary Programming and Targeting

The transition from direct to indirect instruments will require a change of the programming framework and of operational targets. While the targets of direct instruments must be at the level of the system-wide aggregates or interest rates that they seek to control, the operational targets of indirect instruments should be the narrowly defined aggregates in the central bank's balance sheet that they can control. Volume targets could be net domestic assets of the central bank, currency in circulation, or reserve money, or even excess reserves; price targets could be the rediscount rate or a money market reference rate.

Monetary programming at the level of the central bank's balance sheet rather than broader aggregates is also justified by the fact that during the transition it will not be possible to forecast market behavior due to increased competition, less segmentation, and particularly interest rate flexibility. Old money-demand models are bound to be obsolete and perhaps of little use. Last week, it was interesting to hear that the speakers from Austria, Canada, Italy, and Germany all discarded the use of broad monetary aggregates as targets and instead suggested that the focus be either on the narrowest aggregates of money on the balance sheet of the central bank or a specific target for exchange or interest rates. Clearly, several broad aggregates should be monitored but, in my experience, one need not be too concerned with changes in velocity as long as the narrow monetary aggregates in the central bank's balance sheet are under control.

In programming and targeting, there can be only one anchor. One cannot target both volume and price. It has to be either one or the other. If one targets a price, a volume follows and vice versa. Neither can one target two prices, say, both exchange and interest rates. Inconsistent targets cannot be met and will typically be overruled by market forces. I will not dwell here on the type of target that should be chosen, but I would like to stress that whatever target is used, it should be clearly defined and understood, because it will determine the use of policy instruments and operational decisions, such as cut-off price or cut-off volume, in the primary tenders mentioned above.

We have heard representatives of many countries that use price targets. Perhaps it should be said that Fund-supported stabilization programs normally use a volume target. These targets have been applied increasingly at the level of the central bank and are normally expressed in terms of the net domestic assets of the central bank defined as currency issue, or base or reserve money, less net international reserves valued at a constant exchange rate. My preference would be to define a volume target for net domestic assets based on the most narrow money concept, which is currency issued or in circulation, possibly including excess reserves. This definition would include all monetary instruments under the volume target.

The transition from direct or indirect instruments and particularly to market-based instruments will require changing the frequency of the monetary programming. For system-wide direct instruments, a quarterly programming at the level of a monetary survey or the consolidated banking system would be sufficient. There would typically be little active central bank intervention once the instruments have been announced—the central bank's role would be one of passive monitoring. The use of statutory indirect instruments, such as reserve requirements, would require the central bank to be a little more alert but would not require much change. But the use of market-based instruments would require substantial change, because the programming would need to establish a short-term program path that would provide the central bank with at least monthly and probably weekly intervention targets.

This would require the development of a short-term forecasting framework in the central bank to serve the decision-making process until more reliance can be placed on market signals. In such short-term programming, the liquidity movements in the government's accounts are particularly important. Such movements, which are beyond the control of the central bank, could be very large and unpredictable. There is, therefore, a need for very close coordination with the treasury, and for the treasury to improve its cash management system, which should be integrated into the monetary programming framework of the central bank.

Money Market Development

The use of indirect instruments will require a functioning interbank or money market to clear possible disequilibria between segments of the market and between individual institutions, and to transmit the policy effect and interest rate signals to the rest of the economy. There would be a need, therefore, to establish a market that would bring about meaningful market-determined interest rates, meet the central banks' need for a market-based policy intervention, and meet the banks' need for a mechanism to actively manage their excess liquidity. The redesign of monetary instruments as mentioned above should support market development, reduce market segmentation, and increase competition.

It should be realized that deep money markets such as those in the United States or the United Kingdom, may take a long time to develop, and, in many countries, will never be feasible. At the same time, every country can establish conditions for a basic interbank market and develop a market for certain bills and securities. The proper incentives and conditions for market development should be established. A key condition is free pricing, that is, a money market free from interest rate controls. Even if interest rates elsewhere in the system remain controlled, interest rates in an interbank money market or a bill market could be free. In this connection it should be noted that the more direct and statutory indirect instruments are used, the more distorted that market is likely to be.

Other conditions for market development are reasonable interest rate stability, liquidity, low risk, and a proper regulatory environment. Price stability need not be inconsistent with market pricing, but a central bank should be careful with smoothing operations (for example, using the cut-off price in tenders) so that they do not go too much against market forces. This is always a delicate balancing act—decisions should be made on the basis of the policy targets. To provide liquidity until a secondary market has developed, the central bank may need to establish properly designed rediscounting facilities and perhaps even promote market makers.

Another major force in the development of any money and capital market, of course, is the government. The funding of the government should be increasingly directed to the market at market rates. The government should therefore develop a domestic debt management policy and should seek to design instruments that have market acceptance.

Banking Infrastructure

With use of market-based instruments and mechanisms of intervention, there is a need for constant market contact by the central bank and for up-to-date information. This will normally require changes in the way a central bank operates. I have already mentioned the need for a new short-term programming framework. Policy implementation will have to change from passive and sporadic monitoring of compliance with statutory instruments, to more active and constant involvement. Daily monitoring of exchange rate, interest rate, and money market liquidity developments should signal pressure points in the system and the need for policy action. The central bank could intervene when needed in the money or foreign exchange markets either openly or subtly and indirectly through agents.

The need for constant market presence and intervention will require changes in the decision-making structure, the organization, the information systems, and the human resources management of a central bank. Statutory instruments can be managed with centralized decision making at very high levels, normally involving the governor or the board, often even requiring government involvement. But the use of market-based instruments and mechanisms would require decentralized decision making and delegation of authority. Higher decision-making bodies would lay out objectives and broad outlines of policy intervention, but, within such guidelines, the operational decisions would normally be made by a collegiate body of operational managers, possibly headed by a senior official at, say, deputy governor level. Authority would need to be further delegated to the dealers and other staff manning trading desks—the people who are in direct contact with the market and undertake the actual transactions.

Organizationally, central banks are often compartmentalized into separate departments that manage foreign exchange operations, refinancing, monitoring of reserve requirements, research and monetary programming, etc. These departments often have little interaction on a current basis. With the change of policy approach, there is a need to merge the control of all monetary control instruments into one operations department. Many central banks have gone one step further and merged their foreign and domestic operations departments to assure better coordination. Accounting systems often need to be streamlined and modernized in order to provide the necessary up-to-date information for the short-term management of the main components (instruments) of the central bank's balance sheet.

The human dimension should not be forgotten. The change of instruments and policy approach may require extensive retraining of staff, as the skills to enforce controls may be quite different from those of dealing in a market. The lack of properly qualified central bank staff can be a major stumbling block for a reform of monetary management and of broader financial market reform. The central bank would have to pay substantial attention to specialized staff training and be prepared to provide proper incentives for skilled staff to stay. The central bank most likely would also have to invest in modern technology, such as computers and telecommunications equipment, to facilitate operations. It would need to have independence and authority to make decisions both regarding staffing, salary levels, and material acquisitions.

Changes would also be needed in the banking system outside the central bank. An environment of competition and efficiency based on profitability criteria should be nurtured. Banks might have to be restructured and recapitalized to be able to operate profitably in a new more competitive environment. Government-owned banks may for the first time have to think about profitability rather than political objectives. Prudential control would have to be strengthened in order to foster orderly market conditions within an adequate set of rules and regulations, dependable and transparent market information based on common accounting rules, and proper supervision of the integrity of banking operations.

Concluding Remarks

There are other advantages of a transition to market-based instruments and a more efficient financial system. I would like to suggest that the type of instruments and policy framework used for monetary policy intervention is a major ingredient of central bank independence—one of the key themes of this seminar. The use of indirect instruments will require a clear definition of the monetary policy objective(s) and more explicit delegation of authority from the government to the central bank for short-term policy formulation and implementation. As a result, the central bank is likely to be seen more as an institution implementing an independent monetary policy.

Furthermore, a transition toward a market-based system is likely to put pressures on the government to improve its own financial position and make the budget more transparent. I have mentioned market pricing of the government domestic debt, the transfer of selective credit schemes to the budget, and the need to settle possible quasi-fiscal deficits of the central bank and other state-owned banks (recapitalization). Such changes would create initial pressures on the budget but would put the burden of adjustment back on the government, where it should be.

Finally, it is clear that the transition from direct to market-based instruments in each community involves a large number of country-specific considerations. I have attempted to provide a checklist and give ideas to those of you who may be involved or interested in such a transition. My concluding thoughts are that it is never too late to start the process, and that it is possible for any central bank to successfully implement a transition regardless of the conditions at the starting point—and that once the process is set in motion it will to a large extent build upon itself.

Appendix

Advantages and Disadvantages of Direct and Indirect Control Instruments

Direct Control Instruments

The advantages of direct controls are that they are powerful and effective instruments toward those institutions they seek to control. They are easy to link to a monetary programming format, relatively easy to use, and easy to explain to politicians and to the public. There may be occasions when no other instrument is adequate, and when they could be used on a temporary basis. Direct controls should therefore be part of any central bank's arsenal, even if not normally used.

At the same time, direct instruments have strong disadvantages. It is virtually impossible to establish their appropriate level. They invariably lead to distortions, inefficiency, and resource misallocation, which clearly grow over time. They are inconsistent with the objectives of structural reforms, competition, and market development.

The problems and distortions associated with credit ceilings and interest rate limits typically include the following:

(1) they are inflexible and ineffective, as they are hard to fine-tune and only apply to certain segments of the system;
(2) they discourage savings mobilization and thus total credit available in the economy;
(3) they cause disintermediation from the organized (controlled) financial sector to unofficial domestic markets or foreign markets (capital flight);
(4) they limit competition among banks to historic market shares due to the need for bank-specific ceilings and lack of price; they do not foster competition for new deposits and lending opportunities;
(5) they hinder price competition and the development of a money market;
(6) they require the central bank to become increasingly involved in micromanagement issues related to individual banks, which often conflicts with its macroeconomic role;

(7) they make the determination of the levels of credit and interest rates appear as a political decision and, therefore, prone to political rather than monetary considerations; and
(8) they make monitoring of compliance increasingly difficult, as credit is extended in forms not covered by ceilings or interest is paid or charged in forms other than interest.

In addition, the following further problems and distortions can be associated with credit ceilings:

(1) they may largely eliminate competition because borrowers have few options to switch banking relationships (as banks are locked into historical market shares);
(2) they tend to badly misallocate resources, as banks primarily accommodate old established borrowers at the expense of new, often more dynamic, ones. This is particularly troublesome in banking systems with substantial nonperforming loans, where capitalization and loan rescheduling of existing loans tend to crowd out new borrowers;
(3) they may promote loan delinquency, as borrowers are reluctant to repay loans because they fear reduction in future access—this is a particular problem in countries where overdrafts are a common form of credit; and
(4) they distort "freely" determined interest rates, as competition is limited and lending rates are allowed to stay high and deposit rates low.

Indirect Control Instruments

Indirect controls include statutory instruments that have characteristics similar to those of direct controls. This section will therefore relate only to market-based indirect instruments. Because such instruments work through the market and the interest rate regime is central to the working of the market, the advantages of market-based instruments are similar to those of market-determined interest rates.

Any market-based interest rate structure that equilibrates supply and demand for money and credit in the money market and the rest of the economy is in itself a most efficient monetary control mechanism and greatly reduces the need to rely on any other control instrument. Market-determined interest rates give a central bank the following advantages:

(1) they ensure automatic and immediate adjustment, and, therefore, reduce the risk for policy error;
(2) they transmit the policy signals and effects immediately to all segments of the economy;

(3) they assure an optimal allocation of money and credit based on price and relative risk and return;
(4) they ensure consistency between monetary, fiscal, and exchange rate policies;
(5) they make pressures in the money market immediately apparent;
(6) they support and complement exchange rate management;
(7) they reduce the political sensitivity to interest rate changes; and
(8) they allow the central bank to stand back from the market without losing control.

22

Jamaica's Transition from Direct to Indirect Instruments of Monetary Policy

G. ARTHUR BROWN*

The transition from direct to indirect instruments of monetary policy in Jamaica commenced in 1985 and was a major policy initiative by the Government. It formed an important part of the policy framework that was established within the context of the Financial Sector Reform Program adopted by the Government of Jamaica under the auspices of the World Bank. The program was geared toward eliminating certain macroeconomic impediments to efficient financial sector intermediation. It was also intended to implement certain monetary policy reforms that were deemed necessary for improving resource allocation and mobilization in the monetary and banking system.

Up to 1985, the major factor affecting the efficiency of the monetary and financial sector had been the large fiscal deficits, which required substantial financing by the banking system—provided mainly by the imposition of a liquid assets ratio. This created much difficulty in separating monetary policy from fiscal policy and in enabling the Bank of Jamaica to pursue an independent monetary policy.

Another important aspect of macroeconomic policy considerations in 1985 was the search for a realistic exchange rate determination mechanism. An auction market for foreign exchange had been established since 1983, but over the two-year period, the parity of the Jamaica dollar fell from J$1.78 to US$1.00 in 1983 to J$5.50 to US$1.00 in 1985. As a consequence of this rapid depreciation, the stability of the par value of the nominal exchange rate became a major policy goal of the Government in 1985. This meant that overall economic policy

*The author is Governor of the Bank of Jamaica.

was directed at anchoring the par value of the Jamaican dollar to the U.S. dollar at a fixed rate (J$5.00 = US$1.00 at the end of January 1985), with domestic monetary policy being formulated and implemented to support the achievement of this objective.[1]

Prior to 1985, the Bank of Jamaica relied solely on direct instruments of control to execute monetary policy. The main instruments were variations in the liquid assets ratio of the commercial banks, an administrative floor on the savings deposit rate, and selective and quantitative controls on credit expansion. The liquid assets holdings of the commercial banks were mainly cash reserves, treasury bills, and local registered stock issued by the Government. Treasury bills were short-term government instruments with a 90-day maturity. Local registered stock, which qualified as liquid assets, were long-term government securities with a remaining period to maturity of nine months or less. Variations in the liquid assets ratio of the banks were used to adjust the distribution of credit between the private and public sectors. But the instrument lacked efficiency because it distorted the pattern of credit allocation. The minimum savings deposit rate, because of its direct impact on lending rates, was used as an important support for demand management programs. Quantitative controls on credit were intended to regulate the amount of credit that was available to the private sector and hence to influence monetary expansion. But loopholes existed that led to the avoidance or circumvention of the restrictions.

It was in the context of this exposure with direct controls that a complete revision of the system of monetary management was adopted. Not only was there a need to reverse the inherent distortions in the system but also there was a need to equip the Bank with a range of instruments that had the requisite flexibility and were efficient.

The Bank of Jamaica and the World Bank, therefore, issued a joint memorandum on monetary and fiscal policies that focused on four main areas: (1) the need for base-money management; (2) rediscounting transactions of the Bank of Jamaica; (3) open market operations; and (4) other policy measures to support base-money management and improve financial intermediation in general.

The first section of this paper reviews and analyzes those measures that were undertaken by the Bank of Jamaica to develop open market operations and implement a program of base-money management in the 1985–89 period. The development of open market operations has been the most significant monetary policy initiative undertaken by the

[1]See W. Max Corden, *Exchange Rate Policy in Developing Countries*, Country Economics Department (Washington: The World Bank, April 1990).

Bank of Jamaica in implementing reforms of the financial sector. From the conceptual perspective of base-money control, open market transactions are expected to operate mainly in influencing changes in the monetary base.[2] Other policy instruments relating to the pattern of rediscounting transactions and liquidity support are also briefly examined in this section. These instruments were also expected to have an impact on the monetary base. In the second section, the impact of other instruments of monetary policy is examined. Here, the phasing out of some instruments of direct control is reviewed. This is interpreted as part of the movement toward indirect, rather than direct, monetary policy formulation. The third section deals with some operational procedures, including the prudential supervision of bank risks arising from the changes that were introduced. The last section provides a summary and conclusion in respect of the main findings of the paper.

Transactions Undertaken to Influence Changes in the Monetary Base

In support of the primary objective of exchange rate stability and relatively low inflation, open market operations, which commenced in the fourth quarter of 1985, were designed to contain the monetary base. The initial issue was J$50.0 million, but as demand pressures intensified the stock of the Bank's certificates of deposit expanded to J$2,425.9 million at the end of December 1989. The market for certificates of deposit evolved rapidly in the initial year of operation in 1986, with outstanding certificates totaling J$1,010.0 million. There was a relative slowdown in 1987, but the market expanded sharply in 1988 to reach J$2,299.6 million in outstanding certificates. The year 1989 saw a marginal expansion in their stock, a consequence of intense speculative pressures and the low preference for Jamaican dollar assets.

The certificate of deposit is a short-term instrument with a maturity ranging between one and nine months, but the bulk of the outstanding stock during the period was three-month securities. The rate of interest is generally determined through an auction, but the Bank has at times fixed the yield or placed a cap on the interest rate that it will accept. The amounts offered by the Bank of Jamaica vary on the basis of policy considerations. During 1987, unlimited amounts were

[2]The principle of base-money control is based on the well-known algebraic relationship: $M = k B$ where M is the money supply, k is the money multiplier, and B is reserve or base money. Changes in the money supply are dependent on changes in k, the money multiplier, as well as changes in B, the monetary base.

offered because much emphasis was placed on mopping up excess liquidity in the banking system.

Commercial banks account for the single largest share of the market, or about 45 percent of the volume of outstanding certificates issued over the five-year period. Sales of certificates of deposit by the Bank of Jamaica were expected, in principle, to contract and purchases to expand base money, thereby leading to a corresponding contraction or expansion of the money supply; however, during the period, the Bank made no purchases. Sales of certificates of deposit to the commercial banks were the only type of transaction carried out by the Bank. This situation was linked with the need for sustained demand management action and reflected some substitutes consequent to the phased reduction of the liquid assets ratio.

In the past, the liquid asset requirement had distorted the pattern of credit allocation and provided resources to government at subsidized rates of interest. Its removal was, therefore, one of the major goals of the reform program. The phasing out of the liquid assets ratio was to be achieved according to the following schedule, 48 percent by March 1985; 44 percent by March 1986; 35 percent by March 1987; 25 percent by March 1988; and 20 percent by March 1989.

Open market operations in the period, however, had little impact in influencing changes in base money, since the banks held very little excess cash balances over the statutory cash reserve requirement of 20 percent, which existed for most of the period. This was a very high statutory cash requirement and it imposed substantial costs on the banks. It meant that the banks were inclined to hold only minimal excess balances, under normal circumstances. The restrictive nature of the high cash reserve ratio was emphasized by the requirement that the banks maintain this ratio on a daily basis. Open market operations in certificates of deposit, therefore, had their main influence on the money multiplier, through their impact on short-term interest rates, rather than through variations in reserve balances held by the commercial banks.

The data shown in Table 1 indicate marginal excess cash balances for most of the period that showed no apparent link with the variation in balances of certificates of deposit held by the banks. On the other hand, the large overall excess liquidity could be associated with the change in the statutory requirements (Chart 1). The source of the banking system's liquidity after the third quarter 1988 and part of the buildup of excess liquidity was related to large reinsurance inflows from overseas following the destruction caused by Hurricane Gilbert in September of that year. Certificates of deposit were used extensively

Table 1. Liquid Assets and Currency/Deposit Ratios of Commercial Banks

Quarters	Cash	Deposits with Bank of Jamaica	Treasury Bills	Local Registered Stock	Money at Call	Specified Assets	Total Liquidity	Excess Liquidity	Currency/ Deposit[1]	Excess Cash Reserves
1985										
First quarter	1.2	18.7	12.8	11.1	0.1	4.1	48.0	4.0		
Second quarter	1.1	21.8	14.7	10.0		4.0	51.6	3.6		
Third quarter	1.2	22.5	16.0	9.6		4.1	53.4	5.9		
Fourth quarter	1.4	21.9	13.3	9.8		4.0	50.4	2.4	0.2	1.9
1986										
First quarter	1.2	21.6	15.2	9.3		2.6	49.9	5.9	3.9	1.6
Second quarter	1.2	22.4	14.7	8.1		2.5	48.9	10.9	5.0	2.4
Third quarter	1.3	22.1	13.6	8.1		2.6	47.7	9.7	6.4	2.1
Fourth quarter	1.7	21.2	13.2	7.9		2.5	46.5	8.5	8.1	1.2
1987										
First quarter	1.3	21.0	11.7	7.7		2.2	43.9	8.9	9.2	1.0
Second quarter	1.2	22.7	10.4	6.5		2.1	42.9	7.9	8.9	2.7
Third quarter	1.2	21.6	11.4	6.3		2.1	42.6	7.6	7.0	1.6
Fourth quarter	1.5	21.0	10.7	6.2		1.9	41.3	6.3	8.2	1.0
1988										
First quarter	1.2	20.9	10.3	5.2		1.3	38.9	18.9	8.3	0.9
Second quarter	1.1	21.3	13.4	6.6			42.4	22.4	7.4	1.3
Third quarter	1.4	29.4	11.7	4.0	0.2		46.7	26.7	11.1	9.4
Fourth quarter	1.7	30.9	14.8	2.9	0.7		51.0	31.0	13.2	10.9
1989										
First quarter	1.3	31.4	13.2	2.0	0.2		48.1	28.1	15.0	11.4
Second quarter	1.2	31.9	9.4	0.4	0.4		43.3	23.3	16.7	11.9
Third quarter	1.3	25.8	7.6	0.3	0.2		35.2	15.2	12.1	6.8
Fourth quarter	1.6	26.7	7.3		0.6		36.2	16.2	11.7	7.7

Source: *Statistical Digest*, Bank of Jamaica

[1]Outstanding holdings of certificates of deposit expressed as a percentage of average deposit balances.

Chart 1. Actual and Statutory Liquid Assets Ratio of Commercial Banks
(In percent)

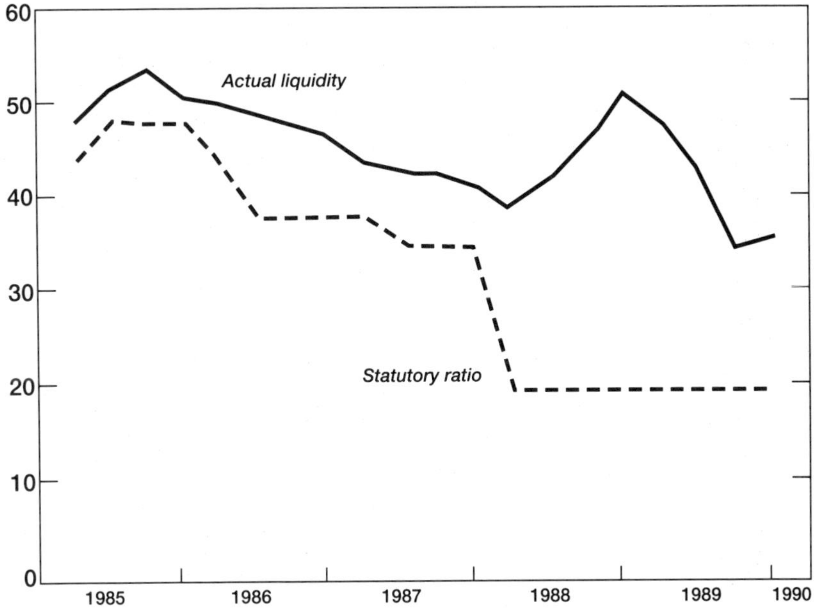

to mop up excess liquidity, but large excess cash and liquid balances still remained in the system. The table also shows some substitution between holdings of certificates of deposit, on the one hand, and treasury bills and local registered stock, on the other.

The excess liquidity that existed in the banking system for most of the period meant that the need for refinancing as a tool for regulating the stock of reserve money was limited. In 1986, a new Liquidity Support Facility was established to manage transactions at the margin. From the facility's inception, access to it was restricted. Support was limited to a maximum of two applications a month, not exceeding a total of five days, and the rate of interest charged was initially $^1/_6$ of 1 percent a day, but later was linked to the highest lending rate charged by the commercial banks.

The factors affecting the demand for currency held by the public—the other component of base money—remained largely outside the direct control of the Bank of Jamaica. Interest rate policy was expected to affect, indirectly, the demand for such balances however. Changes in the exchange rate were also expected to influence changes in the demand for currency. There were also "nonmonetary" factors, such as the cash requirements of a large underground economy, capital flight,

Table 2. Demand for and Supply of Base Money
(In percent)

	Demand			Supply			
Quarters	Commercial Banks' Reserves	Currency	Total	Bank of Jamaica Credit to Public Sector	Other Assets (net)	Foreign Assets (net)	Total
1985							
First quarter	68.1	31.9	100.0	176.0	197.3	−273.3	100.0
Second quarter	72.5	27.5	100.0	144.6	187.9	−232.5	100.0
Third quarter	72.8	27.2	100.0	143.4	191.8	−235.2	100.0
Fourth quarter	68.1	31.9	100.0	111.1	187.9	−199.0	100.0
1986							
First quarter	67.7	32.3	100.0	160.4	149.3	−209.7	100.0
Second quarter	70.6	29.4	100.0	164.3	121.4	−185.7	100.0
Third quarter	70.2	29.8	100.0	180.0	121.6	−201.6	100.0
Fourth quarter	64.7	35.3	100.0	174.3	125.9	−200.2	100.0
1987							
First quarter	69.2	30.8	100.0	128.7	115.5	−144.2	100.0
Second quarter	71.4	28.6	100.0	93.2	109.6	−102.8	100.0
Third quarter	69.1	[illegible]	100.0	98.2	111.6	−109.8	100.0
Fourth quarter	67.4	32.6	100.0	83.4	111.4	−94.8	100.0
1988							
First quarter	69.4	30.6	100.0	55.0	147.5	−102.5	100.0
Second quarter	66.1	33.9	100.0	58.9	149.7	−108.6	100.0
Third quarter	65.0	35.0	100.0	64.4	134.0	−98.4	100.0
Fourth quarter	62.3	37.7	100.0	40.7	121.8	−62.5	100.0
1989							
First quarter	64.0	36.0	100.0	46.4	114.0	−60.4	100.0
Second quarter	65.4	34.6	100.0	47.1	100.8	−48.0	100.0
Third quarter	64.8	35.2	100.0	47.5	123.9	−71.4	100.0
Fourth quarter	61.5	38.5	100.0	60.1	121.2	−81.3	100.0

Source: Monetary Aggregates, Bank of Jamaica.

seasonal demand for transactions balances, etc., which would have caused changes in the demand for currency. The overall impact of these factors has resulted in much variability in this component of the demand for base money. This appears to have been the principal cause of variations in the overall base-money aggregate during the period (see Table 2). The quarterly average proportion of currency to total base money over the period was 32.6 percent, with a significant coefficient of variation (0.10). This indicates the volatility of the currency/deposit ratio and its likely impact on the money multiplier.

In searching for an equilibrium position, the Bank's manipulation of changes in the demand for base money is affected by its capacity to influence the factors relating to the supply of base money. But the characteristics of the supply components of the base shown in Table 2 indicate that only limited control, if any, was possible.

Other Instruments of Monetary Policy

The Bank of Jamaica took some action to remove credit ceilings, but direct controls remained in force for most of the period. For the first half of fiscal year 1985, outstanding credit in the commercial banking system was frozen at the level outstanding at March 31, 1985. But during the second half of the year increases were allowed, which took the outstanding balance to 10 percent above the March 31, 1985 level. In 1986, the global ceilings on bank credit were removed, but ceilings on consumer-oriented credit were retained. These were fixed at the level outstanding at March 31, 1986 and remained at that level until March 31, 1987. For the remainder of 1987 and 1988 global and selective credit ceilings were removed, but in the latter part of 1989 new restrictions were imposed as part of a new stabilization program. Some success can be claimed for the use of these instruments of direct control, if the relative stability of the exchange rate in 1986, 1987, and 1988 is taken as an indicator.

In November 1985, the Bank reintroduced a Pre-Shipment Financing Facility (PSF) and a Bankers Export Guarantee Facility (BEGF) to channel credit to the export sector at preferential rates of interest. The PSF provided credit for raw materials and other intermediate goods to enable companies to meet the demands of the export market. The BEGF provided financial resources to bridge the period between the exports of goods and services and the actual foreign exchange receipts. A Bankers Rediscounting Facility (BRF) was also in operation at the beginning of the period; this was used to channel funds at preferential rates to the agricultural, construction, manufacturing, and tourism sectors. Highly preferential rates of interest were provided for agriculture, but the subsidy for construction, manufacturing, and tourism was less. These were all examples of the use of the rediscounting facility to channel funds to certain preferred areas and to introduce some degree of flexibility into the process of credit allocation so as to stimulate productive activity in the economy. But the use of the discounting facility as a tool of monetary policy, although used several times during the period, had little impact on the overall monetary aggregates.

The cash reserve ratio was used as an active instrument of policy in 1985. During that year, the ratio was changed four times, increasing from 14 percent to 20 percent. It remained at that level until it was reduced to 19.0 percent in July 1989. In July 1986, the Bank of Jamaica commenced paying interest on the cash reserve account up to a maximum of 3 percent of prescribed liabilities held by the banks. The rate of interest was the same as that earned on similar balances. In July 1989, the Bank discontinued the payment of interest on any portion of the cash reserves held by the commercial banks. The inflexibility of the cash reserve ratio as a policy instrument was emphasized by the fact that at 20 percent only a small upward adjustment of the ratio was possible without an amendment of the law. The payment of interest on a proportion of the reserves was intended to reduce upward pressure on interest rates.

Transactions in certificates of deposit were effective in generating market forces that led to changes in short-term interest rates, with the savings deposit rate indexed to a combination of market rates. Interest on savings deposits forms a large component of bank costs, so that changes in these rates were an important instrument for increasing bank lending rates and stabilizing the demand for bank credit. In 1985, for example, when there was an urgent need to reduce domestic demand and stabilize exchange rate movement and balance the external accounts, the minimum savings deposit rate was raised three times, taking the rate from 13 percent to 20 percent. In contrast, there were two reductions in the minimum rate in 1986, which resulted in a reduction of the rate to 15 percent. There were no changes in 1987, but in 1988 the rate was reduced further to 13 percent. In 1989, the rate was again increased, to 18 percent, as the exchange rate came under increased pressure. The savings deposit rate, therefore, assumed the role of a major policy instrument in the manipulation of changes in the level of interest rates. Selected interest rates for the period are shown in Table 3.

A combination of ceilings on bank credit and interest rates contributed to the buildup of liquidity in the banking system and affected the money multiplier when the ceilings forced the banks to hold excess cash balances. Interest rates directly affected the demand for and supply of money and credit and also affected the multiplier when they caused shifts in the proportion of currency to deposits that the public wished to hold. Apart from these factors, there were the nonmonetary factors affecting changes in the money multiplier, such as the seasonal demand for currency. For the 1985–89 period, these factors combined to create much variability in the quarterly money multiplier. Over the period, the average quarterly money multiplier was 2.6628 with a sig-

Table 3. Selected Short-Term Interest Rates

Quarters	Savings Deposit Rate	Certificate of Deposit Rate	Weighted Deposit Rate	Weighted Lending Rate	Treasury Bill Rate
1985					
First quarter	15.00		17.7	20.60	17.13
Second quarter	20.00		18.5	22.27	18.97
Third quarter	20.00		18.5	27.54	19.27
Fourth quarter	20.00		19.6	28.95	21.28
1986					
First quarter	20.00	27.89	20.0	29.20	23.75
Second quarter	16.00	21.00	18.5	26.35	23.17
Third quarter	15.00	18.00	16.1	24.98	17.49
Fourth quarter	15.00	18.00	14.8	24.90	15.93
1987					
First quarter	15.00	18.00	14.4	24.70	16.87
Second quarter	15.00	17.50	14.8	24.91	18.32
Third quarter	13.00	18.00	15.1	24.84	18.76
Fourth quarter	13.00	20.00	15.5	24.59	19.61
1988					
First quarter	13.00	18.37	15.6	24.86	19.68
Second quarter	13.00	18.37	14.9	24.36	19.61
Third quarter	13.00	17.08	14.3	24.35	18.11
Fourth quarter	13.00	17.50	14.3	24.26	18.00
1989					
First quarter	13.00	17.64	14.4	23.68	17.82
Second quarter	13.00	18.54	15.0	23.54	17.91
Third quarter	13.00	20.90	16.2	24.10	19.95
Fourth quarter	18.00	25.11	20.2	28.26	23.59

Source: *Statistical Digest*, Bank of Jamaica.

nificant coefficient of variation. This relatively high degree of variation in the context of base money management indicated the volatile impact of the money multiplier on monetary expansion. The data are shown in Table 4.

The table shows that for most quarters an inverse relationship existed between changes in base money and those in the money multiplier in respect of their impact on the growth of the money supply.[3] This was most evident during the fourth quarters, when large positive changes in base money were associated with the sometimes large con-

[3]The methodology used to separate the impact of the base and the money multiplier on monetary expansion is found in Joachim Ahrensdorf, and S. Kanesathasan, "Variations in The Money Multiplier and Their Implications for Central Banking," *Staff Papers*, International Monetary Fund (Washington), Vol. 8 (November 1960), pp. 126–49.

Table 4. Quarterly Growth Rate of Monetary Variables
(In percent)

Quarters	M2	Base Money	Money Multiplier
1985			
First quarter	5.7	−14.9	20.6
Second quarter	4.7	23.7	−19.0
Third quarter	2.5	3.9	−1.4
Fourth quarter	10.0	17.1	−7.1
1986			
First quarter	6.1	−11.7	17.8
Second quarter	4.8	16.3	−11.5
Third quarter	6.0	1.0	5.0
Fourth quarter	8.2	8.5	−0.3
1987			
First quarter	5.1	3.8	1.3
Second quarter	4.8	11.2	−6.4
Third quarter	−0.1	−5.0	4.9
Fourth quarter	5.3	14.3	−9.0
1988			
First quarter	3.9	−3.5	7.4
Second quarter	8.7	5.1	3.6
Third quarter	9.0	4.4	4.6
Fourth quarter	13.3	24.3	−11.0
1989			
First quarter	−1.0	−3.0	2.0
Second quarter	−0.9	−1.4	0.5
Third quarter	2.9	−3.1	6.0
Fourth quarter	5.3	12.8	−7.5

Source: Monetary Aggregates, Bank of Jamaica.

traction in the money multiplier. During the first quarters, except for 1987, the pattern is reversed, with the changes due to base money being negative while those emanating from the multiplier were positive. A less clear-cut pattern emerges in some of the other quarters but, in most of them, the negative relationship between changes due to the base and those of the money multiplier is evident.

The volatility of the money multiplier appears to be related primarily to changes in the currency/deposit ratio. In the fourth quarters, for example, the public's demand for currency rises sharply to finance a high level of transactions related to the holiday season. This increase in the demand for currency has a positive impact on the expansion of base money but a negative one on the money multiplier. This results from the drawdown of deposit balances by the public and their conversion into currency. As the monetary base expands, the ratio of currency to deposits rises, thereby leading to a reduction of the money multiplier. During the first quarters, the process is reversed. The liquidation of currency holdings is replaced by an increase in business sector deposits in the commercial banks. Hence, base money contracts, but the impact of the money multiplier correspondingly increases as the currency-to-deposit ratio falls. Other factors could possibly offset these changes, but evidence so far indicates the dominance of the currency/deposit relationship.

The thinness of the local money market and the absence of a well-developed secondary market for securities appear to have contributed to the volatility of the changes in the currency/deposit ratio. The existence of a developed capital market in which portfolio balances are more widely spread means that base money expansion arising from an increase in currency demand will have a less direct impact on changes in the currency/deposit ratio. This will also lead to less volatility in the money multiplier. This instability of the money multiplier in Jamaica has complicated the process of base-money management. It could also be an obstacle to the successful implementation of base-money control in other countries where money and capital markets are relatively thin and undeveloped.[4]

Operational Procedures

As part of the operational procedures for monitoring the transition to a more market responsive environment, the Bank of Jamaica established an Open Market Committee comprising its senior managers and chaired by the Governor of the Bank. The Committee supervised the sequencing and supervision of new policy initiatives to ensure their consistency with other aspects of the overall policy framework. In its supervision of open market policy the Committee received weekly reports on money, credit, base money, interest rates, etc., and their performance in regard to prescribed targets, and then advised the Operations Department of the Bank of the targeted open market sales. The Committee also examined applications for liquidity support and other discretionary facilities, such as the discount window, operated by the Bank.

The actual operation of the market for certificates of deposit has been relatively simple, based as it is on only one type of transaction.

---

[4]See Graeme S. Dorrance, "The Instruments of Monetary Policy in Countries Without Highly Developed Capital Markets," *Staff Papers*, International Monetary Fund (Washington), Vol. 12 (July l965), pp. 272–81.

Press releases provide information on the amount of a new offer, the date of issue, the maturity date, and the length of the tenure. Tenders are submitted at least one day before the issue date in sealed envelopes to the Bank. Applicants state the volume that they require, as well as the proposed rate of interest. When the rate is fixed by the Bank, the applicant states only the amount that is required. Applications are vetted by senior administrative personnel of the Operations Department of the Bank to ensure that they comply with the rules of the tender. But the decision concerning the rate of interest to be accepted and the volume of qualified bids is made by the Open Market Committee of the Bank.

The monetary policy changes and other developments in the financial sector have resulted in a revision of the legislation that governs the activities of the Bank of Jamaica and the commercial banks. This is expected to strengthen the legal basis for further development of base-money management. Other amendments will set legal minimum ratios for both reserve and liquidity balances. There are also amendments that are aimed at giving increased powers to the Bank of Jamaica, a move that will increase the independence of the Bank in the implementation of policy.

With regard to the commercial banks, the proposed amendments aim to reduce the growth of monopoly power within the sector by limiting the links with nonfinancial entities. The proposed legislation seeks to prevent large-scale equity participation by commercial banks in nonfinancial entities.

Supervisory operations of the Bank Inspection Department have been increased during the period to allow for increased monitoring of the banks' balance sheets and profit-and-loss accounts. The banks were required to adopt a new reporting format, and accounting guidelines have been revised and updated. Liquidity and interest rate monitoring have also been increased, the main focus being the monitoring of short-run liquidity risks. Banks have also begun to report off-balance sheet items, such as commitments and guarantees, which, if met, affect the banks' liquidity and therefore become balance sheet assets or liabilities. Many of the off-balance sheet commitments are facilities that borrowers may use whenever they wish, and can thus be considered as ways of circumventing the credit restrictions.

Summary and Conclusion

The phasing out of the statutory liquid asset requirement in the commercial banking system was carried out in accordance with the scheduled program that had been agreed to with the World Bank. Because the statutory liquidity requirement was generally below actual levels of liquidity, there was some substitution between treasury bills and certificates of deposit. More substantively, however, in defense of price and exchange rate stability in the Bank of Jamaica's transactions in certificates of deposit, the substitutions were devoted solely to reducing, rather than augmenting, liquidity levels in the banking system. This led to some lack of dynamism in the market for certificates. High levels of liquidity in the banking system also reduced the role of central bank refinancing as an instrument of aggregate monetary policy. Instead, such refinancing as was carried out by the Bank was used mainly as a tool in the allocation of credit.

In spite of the movement to indirect instruments of policy, selective credit ceilings still remained an important direct policy tool. Given the limited range of financial instruments that were available, the credit ceilings formed an effective, although not efficient, instrument of policy. The cash reserve ratio remains a blunt and inflexible instrument, which has been used only once since 1985. Its inflexibility is emphasized by the fact that at 20 percent the ratio is near the maximum that is permitted by law.

The effectiveness of base-money control was hampered by the instability of the money multiplier. An estimate based on quarterly data shows a high degree of variability in the money multiplier. The reasons for this instability can be traced to the volatility of the currency/deposit ratio, which appears to be linked to thinness in the local money market. Other developing countries could experience similar problems where money and capital markets are thin.

Base-money control was also hampered by the inability of the Bank of Jamaica to exercise adequate control over the supply of reserve money. As is shown in Table 2, two of the factors influencing the supply of base money are the Bank of Jamaica's net credit to the public sector and the change in net foreign assets of the Bank. The change in net other assets is the other component in the supply of base money. These net other assets are in fact mainly other elements of credit provided to the public sector by the Bank of Jamaica. They reflect losses of the Bank stemming from policies implemented on behalf of the Government. The nature of these components, together with the absence of any substantial refinancing of commercial banks, indicated minimal control by the Bank over the factors influencing the supply of reserve money. This was an additional difficulty in promoting an effective policy of base-money management.

Interest rate policy reflected a mix of market and nonmarket forces. The savings deposit rate remained an important and frequently used direct instrument of interest rate policy. On the other hand, the rate for certificates of deposit emerged as a freely determined market rate, except in periods when it was fixed by the Bank. In spite of its partially regulated nature, interest rate policy succeeded in generating positive real short-term interest rates in 1986 and 1987. In that sense, the policy could have made a contribution to financial deepening and the long-term development of the money and capital markets in Jamaica.[5]

The attempt at base-money management encountered substantial difficulty in the period under review, although success was achieved in implementing some of the reforms. The need remains to develop and broaden the money and capital markets. A secondary market for securities, as well as a more vibrant interbank market, needs to be developed. Refinancing as a tool of monetary policy represents another instrument that needs to be developed.

[5]See Ronald I. McKinnon, *Money and Capital in Economic Development* (Washington: Brookings Institution, 1973).

23

Kenya's Transition from Direct to Indirect Instruments of Monetary Policy

DAVID FOLKERTS-LANDAU*

Kenya has been engaged in far-reaching financial sector reforms aimed at improving monetary control and at improving the efficiency of financial intermediation. Exclusive reliance on credit ceilings, without an adequate mechanism for implementing such ceilings, combined with controls on interest rates had resulted in the progressive weakening of monetary control and had produced the inefficiencies in financial intermediation that are characteristic of the use of direct monetary policy instruments. This paper discusses the implementation and the sequencing of reform measures that led to the use of market-based techniques of monetary control.

The approach adopted by Kenya in moving from direct to indirect instruments of monetary control is instructive for three reasons. First, it was recognized that the liberalization of interest rates was a necessary prerequisite for the successful use of market operations to control money and credit aggregates. Hence, the authorities undertook a gradual relaxation of interest rate controls, focusing the removal of controls on treasury bill yields. Second, since government securities markets were to a significant degree segmented from other financial markets, the immediate and exclusive reliance on open market operations in government securities for purposes of monetary control was not desirable. Instead, it was necessary to broaden and deepen the market for government securities to remove the segmentation, and thus improve the transmission of policy effects from the monetary to

---

*The author is Deputy Division Chief of the Financial Studies Division of the International Monetary Fund. Peter Garber, Peter Heller, Maurice Kanga, Donald J. Mathieson, and V. Sundararajan provided helpful comments during the preparation of this paper.

the real sector. Third, Kenya introduced an innovative transitional arrangement in the form of a market-based enforcement mechanism for credit ceilings to improve control of money and credit, until open market operations could be used in sufficient volume.

The Issues

In 1989 and early 1990, the Kenyan monetary authorities faced major difficulties in implementing monetary policy.[1] Credit ceilings were, in practice, the main instrument at their disposal to manage liquidity. These ceilings were not fully effective, however, since enforcement was weak; therefore, compliance was poor, and the ceilings could not in any event be used to fine-tune short-term liquidity movements. Furthermore, the monetary authorities were not in a position to sell sufficient government securities in the open market to control liquidity, because of an administered interest rate structure. As a result, any unprogrammed increase in reserve money—frequently due to government borrowing from the Central Bank of Kenya—could not be fully sterilized through the sale of government securities and resulted in a multiple expansion in the money and credit aggregates.

The development of a viable market in government bills and bonds was held back by two major impediments. The first was the growing gap between yields on such securities—particularly treasury bills—and effective bank lending rates. Through the application of fees and charges, banks had been able to increase effective rates above administered rates for a substantial portion of their lending to the private sector. For example, although the maximum rate for short-term lending was 15.5 percent in March 1990, the effective rate was estimated to be in the range of from 20 to 22 percent. At the same time, the maximum yield on treasury bills was about 14 percent and on treasury bonds about 19 percent, that is, not sufficiently high to generate voluntary demand for securities from the financial sector. Similarly, with treasury bill yields below the rate on time deposits of 15–16 percent, the nonfinancial sector also had no incentive to acquire bills on a voluntary basis. Under these circumstances, the sale of government securities was mostly to captive lenders, and actual quantities sold were well below desired levels.[2]

[1]For a detailed review and description of the issues, see Folkerts-Landau and others (1990) and (1991).

[2]Banks and nonbank financial institutions demand treasury bills to satisfy a liquidity requirement; the National Social Security Fund (NSSF) and insurance companies are mandated to hold bills and bonds, and at times, parastatals are directed by the treasury to hold government

On the other hand, although, the spread between the rate on savings deposits earned at banks, and the yield on treasury bonds was about 6–7 percent in favor of treasury bonds, the authorities were not able to sell a sufficient volume at the prevailing bond rate to absorb excess liquidity. Thus, pricing was not the only factor holding back sales of bonds. The second impediment to increasing their sale, therefore, was identified as an insufficiently developed institutional structure in the government securities markets. In particular, the absence of an effective marketing and distribution system, as well as the absence of liquidity caused by the lack of a market maker was hampering the sale of bonds to the nonfinancial sector.

The reluctance to raise yields on government securities was based on the view that demand for such securities could be increased without further increases in yields and that, indeed, further increases in yields would not have much effect on demand. The fact that a yield on treasury bonds of 19 percent exceeded the rate on savings deposits by 6.5 percent, and that real interest rates were in excess of 5 percent, tended to support the hypothesis that informational and institutional shortcomings had effectively *segmented the treasury bond market from other markets*, thus severely hampering the transmission of monetary policy to the real sector.

Hence, rather than allowing yields to find their market-clearing levels in a market that was perceived to be segmented and narrowly based, the authorities undertook an ambitious program to broaden and deepen the market for government securities. Among these were the introduction of bearer bonds to preserve the anonymity of the investor; the expansion of the role of the Central Bank as market maker through outright purchases and sales designed to increase liquidity in securities markets; and finally, the publicizing of the pricing and availability of government securities, particularly to financial cooperatives, public sector employees, and the Asian community. These measures were then reinforced by a gradual increase in yields on treasury securities, particularly those on treasury bills. In late 1990, the authorities implemented the final step in the liberalization process, namely, the freeing of treasury bill rates. Simultaneously, the Central Bank established its operational capabilities in the money market and set up the data gathering mechanism needed to sterilize effectively any disturbances to the monetary base.

It was expected that these efforts to increase the sales of government securities would take some time to become fully effective. In order to

bills and bonds, and at times, parastatals are directed by the treasury to hold government securities.

ensure some degree of monetary control in the interim, the authorities implemented a transitional credit control measure to achieve a higher degree of compliance with the ceilings on bank credit to the private sector. In particular, banks were required to deposit 20 percent of any credit in excess of individual bank credit ceilings into an interest-free deposit with the Central Bank. The size of the deposit in relation to the excess credit was uniform across all banks and was calculated from the credit multiplier so as to reduce the growth in reserve money to levels consistent with credit ceilings. The effect of this penalty deposit scheme was to reduce the income from loans extended beyond the credit ceiling to approximately what could be earned by investing in treasury bonds.

Monetary Policy Problems and Arrangements

A review of monetary developments in Kenya in early 1990 identified two major problems: a permanently high variability in the stock of reserve money and, since the end of 1988, an unprogrammed expansion in monetary and credit aggregates. Both problems raised questions about the efficiency and effectiveness of the monetary policy arrangements. Table 1 illustrates the variability in reserve money and shows that government overdraft at the Central Bank has been one of the main causes of this increase. The monetary data in Table 2 show that growth in liquidity throughout 1989 was increasing rapidly.

Present Policy Arrangements

The main instruments of monetary and credit policy in Kenya are quantitative ceilings on total domestic credit and net bank credit to the Government.[3] The Central Bank controls bank credit to borrowers other than the Central Government through monthly credit ceilings on each bank. In practice, the Central Bank has attempted to enforce observance of these ceilings through moral suasion. The treasury tries to ensure compliance with the credit ceilings on outstanding lending by the Central Bank to the Government by controlling the level of the Government's overdraft with the bank.

The main advantage of credit ceilings was that of a quick-acting, short-term monetary policy measure to restrict money and credit

[3]These ceilings constitute performance criteria for the Fund-supported adjustment program. As a result of the problems mentioned in the previous section, the 1990 Article IV consultation mission recommended a change in the performance criterion for total domestic credit to a ceiling on net domestic assets, which will cover the "Other items net." This, however, will not resolve other more general problems of compliance with the credit ceilings which are discussed below.

Table 1. Sources of Variation in Reserve Money, 1987–89
(In millions of Kenyan shillings; end of quarter)

	1987		1988				1989			
	III	IV	I	II	III	IV	I	II	III	IV
Reserve money	+8	+1,769	−943	−602	+627	+1,137	+771	−707	+702	+1,371
Government overdraft	+1,544	+1,024	−1,664	+425	+396	+1,799	−170	−1,025	+577	−1,128
Net foreign assets	−1,663	+670	−384	−484	−66	−466	+987	+562	−1,272	+431
Advances and discounts to banks	+5	−5	+51	+166	−216	+152	−223	+12	−12	+1,019
Treasury bills and bonds	—	+207	−162	+425	+63	−500	+1,789	−27	+398	−13
Government stock	—	—	—	—	—	—	−2,000	—	—	—
Uncleared effects	−55	+59	+1,264	−1,313	−484	+642	+1,094	−397	+328	+1,274
Other items (net)	+177	−186	−48	+177	+934	−490	−704	+168	+683	−212

Source: Central Bank of Kenya.

Table 2. Monetary Data, 1987–89
(Annual change in percent)

	1987	1988	1989 I	1989 II	1989 III	1989 IV
Reserve money	18.9	1.8	17.3	17.3	16.7	17.3
Net domestic assets	18.1	10.7	11.7	14.2	19.1	14.1
Total domestic credit	20.5	7.2	7.4	8.3	12.8	9.7
Money and quasi-money	12.4	8.3	12.7	17.8	20.7	17.8

Sources: Central Bank of Kenya; and Fund staff estimates.

expansion. Kenya's experience, however, particularly during 1990 and 1991, demonstrated how inefficient and ineffective credit ceilings are as the only instrument of monetary policy. The authorities were unable to reduce fluctuations in reserve money, nor could ceilings contain the significant growth in liquidity that had been building up in the system since the end of 1988. The ineffectiveness of this ceiling is illustrated by the fact that the four major banks in Kenya were in excess of their credit limits to the private sector by K Sh 3.0 billion at the end of January 1990, which is 14.3 percent on average above the ceilings (the banking sector as a whole was 8.5 percent above its aggregate limits).[4]

Credit controls also introduced rigidities and reduced competition in the financial system, and resulted in a misallocation of resources. In addition, borrowers and lenders in the financial markets have been successful in avoiding such controls by channelling lending to wholly owned nonbank financial institutions.

The Central Bank was not able to channel excess liquidity into the treasury bill and bond markets through sales of such securities. Current yields and institutional arrangements made it difficult to sell the necessary volume of government securities into the open market. Demand in these markets has been generated mainly by statutory liquidity requirements placed on the NSSF and insurance companies, and by the minimum liquidity requirements of the commercial banks and nonbank financial institutions. Efforts to achieve better monetary control have, therefore, concentrated on improving the ability of the Central Bank to sell government securities. This aim is being pursued along two avenues. First, yields on treasury bills and bonds are being allowed gradually to reflect market forces fully. Second, the institu-

[4]The banking system as a whole could avoid breaching the credit ceilings only if it were willing to hold non-interest-bearing excess reserves at the Central Bank or to invest in government securities at below bank-lending rates for comparable maturities.

tional structure of the government securities market is being improved.

Simultaneously, the Central Bank is formulating on a continuing basis a reserve money program, entailing projections of the supply and demand for reserve money so as to determine the volume of government securities that must be sold in order to achieve the desired growth in base money. To this end, the bank is establishing a statistical framework for monitoring and forecasting influences on reserve money and has begun compiling on a daily basis the historical data required. This monetary programming framework will consist of a mechanism to (a) smooth short-term liquidity conditions and interest rates in the money markets, which should help the growth of the secondary market; and (b) ensure that monetary expansion occurs in line with its financial program. These statistical data are being supplied by the relevant departments of the Central Bank, the Ministry of Finance, and other government departments.

With a reliable statistical framework in place by mid-1990, the Central Bank started to conduct shadow, open market operations. These operations allowed the relevant central bank departments to gain expertise in monetary programming and in trading with the financial sector. This approach also allowed banks to become accustomed to this type of operation.

Reform of Interest Rate Policies

The Kenyan authorities recognized early that an environment of flexible interest rates is a vital prerequisite for the development of an effective monetary policy framework, operating through market-based instruments. This section reviews interest rate policies and the problems associated with these policies, as well as the reform efforts.

Present Interest Rate Policies

Kenyan authorities had been regulating interest rates of commercial banks since 1974 by imposing a maximum lending rate and a minimum savings deposit rate. In April 1989, the system was amended slightly: the maximum rate was split into a rate for short-term lending and one for lending with maturities of four years or more. This change brought the commercial banks' long-term lending rate in line with that of the nonbank financial institutions. The maximum rate for long-term lending was applied to loans of more than three years in November 1989.

The *effective interest rate structure*, however, differed from this administered framework, mainly because of the existence of an active wholesale market and because of the application of fees and charges (Table 3). Effective interest rates on time deposits in June 1990 were 15–16 percent, and 7–9 percent on wholesale current accounts (current accounts are nominally non-interest-bearing). This implied that roughly 48–50 percent of the banks' funding is at the minimum rate (savings accounts and non-interest-bearing current accounts) against 50–52 percent that is attracted at a higher cost.

Table 3. Interest Rate Structure, October 1989
(In percent)

Effective bank lending rates	22–24
Yield on treasury bonds (two years)	24
Maximum long-term lending rate[1]	19
Maximum short-term lending rate[1]	17
Central Bank rediscount rate[2]	17.5
Interbank rate, overnight	6–19
Discount rate on treasury bills[1]	14
Minimum savings deposits rate[1]	13.5
Wholesale current accounts	7–9
Retail current accounts	0
Certificates of deposit	14–17

[1]Administered rates.
[2]Rediscount of government paper. The rediscount rate for private paper is 1 percentage point higher.

In general, the yields on government securities have been set more or less in line with administered rates. The discount rate on *treasury bills* was, in practice, predetermined by the treasury. Each week, the Central Bank offered for tender K Sh 2 billion in 90–day bills. Tenders were accepted or rejected on the basis of this discount rate. In practice, the accepted rate was only marginally different from the result of the previous week's tender. The actual yield was slightly higher than the accepted discount rate.[5] Bidders were, therefore, very cautious in their bids; and there is evidence that several market participants, who were in need of large amounts of treasury bills in order to comply with regulatory requirements, consulted with the authorities prior to the tender. Since the fourth quarter of 1988, there has been a tendency to

[5]The accepted discount rate for the March 5 tender was 14.0 percent, while the effective yield was 14.3 percent for 91 days.

increase the rate on treasury bills only gradually.[6] As a result of the procedures, the amounts accepted are in most cases much lower than the amounts tendered, as Table 4 shows.

Table 4. Treasury Bill Tenders—Overview of the Amounts Allotted
(In millions of Kenyan Shillings)

	Amount Offered[1]	Amount Accepted	As Percentage of Amount Issued
1989			
September	8,000	6,312.8	78.9
October	10,000	5,749.4	57.5
November	8,000	6,235.8	77.9
December	11,000[2]	8,059.1	73.3
1990			
January	10,000	4,268.1	42.7
February	8,000	5,987.1	74.8

Source: Central Bank of Kenya.
[1]K Sh 2,000 million per tender.
[2]Three tenders of K Sh 2,000 million and one, at the end of the month, of K Sh 5,000 million.

Starting in September 1989, treasury bonds (with maturities of one, two, and five years) have been auctioned on a monthly basis. Previously, the Government only held auctions irregularly. The treasury fixes the amount of the issue, and the effective yield is determined by the price bids that are acceptable to the treasury.

Three important conclusions can be drawn from the preceding overview: (a) effective bank lending rates were significantly higher than the administratively prescribed rates; (b) the yields on government paper—and particularly on treasury bills—were set in line with administered rates; and (c) average savings deposit rates were significantly lower than the yields on government bonds (6–7 percent). Despite this latter yield gap, almost no nonbank savings are channeled into government paper. This fact was taken as indicative of the existence of severe institutional rigidities in the government paper market.

[6]The treasury bill rate is also the benchmark rate for the Central Bank's advances and rediscounts: the Central Bank sets its rate on bank borrowing when treasury bills are used as collateral and its rate for rediscounts of treasury bills at 1.5 percentage points above the maximum rate on treasury bills accepted by the Government in the most recent tender. The comparable rates for private paper are 2.5 percentage points above the maximum rate on treasury bills accepted by the Government in the most recent tender.

Problems Arising from Interest Rate Regulations

That yields on government paper are held closely to the administered bank lending rates creates a growing discrepancy with the effective bank lending rates. This is a major reason why the monetary authorities have been unable to sell sufficient quantities of government securities to control base money growth.

The fact that the yield on bills is 7–8 percent below the effective bank lending rates makes it difficult to attract genuine demand from the banking sector. Yet, in a financial market like Kenya's, where financial intermediation is the predominant way of channeling savings from surplus to deficit units, this sector should be an important source for government borrowing. Second, the fact that the treasury bill rate is 2 percent below the wholesale time deposit rate makes this paper unattractive for other potential investors, such as large companies.

As regards treasury bonds, the fact that five-year bonds are yielding 2–3 percent less than short-term bank lending also means that the financial sector will not voluntarily hold bonds. Another economically relevant aspect of the yield structure, however, is the premium by which the bond yield exceeds the banks' savings deposit rate.

The existing demand for government securities is largely generated by induced purchases by important captive lenders. It can be seen from Table 5 that for bills, bonds, and stock, the "parastatals and others" are by far the most important holders. At the end of the financial year 1988/89, parastatals and others held 52.3 percent of total domestic government debt. The NSSF and insurance companies (private and government owned) are the most important institutions in this category. They are subject to stringent holding requirements for bills and bonds. The parastatals are not subject to legal requirements, but they are frequently urged by the treasury to invest their surplus funds in government securities.

Only 29.8 percent of total domestic government debt is in the hands of banks and nonbank financial institutions. The data indicate that these securities are primarily held to comply with the liquid assets ratio or as a cushion for borrowing from the Central Bank.[7] In June 1989, the commercial banks' treasury bill portfolio amounted to K Sh 4.7 billion. The required amount according to the liquid assets ratio at that time was K Sh 4.2 billion. The residual, K Sh 0.5 billion is the "cushion."

[7]Fifty percent of the commercial banks' liquid assets under this ratio must be held in the form of treasury bills. Treasury bonds maturing within three months are considered equivalent to bills.

Table 5. Outstanding Government Domestic Debt
(June, end of financial year)

	1987/88		1988/89	
	In millions of Kenyan shillings	In percent of total	In millions of Kenyan shillings	In percent of total
Direct Central Bank advances to government	7,756	16.7	8,747	17.9
Treasury bills	15,598	33.6	15,466	31.7
Banks	*4,076*	*8.8*	*4,687*	*9.6*
Nonbank financial institutions	*2,951*	*6.4*	*3,126*	*6.4*
Parastatals and others	*8,571*	*18.4*	*7,653*	*15.7*
Treasury bonds	9,160	19.7	13,169	27.0
Banks	*1,663*	*3.6*	*2,959*	*6.1*
Nonbank financial institutions	*282*	*0.6*	*193*	*0.4*
Parastatals and others	*7,215*	*15.5*	*10,017*	*20.5*
Government stocks	13,928	30.0	11,451	23.4
Banks	*5,428*	*11.8*	*3,428*	*7.0*
Nonbank financial institutions	*71*	*0.1*	*171*	*0.3*
Parastatals and others	*8,429*	*18.1*	*7,852*	*16.1*
Total government debt	46,442	100.0	48,833	100.0

Source: Central Bank of Kenya.

Another problem created by selling securities into captive markets is that—in addition to the lack of volume—the market in its present form is not liquid enough to permit the Central Bank to intervene through short-term purchases or sales to financial institutions. Most of the institutional investors will hold the securities until maturity.

The combination of below-market administered lending rates and credit ceilings has produced excess credit demand. This excess demand has reinforced banks' preferences for safer, connected borrowers, thereby limiting the credit available to long-term projects and to new or more risky, entrepreneurial borrowers. This behavior has resulted in preferential treatment for larger companies and parastatals. A derived effect from this policy may be that the banks' managerial skills are not as developed as they would be in an environment with more diversified investment opportunities.

Below-market administered interest rates have also tended to favor debt financing over equity financing, which, together with other institutional shortcomings, explains the decline of Kenya's equity markets during the last decade. Recently, efforts have been undertaken to revitalize the capital markets, inter alia, through the establishment of a Capital Markets Authority.

Finally, below-market administered interest rates have prevented the authorities from considering the liberalization of exchange controls, because of the fear that this measure would induce large capital outflows.

Recent Policy Measures

The approach to interest rate liberalization has proceeded along two lines:

First is alignment of the administered bank interest rate structure with the market-clearing structure. Effective April 1, 1990, the ceilings on interest rates on deposits and on short- and long-term loans were raised by 1 percentage point, to 13.5 percent, 16.5 percent, and 19.0 percent, respectively. The ceiling on short-term loans was raised by a further 0.5 percentage point at the end of August 1990, to 17.0 percent. More important, the authorities removed the legal requirement stipulating that lending related fees and charges be inclusive of the loan interest rates subject to ceilings. This means that effective interest rates can significantly exceed the formal ceilings and that they are market determined.

Second is that yields on government securities are to be market determined. This was first and foremost required for treasury bills, as this market will be used for open market policy purposes. The same policy also holds for yields on government bonds, although institutional growth in this market is being emphasized equally. The rates on treasury bonds are fully liberalized, and the yields on treasury bills will be liberalized effective November 15, 1990, allowing price to be set by true and proper auction.

The move toward equilibrium interest rates was self-reinforcing: the gap between government securities' yields and the effective bank rates narrowed, and the greater volume of government paper sold reduced the growth in reserve money caused by government borrowing from the Central Bank. Furthermore, the reduction in inflationary expectations lowered the effective bank lending rates and narrow the gap between them and government securities' yields. The reforms of the administered interest rate structure will be completed by June 1991.

Institutional Reform of the Government Securities Markets

The previous section has pointed out that the relatively low yields are a major barrier to the smooth development of government securities markets. In addition, however, institutional and distributional rigidities have the effect of segmenting the government securities markets from other markets, most notably the banking markets. It was, therefore, necessary to undertake measures to broaden and deepen government securities markets before full interest rate liberalization could become effective.

In this regard, it is useful to draw a distinction between the treasury bill market and the bond market, inter alia, because the target group of potential investors differs. The treasury bill market will, at least in the initial stages, be mainly a market for professionals, that is, banks, other financial institutions, and large nonfinancial companies. The treasury bond market, on the other hand, should be adequately developed so as to offer investment opportunities for the nonfinancial sector as well. In this way, the small investor would be in a position to diversify his asset portfolio.

Reforms of the Treasury Bill Market

Although the treasury bill market suffered in the main from a yield that was too low, its development was also hindered by a number of institutional problems.

Tenders

The main institutional problems in the treasury bill market concern the tender method. Efficient tender procedures are the heart of well-functioning government securities markets. They have a bearing on the marketability and the liquidity of the market, and for that reason also on monetary policy. A first requirement is that tenders must be "clean." Currently, the treasury determines the discount rate on bills, and competition is undermined by informal consultations between large bidders and the authorities to determine which bids are acceptable. This has resulted in few bids in excess of the permitted yields, and, consequently, the sales volume has been less than the amounts on offer.

The Central Bank has now begun to preannounce auction dates and amounts on offer and to solicit sealed bids. It is planned to let the treasury bill tender amounts be determined by the reserve money program and not by the needs of the treasury. Bids will be accepted beginning with the highest, until the amount on offer is exhausted. During a transitional period, the Central Bank will seek to prevent excessive rate fluctuations in tenders by limiting the maximum change in the successive tender rates (e.g., 0.5 percent a year in any one direction). The market participants will be informed of this policy and of this range. As the tenders develop, the present practice of irregular "on tap" sales will also cease; a secondary market in treasury bills and bonds will remove the need for this type of operation.

A more competitive primary market should, in principle, provide a sounder foundation for monetary policy operations. Initially, the primary market will be used for monetary policy purposes. But since the use of the primary market for monetary policy purposes may create conflicts between monetary policy and fiscal policy priorities, the Central Bank will conduct monetary policy through the secondary markets.[8]

Primary Dealers

If the first two measures fail to generate turnover in treasury bills, then the Central Bank may ask a group of financial institutions to act as primary dealers. Participation in tenders would then be restricted to such dealers. In return, the dealers would be required to make a two-way market in government securities. The dealers might be established as subsidiaries of the commercial banks. They might serve also as market makers in other segments of the money market. Setting up a dealer network would require, of course, efficient supervisory guidelines, including in particular, minimum capital requirements.

Supplementary Measures

As the treasury bill market develops, the Central Bank will encourage other money market instruments as well. At present, the interbank market is exclusively an overnight market. The development of an efficient interbank market (with a variety of maturities) would allow banks to manage their liquidity more easily and would make the liquidity conditions more homogenous across the financial system. One way to encourage the interbank market is to make the lender-of-last-resort facilities penal. A liquid interbank market could provide also a

[8]No particular institutional or administrative impediment to the development of a secondary bill market exists. The reform measures, and especially the proposed increase in yields, would gradually generate secondary market transactions. In order to prepare for secondary market trading, Central Bank has to convert some or all of the current government overdraft into treasury bills. Proposals along this line have already been formulated. They should be implemented as soon as possible.

benchmark rate for transactions in the fledgling secondary treasury bill market, and for that reason improve the efficiency of the latter.

Reforms of the Treasury Bond Market

The institutional rigidities and shortcomings that prevent the non-financial sector from investing in bonds mainly concern an inadequate marketing and distribution system; the absence of market makers to provide liquidity; the lack of transparency in tenders; and the unavailability of bearer instruments. As a result, the sale of securities to small investors has been minimal, despite the substantial interest differential in favor of government securities. The interaction of these measures with the recommendations regarding the yield should enable the Central Bank to exploit the market for government securities. A deepening of these markets will then allow the authorities to absorb part of the liquidity overhang that is currently in the system.

Special Issue of Treasury Bonds

A special issue of treasury bonds is meant to promote the sale of treasury bonds on a large scale. The target group is the nonbank sector, and especially the personal investor—public sector employees, farmers, and cooperatives. In order to acquaint this group with longer-term types of investment, one-year bonds are suggested for the first time. The Central Bank will fix the conditions of issue, and the bonds will be offered for subscription during a predetermined period.

Depending on the results of this issue, the authorities will decide whether to continue with a series of "special" issues, alongside the auctions for professionals, or to supplement the auction with non-competitive bids for small investors.

Purchase Facility for Small Volumes of Bonds

Holders of small amounts of bonds will want to be reassured on the liquidity of their investment. Professional investors are likely to be unwilling to purchase small quantities from personal investors; and the costs involved in locating a professional counterparty and completing the transaction are likely to be high. One way of enhancing the liquidity of small holdings of securities is for the Central Bank to establish a small-purchase facility. The Central Bank would stand ready (either directly or through the Post Office) to repurchase, on request, treasury bonds at current market rates (perhaps adjusted for a handling fee).

To avoid stifling the secondary market for major investors, and to prevent banks and others from gaining uncontrolled access to central bank funds, repurchases will be restricted, however, to personal investors completing the appropriate "application-to-sell" forms. A facility of this kind can increase the attractiveness of bonds at a low cost without harming the secondary market.

Bearer Securities

Bearer securities, as opposed to registered securities, provide many advantages, and the Central Bank is at present investigating actively their introduction—in particular, the security details of printing and the range of denominations to be offered. The issue of bearer securities should overcome the concern of investors that information regarding their holdings and interest income will be transmitted to the Commissioner of Inland Revenue. Bearer securities should encourage also the holding and trading of paper at places distant from Nairobi and Mombassa.

Effective Price Information

Offering coupon rates of interest that are closer to the effective yield could increase subscriptions. Many people may not realize that rates of return are dependent on the actual price paid for the securities, together with the coupon rate. They could be deterred by apparent returns of only 16 percent a year. The authorities will work toward improving the public's appreciation of the actual yield they will receive on their investment, as part of the marketing campaign. If this does not appear to be successful, the authorities will consider higher coupon rates as a way of encouraging subscriptions.

Consolidating the Maturity Dates

For some time the Government has, on occasion, issued treasury bonds, but in 1989 it began a series of monthly tenders. Each tender included securities with one, two, and five years' maturity. Rigid adherence to these maturities has produced a proliferation of stocks and maturity dates. There are 35 series currently on issue, each with a separate maturity date. Ten series will mature in 1990, eleven in 1991.

This multiplicity of stocks adversely affects their marketability. Reducing the number of series but increasing the volume on issue for each maturity date will widen the number of holders of each stock. The greater the number of holders and the larger the volume of stock, the more likely it is that secondary trading will occur.

This is to be achieved through two steps. First, a single maturity date will be chosen for each month—ideally the same date for each month of the year to simplify the trading process. Any date can be chosen;

however, 10 of the 35 series currently mature on the fifteenth day of the month, so this might be a good initial choice. Second, the authorities will move away from the issue of strict one-, two-, and five-year maturities. By selecting a single maturity date for each month and issuing stocks that do not have an exact number of years to maturity, the authorities can reduce, over time, the number of maturity dates in each year.

An Asset Reserve Requirement

It was recognized that institutional reforms and monetary policy framework development were likely to be slow to take hold; hence, it was necessary to provide a backstop during the transitional period. Better compliance with the ceiling on commercial bank credit to the private sector could provide the necessary control of credit in the interim. Once the Central Bank is in a position to trade government securities in the open market, it will no longer be necessary to rely on credit ceilings to control monetary expansion.

Enforcement would take place by requiring noncomplying banks to place a non-interest-bearing deposit at the Central Bank equivalent to 20 percent of the amount by which the banks have exceeded their credit ceiling. The size of the deposit in relation to the excess credit would be uniform across all banks and would be such as to reduce the banks' reserves at the Central Bank to the level that supports credit extended up to the ceiling only. It was expected that banks with excess credit positions will initially finance the required deposits through increased borrowing from the Central Bank. It was expected that access to such borrowed funds would be administered liberally during the transition phase, that is, prior to May 31, 1990.

A stricter enforcement of the credit ceiling on bank credit to the private sector would most likely also generate additional demand for government securities by financial institutions, in the event of unprogrammed growth in reserve money. Some of the excess liquidity created by government borrowing from the Central Bank would then flow into government securities.

Reserve Money Programming

The Central Bank has begun to develop the statistical base for a monetary programming exercise—to be able to forecast influences on reserve money. Changes in the supply of cash reserves result from transactions between the public (including the banks) and the Central Bank. These transactions can be divided broadly into nondiscretionary factors—those that are largely beyond the short-term control of the bank—and the Central Bank's discretionary operations. Forecasting of influences on reserve money is concerned with the nondiscretionary transactions and the Central Bank's policy action with discretionary operations. Changes in the demand for cash reserves depend on banks' demand for reserve balances. This, in turn, depends on the growth of deposits in the banking system and cash ratio requirements.

The main nondiscretionary transactions are listed below. Depending on their sign, the items will either increase (+) or decrease (−) the cash reserves of the banks:

(1) net purchase (+) or sale (−) of foreign exchange by the Central Bank;

(2) increase (−) in currency in circulation;

(3) net payments (+) by government (increase in overdraft or drawdown of deposits);

(4) net redemption (+) or issue (−) of treasury bills and bonds; and

(5) increase (+) in access to refinancing and advances windows at the Central Bank.

The main discretionary policy actions by the CBK that influence cash reserves are:

(6) sales (−) or purchases (+) of treasury bills;

(7) sales (−) or purchases (+) of treasury bonds; and

(8) central bank lending (+).

The sum of items (1) through (8) determines the overall increase in cash reserves. This increase has to be compared with the additional demand for cash reserves by the banking system to meet required cash ratios and the level of desired precautionary balances. By comparing the level of cash reserves that is likely to be supplied with the level that is forecast in line with the Fund-supported monetary program, the level of bank reserves that needs to be absorbed or injected can be determined. From these calculations, the volume of government securities to be sold or purchased in the Central Bank's open market operations can be determined.

Once all the monetary data is available and in place, the Central Bank can start to train staff for "shadow," open market operations, with a view to daily community operations in 1991. This strategy would, of course, need to be agreed to by the Monetary Policy Committee and other decision makers, and projections would need to be discussed on a regular basis in these forums. The Monetary Policy Committee should receive regular reports on monetary conditions to enable it to assess progress toward its longer-term monetary policy objectives and to assess the success of previous projections and decisions based thereon.

Finally, the Central Bank has undertaken efforts to ensure that its operation of monetary policy is well understood in the financial markets, including those parastatals who have invested a considerable amount of their portfolio in government securities. To this end, the objectives of monetary policy will be stated clearly, and any relevant information on monetary conditions publicized.

Bibliography

Folkerts-Landau, David, Marc Quintyn, and Richard J. Walton, "Kenya: Toward Improved Monetary Control" (unpublished, Washington: International Monetary Fund, 1990).

Folkerts-Landau, David, Peter M. Garber, and Aftab S. Ahmed, "Kenya: Development of Money and Capital Markets" (unpublished, Washington: International Monetary Fund, 1991).

Background Papers

24

Effectiveness and Implications of Limits on Central Bank Credit to the Government

ALFREDO LEONE*

The main purpose of this paper is to explore the role and consequences of limiting central bank lending to the government. In the first section, the legal provisions that were in force in the mid-1980s for a sample of over 100 countries are surveyed. Also, data from 22 industrial countries and 22 developing countries are analyzed to investigate actual central banks' behavior regarding credit operations with governments. In the second section, an analytical framework, describing the budget constraints of the central bank and the government together with a consolidated budget constraint, is presented to investigate the contribution of these limitations to preserve the independence of central banks and the value of local currencies. The third section considers several issues related to the difficulties in designing and enforcing limits on outstanding central bank lending to governments. In particular, it deals with (a) the vulnerability of these limitations, (b) the implications of foreign exchange losses, and (c) possible inconvenience that these limitations may pose for central banks in conducting open market operations. The last section, taking account of previous discussions, states some conclusions and provides some suggestions for more appropriate limitations.

*The author is Senior Economist in the Central Banking Department of the International Monetary Fund. The author is grateful to Alex A. Cukierman, Patrick Downes, Douglas A. Scott, and V. Sundararajan for their helpful advice and comments and to Caroline Cox and Amelita Concepcion for their secretarial assistance.

Common Regulations and Decision-Making Processes

The establishment of limits on central banks' advances to the government or central banks' holdings of government securities, or both, is a very common practice all over the world.[1] These limitations take different forms, however, ranging from strict explicit rules to vague regulations that leave wide scope for discretion.

Common Rules

Limits on cash advances usually differ from those on holdings of government securities, particularly when the securities are purchased by the central bank in the open market. Also, the cost to governments, repayment conditions, and maturity features of the government securities that central banks are allowed to hold are usually explicitly established. The more common among these forms are as follows.

Limits on Cash Advances

(1) Net outstanding central bank loans to the government (in the form of cash advances) should be zero (Austria, Switzerland).

(2) No explicit limits are established, but advances to the government by the central bank require approval by the legislature (France, Norway, Korea) or a federal agency (United States) or the Central Bank Board (Turkey).

(3) No explicit limits are established, but the circumstances under which the central bank may make advances or the purposes of such advances are specified in the central bank's law (United Kingdom, New Zealand).

(4) No explicit limit is established (Japan).

(5) An explicit limit expressed as an absolute amount in domestic currency is established, usually by a legislative body. This amount may be revised, from time to time (Germany, Greece, Sweden).

(6) A limit is established in the form of a proportion of the central bank's liabilities (The Gambia, Mozambique).

(7) A limit is established as a percentage of government revenues (Algeria, Argentina, Canada, Israel, Venezuela).

(8) A limit is established as a percentage of government expenditures (Thailand, Spain).

[1]Appendix I summarizes the regulations and decision-making processes related to limitations on central bank credit to governments in different countries. The summary was prepared with the research assistance of Ms. Anne Johannessen of the Central Banking Department of the International Monetary Fund.

Limits on Holdings of Government Securities

(1) No explicit limit is established (Italy, Norway, Sweden).

(2) No explicit limit is established for open market operations (Canada, Iceland, Ireland, the Netherlands).

(3) No explicit limit is established, but purchases and holdings of government bonds require approval by a legislative body (Korea, Switzerland) or a federal agency (United States).

(4) An explicit limit is established expressed as a proportion of the central bank's capital and reserves (Belgium, Turkey).

(5) An explicit limit is established by the legislative body, expressed as an absolute amount in domestic currency (Germany).

(6) An explicit limit is established expressed as a percentage of central bank liabilities (Cyprus, Malta, Nigeria).

(7) An explicit limit is established expressed as a percentage of government revenues (Austria, Ethiopia, Paraguay, Peru, Tanzania).

(8) An explicit limit is established expressed as a percentage of government expenditures (Jamaica).

We now turn to real life trying to assess how these legal limitations have worked in practice in a sample of industrial and developing countries.

Common Practices: Empirical Evidence

Among the countries considered in Table 1, there is no uniform design of limits making cross-country comparisons difficult. Some countries have established separate limits for each type of government debt. Other countries use limits on advances alone, or one single limit covering different types of government debt. In some countries, the securities purchased in the open market are excluded from the limits. There are also differences with regard to the base variable used in establishing limits. Some countries use different bases for establishing limits on different types of debt, but government revenues appear to be the most commonly used base variable for these purposes.[2]

Table 1 gives information on the behavior of six different ratios. The information on outstanding central bank claims and net claims on governments used in the calculation of those ratios presented covers all categories of central government debt, such as advances, treasury bills, and other government or government-guaranteed paper. The

[2]In addition, the average government revenues or expenditures during a previous period (the past three or five years) is usually the base variable in practice. This procedure differs from the one used in calculating the ratios in Table 1 where the current levels of revenue, expenditure, or base money were used instead.

Table 1. Central Bank Claims on Central Governments in Industrial and Developing Countries, 1975–87

(In percent)

Country	(1) Claims/Base Money		(2) Claims/Revenues		(3) Claims/ Expenditures		(4) Net Claims/Base Money		(5) Net Claims/ Revenues		(6) Net Claims/ Expenditures	
	M	SD	M	SD	M	SD	M	SD	M	SD	M	SD
Industrial Countries												
Australia	84.3	22.9	17.2	6.0	16.3	5.6	n.a.	n.a.	n.a.	n.a.	n.a.	n.a.
Austria	5.5	1.0	1.9	0.6	1.7	0.5	3.0	0.8	1.0	0.3	0.9	0.2
Belgium	21.2	1.8	5.0	0.9	4.2	0.9	n.a.	n.a.	n.a.	n.a.	n.a.	n.a.
Canada	67.3	13.0	18.4	3.9	15.7	3.3	n.a.	n.a.	n.a.	n.a.	n.a.	n.a.
Denmark	195.5	194.7	19.9	17.7	17.6	14.8	−92.9	61.3	−10.2	5.5	−10.0	6.1
Finland	12.1	4.6	1.6	0.6	1.5	0.6	−7.7	9.1	−1.2	1.3	−1.2	1.3
France[1]	14.9	4.7	2.5	0.7	2.4	0.7	−1.8	7.6	−0.3	1.3	−0.3	1.3
Germany	13.6	1.8	4.8	0.7	4.5	0.6	4.5	2.1	4.2	0.6	3.9	0.5
Greece	70.1	20.5	60.1	20.5	45.7	13.8	56.3	21.0	47.8	18.0	36.1	11.8
Iceland	63.7	26.0	20.5	7.6	20.0	7.5	27.3	26.7	8.6	8.1	8.2	7.9
Ireland	21.8	6.3	7.4	1.4	5.5	1.0	3.7	14.1	0.5	5.4	0.3	4.0
Italy	n.a.	n.a.	n.a.	n.a.	n.a.	n.a.	89.4	9.4	69.0	29.3	48.9	20.2
Japan[2]	46.8	8.4	15.1	2.7	13.7	2.0	38.8	10.3	12.5	3.3	11.3	2.7
Netherlands	8.9	2.4	1.3	0.4	1.2	0.3	−9.0	11.3	−1.3	1.6	−1.2	1.6
New Zealand	130.2	28.4	14.4	4.9	13.2	4.3	7.6	94.3	3.1	9.8	3.0	8.9
Norway	61.8	32.1	11.3	5.1	12.1	5.2	−61.4	123.5	−7.2	16.4	−8.8	18.8
Portugal	105.0	45.0	69.7	16.3	54.7	12.3	95.1	44.2	62.7	15.9	49.2	12.4
Spain	53.1	17.1	35.4[3]	13.0[3]	31.1[3]	9.3[3]	47.7	17.0	31.8[3]	12.7[3]	27.9[3]	9.6[3]
Sweden	97.0	29.7	18.3	3.8	17.3	3.3	n.a.	n.a.	n.a.	n.a.	n.a.	n.a.
Switzerland	6.8	2.0	15.2	3.0	14.8	3.3	2.1	4.7	3.7	11.0	4.0	10.7
United Kingdom	n.a.	n.a.	n.a.	n.a.	n.a.	n.a.	54.0	32.8	8.8	8.1	8.1	7.3
United States	83.8	1.9	26.5	3.5	23.0	3.4	78.7	1.4	24.9	3.1	21.6	3.2

Developing Countries												
Argentina[4]	76.4	48.2	66.3	40.8	55.5	30.9	74.6	47.8	63.7	38.9	53.5	29.8
Brazil[5]	108.4	57.2	19.4	6.1	22.4	5.9	11.6	42.1	0.9	7.3	1.1	8.5
Chile[6]	185.2	120.7	40.2	21.4	39.5	19.8	141.6	127.1	29.7	21.3	28.6	18.8
Colombia	26.2	21.3	25.1	18.6	21.4	14.9	12.5	21.7	10.7	19.3	8.7	15.7
Egypt	114.7	25.1	103.3	23.1	90.9	26.1	108.3	22.1	97.3	20.0	85.6	23.4
Ghana	135.0	41.5	189.6	64.1	119.4	24.3	127.3	40.5	178.5	62.3	112.5	25.0
India	93.4	16.4	93.0	19.1	83.3	12.7	91.7	15.6	91.3	18.3	81.8	12.1
Indonesia	28.2	7.3	10.6	3.6	9.9	3.2	−63.0	46.1	−20.9	14.9	−19.8	13.9
Israel	49.1	16.7	35.8	14.0	26.5	9.6	40.4	14.4	29.8	12.2	21.8	8.0
Kenya	88.4	39.3	34.4	15.1	27.6	11.2	85.0	44.7	32.6	17.7	26.1	13.5
Malaysia	21.0	13.3	10.3	5.6	8.3	4.7	−6.4	25.2	−3.9	13.1	−3.2	10.8
Mexico	97.1	12.3	96.0	20.9	71.6	19.3	n.a.	n.a.	n.a.	n.a.	n.a.	n.a.
Morocco	84.8	22.8	50.8	12.3	36.9	10.5	83.3	22.8	49.9	12.3	36.2	10.4
Nepal	95.5	26.8	117.6[7]	37.0[7]	61.6[7]	11.8[7]	52.8	26.6	62.7[7]	34.7[7]	31.9[7]	13.8[5]
Pakistan	92.4	7.6	93.6	7.7	77.1	9.0	83.1	8.9	84.5	11.9	69.6	11.8
Peru	29.3	18.9	27.8	21.4	19.7	12.2	28.4	19.0	27.0	21.4	19.1	12.3
Philippines	70.0	25.7	39.6	18.9	39.4	19.0	47.1	25.9	26.6	17.0	26.6	16.9
Tanzania	113.6	35.2	79.1	35.8	53.4	25.1	n.a.	n.a.	n.a.	n.a.	n.a.	n.a.
Thailand	96.6	27.9	57.9	10.5	45.2	6.8	84.9	31.7	50.3	14.1	39.1	10.1
Venezuela	17.8	8.0	7.5[8]	3.2[8]	8.5[8]	3.7[8]	−8.5	11.5	−3.1[8]	5.6[8]	−3.7[8]	6.3[8]
Zambia	283.0	138.1	124.9	54.1	88.9	40.6	280.2	140.6	123.7	55.2	88.0	41.4
Zimbabwe[9]	49.2	21.9	13.1	6.0	10.6	5.2	39.2	26.0	10.1	6.7	8.4	5.8

Source: International Monetary Fund, *International Financial Statistics*.

Note: (1) the ratio of central banks claims on government to the stock of reserve money; (2) the ratio of central bank claims on government to government revenues; (3) the ratio of central bank claims on government to government expenditures; (4)–(6) similar ratios with central bank net claims on government replacing gross claims in the numerator of ratios (1)–(3). M = Mean; SD = Standard Deviation; net claims are defined as central bank claims to the government less government deposits with the central bank.

[1]1977–87.

[2]1979–87, data on government revenues and expenditures provided by the Asian Department of the International Monetary Fund.

[3]1975–86

[4]1977–86

[5]1978–85

[6]1978–84

[7]1975–85

[8]1975–86

[9]1976–87

table consists of the means and standard deviations of those different ratios for the period 1975–87. Low values for means imply that on average central banks were able to enforce narrow limits in their lending to governments during the period considered. Low values for means, together with low values for standard deviations, imply that those limits were generally kept narrow at all times over the 1975–87 period. The importance of keeping narrow limits on central bank lending to governments at all times will be underscored below. High values of means combined with high standard deviations imply, on the contrary, very permissive and erratic central bank policies regarding government financing.

It is clear that the behavior of these ratios differs substantially among the countries included in the sample. Some countries (such as Austria, France, Germany, the Netherlands, and Switzerland) have kept limits narrow and stable. Others (noticeably Greece, Italy, Portugal, and most developing countries) showed relatively high and variable observed ratios. Some countries showed low and stable ratios even though the explicit legal limits did not appear to be very strict (the Netherlands). In some others, the ratios attained such high levels that it is very likely that legal allowances were transgressed. The next section attempts to analyze the implications of these different behaviors.

The available data from the countries in the sample also show a high correlation between means and standard deviations of ratios. This implies that generally more permissive access to central bank credit by governments had led to more instability in the ratios making central bank policies regarding government financing more uncertain.[3] Table 2 and Chart 1 illustrate this point by analyzing the behavior of the ratio of

Table 2. Central Bank Net Claims in Terms of Government Revenues
(Regression outputs for the relationship between mean and standard deviation)[1]

	All Countries	Industrial Countries	Developing Countries
Constant	6.000337	4.093562	9.934198
Standard deviation of *Y* Est	8.146406	5.286622	9.845206
R squared	0.651413	0.496195	0.581942
Number of observations	44	22	22
Degrees of freedom	42	20	20
X coefficient(s)	0.267251	0.240282	0.234973
Standard deviation of coefficient	0.030166	0.054139	0.044532

[1]Simple ordinary-least-squares regressions were run of the form: Standard deviation = a + b Mean.

[3]This finding is consistent with the analysis of Cukierman (forthcoming), Chapter 18.

Chart 1. Central Bank Net Claims in Terms of Government Revenues
(In percent)

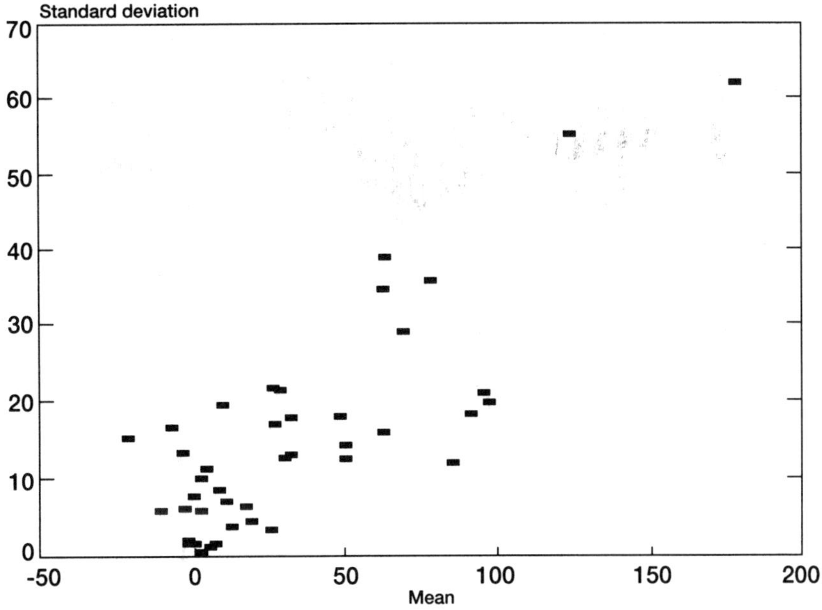

net outstanding central bank credit to the government over government revenues for the sample of countries considered in this paper.

An Analysis of the Effectiveness and Implications of Limits

In this section the effectiveness and implications of limits on central banks lending to governments will be analyzed using as the starting point the budget constraints specified in detail in Appendix II.[4]

On Budget Constraints and Limits

For the purposes of this section the three equations for budget constraints will be written in a more simplified way than in the appendix, as follows:

[4]Appendix II, equations (3), (4), and (5).

Government budget constraint

Net credit from central bank + government foreign and domestic net borrowing = government operational budget deficit + interest payments on outstanding net government debt + acquisition of foreign assets and other net assets by the government. (1)

Central bank budget constraint

Printing of base money + central bank foreign and domestic net borrowing = central bank operational expenditures + interest payments on outstanding net central bank debt + net credit to the government + credit to the economy + acquisition of foreign assets and other net assets by the central bank. (2)

Consolidated budget constraint

Given that

net credit from central bank (in equation (1)) = net credit to the government (in equation (2)),

it follows that:

printing of base money + consolidated foreign and domestic net borrowing = consolidated budget deficit + interest payments on outstanding consolidated net debt + central bank credit to the economy + acquisition of foreign assets and other net assets by the government and the central bank. (3)

Equation (1), the government budget constraint, shows that the government current operational deficit, the interest payments on outstanding government net debt (the accumulated result of government deficits incurred in the past), and the acquisition of foreign assets and other net assets by the government determine its total financial requirements. To satisfy these requirements, the government may borrow domestically or abroad, facing the market demand functions and implied costs for its debt instruments, or may borrow from the central bank.[5]

As shown by equation (2) the central bank will increase its own financial requirements in increasing its lending to the government. Its financial requirements will also be affected by its operational expenditures, the interest payments on outstanding central bank net indebtedness (domestic and foreign), its lending to the economy (financial

[5]It is convenient to emphasize that current borrowing will contribute to future financial requirements through interest payments and debt servicing of outstanding debt.

and other institutions), and the acquisition of foreign assets and other net assets. To satisfy these requirements, the central bank may borrow domestically or abroad or may print money, facing the market demands for its debt instruments and for base money, respectively.

The consolidated budget constraint, equation (3), shows that the aggregate financial needs of the government and the central bank result from their operational deficits, the interest payments on the outstanding consolidated net debt, the central bank credit to the economy, and the acquisition of foreign assets and other net assets by the government and the central bank. To satisfy these aggregate financial requirements, the consolidated public sector (government and central bank) may borrow domestically or abroad or may print money, facing the demand functions for their debt instruments and for base money, respectively.

Thus, the availability of credit from the central bank represents an alternative for governments to satisfy their financial requirements. It may represent a very convenient alternative if costs and conditions on borrowing from the central bank are more favorable than those prevailing in domestic or foreign financial markets. The availability of cheap central bank credit for the government will not reduce financial costs for the consolidated public sector but will imply lower costs for the government and higher costs for the central bank, which will face market conditions for its financial needs or may result in a higher inflation rate when government financing is not appropriately sterilized. Moreover, the availability of cheap central bank credit may encourage governments to increase expenditures, jeopardizing macroeconomic stability and deteriorating the financial position of central banks.[6]

From the previous analysis, it is clear that governments' fiscal decisions may limit the independence of central banks by affecting their monetary policy decisions and their financial positions. Thus, the existence of legal limits on central bank lending to governments may represent a protective barrier that will contribute to guaranteeing a certain degree of independence for central banks. Appropriately defined limits would allow central banks to follow monetary policies independent of government fiscal decisions and protect their financial positions, particularly when access to central bank credit by governments is cheap relative to market conditions.

Traditionally, as explained before, central bank laws have established limits on the total amount of outstanding central bank credit to the government. Most commonly, these limits have taken the form of a

[6]These issues relate to the problem of coordination of fiscal and monetary policies. See, for example, Alesina and Tabellini (1987).

fixed amount in domestic currency (determined periodically) or a proportion of government revenues. These limits imply that the flow of central bank credit to the government during a given period is also limited. It is limited to a fixed amount in domestic currency (equivalent to the difference between the annual limit established for the current year and the outstanding debt at the end of the previous year) as shown in the following relationships:

$$\text{Credit to the government} \leq \bar{L}(t) - L^*(t-1),$$

or

$$\text{credit to the government} \leq \alpha T(t) - \alpha a T(t-1) = \alpha[T(t) - T(t-1)] \leq \alpha T(t) - L^*(t-1)$$

where

$\bar{L}(t)$ = maximum stock of outstanding government debt with the central bank allowed at the end of period t,
$L^*(t-1)$ = outstanding stock of government debt with the central bank at the end of period $t-1$,
$T(s)$ = total government revenues during period s ($s = t$ or $t-1$); and
α = a constant.

Effectiveness of the Limits and the Independence of Central Banks

Are the kinds of limits commonly established in central bank laws effective enough to guarantee their independence from fiscal decisions and to promote macroeconomic stability? In this section, the question will be addressed from an analytical perspective leaving other aspects for the following section.

Let us first suppose that, at a given time t, all interest-bearing outstanding debt is of the same maturity period. Suppose also that the government runs a deficit at that time and that credit from the central bank is interest free. Then the government budget constraint (equation (1)) can be rewritten as follows:

$$CBCG(t) + [GD(t) - GD(t-1)] = D(t) + R^*GD(t-1) + AOA(t) \quad (4)$$

where

$CBCGt(t)$ = flow of central bank net credit to the government at time t;

$[GD(t) - GD(t-1)]$ = change in outstanding government net debt outside the central bank: Net borrowing at time t;

$D(t)$ = government deficit at time t;

R = nominal interest rate on outstanding government debt outside the central bank;

$AOA(t)$ = net acquisition of foreign assets and other assets at time t.

Rearranging and dividing all terms by the nominal gross domestic product at time t, that is, by GDP(t), the following first-order difference equation results:

$$gd(t) = [d(t) + aoa(t) - cbcg(t)] + \frac{(1+r)}{(1+y)} gd(t-1) \tag{5}$$

where lower-case letters represent the ratio of the nominal variables with regard to nominal GDP, and

y = rate of growth of real GDP;

r = real interest rate.

Equation (5) shows that if the government deficit and the net acquisition of other assets exceed the availability of credit from the central bank and the real rate of interest exceeds the economy's rate of growth, then the government debt-to-GDP ratio will grow without limit as shown in Chart 2. Given that the demand for government debt is finite, it will be impossible for the government to sustain this process forever. At some point in the future, it will have to take a decision of reducing the deficit, selling foreign or other assets, or increasing its demand for central bank credit. Let us next see which are the alternatives for the central bank when the government decides to follow the last mentioned, and usually easiest, route.

Following similar procedures as in the case of the government budget constraint, the central bank budget constraint (equation 2) can be rewritten as follows:

$$cbd(t) = [cboe(t) + cbaoa(t) + cbcg(t) + cbce(t) - pbm(t)] + \frac{(1+r)}{(1+y)} cbd(t-1) \tag{6}$$

where

$cbd(s)$ = ratio of outstanding central bank debt-to-GDP at time s ($s = t$ or $t-1$);

$cboe(t)$ = ratio of central bank operational expenditures to GDP at time t;

$cbaoa(t)$ = ratio of flow of central bank acquisition of foreign and other assets to GDP at time t;
$cbcg(t)$ = as before;
$cbce(t)$ = ratio of central bank credit to the economy to GDP at time t;
$pbm(t)$ = ratio of printing of base money to GDP at time t.

Equation (6) is also a first-order-difference equation. It tells us that if central bank expenditures and central bank financing of the economy and the government exceed the printing of base money and, as before, the real interest rate exceeds the economy rate of growth, the central bank interest-bearing debt will grow without limit, as shown in Chart 2. This process is not sustainable in the longer run given the finiteness of the demand for any kind of debt. At some point in the future, the central bank will be forced to reduce its expenditures, sell some of its foreign or other assets, reduce the financing to the economy (crowding-out effect) or the government, or increase the printing of money in order to reverse the process of ever-increasing debt.

The increase in the printing of base money appears to be the easiest route for the central bank to attend the financing requirements of the

Chart 2. The Debt Growth Process: An Example
(In percent of gross domestic product)

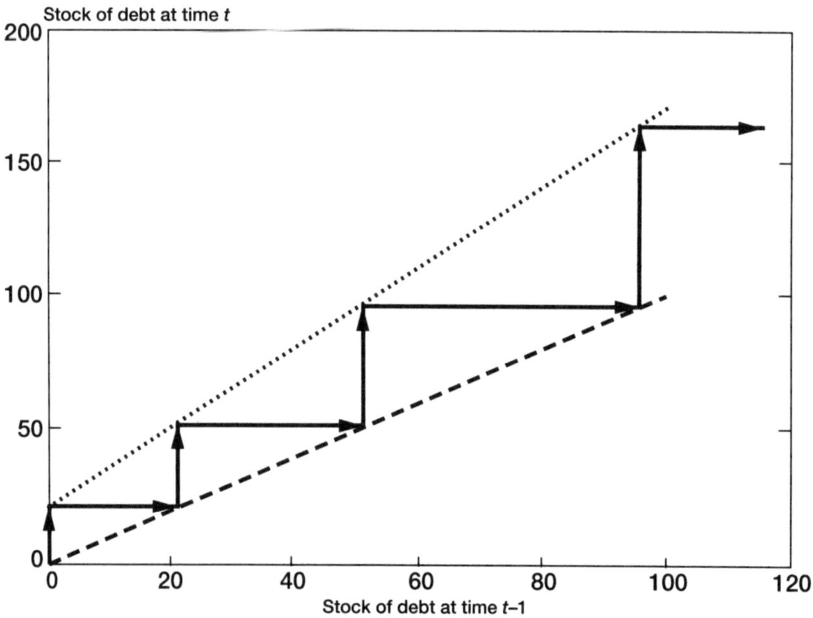

government and the economy without increasing its own interest-bearing debt and drifting into the explosive process depicted above. But, can the central bank increase the printing of base money without limit? To answer this question let us rearrange equation (6) a little bit, as follows:

$$bm(t) - \frac{bm(t-1)}{(1+p^*)(1+y)} = G(t) \tag{7}$$

where

$[bm(t) - bm(t-1)/(1+p^*)(1+y)] = pbm(t)$;

$bm(s)$ = the stock of base money in terms of GDP, at time s (s: t or $t-1$);

p^* = $p(t)/p(t-1)$ = the inflation rate;[7]

$$G(t) = [cboe(t) + cbaoa(t) + cbce(t)] - \left[cbd(t) - \frac{(1+r)}{(1+y)} cbd(t-1) \right];$$

y = as before.

Next, let us define $q(t)$ as the demand for base-money holdings in terms of GDP. Let us adopt the conventional assumption that $q(t)$ is a negative function of the inflation rate:

$$q(t) = q[p^*] \tag{8}$$

where

$$q' < 0.$$

In equilibrium the demand for base-money holdings should be equal to the observed stock of base money. Also, the assumption of a constant inflation rate implies that $q(t)$ will also be a constant in this equilibrium. Then replacing equation (8) into equation (7) and rearranging, the following expression results:

$$q(p^*)\left[1 - \frac{1}{(1+p^*)(1+y)}\right] = G(t) \tag{9}$$

A specific case of equation (9) is presented in Chart 3. It can be observed that there is a maximum revenue that the central bank may collect by printing base money.[8] Beyond that maximum, any increase in the supply of base money will result in more inflation and less revenue.

---

[7]An equilibrium with a constant inflation rate is considered for the purposes of this analysis.

[8]This curve has been derived elsewhere in the literature, see for example, Bailey (1956), Cagan (1956), and Wallace (1980).

Chart 3. Central Bank Revenue from Printing Money: An Example

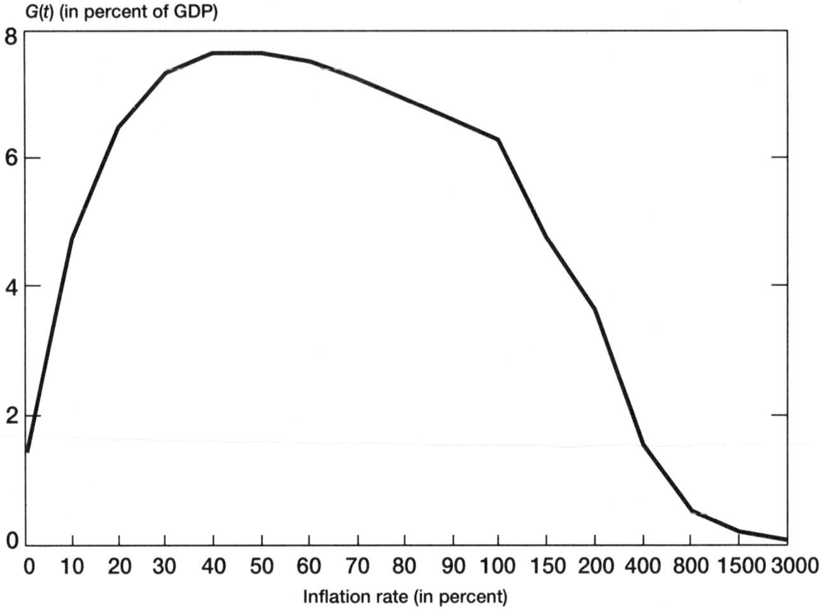

In summary, both governments and central banks face structural constraints that limit their financing possibilities. Going beyond those structural constraints will produce explosive processes of debt growth or serious inflationary problems. These constraints are best represented by the following consolidated budget constraint (a transformation of equation (3)):[9]

$$cgd(t) = [cdef(t) + caoa(t) + cbce(t) - pbm(t)] + \frac{(1 + r)}{(1 + y)} cgd(t - 1) \tag{10}$$

where

$cgd(s) = gd(s) + cbd(s)$, s: t or $t - 1$;
$cdef(t) = d(t) + cboe(t)$;
$caoa(t) = aoa(t) + cbaoa(t)$;
$cbce(t) =$ as before;
$pbm(t) =$ as before.

[9]Fischer (1990) uses a form of this equation to analyze the dynamics of the (consolidated) government debt.

Thus, limiting the scope for central bank lending to governments to very narrow limits would force governments to pursue prudent fiscal policies in order to avoid explosive episodes of government debt growth. In this way, the limits would help central banks to avoid inflationary processes or the explosive growth of their own debt.

The existence, however, of narrow limits on a government's access to central bank credit at a given time t is only a necessary condition to avoid the kind of explosive and inflationary processes mentioned before. Unfortunately, it is not a sufficient condition. For those processes to be avoided, the scope for central bank lending to the government should be kept within very narrow limits *at all times*. This requires institutional arrangements that effectively discipline the fiscal authority. As shown before, bond-financed expansive fiscal policies may not be sustainable in the longer run. Under these circumstances, central banks will be unable to control either the growth rate of the monetary base or inflation forever if it is known that sooner or later governments will be financed by printing money when placement of additional government or central bank debt becomes unfeasible. This was already clearly understood at the time of the currency reform taken in Germany, against a background of historical experience with two hyperinflations.[10] This is also the message of a theoretical paper by Sargent and Wallace (1981).

Some Cross-Country Experience on Deficits, Debt Growth, and Government Borrowing from Central Banks

Let us now illustrate the analytical framework considered above with the experience in some industrial and developing countries regarding government deficits and central bank behavior. For these purposes, Table 3 presents information on the average values for government deficits, government borrowing from central banks, and printing of money, all in terms of GDP, and the economy growth and inflation rates corresponding to the 1975–87 period in industrial and developing countries, respectively.

Chart 4 illustrates the observed relationship between government deficits and borrowing from central banks in the sample of countries selected.[11] It can be observed that in countries with relatively low government deficits, say of less than 5 percent of GDP, most central banks were able to keep relatively low lending-to-GDP ratios. On the

[10]See Deutsche Bundesbank (1986).

[11]The distance between each point in the graph and the diagonal represents government net borrowing outside central banks (in terms of GDP).

Table 3. Government Deficits and Central Bank Behavior in Industrial and Developing Countries, 1975–87

	Deficit[1]	Government Net Borrowing from Central Banks	Printing of Money	Growth in Gross Domestic Product	Inflation Rate
	(In percent of GDP)			(In percent)	
Industrial Countries					
Australia	2.5	0.53	0.6	3.0	9.8
Austria	4.5	0.02	0.6	2.0	4.8
Belgium	9.0	0.11	0.4	2.2	6.4
Canada	4.3	0.37	0.4	3.4	7.7
Denmark	2.3[2]	− 0.50	0.5	2.2	8.4
Finland	1.5	0.06	0.7	2.9	9.3
France	2.1	− 0.14	0.4	2.2	9.1
Germany	2.0	0.02	0.5	1.9	3.5
Greece	6.8	2.44	3.4	2.7	18.3
Iceland	2.9	0.72	2.7	3.9	42.1
Ireland	12.3	− 0.14	1.3	3.2	12.3
Italy	11.9	1.87	2.2	2.7	13.7
Japan	2.6[3]	0.22	0.6	4.4	4.6
Netherlands	4.6	0.15	0.5	1.6	4.7
New Zealand	6.3	− 0.14	0.1	1.5	13.7
Norway	1.3	− 1.46	0.6	3.9	8.8
Portugal	10.6	4.96	3.6	2.8	20.5
Spain	4.3[2]	1.39	2.1	2.0	14.1
Sweden	4.8	0.89	0.6	1.8	8.9
Switzerland	0.4	0.05	0.6	1.1	3.2
United Kingdom	4.1	− 0.35	0.4	2.0	10.8
United States	3.7	0.33	0.4	2.7	6.7
Developing Countries					
Argentina[4]	5.9	8.4	10.7	0.0	271.0
Brazil[5]	3.7	0.4	2.7	3.4	116.1
Chile[6]	0.1	2.4	0.6	3.1	26.5
Colombia	1.7	0.3	2.3	4.0	23.0
Egypt	13.0	7.6	7.0	n.a.	14.9
Ghana	5.1	5.4	3.9	0.05	58.2
India	6.3	1.8	1.8	5.0	7.0
Indonesia	1.3	− 0.9	1.3	6.1	12.2
Israel	14.3	8.0	21.1	2.8	125.5
Kenya	4.4	1.4	1.1	5.1	12.3
Malaysia	10.6	− 0.04	1.2	5.8	4.0
Mexico	7.1	4.7	4.7	3.5	53.0
Morocco	10.0	1.5	1.7	4.0	9.0
Nepal	4.3[7]	1.3	1.5	3.5	8.9
Pakistan	7.6	1.9	2.2	6.1	8.4
Peru	4.4	1.4	4.8	2.3	74.4
Philippines	2.2	0.4	1.1	3.2	13.9
Tanzania	7.4	3.3	2.3	2.0	24.1
Thailand	3.9	1.1	0.9	6.7	6.5
Venezuela	−0.7[8]	0.4	1.6	2.1	12.5
Zambia	13.9	5.8	2.1	0.05	21.9
Zimbabwe[9]	8.4	0.3	0.9	2.4	12.7

Source: IMF, *International Financial Statistics*.

[1]Deficit = revenues + grants received − (expenditure + lending − repayments).

[2]The figure is for 1975–86.

[3]The figure is for 1979–87; data on government revenues and expenditures provided by the Asian Department of the International Monetary Fund.

[4]The figures are for 1977–86.

[5]The figures are for 1978–85.

[6]The figures are for 1978–84.

[7]The figure is for 1975–85.

[8]The figure is for 1975–86.

[9]The figures are for 1976–87.

Chart 4. Government Deficits and Credit from Central Banks
(In percent)

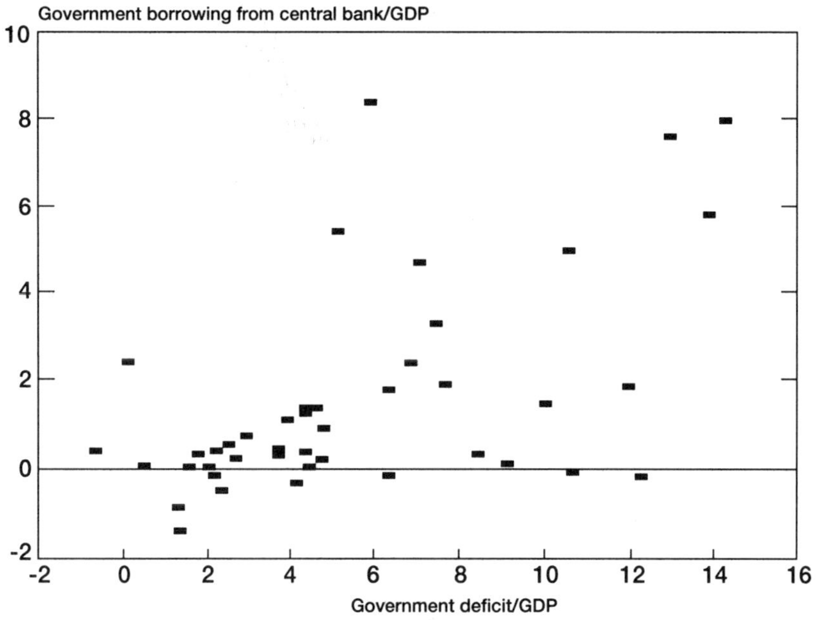

contrary, the proportion of countries enforcing low lending to governments when deficits exceed 5 percent of GDP is much lower.

Chart 5 shows the relationship between central bank lending to governments and printing of base money.[12] It seems that a close positive association exists between these two variables. In fact, in many countries in the sample, the printing of base money has been, on average, equal to government borrowing from central banks over the 1975–87 period. One possible interpretation of this result is that, in the long run, other sources of base-money expansion were relatively insignificant.

Chart 6 offers a sort of consolidated picture. Again, government deficits representing less than 5 percent of GDP seem to have no effect on the printing of money. This means that in these cases governments have, so far, been able to place debt instruments outside the central bank without facing the structural constraints underscored in the previous subsection or that the rate of growth in those economies has exceeded, so far, the real interest rate on government debt instru-

[12]Printing of base money may also originate in other central bank operations (foreign exchange purchases, credit to the economy, etc.) and in central bank losses.

Chart 5. Central Bank Credit to Government and Printing of Money
(In percent)

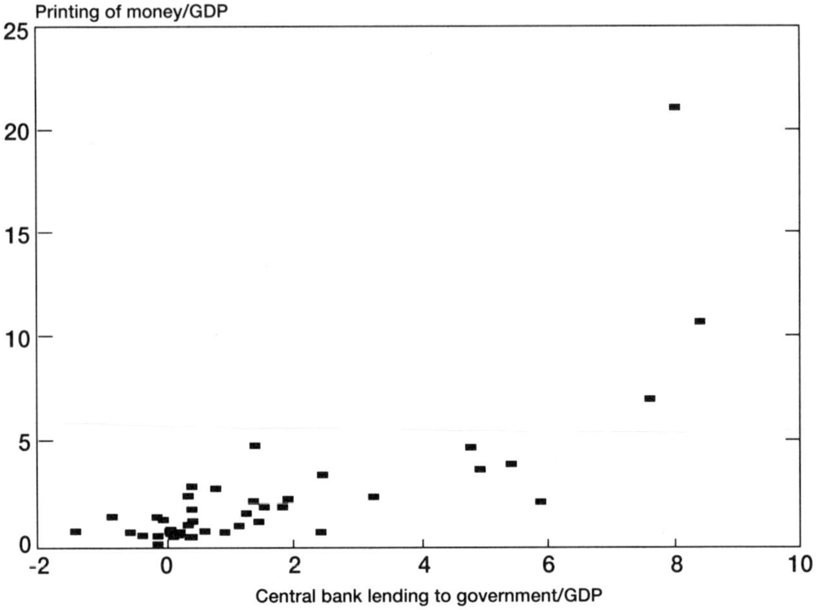

Chart 6. Government Deficits and Printing of Money
(In percent)

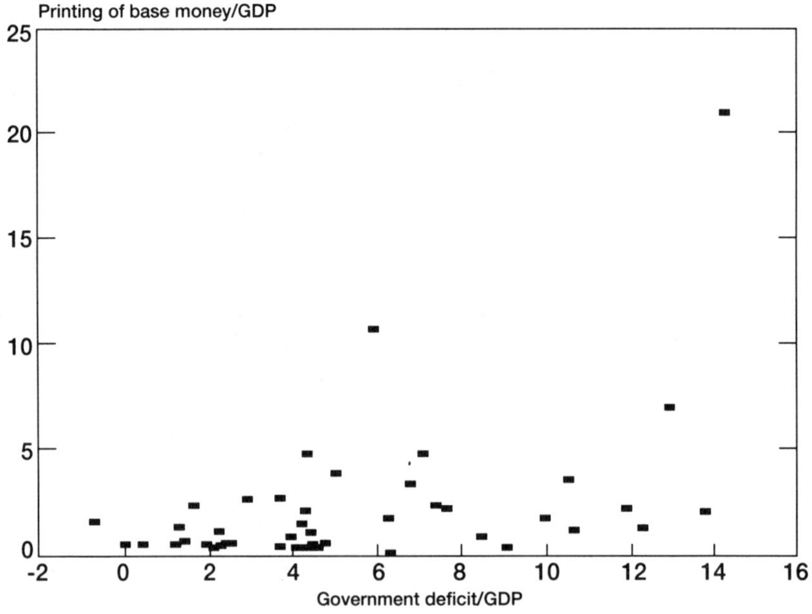

ments. For deficits exceeding 5 percent of GDP, it seems likely that the monetary authorities will end up printing money. In addition, Chart 7 shows that, among the countries in the sample selected, printing money in excess of 2 percent of GDP a year may become troublesome in terms of inflation rates.

There are some countries in the sample, however, that have relatively high government deficits and relatively low printing of money,[13] that is, relatively high government borrowing outside the central bank (Belgium, Ireland, Italy, Malaysia). Taking account of the different growth rates presented in Table 3 and assuming a real interest rate of about 3 percent, it seems possible that some of these countries may be facing in the medium-term debt-growth processes of the kind depicted above, requiring significant fiscal adjustments.[14]

Complexities in Designing and Enforcing Limits for Central Banks' Lending to Governments

Vulnerability of Legal Limits

The establishment of legal limits on central bank claims on governments does not necessarily guarantee that central banks will be safe from pressure from governments looking for borrowing alternatives. Even in cases where the established limits are entirely respected, central banks may end up providing the required financing to governments through indirect mechanisms that "legally" circumvent the legal constraints.

If the legal limits are not clearly defined or they do not include all possible forms of government debt with the central bank, it will be relatively easy for governments to issue debt instruments not affected by the limitations and sell them to central banks particularly when financial needs exceed other available borrowing alternatives. Also, central banks may provide financing to banks (private and public) or to business or individuals for them to buy government debt. These operations will be reflected in an increase in central bank credit to the economy (or in the acquisition of other net assets) in the central bank

[13]Relative, for example, to the sample means.

[14]For many countries, it is difficult to obtain real interest rates values reflecting realistic market conditions, mainly because of the implementation of price and interest rate controls. For the period considered here, real average yield to maturity for government bonds was 3.9 percent in Germany, 2.7 percent in Japan, and 3.2 in the United States. Average treasury bill real rates were 2.1 percent in Germany and 1.5 percent in the United States (not available for Japan). The assumption of a 3 percent average real rate of interest for the 1975–87 period seems then reasonable.

Chart 7. Inflation and Printing of Money
(In percent)

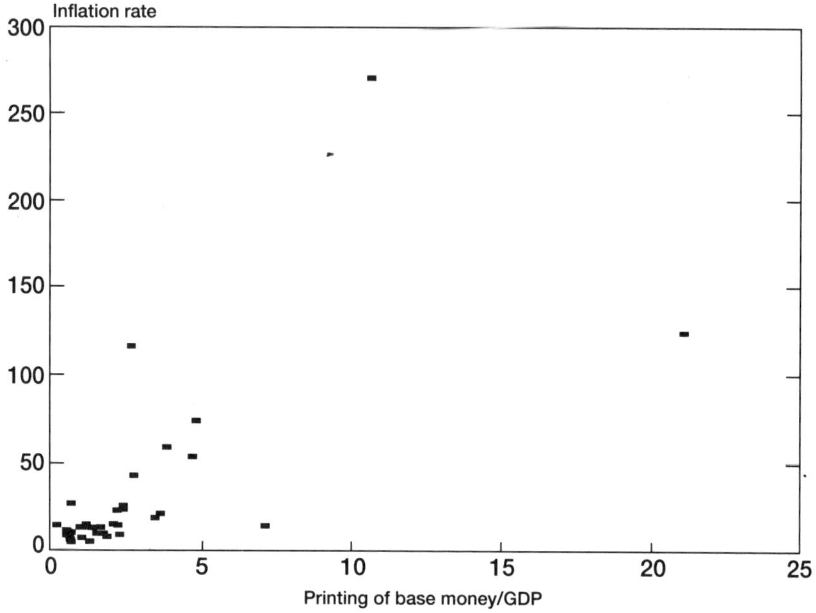

accounts and would not be affected by the usual legal limitations on central bank credit to the government.

In some countries, governments have forcefully placed long-term debt instruments in the portfolio of different institutional investors (particularly, in social security systems or provident funds) at low interest rates. In this way, governments were able to avoid both limitations on financing from central banks and, also, market-related interest rates when borrowing. The main implication of this procedure is the decapitalization of those institutional investors. The limit to this source of deficit financing is given by the size of the capital of these institutions, and sooner or later the government will have to recapitalize them. From this perspective, and particularly if this debt is not marketable and not remunerated at market rates, the placement of government debt under these conditions is another way of postponing fiscal discipline.

The experience of some countries shows that imagination to circumvent legal limits on central bank lending to governments has proved to be almost unlimited. Following the analysis of the previous section, we should emphasize, however, that circumvention of legal limits only transfers to central banks the task of looking for borrowing alternatives. At an aggregate level, the public sector will have to limit its financial requirements to the structural constraints imposed by the demands for money and government debt or the economy will drift into explosive debt-growth and inflationary processes. Moreover, it is frequently the case that central banks' profit-and-loss accounts deteriorate as a consequence of this intermediate activity tailored to finance governments.

Implications of Foreign Exchange Losses

In many countries, central banks have also been intermediaries for foreign financial resources. In many cases, central banks have on-lent foreign financial resources to the government and other domestic borrowers in domestic currency and at low interest rates. These on-lending conditions were generally insufficient to cover the costs of borrowing abroad and the credit and exchange rate devaluation risks leading to foreign exchange losses for the central bank.

Central banks in many countries have also incurred foreign exchange losses by extending exchange rate guarantees for payments related to imports and foreign borrowing by domestic borrowers (both public and private). Under this scheme, central banks grant (generally for a specified premium) a guarantee of foreign exchange at a certain price on a given future date. These guarantees have no immediate significant effect on either the profit-and-loss account or the balance sheet of central banks. In many countries, however, where the exchange rate devaluation exceeded the premium, exchange rate guarantees have eventually resulted in very large losses for central banks.

Foreign exchange losses usually become an important item among the assets of central banks. This is so because, in fact, the accumulated losses represent an additional form of government debt with central banks. Recalling the discussion earlier, it is clear, however, that at a consolidated level foreign losses arise from the misallocation of foreign financial resources (which made foreign currency liabilities greater than foreign currency assets[15]) or the unrealistic pricing of exchange guarantees (which made expenditures in foreign currency higher than income in foreign currency). Sooner or later, through increased taxes or reduced government expenditures or experiencing explosive inflationary processes, society will have to bear these losses.

The most significant impact of foreign exchange losses occurs when foreign debts or exchange guarantees become due. At that time, the

[15]And income from these foreign assets lower than expenditures related to foreign liabilities.

government will have to buy foreign exchange at the current exchange rate to honor foreign debts or exchange guarantees. If, because of misallocation or mispricing, the government is not able to generate enough resources from the investment of its foreign liabilities or from premiums on exchange guarantees, a fiscal surplus in other government operations will be needed to compensate foreign exchange losses. Otherwise, the government will increase its borrowing from domestic or foreign lenders, or from the central bank, contributing to the kind of debt-growth or inflationary processes depicted above.

When foreign exchange losses of significant magnitude arise, governments usually appeal to central banks for financing. The usual case is that central banks end up honoring government liabilities in foreign currency while governments do not provide the necessary counterpart in domestic or foreign currency. In these cases, existing legal limits on central bank lending to the governments may be transgressed. Presumably, this explains why in many countries government debt to central banks arising from these losses were usually explicitly or implicitly disregarded for the purposes of the legal limits. In addition, if this form of government debt becomes nonperforming or its pricing is unrealistic relative to the costs that the central bank faces for borrowing from domestic or foreign markets to compensate the impact of government losses, then the central bank will incur losses of its own.[16]

The main conclusion of this section is that foreign exchange losses represent a fiscal problem: sooner or later they will require a fiscal solution. Otherwise, either directly (by increasing government debt) or indirectly through the central bank (by increasing central bank debt or the printing of money) foreign exchange losses will contribute to unsustainable debt-growth or inflationary processes. From this perspective, government debt with central banks arising from these losses should be included in the legal limitations to central banks lending to governments. Permanent regulations of this kind will encourage governments to avoid misallocation of resources and mispricing of government services.

The main message is, thus, that foreign exchange losses should be avoided. Many countries, however, are surely incurring foreign losses today as a consequence of past decisions. At the time, when these losses are realized they will probably exceed any (existing or potential) reasonable limitation on government borrowing from central banks. It is obvious that this legacy cannot be absorbed, at least completely, by

[16]This is valid for any other government or nongovernment debt with the central bank.

current limitations. It will be important in this case to set up a strategy to absorb them over time without generating losses to central banks.

These inherited losses should be considered by the fiscal authorities when elaborating the government budget. They should be able to determine, given structural constraints,[17] how these losses will be borne by current and future generations through increasing taxes (or reduced current government expenditures) or increasing borrowing. At the same time, any required financing from the central bank should be remunerated at market rates and honored timely.[18]

Implications for Open Market Operations

Limits on central bank lending to the government may also become binding when the central bank implements open market operations with treasury bills or other government paper for monetary policy reasons or it intervenes in the secondary market to support the prices of government debt instruments.[19]

We have already seen that central banks' open market operations and other interventions in government securities markets may imply an indirect way of government borrowing from the central bank resulting from permanent deficient fiscal conditions. In this section, it is assumed that central bank intervention is required "temporarily" to offset excessive fluctuation of security prices reflecting either an excess or a shortage of liquidity, which are not a consequence of the fiscal position of the government.

Let us suppose that an exogenous shock creates excess liquidity in the economy. Then, short-term interest rates will tend to fall. The fall in interest rates may encourage consumption, creating short-term pressures in the goods markets and in the current account of the balance of payments. It may also promote capital outflows of short-term funds. Moreover, the fixed interest rate on long-term government securities will become more attractive, encouraging the demand for these papers and increasing excessively their price. In this case, the

---

[17]Including those constraints depicted above.

[18]In many countries, a proportion of central bank profits are distributed to the government. Then, the need to remunerate central bank loans to the government at market-related rates does not seem necessary at a first look: if, because of mispricing, central bank income from government debt is lower than otherwise, so will be central bank profits and the proportion to be distributed to the government. However, legal provisions in the case that central banks incur losses are not symmetric: in these cases central banks' capital will be affected. It is in these cases when it becomes important to find the causes of central bank losses and determine the responsibility of fiscal authorities. The appropriate remuneration of government debt with the central bank will make this process more transparent.

[19]Such intervention may be needed in the case of long-term papers that carry larger risk of price variability, particularly in the early stages of market development.

central bank will have to intervene by selling part of its stocks of bills and securities. This case, of course, does not pose any problem for the central bank with regard to the legal limits on its holdings of government paper.

Problems may, however, arise under conditions of liquidity shortages. Then short-term interest rates will make the interest rate on long-term paper increasingly unattractive. This will lead to a fall in the demand for long-term paper. This may also discourage consumption and encourage inflows of short-term capital, hence, creating offsetting forces that will gradually push the short-term interest rates to lower levels. However, this adjustment path may take a long time, and the price of long-term government paper meanwhile may decrease excessively. To avoid this effect, the central bank may be forced to intervene by acquiring bills and securities from the market.[20] In this case, however, the required action of the central bank may be limited by the prevailing legal limits on its holdings of government paper.

Thus, the main issue to be considered with regard to the implications of legal limits on central bank intervention in the open market is how these limits may be modified or interpreted to allow more flexible monetary management while, at the same time, assuring long-term monetary control.

A technique that helps to minimize excessive but transitory fluctuations in interest rates on government paper when various lending limits and other liquidity requirements are in effect is the use of "repurchase agreements" supported by appropriate accounting conventions. A repurchase agreement is the purchase of a security from another party, who agrees to buy it back at a specified future date and price. In practice, the repurchase agreement is equivalent to a loan from the buyer to the seller of the securities, with government paper serving as collateral. For example, if a liquidity shortage emerges, the central bank may select competitive offers to buy government paper, with the agreement to sell the securities back to the original sellers at a specified future date.

This mechanism will allow central banks to avoid excessive interest rate volatility and, particularly, excessive fluctuation in the price of long-term government paper. Moreover, under generally accepted accounting conventions, government securities acquired by the central bank with a repurchase agreement would be excluded for the purposes of the legal limits on the central bank holdings of govern-

[20]It should be recognized that by intervening in this way the central bank will reduce the incentives for the offsetting forces (reduced consumption and inflows of short-term capital) to take place.

ment paper. Under these conditions, central bank sales of government securities would not reduce the central bank's holdings of government paper and, likewise, central bank purchases of government paper would not increase its holdings of government paper. This is so because the ownership of a paper sold under a repurchase agreement remains with the seller, even though it may be temporarily deposited with the buyer.

While this mechanism of repurchase agreements is useful to deal with temporary shortages and surpluses of liquidity, it is not prudent to use them (possibly exceeding legal limitations on central bank holdings of government paper) for permanent shortages or surpluses of liquidity. Liquidity problems of a permanent nature should be clearly identified by central bankers and trigger correcting mechanisms of a permanent nature, such as the modification of reserve requirements, sales of long-term central bank paper, or changes in the rediscount policy.

Recommendations

The problem then is how to design appropriate limitations that will contribute to macroeconomic stability and, at the same time, will allow central banks to perform monetary policy independent of fiscal actions while protecting their financial positions. Previous discussions suggest that it is unlikely to attain these objectives by limiting only government borrowing from central banks without having some kind of limitation on the growth of net government debt. Previous discussions also suggest that limitations on central bank lending to governments should be carefully designed to protect central banks from excessive and cheap financing of governments but, at the same time, without limiting the independence of central banks to perform monetary policy appropriately (which may require operations with government securities).

Thus, in looking for a solution to this problem, it seems appropriate to consider two different kinds of limitations: (a) some form of limitation on total government debt; and (b) appropriately defined limits on central banks lending to governments.

Design of Limitations

The design of the suggested limitations requires careful consideration. In the light of previous discussion, it seems important to address the following questions: (a) How should limits be defined and which variables should be involved in the definition of these limitations?

(b) How comprehensive should the limitations be? and (c) How could legal limits be complemented to protect the financial position of central banks?

Definition of Limits

Suggestions for the definition of limits on total government debt and on government borrowing from the central banks is discussed next. The implications of these suggestions for fiscal discipline and central bank independence are also considered.

Limits on Total Government Debt

A prudent and elemental principle in lending establishes that the ratio of payments of loans installments to income should not exceed a certain given percentage. In addition, the amount of payments is a proportion (which depends on interest rate levels and debt maturity) of the total outstanding debt. Appendix III shows that application of these elemental principles and relationships to government borrowing results in a particular form of limitation: total outstanding government debt should not exceed a proportion of government revenues.[21]

Thus, simple prudential principles make it recommendable to link total outstanding government debt (government debt outside the central bank plus central bank holdings of government debt) to government revenues.[22] From this perspective, it does not seem to be safe to link total outstanding government debt to other variables, such as government expenditures or central bank liabilities.

Given the diversity of possible economic environments, it seems difficult to establish a precise proportion of general validity linking total government outstanding debt to government revenues. It does seem possible, however, to state some general principles based on the previous analysis.

In countries facing economic growth rates lower than real interest rates, governments should not borrow. In these cases, the equilibrium value for the stock of government debt is zero. In fact, they should make a fiscal effort to avoid deficits. Even in countries where real interest rates are lower than the economy's growth rate, increasing borrowing requirements by governments may end up by increasing market interest rate levels more than the growth rate and, thus,

[21]It is also shown in Appendix III that this form of limitation implies a limit on the growth of government debt.

[22]This kind of link resembles some of the limitations that are found in actual central bank laws governing the lending to governments.

increasing the likelihood of drifting into explosive processes. Thus, a limit on outstanding government debt should also be established in these cases.

Limits on Government Borrowing from Central Bank

Even if a limit on total government debt is set along the lines suggested in previous discussions, it is also important to set limits on government borrowing from the central bank. This is so because at any time the monetary authority could be forced to purchase all the fiscal authority's outstanding bonds. This would create a dangerous expansion of the monetary base or of interest-bearing central bank debt even within the margins allowed by the previously suggested limit on total outstanding government debt.

The experience in the sample of countries considered in this paper shows that, in general, government borrowing from central banks has translated into monetary accommodation, that is, the expansion of the monetary base. It also shows that the margins for monetary accommodation without troublesome inflationary consequences are indeed very narrow. At the same time, any limitation on governments borrowing should leave central banks enough flexibility to perform open market operations as required by the main objective of monetary policy, that is, the safeguarding of the internal and external value of domestic currency.

These considerations lead us to the following set of general principles for limiting government borrowing from central banks: (a) the government should undertake its financing mainly in the open market; (b) only a very limited amount of direct lending to the government by the central bank should be permitted. This limit will represent the maximum degree of monetary accommodation allowed to finance the government. Given that a prudent limit to monetary base expansion is represented by the economy's real rate of growth, it seems advisable to limit total direct (nominal) government net borrowing from central banks to the economy's real rate of growth;[23] and (c) the central bank should be allowed to buy and sell government securities in the open market as required by its monetary policy objectives. It is recommended that total outstanding net government debt in the central bank (cash advances plus holdings of government paper by the central bank) should not, however, exceed a proportion of total government revenues. Any additional requirement for purposes of monetary policy could be handled through transitory repurchase agreements in conjunction with appropriate accounting conventions.

[23]Notice that this is a limit on the growth of government debt with the central bank.

Implications of Suggested Limitations

It is clear that, according to the budget constraint (equation (1)), the first limitation (the limit on total outstanding government net debt) implies a limit on total government financial needs (the sum of (1) the government operational budget deficit; (2) interest payments on outstanding net government debt; and (3) the acquisition of foreign and other net assets by the government). Thus, this limitation is intended to contribute to macroeconomic stability. It does not, however, provide any guidance to regulate government borrowing from central banks. This role is played by the other two limits.[24]

Limiting the growth of net government debt will contribute to making limits on government borrowing from central bank credible and sustainable in the long run. The suggested limits on central bank lending to governments will protect central banks' independence without curtailing their ability to perform monetary policy appropriately. The conjunction of these limitations will contribute to fiscal discipline at all times.

Comprehensiveness of Limitations

The limits previously suggested should be clearly specified so as to minimize the likelihood of cheating, constrain discretionary management, and permit appropriate scrutiny. This requires the specification of rules defining the forms of government debt affected by the limitations and the methodology guiding the calculations.

The limit on total outstanding government debt should comprehend all forms of outstanding government and government-guaranteed debt (foreign or domestic) net of government financial assets (foreign or domestic). Limits on total net government outstanding debt with the central bank[25] should also comprehend all forms of government debt with the central bank, such as advances, treasury bills, government and government-guaranteed paper, and other forms of credit originating, for example from foreign exchange losses.

For the purposes of these limits, government revenues could include both tax and nontax revenues. Also, government revenues should be calculated as the average value of total tax and nontax collections during some previous period (for example, the three previous fiscal years). For the purposes of the limit on government direct borrowing from the central bank (in nominal terms), the rate of the economy

---

[24]All three limitations taken together impose some constraints to government borrowing outside the central bank.

[25]Net of government deposits with the central bank.

growth should be calculated as the average annual growth rate of real GDP during previous years (for example, during the last three years).

Complementary Regulations

The previous limitations will contribute to long-run macroeconomic stability and central bank independence. Even within these limits, the financial position of central banks may still be threatened if lending to governments is made under inappropriate conditions. To minimize this possibility, some complementary regulations may be useful.

Within the margins allowed by the limits previously suggested, central banks should preferably acquire government securities in the open market. Any other form of government borrowing from the central bank should be exceptional and bear market-related interest rates and conditions.

Conclusions

At least in the sample of countries selected in this paper, the experience with legal constraints to limit central banks' lending to governments has been diverse. In some countries where laws apparently leave more scope for discretionary management, actual central bank lending to governments has remained within narrow and stable limits. On the contrary, in some other countries where legal limitations look more strict, the available data seem to indicate that those limits have been transgressed.

The determination of maintaining fiscal discipline at all times, that is, to keep public sector financial needs within the margins allowed by the kind of structural constraints underscored earlier, seems to have played a key role in facilitating a predictable and prudent central bank behavior regarding the financing of governments. From the experience of the countries selected in this paper, it is difficult, however, to determine if actual legal limitations on central banks lending to governments have contributed to encouraging fiscal discipline. In some cases, these limitations seem to have contributed to limiting government financial needs. In countries with chronic fiscal deficits, legal limits have become unsustainable in the long run. In some others, where fiscal discipline has been a permanent feature of actual behavior, legal limitations appear to be unnecessary.

It has also been underscored that, in general, central bank financing of governments has been a major source of monetary base expansion. In addition, the experiences of the countries in the sample shows that whenever the expansion of the monetary base exceeded some structural constraints, it resulted in relatively high inflation.

In summary, the establishment of legal limitations on government borrowing from central banks looks like a necessary condition to avoid excessive expansion of the monetary base or central banks interest-bearing debt and, thus, to avoid troublesome debt-growth or inflationary processes in the long run. The experience of some countries, particularly those with chronic fiscal deficits, seems to indicate, however, that the establishment of this kind of limitation has not been sufficient to guarantee fiscal discipline. Persistence of fiscal disorder usually makes these limits unsustainable in the long run.

Bibliography

Alesina, Alberto and Guido Tabellini, "Rules and Discretion with Noncoordinated Monetary and Fiscal Policies," *Economic Inquiry* (U.S.), (October 1987), pp. 619–30.

Bailey, Martin J., "The Welfare Cost of Inflationary Finance," *Journal of Political Economy*, (April 1956), pp. 93–110.

Cagan, Phillip, "The Monetary Dynamics of Hyperinflation," in *Studies in the Quanity Theory of Money*, ed. by M. Friedman (Chicago: University of Chicago Press, 1956).

Cukierman, Alex, "Central Bank Behavior, Credibility, Accommodation, and Stabilization" (MIT Press, forthcoming).

Deutsche Bundesbank, "Bundesbank Cash Advances to the Federal Government and the Länder Governments," *Monthly Report* (May 1986), pp. 22–26.

Fischer, Stanley, *The Economics of the Government Budget* (Bombay: Reserve Bank of India, February 1990).

International Monetary Fund, *International Financial Statistics.*

Parkin, Michael, "Domestic Monetary Institutions and Deficits," in *Deficits*, ed. by J.M. Buchanan, C.K. Rowley, and R.D. Tollison (New York; Oxford: Basil Blackwell, 1987), pp. 310–37.

Sargent, Thomas J., and Neil Wallace, "Some Unpleasant Monetarist Arithmetic," *Quarterly Review*, Federal Reserve Bank of Minneapolis (Fall 1981), pp. 1–17.

Wallace, Neil "Integrating Micro and Macroeconomics: An Application to Credit Controls," *Quarterly Review*, Federal Reserve Bank of Minneapolis (Fall 1980), pp. 16–29.

The central bank laws of individual countries were also used in this paper:

Country	*Statute*	*Statute Date*
Anguilla[1]	East Caribbean Central Bank Agreement	1983
Algeria	Statutes of the Central Bank of Algeria	1962
Antigua and Barbuda[1]	East Caribbean Central Bank Agreement	1983
Argentina	Charter of the Central Bank, Argentine Republic	1977
Australia	Reserve Bank Act 1959	1982
Austria	National Bank Law, 1955	1984
Bahamas	The Central Bank of Bahamas Act, 1974	1974
Bahrain	Decree law No. 23 of 1973	1981
Belgium	The Organic Law of the Bank of Cape Verde, 1976	1976
Belize	Central Bank of Belize Act 1982	1982
Benin[2]	Charter of the Central Bank of West African States	1981
Burkina Faso[2]	Charter of the Central Bank of West African States	1981
Burundi	Statutes of the Bank of the Republic of Burundi	1976
Cameroon[3]	Articles of the Bank of Central African States	1984
Canada	Bank of Canada Act	1980
Cape Verde	Organic Law of the Bank of Cape Verde, 1976	1976
Central African Republic[3]	Articles of the Bank of Central African States	1984
Chad[3]	Articles of the Bank of Central African States	1984
Congo[3]	Articles of the Bank of Central African States	1984
Côte d'Ivoire[2]	Charter of the Central Bank of West African States	1981
Cyprus	Central Bank of Cyprus Laws of 1963 and 1979	1979
Denmark	The National Bank of Denmark Act, 1936	1966
Dominica[1]	East Caribbean Central Bank	1983
Ecuador	Law on the Monetary System	1981
Egypt	Charter of the Central Bank 1957 with Decree No. 488 of 1976	1976
El Salvador	Central Reserve Bank of El Salvador	1982
Equatorial Guinea[3]	Decree Law No. 1/1980 of February 9	1980

Ethiopia	Monetary and Banking Proclamation No. 99/1976	1976
Finland	Regulations for the Bank of Finland	1966
France	Law No. 73-7 of January 3, 1973 with Decree No. 73-102 of January 30, 1973	1973
The Gambia	The Central Bank of The Gambia Act, 1971 with The Central Bank of the Gambia (Amendment) Act, 1978	1978
Germany	The Law Concerning the Deutsche Bundesbank, 1957	1978
Ghana	Bank of Ghana Act, 1963	1971
Grenada[1]	East Caribbean Central Bank Agreement	1983
Greece	The Statutes of the Bank of Greece	1966
Guinea	Decree No. 126/PRG	1960
Guyana	Bank of Guyana Act	1982
Iceland	The Central Bank of Iceland Act	1979
Iraq	Law No. 64 of 1976	1976
Ireland	Central Bank Act, 1971	1971
Israel	Bank of Israel law	1982
Italy	The Statute of the Bank of Italy, 1936	1978
Jamaica	Bank of Jamaica (Schedule)	1977
Japan	The By-Laws of the Bank of Japan	1960
Jordan	The Central Bank of Jordan law, 1971	1979
Korea	The Bank of Korea Act	1977
Kuwait	Law No. 32 of 1968	1980
Lao People's Democratic Republic	Statutes, National Bank of Laos (New Law 1990)	1955
Lesotho	Central Bank of Lesotho Act 1982	1982
Libya	Banking Law No. 4 of 1963	1971
Madagascar	Ordinance No. 73–025	1973
Malawi	Reserve Bank of Malawi Act	1982
Malaysia	Central Bank of Malaysia Ordinance, 1958	1982
Mali[2]	Charter of the Central Bank of Mali	1973
	Charter of the Central Bank of West African States	1981
Malta	Central Bank of Malta Act, 1967	1981
Mauritania	Statutes of the Central Bank of Mauritania	1975
Mauritius	Bank of Mauritius Act	1981
Montserrat[1]	East Caribbean Central Bank Agreement	1983
Morocco	Statutes of the Bank of Morocco	1962
Mozambique	Charter of the Central Bank	1975
Myanmar (Burma)	The Union Bank of Myanmar Act, 1952 (New Law 1990)	1952

Netherlands	Bank Act 1948	1980
Netherlands Antilles	The Central Bank Statute 1985	1985
New Zealand	The Reserve Bank of New Zealand Act, 1964 (New Law 1989)	1974
Niger[2]	Charter of the Central Bank of West African States	1981
Nigeria	Central Bank of Nigeria Act, 1958	1962
	Central Bank of Nigeria By-Laws, 1959	1962
Norway	Act relating to Norges Bank and the Monetary System	1985
Oman	Laws of the Sultanate of Oman, 1974	1975
Papua New Guinea	Central Bank Act, 1973	1977
Paraguay	Decree Law No. 18	1952
Peru	Organic Law of the Central Reserve Bank of Peru	1983
Philippines	The Central Bank Act	1979
Portugal	Banco de Portugal Organic Law (No. 644/75)	1976
Rwanda	Decree-law No. 06/81 of February 16, 1981	1981
Sao Tome and Principe	Organic law National Bank of Sao Tome and Principe	1976
Senegal[2]	Charter of the Central Bank of West African States	1981
Sierra Leone	Bank of Sierra Leone (Amendment) Act, 1978	1978
Somalia	Somalia National Bank Law, 1968	1968
Spain	Bank of Spain Law, 18/1962	1975
Sri Lanka	Monetary Law Act	1979
St. Kitts and Nevis[1]	East Caribbean Central Bank Agreement	1983
St. Lucia[1]	East Caribbean Central Bank Agreement	1983
St. Vincent[1]	East Caribbean Central Bank Agreement	1983
Sudan	Bank of Sudan Act, 1959	1962
Suriname	Bank Ordinance Act, 1959	1962
Sweden	Sveriges Riksbank Act	1983
Switzerland	National Bank Law, 1953	1982
Tanzania	The Bank of Tanzania Act, 1965	1971
Thailand	Bank of Thailand Act, B.E. 2485 (1942)	1962
	Royal Decree Reg. Bank of Thailand, B.E. 2485	1979
Togo[3]	Charter of the Central Bank of West African States	1981
Trinidad and Tobago	Central Bank Act, 1964	1978
Tunisia	Central Bank of Tunisia Law No. 58-90 of 1958	1975

Turkey	Law No. 1211	1970
Uganda	The Bank of Uganda Act, 1966	1971
United Arab Emirates	Central Bank Law	1980
United Kingdom	The Bank of England Act, 1819	1819
	The Bank of England Act, 1946	1946
United States	Federal Reserve Act	1983
Vanuatu	The Central Bank of Vanuatu Act	1982
Venezuela	Law of the Central Bank of Venezuela	1984
Viet Nam	Ordinance No. 48, 1954	1954
Western Samoa	Central Bank of Samoa Act 1984	1984
Yemen Arab Republic	Central Bank of Yemen Law, 1971	1971
Yemen People's Democratic Republic	Banking System Law (No. 36 of 1972)	1973
Zaïre	Bank of Zaire Statutes	1976
Zambia	Bank of Zambia Ordinance, 1965	1971
Zimbabwe	Reserve Bank of Zimbabwe Act	1984
	New Laws 1989 and 1990	
Chile	Organic Law Establishing the Central Bank of Chile	1989
Lao People's Democratic Republic	The Law Conc. with Creation of The Bank of Lao People's Democratic Republic	1990
Myanmar (Burma)	The Central Bank of Myanmar Law	1990
Namibia	Central Bank of Namibia Act	1990
New Zealand	Reserve Bank of New Zealand Act	1989

[1]A member of the East Caribbean Central Bank.
[2]A member of the Central Bank of West African States.
[3]A member of the Bank of Central African States.

Appendix I
Limitations on Lending from the Central Bank to the Government

Country	Type of Loan	Decision Process and Regulations
		A. *Limit: As Described*
Austria	Loans to the government	The Federal Republic, the Länder or the municipalities *in no way*, either directly or indirectly, may draw on the National Bank's funds for their own purposes, without providing the counterpart in gold or foreign exchange.
Belgium	Government securities	The National Bank may discount, buy and transfer short- and medium-term securities issued or guaranteed by the Belgian State or the Luxembourg State or issued by institutions whose liabilities are guaranteed by the Belgian State or the Luxembourg State. It may also buy and sell national long-term public securities quoted on the Stock Exchange. Holdings of national public securities may not exceed an amount equal to its capital, reserves and amortization accounts.
Canada	Securities issued or guaranteed by the government	For the purposes of its open market operations there is no established limit.
France	Advances and loans to the state	Agreement drawn up by the Ministry of Economy and Finance and the Governor of the Bank of France, authorized by the Board of Directors and approved by the legislature.
Iceland	Advances	The Central Bank may advance short-term loans to the treasury. Such loans shall be paid up within three months after the end of each fiscal year through borrowing or other acquisition of funds *outside of the Central Bank*.
	Government securities	Treasury bills, bonds, and other securities, which are issued by the treasury and bought by the Central Bank in the securities market or from financial institutions in order to promote balance in the money market, shall not count *as loans to the treasury*.
Ireland	Government securities	The Central Bank may buy, hold, or sell securities of or guaranteed by the state which have been offered from public subscription or tender before being bought by the Bank, and are officially quoted on stock exchanges.
Italy	Government securities	The Bank of Italy may invest funds in securities issued or guaranteed by the state.
Japan	Advances to the government	The Bank of Japan may make advances to the government without collateral and may subscribe to or take up government loan issues.
Korea	Advances and holdings of government bonds	Authorization by the National Assembly.
Netherlands	Government securities	The central bank may buy and sell Dutch Treasury paper and debt instruments quoted on the Amsterdam Stock Exchange and issued or guaranteed as to interest and principal by the government.

Appendix I (*continued*)

Country	Type of Loan	Decision Process and Regulations
New Zealand	Loans to the government	The Reserve Bank shall make loans to the government and on such conditions as the minister decides from time to time, in order to ensure the continuing full employment of labor and other resources of any kind. The Bank may also buy and sell securities issued or guaranteed by any government or issued by any local authority or public body, and such other classes of securities as may be approved from time to time by the minister.
Norway	Short-term credits to the government	The Norges Bank may grant *seasonal* and other *short-term* credits direct to the government within specific limits stipulated by the Storting. In *special* cases, it may also grant *long-term* credit direct to the government within specific limits stipulated by the Storting. The Bank may also purchase and sell treasury bills and government and government-guaranteed bonds. Purchases of these instruments are not covered by the previous limitations.
Portugal	Government securities	In accordance with the guidelines for monetary, financial, and exchange rate policy established by the appropriate authorities, the Bank of Portugal may buy and sell securities issued by the Portuguese State.
Switzerland	Advances and government securities	The National Bank may make payments on behalf of the Confederation but *only* up to the limit of the credit balance of the Confederation with the Bank. Moreover, to prevent excessive recourse to the money and capital market, the Federal Council may require authorization of public issues of domestic treasury bills and debt instruments of any kind. The National Bank shall establish the overall amount of issues to be authorized in a given period.
Turkey	Advances to state economic enterprises and administrations	These advances should be made against bills or treasury-guaranteed bills of a maximum of nine months' maturity. The maximum limits of the bills that may be accepted in this manner and applicable discount and interest rate shall be decided by the Board of Directors.
	Purchases of state bonds	In order to regulate money supply and the liquidity requirements of the economy the Bank may purchase and sell state bonds, state internal loan bonds, bonds of the public agencies and institutions, and the sound bonds quoted on the stock exchange. These open market operations shall not exceed five times the total of the bank's capital and reserve funds.
United Kingdom	Loans to the treasury	The Bank of England may lend any sums that the treasury has the power to borrow under the National Loans Act, 1968, for providing the sums required to meet any excess of payments out of the National Loans Fund (the account of the treasury at the Bank of England), over receipts into the National Loans Fund, and for providing any necessary working balance in the National Loans Fund.

United States	Holdings of government securities	Every Federal Reserve bank may buy and sell bonds, notes, or other obligations that are direct obligations of the United States or that are fully guaranteed by the United States as to the principal and interest, *without regard to maturities*, *but only in the open market*. Besides, Federal Reserve banks may buy and sell, at home or abroad, bonds and notes of the United States having maturities from date of purchase that do *not exceed six months*, and bills, notes revenue bonds and warrants with a maturity from date of purchase *of not exceeding six months*, issue in anticipation of the collection of taxes or in anticipation of the receipt of assured revenues by any state, county, district, political subdivision, or municipality in the continental United States. They may also buy and sell *in the open market*, under the direction and regulations of the Federal Open Market Committee, any obligation that is a direct obligation of, or fully guaranteed as to principal and interest by, any agency of the United States.
	Treasury borrowing	Moreover, the Secretary of the Treasury *may borrow* from any Federal Reserve bank, subject to the approval and rules and regulations of the Federal Open Market Committee, any obligation of, or fully guaranteed as to principal and interest by, any agency of the United States, and to sell any such obligation in the open market *for the purpose of meeting the short-term cash needs of the treasury*. Not later than six months after the date of sale of such an obligation, the Secretary of the Treasury shall repurchase such obligation and return such obligation to the Federal Reserve bank from which such obligation was borrowed. The aggregate of the face amount of obligations borrowed under their authority shall be included during the period of such borrowing as part of the public debt subject to the limitation imposed by Section 21 of the Second Liberty Bond Act (a fixed amount in U.S. dollars).

B. *Limit: Absolute Amount in Domestic Currency*

Germany	Cash advances	The maximum limit on the cash advances is set annually by the legislative body and includes such treasury bills as the Deutsche Bundesbank has purchased for its own account or to the purchase of which it has committed itself.
	Holdings of treasury bills and treasury bonds	The Bundesbank may, for the purpose of regulating the money market, purchase and sell on the open market at market prices treasury bills and treasury bonds issued by the Federation (mobilization paper). Mobilization paper shall not be counted toward the credit ceiling mentioned before, but there exists also a maximum limit (set by the legislative body) for the holdings of mobilization paper by the Deutsche Bundesbank.
Greece	Advances	The Bank of Greece may make temporary advances in drachmas to the government for expenditure in the annual state budget, provided that the whole of the advances outstanding at any one time shall not exceed a given amount in domestic currency. All advances shall be repaid not later than at the end of the quarter following the close of the fiscal year in respect of which such advances were made.

Appendix I (*continued*)

Country	Type of Loan	Decision Process and Regulations
Netherlands	Advances	For the *temporary* strengthening of the treasury's position the central bank may make advances to the government against sufficient security of treasury notes provided that the issue or pledge of such notes has been permitted by law.
Sweden	Credits	The Riksbank may open credits in current account for a period not exceeding 12 months against the pledge of the Swedish State up to a fixed amount in kronor.
	Government securities	The Riksbank may buy and sell Swedish Government bonds and other Swedish Government securities.

Country Name	Type of Loan	Percent	Base for Calculation	Cost	Repayment	Days to Maturity
	C. Limit: Percentage of Central Bank Liabilities					
Cyprus	Holdings of government and government-guaranteed securities	20	Total sight liabilities			
Equatorial Guinea	Holdings of government securities	20	Total liabilities			
	(max. annual increase)	(5)	(Monthly average previous 12 months)			
Gambia, The	Advances and holdings of government securities	50	Average demand liabilities previous fiscal year			
Malawi	Holdings of government securities	25	Total demand liabilities			More than 2 years, less than 25 years.
Malta	Holdings of treasury bills and holdings of publicly issued securities of or guaranteed by the government, including any security held as collateral	20	Total central bank demand liabilities			For treasury bills, 93 days and not more than 20 years for other government securities.

Mozambique	Line of credit	10	Average monthly sight liabilities of first 9 months of previous fiscal year	Free	End of current fiscal year	
Nigeria	Holdings of government securities	75	Total demand liabilities			More than 2 years, less than 25 years.
D. *Limit: Percentage of Government Revenue*						
Algeria	Overdrafts	5	Previous fiscal year	Service charge	Maximum 240 days each fiscal year	
Argentina	Advances	30	Previous fiscal year	Discount rate or higher	Twelve months after fiscal year	
Austria	Holdings of short-term treasury certificates and other bonds of the Federal Republic	5	Current fiscal year	Discount rate		
Bahamas	Advances	10	Least of previous and current fiscal year			
Bahrain	Advances	10	Previous fiscal year	As agreed by the authorities	Three months after fiscal year	
	Holdings of government securities and other loans	25	Previous fiscal year			
Belize	Advances	15	Current fiscal year		Three months after fiscal year	
Botswana	Advances and holdings of government securities	20	Average three preceding fiscal years	As agreed by the authorities	Six months after fiscal year	
		+ 10	(In exceptional circumstances)			
Burma	Advances	15	Current fiscal year			Maximum six months
Burundi	Advances	50	Previous fiscal year	Minimum 3 percent		
Canada	Advances to the government	33	Current fiscal year		Three months after fiscal year	
	Advances to any provincial government	25	Current fiscal year		Three months after fiscal year	

Appendix I (*continued*)

Country Name	Type of Loan	Percent	Base for Calculation	Cost	Repayment	Days to Maturity
Cape Verde	Overdraft holdings of loans against treasury notes	15	Previous fiscal year	Free	End fiscal year	
Central African States	Overdraft	20	Previous fiscal year		Maximum 12 months	
Cyprus	Advances	25	Current fiscal year		Six months after fiscal year	Maximum 12 months
	Holding of treasury bills	30	Current fiscal year			
East Caribbean Currency Board	Temporary advances	5	Average three preceding fiscal years			
	Holdings of treasury bills	10	Average three preceding fiscal years			Maximum 91 days
Ecuador	Advances	10	Average three preceding fiscal years		End fiscal year	Maximum one year
Egypt	Loans	10	Average three preceding fiscal years			Maximum 12 months
El Salvador	Advances and loans	30	Average five preceding fiscal years			Maximum 12 months
Ethiopia	Advances	25	Previous fiscal year	Maximum 3 percent	Six months after fiscal year	
	Holdings of treasury bills and government bonds	50	Previous fiscal year			Maximum 10 years
Ghana	Advances	10	Current fiscal year	As agreed by the authorities	Three months after fiscal year	
		15	(In exceptional circumstances)			
Greece	Overall amount of advances, guarantees and discounted treasury bills	10	Current fiscal year			

Guinea	Overdraft	10	Previous fiscal year	Service charge	Maximum 240 days each fiscal year
Guyana	Advances	15	Average 3 preceding fiscal years	Minimum 3 percent	Maximum 350 days each fiscal year
Iraq	Advances	15	Current fiscal year		Three months after fiscal year
Israel	Advances	20	Current fiscal year		End fiscal year
Jamaica	Advances	30	Current fiscal year		Three months after fiscal year
Jordan	Advances	25	Current fiscal year	Free	
Kuwait	Advances	10	Previous fiscal year		End of next fiscal year
Lao People's Democratic Republic	Advances	25	Previous fiscal year	As agreed by the authorities	As agreed by the authorities
		50	(In exceptional circumstances)		
Lesotho	Advances	5	Current fiscal year		
Libya	Advances	10	Current fiscal year		End of fiscal year
Madagascar	Advances	15	Previous fiscal year		6 months after fiscal year
		(20)	(In exceptional circumstances)		
Malawi	Advances	10	Current fiscal year	Determination by central bank	Four months after fiscal year
Malaysia	Advances	12.5	Current fiscal year		Three months after fiscal year
Mali	Overdrafts	10	Previous fiscal year	Discount rate	Maximum 240 days each fiscal year
		15	(In exceptional circumstances)		

Appendix I (continued)

Country Name	Type of Loan	Percent	Base for Calculation	Cost	Repayment	Days to Maturity
Malta	Advances	15	Current fiscal year	As agreed	End fiscal year. If after that date such advances remain unpaid, the power of the central bank to grant further advances shall not be exercisable until the outstanding advances have been repaid.	
Mauritania	Overdrafts and loans	15	Previous fiscal year			
		20	(In exceptional circumstances)			
Mauritius	Advances	25	Current fiscal year		Four months after fiscal year	
Morocco	Advances	10			Maximum 240 days each fiscal year	
Mozambique	Overdrafts and loans	8.3	Current fiscal year	Maximum discount rate		Three months
Netherlands Antilles	Advances	10	Previous fiscal year	Free		
Nigeria	Advances	25	Current fiscal year	Determined by the Central Bank	End fiscal year	
Oman	Advances	10	Current fiscal year			Ninety days
Papua New Guinea	Advances and holdings of government securities	20		As agreed	As agreed	
		25	(In exceptional circumstances)			Maximum six months

Paraguay	Holdings of treasury bills	20	Average three preceding fiscal years			Maximum one year
Peru	Holdings of treasury bills	8.3	Current fiscal year			Maximum 90 days
Philippines	Advances	20	Average three preceding years		Three months after fiscal year	
Portugal	Overdrafts	10	Previous fiscal year	Free	End of fiscal year	
Rwanda	Overdrafts	5	Average three preceding fiscal years	3.0 percent		
		+ 5		4.5 percent		
		+ 1		6.0 percent		
Sao Tome and Principe	Overdrafts	5	Previous fiscal year	Free	End of fiscal year	
	Short-term loans	8.3	Current fiscal year	Maximum discount rate		Maximum three months
	Special purpose loans	20	(In exceptional circumstances)			
Sierra Leone	Advances	20	Current fiscal year		End of fiscal year	
Somalia	Advances and holdings of government securities	35	Average three preceding years	Minimum 2.5 percent		
Sri Lanka	Advances	10	Current fiscal year			Maximum six months
Sudan	Advances	15	Current fiscal year	Determined by the Central Bank	Six months after fiscal year	
Suriname	Advances	10	Current fiscal year	Free up to 1 million guilders		
Tanzania	Advances	20	Current fiscal year	Minimum 3 percent	Maximum 300 days each fiscal year	
	Holdings of government securities	25				Maximum 12 months
Trinidad and Tobago	Advances	15	Current fiscal yar		End fiscal year	
Tunisia	Overdrafts	5	Previous fiscal year	Service charge	Maximum 240 days each fiscal year	
Turkey	Advances	15	Current fiscal year	As agreed between the Ministry of Finance and the central bank		

Appendix I (*concluded*)

Country Name	Type of Loan	Percent	Base for Calculation	Cost	Repayment	Days to Maturity
Uganda	Advances	18	Current fiscal year	As agreed by the authorities	End fiscal year	
United Arab Emirates	Advances	10	Previous fiscal year		End of next fiscal year	
Vanuatu	Advances and holdings of government securities	15	Average three preceding fiscal years			Maximum six months
Venezuela	Advances and holdings of government securities	10 20	Average five preceding fiscal years (In exceptional circumstances)		End of fiscal year	
Viet Nam	Advances	25	Previous fiscal year			
West African Monetary Union	Advances	20	Previous fiscal year			
Western Samoa	Advances	25 35	Current fiscal year (In exceptional circumstances)	Determined by the central bank	Six months after fiscal year	
Yemen Arab Republic	Advances	20	Current fiscal year	Service charge mimimum 3 percent	As agreed	
	Holdings of government securities	15				Maximum 12 months
Yemen People's Democratic Republic	Advances	15	Current fiscal year		End of fiscal year	
	Holdings of government securities	25	Current fiscal year			

Zaïre	Advances	15	Average three preceding fiscal years	Minimum 3 percent	Maximum 300 days each fiscal year	Holdings of treasury notes
		20	Average three preceding fiscal years			
Zambia	Advances and holdings of government securities	50	Current fiscal year	Minimum 3 percent	Maximum 300 days each fiscal year	Holdings of treasury notes
Zimbabwe				Twelve months after fiscal year		
E. *Limit: Percentage of Government Expenditure*						
Jamaica	Holdings of government securities	40	Current fiscal year			
Thailand	Advances	25	Current fiscal year		Three months after fiscal year	
Spain	Advances to the treasury	12	Current fiscal year	Free		

Appendix II

Analytical Framework

We will start with the following general expression for the budget constraint faced by a typical economic unit:

$$Ex + \Delta A = In + \Delta L \tag{1}$$

where

Ex = expenditures;
ΔA = change in assets;
In = income; and
ΔL = change in liabilities.

We can use expression (1) to specify the government budget constraint as follows:

$$GOE = r^G CBNCG + r^D GDD + \Delta GNFA + \Delta GONA$$
$$= T + r^* GNFA + r^{**} GONA + \Delta CBNCG + \Delta GDD \tag{2}$$

where

GOE = Total government current operational expenditures (including investment);
r^G = $a(1 \times m)$ vector of nominal interest rates on government net liabilities with the central bank;
$CBNCG$ = $a(m \times 1)$ vector of outstanding government net liabilities with the central bank;
r^D = $a(1 \times m)$ vector of nominal interest rates on government domestic debt instruments outside the central bank;
GDD = $a(m \times 1)$ vector of outstanding government domestic debt instruments outside the central bank;
$\Delta GNFA = \sum_i (GFA_{it} - GFA_{it-1}) - \sum_j (GFL_{jt} - GFL_{jt-1})$
GFA_{is} = stock of government foreign asset type i, valued in local currency, outstanding, at time s ($i = 1, \ldots, m$; $s = t, t-1$);
GFL_{js} = stock of government foreign liability type j, valued in local currency, outstanding at time s ($j = 1, \ldots, m$; $s = t, t-1$);
$\Delta GONA = \sum_i (GOA_{it} - GOA_{it-1}) - \sum_j (GOL_{jt} - GOL_{jt-1})$
GOA_{is} = stock of other government asset type i outstanding at time s ($i = 1, \ldots, m$; $s = t, t-1$);

GOL_{js} = stock of other government liability type j outstanding at time $s(j = 1, \ldots, m; s = t, t - 1)$;
T = tax revenues;
r^* = $a(1 \times m)$ vector of (local currency equivalent of) nominal international interest rates on government net foreign assets;
$GNFA$ = $a(m \times 1)$ vector of outstanding government net foreign assets valued in local currency;
r^{**} = $a(1 \times m)$ vector of nominal interest rates on other net government assets;
$GONA$ = $a(m \times 1)$ vector of outstanding other net government assets;
$\Delta CBNCG = \sum_i (CBCG_{it} - CBCG_{it-1}) - \sum_j (GDCB_{jt} - GDCB_{jt-1})$
$CBCG_{is}$ = stock of central bank credit (type i outstanding at time s) to the government $(i = 1, \ldots, m; s = t, t - 1)$;
$GDCB_{js}$ = stock of government deposits (type j outstanding at time s) with the central bank $(j = 1, \ldots, m; s = t, t - 1)$;
$\Delta GDD = \sum_i (GDD_{it} - GDD_{it-1})$
GDD_{is} = stock of government domestic debt instrument type i outstanding at time s $(i = 1, \ldots, m; s = t, t - 1)$ outside the central bank.

Rearranging expression (2) we get:

$$\Delta CBNCG + (\Delta GDD - \Delta GNFA) = (GOE - T) + (r^G CBNCG + r^D GDD - r^* \mathrm{GNFA} - r^{**} GONA) + \Delta GONA. \quad (3)$$

A similar expression can be derived for the central bank budget constraint as follows:

$$\Delta RM + (\Delta CBB - \Delta CBNFA) = CBOE + (r^B CBB - r' \mathrm{CBNFA} - r'' CBONA - r^G CBNCG - r^e CBCE) + \Delta CBNCG + \Delta CBCE + \Delta CBONA \quad (4)$$

where

$\Delta RM = RM_t - RM_{t-1}$;
RM_s = stock of reserve money outstanding a time s $(s = t, t - 1)$;
$\Delta CBB = \sum_i (CBB_{it} - CBB_{it-1})$

CBB_{is} = stock of type i central bank bond (or bill) outstanding at time s (i: 1, . . . , m; $s = t, t-1$);

$\Delta CBNFA = \sum_i (CBFA_{it} - CBFA_{it-1}) - \sum_j (CBFL_{jt} - CBFL_{jt-1})$

$CBFA_{is}$ = stock of type i central bank foreign assets, valued in local currency, outstanding at time s ($i = 1, \ldots,$ m;
$s = t, t-1$);

$CBFL_{js}$ = stock of type j central bank foreign liability, valued in local currency, outstanding at time s ($j = 1, \ldots,$ m; $s = t, t-1$);

$CBOE$ = current operational central bank expenditures;

r^B = $a(1 \times m)$ vector of nominal interest rates on central bank bonds or bills;

CBB = $a(m \times 1)$ vector of outstanding central bank bonds or bills;

r' = $a(1 \times m)$ vector of (local currency equivalent of) international nominal interest rates on outstanding central bank net foreign assets;

r'' = $a(1 \times n)$ vector of nominal interest rates on other outstanding central bank net assets;

$CBONA$ = $a(m \times 1)$ vector of other outstanding central bank net assets;

r^e = $a(1 \times m)$ vector of nominal interest rates on outstanding liabilities of the economy with the central bank;

$CBCE$ = $a(m \times 1)$ vector of outstanding debt instruments of the economy (banks and private sector) with the central bank;

$\Delta CBCE = \sum_i (CBCE_{it} - CBCE_{it-1})$;

$CBCE_{is}$ = stock of the liability type "i" of the economy with the central bank outstanding at time s ($i = 1, \ldots,$ m;
$s = t, t-1$);

$\Delta CBONA = \sum_i (CBOA_{it} - CBOA_{it-1}) - \sum_j (CBOL_{it} - CBOL_{jt-1})$

$CBOA_{js}$ = stock of other central bank assets (type i) outstanding at time s (i: 1, . . . , m; $s = t, t-1$);

$CBOL_{js}$ = stock of other central bank liabilities (type j) outstanding at time s ($j = 1, \ldots, m$; $s = t, t-1$); and r^G, $CBNCG$ as before.

Using (3) and (4) we can obtain an expression for the consolidated budget constraint of the government and the central bank as follows:

$$\begin{aligned}\Delta RM + (\Delta GDD + \Delta CBB - \Delta GNFA - \Delta CBNFA) \\ = (GOE + CBOE - T) + (r^{D}GDD + R^{B}CBB \\ - r^{*}GNFA - r'CBNFA - r^{**}GONA - r''CBONA \\ - r^{e}CBCE) + \Delta CBCE + \Delta GONA + \Delta CBONA \quad (5)\end{aligned}$$

Appendix III

Suggested Limitations

Limit on total outstanding government debt

A prudent and elemental principle in lending establishes that the ratio of payments of loans installments to income should not exceed a certain given constant. For government debt, this relationship can be written as follows:

$$Pt \leq k_1 T_t \quad (1)$$

where

Pt = payments at time t;
Tt = government revenues at time t;
k_1 = a constant.

A relationship linking the amount of payments to the total amount of government debt also exists. Assuming, for simplicity, that only one outstanding loan to the government exists, this relationship can be written as follows:

$$P(t) = \beta D(t) \quad (2)$$

where

$D(t)$ = amount of the loan or outstanding debt;
$\beta = \dfrac{i}{[1 - (1 + i)^{n}]}$,
i = interest rate per payment period;
n = number of payment periods.

Thus, relationship (1) can be rewritten as follows:

$$D(t) \leq \frac{k_1}{\beta} T(t) \quad (3)$$

Inequality (3) limits total outstanding debt to a proportion of total government revenues. This proportion is decreasing in the interest rate on government debt and increasing in the maturity of loans to the government. To some extent, a limitation of the form in equation (3) derived from simple prudential principles resembles some of the limitations we found in actual central bank laws governing the lending to governments.

The relationship expressed in equation (3) implies a limit on government-debt growth of the form:

$$\Delta D \leq \frac{k_1}{\beta} \Delta T \leq \frac{k_1}{\beta} T(t) - D(t-1) \tag{4}$$

Limits on Governments Borrowing from the Central Bank

Limit on Total Outstanding Net Government Debt with the Central Bank

This limit is similar to the one suggested for total outstanding government debt and can be expressed as follows:

$$D_{cb}(t) \leq \frac{k_2}{\beta} T(t) \tag{5}$$

where

$D_{cb}(t)$ = outstanding total government net debt with the central bank.

The relationship expressed in equation (5) implies a limit on the growth of government debt with the central bank of the form:

$$\Delta D_{cb} \leq \frac{k2 \Delta T}{\beta} \leq \frac{k2}{\beta} T(t) - D_{cb}(t-1) \tag{6}$$

Limit on Government Direct Borrowing from the Central Bank

The purpose of this limiting direct borrowing from the government is to indicate the maximum allowed amount of direct central bank lending to the government. This amount is also constrained by the limits given by the relationship shown in equation (6). The proposed limit takes the form:

$$CBDCG(t) \leq (1 + y(t))\, CBDCG(t-1) \leq \Delta D_{cb} \tag{7}$$

where

$CBDCG$ = outstanding direct central bank net credit to the government at time t (in nominal terms)

$y(t)$ = rate of growth of real GDP at time t.

25

Central Bank Independence and Central Bank Functions

MARK SWINBURNE AND MARTA CASTELLO-BRANCO*

During the 1970s and 1980s, important changes were made in the way a number of countries operated and presented monetary policy. A major reason for such changes appears to have been a recognition of the value of monetary policy "credibility" and transparency for achieving policy objectives effectively and efficiently. More recently, a similar reason seems to have motivated renewed interest in a few countries in examining fundamental changes in central banking legislation with the general aim of allowing greater monetary policy autonomy for the central bank. Chile has just enacted new legislation, New Zealand is on the point of enacting its new legislation, and Argentina is in the process of developing specific proposals. In Venezuela, a larger degree of independence for the central bank is expected to result from the ongoing reform of the financial system, and in Hungary legislation has been drafted granting more autonomy to the central bank. There have also been calls for increased central bank autonomy in Brazil, the United Kingdom, Australia, and Italy.

Such changes naturally raise fundamental questions about the appropriate relationship between central banks and governments, and this is one focus of this paper. But they also raise fundamental and related questions about the appropriate role of modern central banks: what functions (other than monetary policy itself) should central banks undertake, and how does the allocation of functions affect a

---

*Mr. Swinburne and Ms. Castello-Branco are Economists in the Central Banking Department of the International Monetary Fund. An extensively revised version of this paper has been issued as "Central Bank Independence: Issues and Experience," IMF Working Paper, No. 91/58 (unpublished, Washington: International Monetary Fund, 1991).

central bank's monetary policy independence? Such questions are the other focus of the paper.

These issues are examined with reference to arrangements in a limited initial sample of countries, including Chile and New Zealand because of the recent changes in their central banking legislation.[1] Obviously, the practical effect of the changes in these two countries has yet to be tested, but the nature of the changes is of interest in itself. It is also of interest to note two other points about these countries. First, the changes to central banking legislation reflect a common perception that monetary policy had been misused in the past and had come against the background of major stabilization and structural adjustment programs, which have already had significant success in reining in inflation. Second, while the changes in New Zealand immediately gained broad political support, this was not initially the case in Chile: until specific appointees to the central bank's governing board were finalized, early amendments to the Chilean arrangements seemed a possibility.

The structure of this paper is as follows. The first section provides a highly summarized review of the historical development of central banking and monetary policy, as background for the rest of the discussion. The second discusses the case for central bank independence in monetary policy, with reference to the thrust of recent theoretical and empirical work in the professional literature. The third considers the dimensions of monetary policy independence in practice, based on the initial survey of arrangements in eight countries. The fourth considers the relationship between monetary policy autonomy and other common functions of central banks, again with reference to arrangements in the surveyed countries. Concluding observations are made in the last section.

Central Banking and Monetary Policy—A Brief Review

In considering the monetary policy role of central banks, it is useful to keep in mind the long history of central banking.[2] The original impetus to the development of the first central banks—in Europe—seems to have come from two main sources. First, governments began

[1]The other countries in the survey are Germany, Switzerland, the United States, the United Kingdom, France, and the Netherlands. The preliminary conclusions and generalizations will be modified at a later stage based on a more comprehensive survey of key factors affecting independence, and of the more recent empirical literature.

[2]For a more detailed historical analysis of the development of central banking, see, for example, the interesting study by Goodhart (1988), on which the following discussion is partly based.

to realize that they could obtain financial assistance and advantages in return for supporting a particular bank in various ways. Such favoritism, often supported by legislation, could involve either a private bank (as with the Bank of England) or a specially established state bank (such as the Prussian State Bank).

Second, some early central banks (e.g., in Switzerland, Italy, and Germany) were founded specifically to unify the note issue system, manage and protect the metallic reserve of the country, and improve the payments system. Although broader economic benefits were seen in such moves—that is, economies of scale and increased confidence from the unification of the note issue system—there were also clear political attractions, especially, access to seigniorage revenue.

Through the first half of the nineteenth century, at least, these two areas largely defined the role of the then existing central banks. Even up to the early twentieth century, most economic analysis of central banking concentrated on the advantages or disadvantages of the note issue monopoly. What followed from these functions of early central banks seems to have been largely unrecognized by policymakers for some time.

Once central banking institutions existed with privileged legal positions as banker to the government and as currency issuer, these institutions began to develop into "bankers' banks." Their position as monopoly supplier of currency and as the government's bank led to a concentration of the banking system's cash reserves at the central bank. This, in turn, enabled individual banks to call on the central bank for temporary additional liquidity when required.

Moreover, since the existence of a central source of reserves enabled commercial banks to economize, on their own, individual cash holdings, there were marked tendencies for quasi-central banking mechanisms to develop in countries without central banks as such. In the United States, for example, clearinghouse associations and some large commercial banks used to provide these services for other banks. This suggests that government intervention to create a specific central bank, or to endow a pre-existing bank with monopoly currency issue and government banking privileges, may have served mainly to determine the particular form of central banking arrangement—which institution would be the central bank—rather than whether there would be such an arrangement at all.

In any event, their position as the ultimate source of domestic liquidity for the banking system meant that central banks became increasingly tied to two closely related areas of broader concern—a more micro concern for the health of the banking system, and a more macro concern for the state of monetary conditions in the economy in general. Because of perceived conflicts between these broader concerns and their competitive commercial banking operations, central banks eventually had to move out of their former competitive activities and concentrate on the "true" central banking functions. With the Bank of England and the Banque de France, for example, this took place in the second half of the nineteenth century.[3] For similar reasons, most of the central banks established in the twentieth century were set up as entirely new and noncompetitive institutions (and where this was not the case initially, such as in Australia, a separate central bank was split out subsequently).

Compared with the long history of central banking, the development of a distinctive monetary policy function for central banks, built on top of their traditional functions, is relatively recent. Specifically, discretionary monetary policy developed into a defining feature of modern central banking following the abandonment of guaranteed convertibility of national currencies into gold at fixed exchange rates. In the absence of an external standard of value, the key determinant of the exchange value of money (i.e., the price level) became the rate of expansion of money itself. Governments thus became faced with the need to manage their currency, to some extent at least, on a discretionary basis.

The idea that central banks should have independence from political influence also has rather long historical roots and featured clearly in the discussions leading up to the establishment of many twentieth century central banks. In the past, the concern was that limits were needed on the government's ability to fund itself through seigniorage. The more common contemporary interpretation of the problem is that the political leadership tends to take too short-term a view on the appropriate stance of monetary policy at any particular time: monetary policy consequently tends to take on a stop-and-go nature, reflecting excessive interest in fine-tuning. Monetary stability is, therefore, according to this view, more likely to be achieved over time when monetary policy is in the hands of apolitical central bankers who can afford to take the longer view.

Here, a distinction should be drawn between two different notions of monetary policy independence. First, monetary policy can be insulated from day-to-day political pressure by the relatively simple expedient of legislating some form of monetary policy "rule." In the past, the gold standard was just such a rule. In recent times, there have been numerous proposals for new types of monetary policy rules to be established, and there is extensive literature on the long-running

[3]However, during the Great Depression of the 1930s, the Banque de France resumed its competitive activities.

"rules-versus-discretion" debate. Under a rule, a central bank has monetary policy independence in only a limited sense—its freedom to devise and implement its own view of a desirable monetary policy may not be constrained by the political leadership, but it is heavily constrained by the rule.

Second, central banks can be endowed with monetary policy independence in a fuller sense when they are both insulated from political pressure and have considerable discretion in the determination and operation of monetary policy. This second notion of central banks' monetary policy independence is clearly the more relevant concept in terms of current central banking practice, and it is monetary policy independence in this sense that is the subject of this paper.

Even in the situation where binding monetary policy rules do not apply, there may, however, still be important issues about the extent of a central bank's discretion and how this relates to central bank independence. There is a wide middle ground between complete discretion and completely binding rules: commitments to monetary targeting and pegged but adjustable exchange rates, such as under the European Monetary System (EMS), are but two examples of a range of possibilities in this middle ground.

The problem for monetary policy today is to design an arrangement that makes the maximum contribution to achieving stability, built on monetary policy credibility, taking into account two inherent characteristics of the policy environment. First, no modern government appears willing to completely concede flexibility by committing itself to a binding monetary rule. Second, there will always be an element of difficulty in monitoring monetary policy performance, because the underlying monetary relationships are only imperfectly understood, do not work mechanically, can change over time (possibly quite sharply), and tend to involve long and variable lags between policy changes and final outcomes.

The Case for Monetary Policy Independence

The conceptual case for central bank independence in monetary policy is based on the view that policy credibility could improve the effectiveness and efficiency of monetary policy. Although the concept is not new, only in recent years has it been defined and analyzed in rigorous terms.[4] A key feature of the new literature on credibility is the explicit modeling of the motives of policymakers and the constraints

[4]See, among others, Cukierman (1986) and Blackburn and Christensen (1989) for surveys of the new extensive literature in this field.

they face in a world where the public learns from experience and adjusts its expectations fairly rapidly. The value of this work is that it directs attention to the central importance of the actual and perceived objectives of monetary policymakers, and the mechanisms for establishing and protecting public trust in the operation of monetary policy.

Starting from the proposition that real output in the economy is invariant to anticipated inflation (and monetary growth) but increases temporarily with unanticipated inflation, it can be shown that when the policymaker has both inflation and employment and output goals, a "time inconsistency" problem arises for monetary policy. Specifically, although the policymaker may adopt an anti-inflationary monetary policy in one period, an incentive exists to reverse that policy at some stage in the future in order to engineer an inflation surprise and achieve short-term output gains. Furthermore, if the private sector recognizes the time inconsistency, and if the policymaker cannot make a credible precommitment to a lasting anti-inflationary policy stance, the monetary deflation (while it lasts) will make slower progress than otherwise and, in particular, will involve higher real sector costs. The reason is that inflation risk premiums will be incorporated into interest rates and price and wage decisions, and inflation expectations will decline only slowly. From a longer-term perspective, the economy would be seen to remain around the "natural rate" of output and employment with an inherent inflationary bias.

One potential solution is for a "reputational equilibrium" to be established over time. The policymaker builds a reputation for consistency and determination in monetary policy, possibly as much by actions taken in other economic policy areas as in monetary policy itself. The policymaker demonstrates willingness and ability to stay on the anti-inflationary course for a sufficiently long time, despite the costs, to establish credibility. This sort of solution, however, begs important questions. For example, if monetary policy credibility has to be earned by bearing additional real sector costs until the private sector changes its perception of the policymaker's nature, what, if anything, can be done to hasten that process and reduce the costs? Additionally, since the private sector has to believe that the policymaker places a great weight on the cost of a damaged reputation, compared with the temporary gain from reneging on the anti-inflationary policy, how can the private sector be convinced that this is indeed the case?

Similar questions arise in considering possible solutions. Essentially, these other solutions seek to establish some form of institutional arrangement that would be seen by the public as a (more) credible precommitment to anti-inflationary monetary policy. Given that some measure of discretion in monetary policy is generally seen to be necessary, it might be possible to enhance credibility by ensuring that monetary policy is under the auspices of an independent authority that does not possess the same objectives and incentives as the political leadership. The key issues, then, become how to convince the public that such an authority is in fact independent, does in fact have the appropriate objectives, and is in fact motivated to achieve those objectives.

These are not straightforward issues. They force an explicit consideration of the actual behavior of central banks. As discussed further, below, studies that have examined actual central bank behavior indicate that it cannot be automatically assumed that central banks are motivated to consistently pursue appropriate monetary policy.

Some recent empirical work directly tests and lends limited support to the notion that countries with more independent central banks tend to deliver better inflation outcomes, and also that they have smaller and less variable fiscal deficits. While these results are suggestive and, to many, intuitively plausible, closer examination indicates that the evidence so far is less than compelling. There is also some indirect evidence drawn from studies of the end of past hyperinflations, but this may say more about the value of monetary policy "rules," such as the gold standard, than central bank independence as such. Moreover, desirable arrangements for ending hyperinflations may not also apply to less extreme situations.

There are two main problems with empirical evidence produced so far: measurement and causation. First, with regards to measurement, formal legislative arrangements are not always a good indicator of actual independence; a number of less formal arrangements and practices may be more important. The political leadership often has a range of methods for exerting influence, irrespective of formal mechanisms. As a result, monetary policy outcomes are often seen to depend critically on the particular personalities involved at the time.

Second, with regard to causality, rather than central bank independence leading to lower inflation and better fiscal policy, it may be that both are due to a third factor. For example, it might be argued that the German public's often quoted deep-seated fear of inflation has exerted a strong direct influence on the decisions of policymakers, as well as being behind the creation of an independent Deutsche Bundesbank.

Although the analytical case for central bank independence is now on rather firmer ground than previously, the view that such independence is necessarily desirable is far from universal. At one level, the notion of unelected central bankers determining a major element of economic policy is sometimes seen as contrary to democratic principles. At a different level, the value of independent central banks may be questioned on the grounds that they may not actually deliver superior monetary policy outcomes.

Although the "undemocratic" view is understandable, it is somewhat misdirected. It ignores the fact that no central bank is ever completely independent of government, if for no other reason than that the government, if political support is sufficient, can always change the legislation granting independence. On a more everyday level, governments can always exert influence over the policies implemented by central banks, over the longer run at least, through a variety of formal and informal mechanisms.

A more helpful way of analyzing the independence issue is to ask what, given the technical features of monetary policy, is a desirable degree of delegated responsibility for the central bank, and what are the desirable arrangements to establish it, recognizing that ultimate responsibility rests with the political leadership. To convey this sort of thought, some previous writers have referred to central bank independence within government, rather than independence from government.

A more substantial variant of the "undemocratic" criticism has to do with possible conflicts between an independent central bank's monetary policy and other areas of economic policy, especially fiscal policy. When such a conflict arises, some would say, it is not appropriate for monetary policy to be unyielding. A related point in the analytical literature emphasizes that monetary policy credibility does not depend on monetary policy alone, but rather upon the government's macroeconomic program in its entirety. In particular, when fiscal policy involves a stream of large deficits while an independent central bank pursues tight monetary policy, the economic program as a whole is not credible because eventually either fiscal or monetary policy has to give way. As Blackburn and Christensen (1989, p. 28) put it "[since] it matters considerably for inflation which of them does so, . . . [s]uch coordination problems generate uncertainty for private agents and invite speculation over how and when the conflict . . . will be resolved."

A counter to this argument is that it may well be desirable for monetary policy to be independent, notwithstanding the potential costs of conflicts with other areas of policy, precisely because it makes transparent the costs of inappropriate policy in these other areas. For example, depending on the sensitivity of those responsible for fiscal policy to such visible costs, an independent monetary policy may have the advantage of providing a disciplinary check on other policies. As noted previously, there is some suggestive, but not conclusive, evidence in support of this view.

The other view of independent central banks not actually achieving superior monetary policy outcomes depends on the central objectives and motivations; they might conflict with the appropriate stance of monetary policy. The U.S. Federal Reserve, for example, is usually considered one of the most independent of central banks, but its revealed or actual independence may be less than commonly thought. A number of studies have argued that the Federal Reserve responds to political pressure because it values its formal independence, and, to protect that independence, it tries not to alienate the U.S. Congress or the administration. One study, for example, concluded that, in practice, ". . .[Federal Reserve] officials attempt to preserve its political power by such actions as following the monetary policies of the U.S. President."[5]

If supposedly independent central banks in reality are motivated to follow the monetary policy of the political leadership in this way, independence may be even more harmful than a lack of it is purported to be. Formal independence that permits substantial backdoor political influence on monetary policy is likely to assist the political leadership in escaping its responsibility and accountability for monetary policy because of the nontransparency of the actual relationships involved. Monetary policy may still take on a stop-and-go nature in response to changing political winds, but the pretense of central bank independence could mean that the attention of the public and its elected representatives tends to be diverted from the medium-term performance of monetary policy so that it does not receive the analysis and review it deserves. In addition, this sort of situation may cause the central bank to employ nontransparent and suboptimal implementation procedures. It has been suggested that the tension between formal independence and actual, but unacknowledged, dependence may explain the Federal Reserve's well-documented "noisy" operating procedures and its preoccupation with secrecy.

The foregoing discussion suggests that two main questions are to be considered in establishing or reviewing central bank independence arrangements. The first is what degree of formal independence ("delegated authority") is likely to be considered desirable and realistic by politicians and society in general in the country in question? The second is, given the intended degree of central bank independence, what are the detailed arrangements that will be needed to put that independence in place, including especially the appropriate account-

[5]Auerbach (1985), p. 57.

ability arrangements? Even if the credibility argument for central bank independence is accepted in principle, the desired degree of independence is likely to depend on a number of country-specific factors. We could speculate that such factors might include a country's inflation history, the nature of existing checks and balances in the political system,[6] the level of public awareness and debate of economic issues, the state of development of financial markets, and so on. The next section examines the practice with respect to these questions.

Dimensions of Monetary Policy Independence

The discussion above suggests that the detail of the arrangements governing the relationship between central banks and governments may be particularly important if the potential credibility benefits of central bank independence are to be captured. The following sections discuss key aspects of these arrangements.

Formal Monetary Policy Responsibility

The central bank's duty to conduct policy at least in consultation with the political authorities is generally accepted, but within that, varying degrees of independence for the central bank are possible. The limited number of countries surveyed in this paper appears to cover the whole range of established arrangements.

At one extreme are central banks with a great deal of formal independence. The Deutsche Bundesbank has the statutory responsibility to determine monetary policy, but also the obligation to support the general economic policy of the government to the extent that this is compatible with the Bundesbank's statutory objectives. The Swiss National Bank, in its determination of monetary policy, is constitutionally independent of the political authorities, but the Bank and the government are obliged to consult each other before implementing policies. In neither case is approval by the second party necessary. In practice, the Bank and the government work closely together.

At the other extreme, such formal independence is explicitly denied in the legislation of some central banks. In France, the Ministry of the Economy decides on the stance of monetary policy. In the United Kingdom, the treasury has the power (so far apparently unused) to issue formal but unpublished directives to the Bank of England. In

[6]In the context of political checks and balances, it is interesting to note that the three most formally independent central banks (i.e., those in Germany, Switzerland, and the United States) have been established in federal systems, where a wish to constrain the powers of the national government has played a central role in political history.

practice, the treasury is in control of monetary policy at the officials' level, and the Bank of England is the agent that implements monetary policy in consultation with the treasury.

Between these extremes is the U.S. Federal Reserve, which is explicitly independent of the Executive Branch in determining and implementing monetary policy, but must report twice a year to Congress. In practice, the Federal Reserve is in continuous contact with all policymaking bodies of the government. A 1984 survey of central bank relationships with government notes that because the Federal Reserve's position is based on a delegation of the powers of Congress, Congress retains the right to instruct it. In general, Congress has apparently restrained itself in this respect but, according to the survey, has on occasion expressed itself in a form considered as being fairly close to a directive. In the Netherlands, the government has the right to issue formal directives to the Nederlandsche Bank and the Bank has the right to request publication of a conflict of views. In practice, the Bank has a high degree of independence in the determination of monetary policy (within the limits arising from membership in the EMS), except that the size of the note issue is set by the government after advice from the Bank.

In the two countries with major recent changes in their central bank legislation, formal independence is tempered by cooperating with the government. In Chile, the central bank has the authority to design, implement, and operate monetary policy, but is required to take into account the general direction of government economic policy. The central bank also has a duty to advise the President of the Republic, on request, on matters relating to its functions. In New Zealand, the new legislation gives the Reserve Bank of New Zealand the responsibility for formulating and operating monetary policy, in line with published policy targets agreed between the Bank's Governor and the Minister of Finance and directed toward the Bank's single statutory objective of price stability. The government has the right to override temporarily the Bank's statutory objective and to negotiate revised policy targets, but such actions have to be made public. The Bank is required to consult with and give advice to the government and any other parties that the Bank considers can assist it to achieve its statutory objective.

There is considerable variation in the openness of arrangements for the resolution of conflicts between the central bank and government. In terms of formal arrangements, at least, such openness is irrelevant in countries with the least independent central banks. In the countries surveyed that have the most independent central banks, no formal mechanisms exist for bringing policy conflicts into the open. In some other countries, represented by the Netherlands and New Zealand in this survey, the legislation attempts to provide for transparency in the resolution of conflicts.

In light of the fact that governments in the Netherlands and similar countries have apparently never used their power to issue published directives (and the New Zealand arrangements are yet to be tested), an important issue is whether this is because the formal mechanisms have actually been effective as a constraint on governments or because other channels for influencing the central bank have been used instead.

Similarly, in the case of the most independent central banks, a related question is whether the banks actually have sufficient formal and practical independence to resist the government in the event of a conflict, so that transparent resolution mechanisms would not be seen as necessary. Or alternatively, is it that the influence of public opinion is sufficient to impose a direct constraint on governments? A closer examination of other aspects of central banking arrangements may shed some light on these issues, to the extent that these other aspects help to define the incentive and accountability structure under which central banks operate.

Limits on Financing of Government

An important facet of formal monetary policy independence is the extent of legal constraint on central bank funding of the government. Of the countries surveyed in this paper, Chile has the tightest legal restrictions: no public expenditure may be financed directly or indirectly by credit from the central bank (except under wartime conditions), and the bank cannot purchase paper issued by the government, its agencies, or enterprises. In Germany, Switzerland, and the Netherlands, the legislation sets strict limits on direct central bank credit to government, but allows government paper to be acquired in the course of open market operations.[7] With the Bundesbank, it is explicit that such secondary market purchases can only be for monetary control purposes, and the Bank is not otherwise able to acquire government paper on its own account. In New Zealand, there are legal limits on the size and duration of any government overdraft at the Reserve Bank, but no other specific limits on direct and indirect credit to government. In the United States and the United Kingdom, there are no specific legal limits. In France, limits are agreed upon between the Bank and the minister and presuppose the approval of Parliament.

[7]In Germany, the limits on direct Bundesbank credit to the government are fixed in absolute deutsche mark terms and have not been changed since 1967.

Statutory Objectives

In general—and at the risk of oversimplification—central banks that have little policy independence tend to have statutory objectives that are more broadly defined—for example, the Bank of England's legislation refers only to promoting the "public good"—or defined in terms of functions, rather than goals. Banks with greater formal independence tend to have a statutory objective with a somewhat narrower focus, emphasizing stability in the domestic or external value of the currency (Germany, Netherlands, New Zealand, and Chile). The central banks of Switzerland and the United States could be viewed as exceptions to this generalization. Although Swiss legislation does not narrowly define an objective for the Swiss National Bank, the Bank has apparently done so on its own behalf. At first sight, the purpose stated in the Federal Reserve's legislation appears to approximate a fairly classical expression of a longer-term price stability objective, but the legislation is open to other interpretations in terms of day-to-day implementation.

Based on conceptual analysis, one would expect more independent central banks to have more narrowly defined statutory objectives, for several reasons. First, since monetary policy influence is essentially a single policy instrument, it cannot be simultaneously assigned to more than one policy target, especially when conflicts between those targets are possible in the short term.

Second, it is now widely accepted that active monetary policy manipulation cannot achieve sustainable, worthwhile aggregate real sector effects, but that, on the other hand, a firm and stable monetary policy is necessary for longer-term price stability. In short, therefore, monetary policy has a comparative advantage in achieving price stability relative to "real" economic objectives.

Third, central bank independence in monetary policy does not make sense if the central bank has multiple macroeconomic objectives, such as growth and employment, balance of payments, or distribution, as well as stabilizing the value of the currency. In this case, effective coordination and accountability would appear to require that the central bank be firmly under government control, since different organs of government would then be pursuing different mixes of essentially the same group of objectives.

Fourth, multiple objectives would reduce the transparency of monetary policy, and, for this reason too, would weaken the accountability of both the central bank and the political leadership. With multiple objectives, policy failure with respect to one objective can be too easily excused by reference to other objectives. Similarly, if the objectives are not clearly defined, those responsible for monetary policy cannot be effectively accountable.

Finally, and perhaps most important, it is the public perception of risks of policy reversals, and of changing policy targets, that weakens the credibility of monetary policy. Multiple or unclear objectives, therefore, do not seem likely to be consistent with the desire for monetary policy credibility. It is this credibility, however, that ultimately is the basis of the argument for central bank independence.

These arguments point to the desirability of a single, clearly defined price stability objective for an independent central bank's monetary policy. A bank's statutory objective does not have to be so specified, as long as a mechanism for clearly establishing the objective to which monetary policy will be aimed is available (compare Switzerland). Nevertheless, a single, clear, statutory objective is likely to be helpful.

Monetary Policy Accountability

Defining clearly the objective of monetary policy goes only part way toward promoting increased monetary policy credibility. The public also has to have some degree of certainty that an independent central bank is in fact being motivated to achieve that objective. This requires that the public is able to adequately monitor the performance of monetary policy and, directly or indirectly, hold accountable those responsible for its formulation and implementation. It seems clear that transparency in the relationship between the central bank and the political leadership is a precondition for effective accountability.

In general, and with the notable exception of New Zealand, the legislation of the surveyed central banks does not establish strong accountability mechanisms. In New Zealand, accountability focuses more on an individual, the governor, than on the central bank as a whole and is based on published policy targets, agreed upon between the governor and the minister, to be achieved during the governor's term of office. Formal monitoring of performance, relative to the policy targets and the Bank's statutory objective, is through the Bank's annual report to the minister (tabled in Parliament) and, more especially, through six-monthly "policy statements" to the minister (also tabled in Parliament), and through the Bank's board.

For the Bank of England and the Banque de France, with no formal independence, a lack of strong accountability mechanisms for the banks themselves in relation to the direction of monetary policy is perhaps not surprising. There is no doubt that the relevant minister, and the government as a whole, bears responsibility for formulation and implementation of monetary policy, and parliamentary review proceeds accordingly. In the United Kingdom, a parliamentary committee examines the governor or other officers of the Bank regularly with particular attention to the implementation, rather than the direction, of monetary policy. Parliamentary examination is less frequent in France. The banks' annual reports are the main formal instruments of accountability, presented to the president, in the case of France, and to Parliament through the minister, in the case of the United Kingdom. Parliamentary review of monetary policy in the Netherlands is less direct, with the Nederlandsche Bank reporting to the Bank Council, which is chaired by the Royal Commissioner, appointed by the Crown to supervise the Bank's affairs and formally accountable to the Crown.

In the United States and Chile, the legislature has an important direct role. The Federal Reserve is required to report to Congress semiannually. While the legislation still requires the Federal Reserve to discuss monetary aggregate targets, it is not bound by its statements about its targets. In addition, the Chairman and other members of the board frequently testify before various congressional committees. In Chile, the central bank reports annually to the president and the senate; the reports include the policies and programs to be adopted in the following year.

The central banks in Germany and Switzerland are not formally accountable to any arm of government, but have instead put considerable weight on the publication and attainment of monetary aggregate targets since the mid-1970s, thereby facilitating monitoring of monetary policy performance directly by the public. The Bundesbank is required to publish an annual report, but it is not presented to the government or parliament. The Swiss National Bank reports annually to its shareholders (which do not include the federal government).

Quantity targets for monetary policy are also set and published in other countries in this survey. In France and the United Kingdom, targets are set and announced by the government and, in terms of establishing monetary policy credibility, may partially compensate for the lack of an independent central bank. In the Netherlands, Germany, and Switzerland, it is the central bank that sets the targets, but in the Netherlands targets are not published because of the need to also maintain exchange rate stability within the EMS. Although the new law in Chile does not state operating procedures for monetary policy, in practice the central bank sets the targets. In New Zealand, it is a legislative requirement that monetary policy targets be set. Although the legislation does not specify the nature of the targets to be set, it requires that all key documents relating to central bank accountability (including in particular those setting out the policy targets) be published and tabled in Parliament.

In the United States, the Federal Reserve used to stress its quantity targets, but since the early 1980s has been de-emphasizing these targets citing instability in behavioral relationships due to technological, regulatory, and institutional factors. The Federal Reserve is, however, required to publish the minutes of its main decision-making body, the Federal Open Market Committee (FOMC), but with a six-week delay.

Role and Composition of Central Bank Boards

The role and composition of central bank boards can have an important influence on the nature of the relationship between central banks and governments. In some cases, the boards are a formal channel for the government to exert influence directly, albeit temporarily, on central bank decisions.

The board structure may have up to two or three tiers. Switzerland and the Netherlands both have a three-tier structure. The Swiss structure consists of a three-man Directorate conducting day-to-day policy and administrative business; a 40-member Bank Council, which is the general supervisory body responsible to shareholders and meets at least quarterly; and the Bank Committee, a subcommittee of the council with up to ten members, carrying out a more detailed supervisory function and meeting monthly. The committee also advises the directorate. In the Dutch structure, an executive Governing Board is responsible for ongoing management of the bank and reports to a 12-member Supervisory Board. There is a 17-member Bank Council, which advises the minister on the guidelines that the bank should follow in its policy. The Council is chaired by the Royal Commissioner, whose role is to supervise the affairs of the bank. The commissioner also attends meetings of the governing and supervisory boards in an advisory capacity.

In the United States, Germany, and Chile, there are two-tier structures; one level is supervisory, and the other is a regular decision-making (executive) body. In the United States, the decision-making body (the FOMC) is larger than the governing body (the Board of Governors) and includes all the members of the latter. In France, New Zealand, and the United Kingdom, there are executive committees for day-to-day management, but these are not formally established by legislation, which only covers the supervisory board. In New Zealand, the responsibilities of directors are clearly defined to emphasize their duty to monitor, on behalf of the minister, the performance of the governor, and the Bank as a whole, in relation to the agreed policy targets and the Bank's statutory objective.

In all cases, the government appoints the majority, if not all, of the members of these bodies (see below), but there may also be ex officio or advisory board members representing the government or treasury explicitly. In Germany and France, the government representative can request that a board decision be temporarily deferred or (in France only) reconsidered. In Chile, the minister or his deputy may attend council meetings and request a temporary deferment, unless at least four council members insist otherwise. In other countries (the United Kingdom and New Zealand), explicit government representation is directly ruled out.

The spread of sectoral and regional representation is often seen as an important criterion for the composition of the board (France, United Kingdom, Switzerland, United States, and the Netherlands), but in other cases, general business or financial knowledge and experience (New Zealand), or even "special professional qualifications" (Germany) are specified.

Appointment and Dismissal of Management and Directors

The fact that governments have the primary role in the appointment of directors and management in all countries reflects a broad recognition that monetary policy is ultimately a government responsibility, even where the central bank has considerable statutory independence. Nevertheless, in banks that have a greater degree of independence, the government's appointment (and dismissal) powers generally have more limitations. Such limitations include a proportion of nongovernment appointments;[8] nongovernmental nomination of candidates; or terms of office that are relatively long compared with the electoral cycle, and, in the case of board members, staggered to reduce the ability of governments to quickly place their own appointees in a dominating position.

For the two least independent central banks in the survey, the head of state makes all the appointments, either on the recommendation of (United Kingdom) or in consultation with (France) the cabinet, and without formal reference to other parties. The only exception is that one Banque de France director is elected by the staff. In the United

[8]Nongovernmental appointment of board members occurs in countries where the central bank is not fully owned by the government—Switzerland and the United States, in this current survey. A minor side issue here is whether ownership of the central bank is important for policy independence. The short answer seems to be that ownership does not necessarily make any difference: the Bundesbank, which is fully owned by the state, is perhaps the most independent of central banks.

Kingdom, the governor and deputy governor have five-year terms, and directors have staggered four-year terms. In France, directors have staggered six-year terms, and the governor and deputies are appointed for indefinite terms, which are, in practice, limited to five to seven years (the seven-year term is of equal length to but not necessarily concurrent with the French president's term).

In other countries, bank boards have an important role in appointment procedures. In New Zealand, the government appoints directors for staggered five-year terms, and appoints the governor on the recommendation of the board, also for a five-year term. The deputy governor is appointed by the board, on the recommendation of the governor, again for a five-year term. In the Netherlands, individual members of the Governing and Supervisory Board are appointed by the government, on the joint recommendation of the current members of these boards, for staggered terms of seven years for governing board members and four years for supervisory board members. Four of the seventeen bank council members are appointed by the Supervisory Board for the remainder of their terms as directors, and twelve others are appointed by the government for staggered four-year terms. The final member of the council, its chairman, is the Royal Commissioner, also appointed and dismissed by the government.

In Chile and the United States, board members are appointed by each country's president, subject to senate approval, for terms of 10 and 14 years, respectively. The bank president in Chile and the U.S. Federal Reserve chairman and vice chairman are appointed by the country's president, subject to senate approval, from the ranks of the respective boards for five- and four-year terms, respectively.[9] In the United States, the presidents of the regional reserve banks who, together with the board, make up the FOMC, are appointed by the regional bank boards. The regional bank boards themselves are made up of equal numbers of directors representing member commercial banks, directors who are nonbankers but who are elected by member banks, and directors appointed by the Federal Reserve Board. The regional bank presidents have to be drawn from this latter group.

In Switzerland, the members of the Directorate (the governor and two deputies) are appointed by the Senate, on the recommendation of the Bank Council, for six-year terms. The governor and one deputy become president and vice president of the Bank Council and Bank Committee. Other bank committee members have four-year terms,

[9]In practice, in the United States, when a vacancy on the Board has arisen as a result of the chairman resigning, the president has, subject to Senate approval, appointed an individual both as board member and chairman.

and are appointed by the council from among its own ranks. Of the 40 council members, 15 are elected by the shareholders. (As already noted, the federal government is not a shareholder.)

In Germany, the Bundesbank president, the other members of the Directorate (the executive body), and the Länder bank presidents are almost invariably appointed for the maximum eight-year term. The president and the other directorate members (up to eight) are appointed by the German president, on the nomination of the federal government, after consultation with the Bank Council, the supervisory body comprised of the Directorate and the eleven Länder bank presidents. The Länder bank presidents are appointed by the federal president, on the nomination of the federal parliament, in turn based on recommendations from provincial governments and after consultations with the Bank Council.

Directors or governors can generally be removed for relatively technical causes, such as bankruptcy, criminal offenses, major conflicts of interest, and so on. There does not seem to be a clear pattern with respect to dismissal on other grounds. In Germany and the United Kingdom, the legislation contains no other grounds for dismissal. In France, there is no limit on the president's ability to remove incumbents, and in the United States, the president may remove board members "for cause." In Chile and the Netherlands, the government may remove incumbents on the recommendation of the board (at least three council members, in Chile) or for a justified cause. In New Zealand, the government can remove directors for unsatisfactory performance (relative to the defined role of the board), and can remove the governor or deputy for unsatisfactory performance in relation to achieving agreed policy targets in particular, whether or not recommended by the board.

Central Bank Budgetary Independence

Except in France and New Zealand, the central banks covered in this survey have substantial financial independence from government across all of their functions, irrespective of the degree of monetary policy independence. This is due mainly to their ability to determine their own current expenditures, and the knowledge that in most cases, their revenue is unlikely to present a constraint on their spending. Even when a bank is required to provide concessional finance of some sort, this is still likely to be the case in the countries surveyed.

Central bank income usually arises from seigniorage revenue in the form of interest earnings on assets backing the note issue. Often, assets backing nonremunerated reserve deposits at the central bank also provide such revenue. In the United Kingdom, for example, it is widely acknowledged that the 0.5 percent cash-reserve requirement imposed on banks is a funding mechanism for the Bank of England and has no real monetary policy significance.

Central bank profits, after allocations to reserve funds and any dividend payments, are invariably transferred back to the treasury. This appears entirely appropriate, given that it is governments that have granted central banks monopoly note issue privileges and the ability to impose effectively binding reserve requirements. There are usually arrangements specified in the legislation for the distribution of central bank profits, though in some cases (e.g., the United Kingdom and France), the distribution is specified by, or negotiated with the government. An exception is the United States, where the Federal Reserve banks themselves decide what amounts should be set aside in reserve funds.

There are several issues to be considered in relation to budgetary independence. First, to what extent is such independence required to support policy independence? A potential concern for a bank with policy independence is that a government could indirectly exert undue influence on the bank's policy by restricting its access to resources. On the other hand, when a central bank is clearly carrying out the government's monetary policy, there appears to be no compelling policy argument for financial independence.

A second question relates to the form of funding for the central bank. How much does it matter if an independent central bank's revenue appears to provide a financial incentive structure inconsistent with the presumed goal of monetary stability, that is, if a central bank's revenue in real terms rises with inflation. It has often been noted that seigniorage revenue has this feature, as does the similar revenue from reserve requirements. The reason is that if inflation is accelerating, such revenue increases faster than the general price level: not only does revenue increase as the note issue and required reserves grow more or less in line with inflation, but it increases even further if nominal interest rates also rise in line with higher inflation. In such a situation central bank revenue would be doubly compensated for inflation. The concern here has more to do with how the inconsistent incentive structure might be publicly perceived, rather than about whether independent central bankers would consciously soften monetary policy as a result of revenue considerations.

A third issue is how to ensure that the central bank, if it has budgetary independence, nevertheless achieves the same sort of financial efficiency that is expected of any other public policy organization. The response in most countries has been to rely on the banks' boards to ensure financial efficiency. There is always a risk, however, of a board being "captured" by the organization it monitors if the incentive and accountability structure is not well designed. In practice, and justifiably or not, it is sometimes a point of some sensitivity that central banks frequently offer considerably better facilities, salaries, and benefits than the civil service.

In an attempt to seek an appropriate balance between considerations such as the above, the new central bank legislation in New Zealand takes a course on budgetary independence quite different from arrangements in the other central banks surveyed. Reflecting the desire to ensure financial efficiency and remove inconsistent financial incentives, all public policy functions of the Reserve Bank will be funded under an agreement between the minister and the governor, ratified by Parliament.[10] Reflecting the need to support policy independence, however, this agreemnt covers Reserve Bank expenditure over a five-year period, rather than requiring approval of expenditure budgets on a year-by-year basis.

Constraints on the Use of Monetary Policy Instruments

In some contexts, monetary policy independence could be seriously impaired if the central bank did not have the freedom to manipulate the instruments of monetary policy as it sees fit, and without the need for approval by the government. This does not appear to be a problem for the most independent central banks in this survey, but could affect some of the other countries surveyed. In addition, in some developing countries, monetary policy independence has been reduced, owing to a lack of well-developed financial markets and money market instruments and the consequent need to rely on coordination with government debt management. For example, the use of treasury bill auctions for monetary policy purposes requires close coordination with fiscal authorities; this could often constrain the freedom of action by the central bank.

There are often limits on the ability of central banks to vary reserve requirements, but since the general trend is away from actively using these in monetary policy, this is unlikely to be a constraint for the countries involved. The most obvious example here is New Zealand, where reserve requirements were removed in 1985; new legislation would be required to reintroduce them. The view was that the normal

---

[10]Commercial activities, mainly the Reserve Bank's debt registry operation, will be required to be fully costed and charged out, and will operate on a fully commercial and competitive basis. The government will be free to take its debt registry business elsewhere on commercial grounds, while the bank's registry service will be free to compete for nongovernment registry business.

legislative procedures should be followed if it was thought necessary to return to an instrument involving compulsion. In the United Kingdom and the Netherlands, the central banks would be able to vary reserve requirements, if they wished to, by making "recommendations" to bankers: but if agreement could not be reached with the bankers, government approval would be required before legally binding directives could be issued. In France, a change in reserve requirements needs to be approved by government, through the National Credit Council. In Germany, the United States, and Chile, the central banks are able to vary reserve requirements: the Federal Reserve has not actively varied requirements in the past, but the Bundesbank has.

Associated Functions of Central Banks

The major functions undertaken by central banks at different times and in different countries vary in a number of respects. These functions can be broadly divided into those directly involved in monetary policy operations and those of other associated functions:

Functions most closely related to the conduct of monetary policy include

- bankers' bank;
- management of the currency issue; and
- government's bank.

Other functions include

- supervision of financial institutions and markets;
- lender of last resort;
- carrying out exchange rate policy, including foreign exchange market management and control;
- holding and managing international reserves;
- fiscal agent and management of public debt;
- quasi-fiscal functions, such as subsidization of specific sectors, equity participation in financial institutions, etc.;
- deposit insurance; and
- participation in clearing and settlements.

In the first group of functions, the bankers' bank role and currency issue are fundamental to central banking and are at the very core of monetary policy.[11] In many countries, the role of government banker has also been close to the core of monetary policy, although it seems clear that this is not an essential central bank function.

The functions in the second group are not so closely related to monetary policy; however, they are associated with central banks to some extent at least. The purpose of this section is to examine the extent to which these associated functions are, or should be, undertaken by central banks, and, if undertaken, the extent to which they constrain or complement monetary policy independence.

Exchange Rate Policy

At the broadest level, the practical independence of monetary policy depends on the nature of the exchange rate regime. The more that the exchange rate is managed, the less is the freedom to choose a monetary policy that differs from that prevailing internationally. Furthermore, exchange rate policy and monetary policy are very closely linked at both the level of objectives and of operation. In the countries surveyed here, intervention in both money and foreign exchange markets can be used to achieve either exchange rate or monetary policy goals. As an example of the closeness of such links, liquidity management operations in Switzerland are mainly carried out through foreign currency swaps, rather than operations in normal domestic securities. The implication is that the two policies need to be very closely coordinated. Effective central bank independence requires as a minimum that the central bank be closely involved in the choice of exchange rate regime.

In no country surveyed has the government been prepared to completely delegate authority for major exchange rate decisions to the central bank—either on the regime itself, or on the appropriate level of the exchange rate under anything less than a "clean" float. Perhaps the clearest statement of this is in the New Zealand legislation: even though a remarkably clean float has operated since 1985, the law states that the government retains the right to formally direct the Reserve Bank to intervene in the market or to fix exchange rates. In the absence of such directives, the Bank can operate in foreign exchange as it sees fit, in relation to its monetary policy targets and its statutory objective. A somewhat similar situation exists in Germany and Chile. In the latter, the central bank, taking into account the general economic policy of the government, can intervene in the market and even

[11]This is not to say, however, that a central bank is required to run the currency issue—alternative arrangements have been and still are in place in some countries. Under such alternative arrangements, the scope for discretionary monetary policy is limited.

introduce certain restrictions on capital movements. Such measures are subject to ministerial veto, which can, however, be overridden by unanimous decision of the Central Bank Council.

Where intervention is required for a reason other than a strictly monetary policy consideration, the central bank acts as an agent for the government and treasury. Given the lack of authority delegated to central banks in this area, it is under a managed float or a fixed rate regime with reasonably wide margins that there is the greatest need for coordination and cooperation between the central bank and the government and treasury. An important issue is whether the central bank will sterilize the foreign exchange intervention. Sterilized intervention involves offsetting the changes in net foreign assets through open market operations so as to keep the money base unchanged. This will preserve the intentions of monetary policy, but is unlikely to have more than a transitory effect on the exchange rate; conversely, unsterilized intervention has a better chance of influencing the exchange rate but may compromise monetary policy targets.

Lender of Last Resort

In some cases, central banks' legislation does not define or even mention a lender-of-last-resort function. From an historical perspective, however, it can be seen that the lender-of-last-resort function has been one of the most important features of the central bank's role as bankers' bank, the ultimate source of domestic liquidity.

It is useful to distinguish between two very different notions of this function. First, the classical notion of lender of last resort has to do with the central bank temporarily providing extra reserves in the event of a sudden loss of confidence in the banking system, reflected in large cash withdrawals from some, or many, banks, and not redeposited elsewhere in the banking system—the "flight-to-cash" situation.

In the absence of offsetting action by the central bank, the loss of bank reserves would be translated into a multiple contraction in broad money and credit aggregates. Although rare, such an event can have potentially severe real sector effects. The effects of the failure of the Federal Reserve to suitably fulfill this function in the 1930s demonstrates this. More recently, the stock market declines of October 1987 and 1989 led many central banks around the world to make clear their intention to act as lenders of last resort to prevent any question of confidence in their financial systems from arising.

Acting as lender of last resort in this classical sense can be seen as a temporary suspension of previous monetary policy targets to accommodate a sharp change in the public's demand for cash. As such, it is clear that this is a natural central bank function, inseparable from monetary policy. Every central bank has this function, whether or not it is explicit in its legislation.[12] In a few cases (Chile and New Zealand), this function is explicitly mentioned in the context of concern about the stability of the financial system, which is presumably meant to distinguish the classical meaning from, and perhaps preclude, the second notion of lender of last resort.

The second notion relates to central bank lending to an individual troubled institution when the system as a whole is not troubled, a few examples of which come to mind (e.g., Continental Illinois in 1984 in the United States). Consistent with the classical guidelines for central banking, few would suggest that it is appropriate for central banks to lend (take on a credit risk) to an insolvent financial institution because of the risks to its own balance sheet. If the institution is only illiquid, the grounds for the central bank lending are reduced because the institution may still be able to borrow on the market provided its solvency is recognized by other institutions. Given the political sensitivities that can be involved in decisions on support for an individual institution, there may well be an argument for separating this second notion of the lender-of-last-resort function from the central bank, with the decision on lending clearly being made by the government. For example, it may be considered whether such action is best left for the deposit insurance authority (where applicable), or left to the government and funded directly from the budget.

Prudential Supervision

While the location of the supervisory responsibility varies among countries, the central bank assumes significant supervisory functions in all of the surveyed countries except Switzerland and Chile. Of the countries included in this survey, the central bank has the sole or major responsibility for bank supervision in the United Kingdom, the Netherlands, and New Zealand.

In France, supervision is the responsibility of the Banking Commission, but this is chaired by the Governor of the Banque de France and staffed by employees of the Bank, so there is only a legal, but not practical, distinction between the two. There is also a close relationship in Germany between the Bundesbank and the Federal Banking

---

[12]Although it is clear that acting as lender of last resort in a flight-to-cash situation is a central bank function, one can conceive of the decision to act as lender of last resort (and to suspend previous money-base growth targets) being a government responsibility, rather than a central bank responsibility.

Supervisory Office. Although legal and constitutional considerations about who should have the ultimate responsibility for supervision are the main factors behind these arrangements, they also serve to insulate the central bank itself from legal action in a potentially very sensitive area.

In the United States, responsibility is shared among the Federal Reserve, the Federal Deposit Insurance Corporation (FDIC), and the Comptroller of the Currency. In Switzerland, the Federal Banking Commission has supervisory responsibility, with very limited involvement on the part of the Swiss National Bank. In Chile, the Superintendency of Banks and Financial Institutions is in charge of supervision.

The fact that most of the surveyed central banks are involved in supervision, even if only minor as in the Swiss and Chilean cases, appears to reflect the need to be at least broadly aware of the prudential consequences of monetary policy, plus the need to be forewarned in the case of a call on the central banks' last resort facilities and to coordinate with supervisors when such a call is actually made. Given that substantial prudential involvement is normal, the implication may be that central banks consider it important to be able to assess the impact of monetary policy on different institutions. Another motivation for close central bank involvement may be the fact that there are close linkages between specific instruments of prudential supervision—liquidity guidelines, accounting standards, capital adequacy rules, etc.—and monetary policy.

A reason often cited for supervision being entirely carried out by the central bank is that there is a potential conflict between supervisory and monetary policy concerns, and coordination between the two would be more efficient if they were both in the same organization. This suggestion appears overstated for the countries surveyed here, however, because prudential difficulties rarely arise from tight liquidity, but rather from poor asset quality, inadequate capital, fraud, and so on. The argument might be more applicable in less developed financial markets.

But even if we accept the suggestion of important conflicts, an important question is who should make the trade-offs between supervisory and monetary policy concerns? If the central bank has monetary policy independence, having the bank make the trade-off internally would reduce monetary policy transparency and accountability. It might be better for the trade-off to be made at the political level, based on two clear streams of advice from separate organizations.

An additional consideration is that having supervisory responsibility in the central bank makes the bank potentially vulnerable to considerable political pressures in the broadest sense, in the event of a bank failure. This could well infringe on monetary policy independence. The Swiss, German, Chilean, and possibly French arrangements may partly reflect this sort of concern.

Another argument is that there are efficiency gains from placing supervision in the central bank. Given that a central bank will want to have some involvement anyway because of its traditional last resort function, there may be efficiencies in the use of information that can be obtained from placing supervision in the central bank. However, there may also be efficiency arguments for placing supervision outside the central bank: namely, where there are other supervisory bodies outside the central bank, concerned with nonbank institutions, securities markets, and the like, then there may be greater efficiencies to be obtained by combining bank supervision with these bodies instead of placing it in the central bank. Although this has not actually occurred in any of the surveyed countries, the possibility of a future move in this direction was acknowledged in New Zealand, and the new legislation explicitly allows for a future shift of bank supervision outside the central bank.

In short, there are arguments both for and against a central bank having the primary responsibility for supervision. The central bank does need to be involved to some extent at least, but this does not in itself imply that the bank needs to be the main supervisory authority. Other things being equal, the arguments against the central bank having the main responsibility gain more weight for independent central banks, where the need to avoid conflicting objectives and to reduce undesirable political pressure becomes particularly important.

Deposit Insurance

Formal deposit insurance schemes exist in all the countries surveyed in this paper, except New Zealand.[13] In most of these cases, however, the central bank is not involved in deposit insurance and separate agencies have been established for that purpose; in the Netherlands and in the United Kingdom, some degree of involvement of the central bank is observed. In the Netherlands, the deposit insurance scheme is managed, but not funded, by the central bank. In the United Kingdom, the Deposit Protection Fund is managed by a board including the central bank governor, deputy governor, and chief cashier.

There are several possible arguments for including a deposit insurance function in the central bank, but these may be of more relevance

[13]In Germany, Switzerland, and France, however, the deposit insurance schemes are run by the relevant banking industry associations, rather than an official body.

in some countries outside this survey than for those in it. These arguments include the following: when the bank already has a major supervisory function, economies of scale can be obtained; that as with a supervisory responsibility, central bank responsibility for deposit insurance could allow better coordination with last resort lending; and central bank responsibility for deposit insurance could remove or reduce doubts about the ability of the insurance fund to cope with major failures.

Counterarguments mainly revolve around the political and monetary policy risks for the central bank in being involved in deposit insurance. These risks may well be more severe in the case of involvement in deposit insurance than involvement in supervision. When deposit insurance and supervision exist, the agency responsible for the former may be the more vulnerable because its public profile in handling failing banks is likely to be higher. Also, if there are indeed conflicts between prudential and monetary policy considerations, these are likely to be more sharply felt if the central bank assumes deposit insurance functions than in the case when the bank only supervises. Again, this would not be desirable from the point of view of monetary policy independence and accountability.

Other Financial Sector Regulation

When the central bank has responsibility for supervision already, it can be argued that efficiency gains can be obtained by including other aspects of financial sector regulation among the central banks' functions. The most important of these other regulatory responsibilities is licensing of financial institutions. In the United Kingdom, the United States, New Zealand, and the Netherlands, the central banks have sole or shared responsibility for bank licensing. In Switzerland, Chile, and Germany, the licensing authority is the supervisory body mentioned in the section on supervision, above, rather than the central bank; in France, it is the Committee on Credit Institutions (like the Banking Commission, chaired by the Governor of the Banque de France).

Although there do not appear to be major problems for monetary policy if a central bank licenses banks, an interesting side issue is whether there might be problems if the same agency performs both licensing and supervision. Under some circumstances, the combination of these two functions could create conflicting internal incentives. For example, the supervisor might be more inclined than otherwise to intervene in a particular institution's affairs if it has also licensed that institution.

Fiscal Agent

Central banks often act as governments' fiscal agents, advising on (in conjunction with the treasury) and implementing domestic and external public debt policy, and managing international reserves. In some countries (such as New Zealand and the United Kingdom), the arrangements relating to domestic public debt policy have been closely entwined with monetary policy. With such an arrangement, there can sometimes be a tendency toward conflict between the two areas—for example, public debt considerations might suggest the issue of short-term public debt at a time when monetary policy considerations require long-term debt.

In general, such conflicts are not helpful from the point of view of monetary policy independence and transparency. Some separation of public debt policy and monetary policy is likely to be desirable to allow clearer objectives to be pursued by each. In the United States, the Netherlands, and France, a large measure of separation exists because the central bank does not act as the government's fiscal agent in the issue of government debt instruments. Some degree of separation has also been recently achieved in New Zealand, with the introduction of central bank bills for liquidity management operations, allowing treasury bill sales to be used more or less exclusively for short-term government funding, rather than serving both purposes.

In most of the countries in this survey, the central bank holds and manages official international reserves. The exceptions are the United Kingdom, where the treasury owns the reserves but the Bank of England manages them, and the United States and New Zealand, where reserves are held by both the treasury and the central bank. The central banks can use these reserves for exchange market intervention on behalf of their governments, and in some cases can also operate in the foreign exchange markets for their own purposes. Of the central banks surveyed, only those in France, Germany, and Chile have a major role in external debt management, but others may have an advisory role (e.g., New Zealand).

Conclusion

Several countries have either recently made or are in the process of considering significant changes to their central banking legislation, generally aimed at making their banks more independent in the formulation and operation of monetary policy. In light of these developments, this paper has reviewed the main issues relating to central bank autonomy, and the potential links between such autonomy and the choice of central bank functions. A limited initial survey of eight countries, including two where new legislation has just been introduced or is about to be enacted, was used as a reference base.

Although the theoretical grounds for central bank independence are now on a rather firmer footing than previously, it is not possible to draw strong conclusions about the desirability of central bank independence in practice. So far, the evidence is not more than suggestive. Nor is it easy to make conclusive inferences about the detailed design of relationships between the central bank and government from a very limited survey such as this. So much depends on the practice of often informal institutional and political arrangements, and both these and formal legislated arrangements vary widely from country to country.

Notwithstanding these reservations, central bank independence does appear to have the potential to improve longer-run inflation performance, or to buttress other arrangements, which provide a disciplinary check on monetary policy. The major point to emphasize, however, is that the detail of the institutional framework is likely to be an important determinant of the contribution that formal central bank independence makes in practice, and indeed to the sustainability of such formal independence. In particular, the legislated framework may need to structure as much as possible these less formal aspects of government–central bank relationships. This is likely to be of particular importance for a country attempting to build monetary policy credibility against an historical background of variable and generally insufficient monetary restraint. In this regard, it will be very interesting to review in the future the experiences of Chile and New Zealand, with their different approaches to central bank independence.

The following additional points seem to be of particular importance in designing central bank independence arrangements. First, for both practical reasons and reasons of constitutional principle, it is not helpful to think of the ultimate responsibility for monetary policy lying anywhere else than with the political leadership. Governments may, however, choose to impose constraints on the extent of their own monetary policy freedom, and that of future governments, by delegating certain authority to central banks. The extent to which they choose to do so is likely to depend on a number of country-specific factors, including past inflation and monetary policy experience, the nature of existing checks and balances in the political system, the economic awareness of the public, and so on.

Second, seen from the perspective of delegated authority, it is clear that central bank autonomy needs to be accompanied by effective monetary policy accountability. Depending on the extent of delegation, such accountability might be to the executive arm of government, to the legislative arm, or direct to the public.

Third, clear, nonconflicting objectives and a structure of incentives and sanctions that align the motivations of the central bank, as monetary policy agent, with what is considered to be welfare-maximizing monetary policy, are important requirements. Without these, the effective execution of the delegated authority and effective accountability may suffer. These considerations are as much a matter of sound management principles as technical considerations from monetary economics.

Fourth, for similar reasons, the respective roles of the central bank and the political authorities need to be clearly set out, and the relationships between the two need to be transparent and consistent. There is unlikely to be any gain in monetary policy credibility from a more autonomous central bank if there are suspicions of backdoor influence.

Fifth, if there are conflicts and trade-offs inherent in a central bank's functions, monetary policy independence and credibility might, in the extreme, require reconsideration of the mix of functions allocated to the central bank. Short of that, there need to be transparent mechanisms for the resolution of such conflicts, with decisions preferably made outside the central bank so that the central bank is not seen to be shifting monetary policy objectives. Even if the inherent conflicts with monetary policy are not substantial, there may sometimes be scope for extreme political sensitivity in relation to some of the nonmonetary policy functions of the central bank, which could impinge indirectly on the monetary policy function. In this case too, the allocation of responsibilities might need to be examined.

Finally, it is worth noting that central bank independence by itself cannot guarantee monetary policy credibility. This depends very importantly on the credibility of economic stabilization and adjustment policy as a whole. For example, where exchange rate policy or fiscal policy is widely seen as inappropriate, the best that can be hoped for is that an independent central bank may help to make the costs of those inappropriate policies more visible.

Bibliography

Auerbach, Robert D., "Politics and the Federal Reserve," *Contemporary Policy Issues* (Long Beach, California), Vol. 3 (Fall 1985), pp. 43–66.

Blackburn, Keith, and Michael Christensen, "Monetary Policy and Policy Credibility," *Journal of Economic Literature* (Nashville), Vol. 27 (March 1989), pp. 1–45.

Cukierman, Alex, "Central Bank Behavior and Credibility: Some Recent Theoretical Developments: Part 1," *Review*, Federal Reserve Bank of St. Louis (St. Louis), Vol. 68 (May 1986), pp. 5–17.

Goodhart, Charles, *The Evolution of the Central Bank* (Cambridge, Massachusetts: MIT Press, 1988).

Selected Bibliography

Part I. Role and Functions of Central Banks

Ahmed, A.K.N., "Role of Central Bank in Economic Development—Financing of Public and Private Sectors," *Commerce* (Bombay), Vol. 154 (January 10, 1987), pp. 14–23.

Albers, Norman, "Electronic Fund Transfers und die Geldpolitik," *Zeitschrift fur das Gesamte Kreditwesen*, Vol. 41 (May 1, 1988), pp. 366–72.

Atkinson, P.E., A. Blundell-Wignall, and J.C. Chouraqui, "Budget Financing and Monetary Targets, with Special Reference to the Seven Major OECD Countries," *Économies et Sociétés* (Paris), Vol. 17, (July/August 1983), pp. 1057–96.

Auernheimer, Leonardo, "The Honest Government's Guide to the Revenue from the Creation of Money," *Journal of Political Economy* (Chicago), Vol. 82 (May/June, 1974), pp. 598–606.

Australian Payment System Council, *The Australian Payment System* (The Council, 1987).

Bank for International Settlements, *Exchange Market Management and Monetary Policy* (Basle, 1988), pp. i-xiii, 11–29, 65–96, 188–200.

Bhatt, V.V., "Financial Innovation and Credit Market Development," Policy, Planning, and Research Working Papers, No. 52 (Washington: World Bank, 1989).

Chandavarkar, Anand G., "Promotional Role of Central Banks in Developing Countries," IMF Working Paper, No. 87/20 (unpublished, Washington: International Monetary Fund, 1987).

Collyns, Charles, *Alternatives to the Central Bank in the Developing World*, Occasional Paper, No. 20 (Washington: International Monetary Fund, 1983).

Cumming, Christine M., "Government Deficits and Monetary Control in Three Industrial Countries," Research Paper, No. 8205, Federal Reserve Bank of New York (January 1982).

Cunningham, Thomas J., "Long-Run Outcome of a Permanent Deficit," *Economic Review*, Federal Reserve Bank of Atlanta, Vol. 71 (May 1986), pp.25–33.

Demopoulos, Georg D., and George M. Katsimbris, "Central Bank Policy and the Financing of Government Budget Deficits: A Cross-Country Comparison," *Economic Papers*, No. 19, European Communities, Commission, Directorate General for Economic and Financial Affairs (September 1983), pp. 1–56.

———, and Stephen M. Miller, "Monetary Policy and Central Bank Financing of Government Budget Deficits: A Cross-Country Comparison," *European Economic Review* (Amsterdam) Vol. 31 (July 1987), pp. 1023–50.

Dowd, Kevin, *The State and the Monetary System* (Hemel Hempstead, England, 1989).

Faulhaber, G.R., A. Phillips, and A.M. Santomero, "Payment Risk, Network Risk and the Role of the Fed," in *U.S. Payment System: Efficiency, Risk and the Role of the Federal Reserve System*, ed. by David B. Humphrey (Boston: Kluwer Academic Publishers, 1989), pp. 197–213.

Fischer, Stanley, "Seignorage and the Case for a National Money," *Journal of Political Economy* (Chicago), Vol. 90 (April 1982), pp. 295–313.

Hodgman, Donald R., and Robert W. Resek, "Central Bank Exchange Rate Policy," BEBR Faculty Working Paper, No. 117, University of Illinois at Urbana—Champaign Bureau of Economic and Business Research (March 1985).

Leone, Alfredo, "Effectiveness and Implications of Limits on Central Bank Credit to the Government" (unpublished, Washington: International Monetary Fund, October 1990).

McEntee, Elliot C., "The Federal Reserve's Role in Controlling U.S. Payment System Risk in the U.S.," *World of Banking* (Rolling Meadows, Illinois), Vol. 7 (May/June 1988), pp. 18–22.

Mengle, David L., "Legal and Regulatory Reform in Electronic Payments: An Evaluation of Payment Finality Rules," in *U.S. Payment System: Efficiency, Risk and the Role of the Federal Reserve System*, ed. by David B. Humphrey (Boston: Kluwer Academic Publishers, 1989), pp. 145–80.

Merrick, John J., Jr., and Anthony Saunders, "Bank Regulation and Monetary Policy," *Journal of Money, Credit and Banking* (Columbus), Vol. 17 (November 1985), Part 2, pp. 691–717.

Meuche, Kurt, "Blueprint for New Domestic and Cross-Border Settlement Systems," *World of Banking* (Rolling Meadows, Illinois), Vol. 9 (January/February 1990), pp. 16–19.

Meyer, Hans, "Implications of the Swiss Interbank Clearing System for Central Bank Policy," *World of Banking* (Rolling Meadows, Illinois), Vol. 6 (January/February 1987), pp. 26–28.

Muller, H.J., "Mr. Muller Discusses Banking Supervision in a Market-Oriented Financial System," *BIS Review*, Bank for International Settlements, (Basle), (January 1990).

Organization for Economic Cooperation and Development, *Budget Financing and Monetary Control* (Paris, 1982).

———, *Exchange Rate Management and the Conduct of Monetary Policy*, OECD Monetary Studies Series (Paris, 1984).

Padoa-Schioppa, Tommaso, "Role of Central Banks: The Issue of Risk in Payment Systems," *World of Banking* (Rolling Meadows, Illinois), Vol. 7 (May/June 1988), pp. 13–17.

Parkin, Michael, "Domestic Monetary Institutions and Fiscal Deficits," Working Paper, No. 8605c, University of Western Ontario, Center for the Study of International Economic Relations (February 1986).

Pecchioli, R.M., *Prudential Supervision in Banking* (Paris: Organization for Economic Cooperation and Development (1987).

Polizatto, Vincent P., "Prudential Regulation and Banking Supervision: Building an Institutional Framework for Banks," Policy, Planning, and Research Working Papers, No. 340 (Washington: World Bank, 1990).

Radcliffe, Nicola, "Towards Uniformity in the Rules Governing Electronic Funds Transfers," *Butterworths Journal of International Banking and Financial Law* (United Kingdom), Vol. 3 (June 1988), pp. 364–66.

Rangarajan, C., "Central Banking and Economic Development: Indian Experience," *Bulletin*, Reserve Bank of India, Vol. 42 (August 1988) pp. 645–48.

Revell, J.R.S., *Banking and Electronic Fund Transfers* (Paris: Organization for Economic Cooperation and Development, 1983).

Rimal, Bimall Nath, *The Role of Central Banks in Development Finance: Experience of South-East Asian Central Banks* (Petaling Jaya, Malaysia: SEACAN Research and Training Centre, 1984).

Robinson, David J., and Peter Stella, "Amalgamating Central Bank and Fiscal Deficits," in *Measurement of Fiscal Impact: Methodological Issues*, ed. by Mario I. Blejer and Ke-Young Chu, Occasional Paper, No. 59 (Washington: International Monetary Fund, June 1988), pp. 20–31.

Tabellini, Guido, "Central Bank Reputation and the Monetization of Deficits: The 1981 Italian Monetary Reform," *Economic Inquiry* (Long Beach, California), Vol. 25 (April 1987), pp. 185–200.

Teijeiro, Mario O., "Central Bank Losses: Origins, Conceptual Issues, and Measurement Problems," Policy, Planning, and Research Working Papers, No. 293 (Washington: World Bank, 1989).

Turnovsky, Stephen J., and Mark E. Wohar, "Alternative Models of Deficit Financing and Endogenous Monetary and Fiscal Policy 1923–1982," NBER Working Paper, No. 2123 (Cambridge, Massachusetts: National Bureau of Economic Research, 1987).

Villanueva, Delano, and Abbas Mirakhor, "Strategies for Financial Reforms: Interest Rate Policies, Stabilization, and Bank Supervision in Developing Countries" *Staff Papers*, International Monetary Fund (Washington), Vol. 37, No. 3 (September 1990), pp. 509–36.

Vinay, B., "Les Banques Centrales de la Zone Franc et le Développement Monétaire," *Revue Juridique et Politique Independence et Coopération* (Paris), Vol. 32 (July/September 1978), pp. 935–48.

Waller, Christopher J., "Deficit Financing and the Role of the Central Bank—A Game Theoretic Approach," *Atlantic Economic Journal* (Worden, Illinois), Vol. 15 (July 1987), pp. 25–32.

"World Development Report: Financial Sector Reform Proves Beneficial when Macroeconomic Environment Is Stable," *IMF Survey* (Washington), (July 10, 1989), pp. 209, 215–17.

Zenkoku Ginko Kyokai Rengokai, *Payment Systems in Japan* (Tokyo: Federation of Bankers Associations of Japan, 1988).

Part II. Central Bank Independence

Adam, Nigel, "Over the Horizon: A European Central Bank," *International Management*, Vol. 43 (April 1988), pp. 39–40.

Aglietta, Michel, "Union Monétaire et Banque Centrale," *Revue d'Economie Financière*, No. 819 (March/June 1989), pp. 150–65.

Arancibia, Sergio, "La Auditoria y los Sistemas: El Caso del Banco Central de Chile," *Monetaria* (Mexico), Vol. 21 (October-December 1988), pp. 462–76.

Auerbach, Robert D., "Politics and the Federal Reserve," *Contemporary Policy Issues* (Long Beach), Vol. 3 (Fall 1985), pp. 43–58.

Axilrod, Stephen H., "Central Bank Credibility: An Alternative to Private Money," *Cato Journal*, Vol. 9 (Fall 1989), pp. 363–66.

Banaian, King, and Leroy O. Laney, "Central Bank Independence: An Analysis," *Auszuge Aus Presseartikeln*, No. 101, Deutsche Bundesbank (October 1983), pp. 9–11.

———, and Thomas D. Willett, "Central Bank Independence: An International Comparison," *Economic Review*, Federal Reserve Bank of Dallas (March 1983), pp. 1–13.

Banque des Etats de l'Afrique Centrale, *La B.E.A.C. à Dix Ans* (Yaoundé, Cameroon, 1983).

———, "Réglementation des Changes et Sorties des Capitaux dans les Etats Membres de la BEAC," Etudes et Statistiques No. 138 (December 1986), pp. 238–66.

Bejot, Jean-Pierre, "CFA, Comment vas-tu?" *Jeune Afrique Economie*, No. 115–16 (January/February 1989), pp. 78–83.

Blackburn, Keith, and Michael Christensen, "Monetary Policy and Policy Credibility: Theories and Evidence," *Journal of Economic Literature* (Nashville), Vol. 29 (March 1989), pp. 1–45.

Bodart, Vincent, "Central Bank Independence and the Effectiveness of Monetary Policy: A Comparative Analysis" (unpublished, Washington: Central Banking Department, International Monetary Fund, August 1990).

"Book Explores Issues Relating to a Centralized European Monetary Authority," *IMF Survey* (Washington), Vol. 27 (November 27, 1989), p. 357.

Burdekin, Richard C.K., "Swiss Monetary Policy: Central Bank Independence and Stabilization Goals," *Kredit und Kapital* (Berlin), Vol. 20, No. 4, (1987), pp. 454–66.

———, and Leroy O. Laney, "Fiscal Policymaking and the Central Bank Institutional Constraint," *Kyklos* (Basle), Vol. 41, No. 4 (1988), pp. 647–62.

Burns, Arthur F., "The Importance of an Independent Central Bank," *Federal Reserve Bulletin*, Board of Governors of the Federal Reserve System (Washington), Vol. 63 (September 1977), pp. 777–81.

Byung-Jong, Lee, "Independence within Government," *Business Korea* (Seoul), Vol. 5 (September 1987), pp. 28–29.

Castello-Branco, Marta, "Central Bank Independence: The Chilean Case" (unpublished, Washington: International Monetary Fund, September 1990).

Christensen, Michael, "Monetary Policy and Policy Credibility: Some Recent Developments," Memo, No. 1986/12, Aarhus Universitet, Okonomisk Institut, 1986.

Cua Dernos de Economia, No. 77 (April 1989), contains several articles on central bank independence in Chile.

Cukierman, Alex, "Central Bank Behavior and Credibility: Some Recent Theoretical Developments," *Review*, Federal Reserve Bank of St. Louis, Vol. 68 (May 1986), pp. 5–17.

Dawe, Stephen, "The Reserve Bank of New Zealand Act 1989," *Bulletin*, Reserve Bank of New Zealand (March 1990), pp. 29–36.

De Cecco, Marcello, and Alberto Giovannini, eds., *A European Central Bank? Perspectives on Monetary Unification after Ten Years of the EMS* (Cambridge, New York: Cambridge University Press, 1989).

Dowd, Kevin, "The Case Against a European Central Bank," *World Economy* (Oxford), Vol. 12 (September 1989), pp. 361–72.

Duisenberg, Wim, "European Central Bank—Five Questions Need an Answer," *European Affairs* (Amsterdam), Vol. 2 (Autumn 1988), pp. 128–34.

Eizenga, Wietze, "Independence of the Federal Reserve System and of the Netherlands Bank: A Comparative Analysis," SUERF Series, No. 41A, Société Universitaire Europëene de Recherches Financières (Netherlands) (1983), pp. 1–17.

———, "Independence of the Deutsche Bundesbank and the Nederlandsche Bank with Regard to Monetary Policy: A Comparative Study," SUERF Papers on Monetary Policy and Financial Systems, No. 2, Société Universitaire Europëene de Recherches Financières (Netherlands) (1987), pp. 1–21.

Epstein, Gerald A., and Juliet B. Schor, "Divorce of the Banca d'Italia and the Italian Treasury: A Case Study of Central Bank Independence," Discussion Paper Series, No. 1269, Harvard Institute of Economic Research (September 1986).

"European Central Bank: A Status Report on Current Institutional Debate," *ECU Newsletter* (Turin), No. 24 (April 1988), pp. 17–21.

European Community, Committee for the Study of Economic and Monetary Union: *Report on Economic and Monetary Union in the European Community* (Brussels: European Communities, 1989) pp. 24–38.

Frenkel, A. Jacob, and Morris Goldstein, "Monetary Policy in an Emerging European Economic and Monetary Union: Key Issues," IMF Working Paper, No. 90/73 (unpublished, Washington: International Monetary Fund, August 1990).

Hardouvelis, Gikas A., and Scott W. Barnhart, "Evolution of Federal Reserve Credibility: 1978–1984," Research Paper, No. 8809, Federal Reserve Bank of New York (March 1988).

Jobert, Michel, "Pouvoir Politique et Banque Centrale Europêene," *Eurepargne*, No. 25 (October 1988), pp. 20–25.

Kloten, Norbert, "A European Central Bank System as a Monetary Policy Alternative," *Auszeuge aus Presseartikeln*, Deutsche Bundesbank (June 23, 1988).

Lhoneux, Etienne de, and Jean-Victor Louis, "Towards a European System of Central Banks," *Journal of International Banking Law* (Oxford), Vol. 5, No. 1, (1990), pp. 8–16.

Llewellyn, David, "Monetary Union in Europe," *Banking World* (London), (November 1988), pp. 30–32.

———, "Monetary Union in Europe: The Problems," *Banking World* (London), Vol. 6 (December 1988), pp. 42–45.

Loehnis, Anthony, "European Currency and European Central Bank: A British View," *Quarterly Bulletin*, Bank of England (London), Vol. 28 (August 1988), pp. 350–55.

MacArthur, Alan, "Monetary Operations, Financial Market Development and Central Bank Independence" (unpublished manuscript, Washington: International Monetary Fund, September 1990).

McCallum, Bennet T., "Credibility and Monetary Policy," NBER Working Paper, No. 1490 (Cambridge, Massachusetts: National Bureau of Economic Research, November 1984).

N'Guessan, Tchetche, "Un Systême de Contrôle du comportement bureaucratique de la banque Centrale," *Revue d'Economie Politique* (Paris), Vol. 99 (September/October 1989), pp. 734–43.

Nascimento, Jean-Claude, "Monetary Policy in Unified Currency Areas: The Cases of the CAMA and ECCA" (unpublished, Washington: International Monetary Fund, September 27, 1990).

O'Brien, Leslie Kenneth, and Baron O'Brien of Lothbury, "The Independence of Central Banks," Comptes Rendus, No. 404 (Brussels: Société Royale d'Economie Politique de Belgique, 1977).

Ola, Olaniyi, "Balancing the Forces," *West Africa*, No. 3741 (May 1-7, 1989), p. 678.

Poehl, Karl Otto, "Rules for Europe's Central Bank," *Journal of Commerce* (New York), February 12, 1990, p. 8A.

Reserve Bank of New Zealand, *Annual Report of the Directors and Statement of Accounts for the Year Ended . . .* (Wellington: Reserve Bank of New Zealand, 1988/89).

———, "Reserve Bank of New Zealand Policy Targets Agreement," *Bulletin*, Reserve Bank of New Zealand (March 1990), pp. 26–28.

———, *Monetary Targets Statement* (Wellington: Reserve Bank of New Zealand, April 1990).

Scharrer, Hans-Eckart, "European Central Bank?" *Intereconomics, Review of International Trade and Development* (Hamburg), Vol. 23 (March/April 1988), pp. 53–54.

Swinburne, Mark, and Marta Castello-Branco, "Central Bank Independence and Central Bank Functions" (unpublished, Washington: International Monetary Fund, December 1989).

Thygessen, Niels, "Propositions pour une Banque Centrale Européene," *Revue Francaise d'Economie*, Vol. 4 (Winter 1989), pp. 3–38.

Waller, Christopher J., "Monetary Policy Games and Central Bank Politics," *Journal of Money, Credit, and Banking* (Columbus), Vol. 21 (November 1989), pp. 422–31.

Wieczorek, Norbet, "Monetary Plan for Europe," *International Economy*, Vol. 11 (November/December 1988), pp. 55–57.

Part III Role of the Central Bank in Financial Crises

Abrams, Burton A., and Cliff J. Huang, "Predicting Bank Failures: The Role of Structure in Affecting Recent Failure Experiences in the USA," *Applied Economics* (London), Vol. 19 (October 1987), pp. 1291–1302.

Bagehot, Walter, *Lombard Street: A Description of the Money Market* (London: John Murray, 1924).

Baliño, Tomás J.T., "The Argentine Banking Crisis of 1980," IMF Working Paper, No. 87/77 (unpublished, Washington: International Monetary Fund, 1987).

Benston, George J., and others, *Perspectives on Safe and Sound Banking: Past, Present, and Future* (Cambridge, Massachusetts, MIT Press, 1986).

Bordo, Michael D., "Lender of Last Resort: Some Historical Insights," NBER Working Paper Series, No. 3011 (Cambridge, Massachusetts: National Bureau of Economic Research, June 1989), pp. 1–31.

Corrigan, E. Gerald, "A Perspective on Recent Financial Disruptions," *Quarterly Review*, Federal Reserve Bank of New York, Vol. 14 (Winter 1989/90), pp. 8–15.

Crockett, John H., "Good Bank/Bad Bank Restructuring of Financial Institutions," *Bankers Magazine*, Vol. 171 (November/December 1988), pp. 32–36.

Hinds, Manuel, "Economic Effects of Financial Crises" Policy, Planning, Research Working Paper, No. 104 (Washington: World Bank, 1988).

Humphrey, Thomas M., "The Classical Concept of the Lender of Last Resort," *Economic Review*, Federal Reserve Bank of Richmond (January/February 1975), pp. 2–9.

Jones, Douglas H., "Powers and Considerations of the Federal Deposit Insurance Corporation for Handling Failing FDIC-Insured Banks" (mimeographed, August 1987).

Lang, William W., and Leonard I. Nakamura, "Optimal Bank Closure for Deposit Insurers," Working Papers, No. 90–12, Federal Reserve Bank of Philadelphia (January 1990), pp. 1–18.

Larrain, Mauricio, "How the 1981–83 Chilean Banking Crisis was Handled," Policy, Planning, and Research Working Papers, No. 300 (Washington: World Bank, 1989).

McMahon, C.W., "Central Banks as Regulators and Lenders of Last Resort: A View from the United Kingdom," in *Key Issues in International Banking*, Conference Series No. 18 (Federal Reserve Bank of Boston, 1978) pp. 102–10.

Nascimento, Jean-Claude, "The Crisis in the Financial Sector and the Authorities' Reaction: The Case of the Philippines," IMF Working Paper, No. 90/26 (unpublished, Washington: International Monetary Fund, 1990).

Negri, Juan Javier, "Argentina's Recent Banking Crisis," *International Financial Law Review* (London), Vol. 4 (August 1985), pp. 6–8.

Office of the Comptroller of the Currency, *An Evaluation of the Factors Contributing to the Failure of National Banks* (Washington, June 1988).

Sheng, Andrew, "Bank Restructuring in Malaysia, 1985–88," Policy, Planning, and Research Working Papers, WPS 54, World Development Report (Washington: World Bank, November 1989).

Velasco, Andres, "Liberalization, Crisis, Intervention: The Chilean Financial System, 1975–85," IMF Working Paper, No. 88/66 (unpublished, Washington: International Monetary Fund, 1988).

Wallich, Henry C., "Central Banks as Regulators and Lenders of Last Resort: A View from the United States," in *Key Issues in International Banking*, Conference Series No. 18 (Federal Reserve Bank of Boston, 1978), pp. 91–98.

Williamson, Stephen D., "Liquidity, Banking, and Bank Failures," *International Economic Review* (Philadelphia), Vol. 29 (February 1988), pp. 25–43.

World Bank, *World Development Report, 1989* (London: Oxford University Press, 1989), see Chapter 5 in particular.

Part IV. Role of Central Bank in Economic Transition and Reform

Ahmed, Sadiq, and Basant Kapur, "How Indonesia's Monetary Policy Affects Key Variables," Policy, Planning, and Research Working Papers, No. 349 (Washington: World Bank, 1990).

Atkinson, Paul E., and William E. Alexander, *Financial Sector Reform: Its Role in Growth and Development* (Washington: Institute of International Finance, 1990).

Blejer, Mario I., and Silvia B. Sagari, "Sequencing the liberalization of Financial Markets," *Finance and Development* (Washington), Vol. 25 (March 1988), pp. 18–20.

Blejer, Mario I., David Burton, Steven Dunaway, and Georg Szapry, "China: Economic Reform and Macroeconomic Management," Occasional Paper, No. 76 (Washington, International Monetary Fund, 1991).

Carrington, Tim, "A Polish Banking System Takes Root, As 'Mattress Money' Economy Wanes," *Wall Street Journal*, February 16, 1990, p. A713.

Cheng, Hang-Sheng, "Money and Credit in China," *Economic Review*, Federal Reserve Bank of San Francisco (Fall 1981), pp. 19–36.

Cole, David C., and Betty F. Slade, "Adapting Monetary Policy Instruments: The Indonesian Experience," Discussion Paper No. 310, Harvard Institute for International Development (June 1989).

———, "Indonesia Financial Development: A Different Sequencing?" paper presented at seminar on Financial Liberalization, Cambridge, Massachusetts, June 10–15, 1990.

Cottarelli, Carlo, and Manuel Sebastiao, "Transition to Indirect Monetary Control: Some Notes on the Case of Portugal," prepared for the International Seminar on Economic and Monetary Union, Portugal, June 8–9, 1990.

De Wulf, Luc, and David Goldsbrough, "The Evolving Role of Monetary Policy in China," *Staff Papers*, International Monetary Fund (Washington), Vol. 33 (June 1986), pp. 209–42.

Dembinski, Pawel H., "Quantity Versus Allocation of Money: Monetary Problems of the Centrally Planned Economies Reconsidered," *Kyklos* (Basle), Vol. 41, No. 2 (1988), pp. 281–300.

Freedman, C., "Structural Changes, Financial Policy, and Bank Regulation," notes for address to IMF Central Banking Seminar, December 7, 1988, Washington.

Friedman, Benjamin M., "Targets and Instruments of Monetary Policy," NBER Working Paper, No. 2668 (Cambridge, Massachusetts: National Bureau of Economic Research, July 1988).

Gelb, Alan H., and Patrick Honohan, "Financial Sector Reforms in Adjustment Programs," Policy, Planning, and Research Working Papers, No. 169 (Washington: World Bank, 1989).

Goldsbrough, David, and Iqbal Mehdi Zaidi, "Monetary Policy in the Philippines during Periods of Financial Crisis and Changes in Exchange Rate Regime: Targets, Instruments, and the Stability of Money Demand," IMF Working Paper, No. 89/98 (unpublished, Washington: International Monetary Fund, 1989).

Hartwig, Karl-Hans, *Monetare Steuerungsprobleme in Sozialistischen Planwirtschaften* [*Monetary Control Problems in Socialist Planned Economies*] (Stuttgart, 1987).

Huszti, E., "Main Trends in the Development of Socialist Banking Systems and Organization: Relations Between the Functions of Issuing (Central) and Credit Banks," *Acta Oeconomica* (Budapest), Vol. 26, Nos. 1/2 (1981), pp. 71–91.

Imai, Hiroyuki, "China's New Banking System: Changes in Monetary Management, *Pacific Affairs* (Vancouver), Vol. 58 (Fall 1985), pp. 451–72.

Johnston, R.B., "Issues in the Design and Implementation of Monetary Control and thc Transition to Indirect Monetary Instruments" (unpublished, (Washington: International Monetary Fund, July 1990).

———, and Anton A.F. Op de Beke, "The Development of Market-Based Instruments of Monetary Control: Issues and Recent Experiences in Developing Countries" (unpublished, Washington: International Monetary Fund, Central Banking Department, November 1988).

———, "Monetary Control Procedures and Financial Reform: Approaches, Issues, and Recent Experiences in Developing Countries," IMF Working Paper, No. 89/48 (unpublished, Washington: International Monetary Fund, 1989).

Junyin, Ren, "The Basis of China's Banking Reform," in *Financial Reform in Socialist Economies*, ed. by Christine Kessides, Timothy King, Mario Nuti, and Catherine Sokil, EDI Seminar Series (Washington: The World Bank, 1989), pp. 205–13.

Kane, Edward J., "Interaction of Financial and Regulation Innovation, *American Economic Review, Papers and Proceedings* (May 1988), pp. 328–34.

Knight, Peter T., "Economic Reform in Socialist Countries: The Experiences of China, Hungary, Romania, and Yugoslavia," Staff Working Papers, No. 579 (Washington: World Bank, 1983).

Lal, Deepak, "The Political Economy of Economic Liberalization," *World Bank Economic Review* (Washington), Vol. 1 (January 1987), pp. 273–99.

Leite, Sergio P., and V. Sundararajan, "Issues in Interest Rate Management and Liberalization," IMF Working Paper, No. 90/12 (unpublished, Washington: International Monetary Fund, 1990).

Nuti, D.M., "Hidden and Repressed Inflation in Soviet-Type Economies: Definitions, Measurements and Stabilization," in *Contributions to Political Economy* (Cambridge) Vol. 5 (1986), pp. 37–82.

———, "Fenghle Financial Innovation under Socialism," in *Financial Reform in Socialist Economies*, ed. by Christine Kessides, Timothy King, Mario Nuti, and Catherine Sokil, EDI Seminar Series (Washington: The World Bank, 1989), pp. 85–105.

Op de Beke, Anton A.F., "IMF Central Banking Department Organizes Aid to National Bank of Poland," *IMF Survey* (Washington), Vol. 18 (August 13, 1990), p. 241, pp. 247–51.

"People's Bank of China to Function Exclusively As Nation's Central Bank," *IMF Survey* (Washington), Vol. 12 (October 24, 1983), p. 337.

Quintyn, Marc, "From Direct to Indirect Instruments of Monetary Policy: Lessons from the French Postwar Experience" (unpublished, Washington: International Monetary Fund, October 10, 1990).

Radecki, Lawrence, and Vincent Reinhart, "Globalizztion of Financial Markets and the Effectiveness of Monetary Policy Instruments, *Quarterly Review*, Federal Reserve Bank of New York, Vol. 13 (Autumn 1988), pp. 8–27.

Robinson, Roger J., and Lelde Schmitz, "Jamaica: Navigating Through a Troubled Decade," *Finance and Development* (Washington), Vol. 26 (December 1989), pp. 30–33.

Sundararajan, V., and Lazaros Molho, "Financial Reform and Monetary Control in Indonesia," IMF Working Paper, No. 88/4, (unpublished, Washington: International Monetary Fund, 1988)

———, "Financial Reform in Indonesia," *Finance and Development* (Washington), Vol. 25 (December 1988), pp. 43–45.

Vigliano, Franco, "China Taps the Capital Markets," *International Financial Law Review* (London), Vol. 6 (February 1987), pp. 31–36.

List of Participants

Guest Speakers

G. Arthur Brown*
Governor
Bank of Jamaica

Charles Freedman*
Deputy Governor
Bank of Canada

Robert Heller
President
Visa International

Tim O'Grady Walshe*
Former General Manager/
Director General
Central Bank of Ireland

Brian Quinn
Executive Director
Bank of England

Bruce Summers
Deputy Director
Federal Reserve Board

Antonio Fazio*
Deputy Director General
Bank of Italy

Alan Greenspan
Chairman
Board of Governors of the
Federal Reserve System

Lindsay Knight
Deputy Governor
Reserve Bank of New Zealand

Andrzej Olechowski*
First Vice President
National Bank of Poland

Maria Schaumayer*
Governor
National Bank of Austria

Hans Tietmeyer*
Member of the Executive Board
Deutsche Bundesbank

Participants

World Bank

Cesare Caranza†*
Executive Director

Deena Khatkhate†
Consultant

Andrew Sheng†
Senior Financial Specialist

International Monetary Fund

Michel Camdessus*
Managing Director

African Department

Emilio Sacerdoti†
Advisor

Asian Department

Tomás Baliño†
Deputy Division Chief

Central Banking Department

Justin B. Zulu*
Director

Douglas A. Scott†
Deputy Director

V. Sundararajan†*
Assistant Director

Patrick T. Downes*
Advisor

Jacque Gautier†
Advisor

Carl-Johan Lindgren†
Advisor

Erik Niepoort*
Advisor

David Folkerts-Landau†
Deputy Division Chief

Barry R. Johnston†
Senior Economist

Reza Vaez-Zadeh†
Senior Economist

Henry N. Schiffman†
Consultant

IMF Institute

Gerard M. Teyssier*
Director

Anthony Lanyi*
Deputy Director

Jeffrey M. Davis
Advisor

Roger Pownall
Division Chief

Observers

Saif Hadif Al-Shamsi
Executive Director
Banking Supervision Department
United Arab Emirates Central Bank

Raja Attar
Director
Internal Control Directorate
Central Bank of Syria

Richard Battellino
Chief Manager
Domestic Markets Department
Reserve Bank of Australia

Omar Rodriguez Bello
Second Vice President
Central Bank of Venezuela

Abdelhaq Benchekroun
Director
Foreign Department
Bank Al-Maghrib, Morocco

Javier Cardenas
Manager
Department of Credit, Legal Deposits, and Financial Markets
Bank of Mexico

Ilmane Mohamed Cherif
Vice Governor
Central Bank of Algeria

Pedro da Neto Cunha
Governor
National Bank of Angola

Sándor Czirjak
Deputy President
National Bank of Hungary

Dariyn Danzan
First Deputy Chairman
Board of Directors
State Bank of the Mongolian People's Republic

Jorge Quiñones del Busto
Deputy Advisor to General Management
Central Reserve Bank of Peru

Naullage Ananda Dharmabandu
Chief Accountant
Banking Department
Central Bank of Sri Lanka

Daniel E. Duenas
Manager
Directorate of Monetary Programming
Central Bank of the Republic of Argentina

A.J. Geerling
Chief
Supervision Department—General Affairs
Netherlands Bank

Clyde Goodlet
Research Advisor
Department of Monetary and Financial Analysis
Bank of Canada

Dan Huan Ha
Assistant Director
External Economic Relations Department
State Bank of Viet Nam

Takis E. Kanaris
Manager
Economic Research Department
Central Bank of Cyprus

Miroslav Kerous
Vice Chairman
State Bank of Czechoslovakia

Bap Kesang
Managing Director
Royal Monetary Authority of Bhutan

Firouzeh Khalatbari
Advisor to the Executive Board
Central Bank of the Islamic Republic of Iran

Pierre Madrieres
Deputy Director
Foreign Relations Department
Bank of France

Mohmoud Qaid M. Naji
Manager
Foreign Department
Central Bank of Yemen

Gata Ngoulou
Central Director
Bank Supervision Department
Bank of Central African States

Harihar Dev Pant
Chief Manager
Banking Development and Credit Department
Nepal Rastra Bank

Franklin Proano P.
Manager
Technical Division
Central Bank of Ecuador

Stefan Schoenberg
Senior Division Chief
Deutsche Bundesbank

Enrique Seguel
Member of the Board
Central Bank of Chile

Yutaka Shiotsu
Manager, Balance of Payments Division
International Department
Bank of Japan

Oumarou Sidikou
Vice Governor
Central Bank of West African States

Ezra Suruma
Deputy Governor
Bank of Uganda

Mengesha Tesfaye
Controller
National Bank of Ethiopia

Andrzej Topinski
Vice President
National Bank of Poland

Iris Teresa Vaz
Executive Director
Reserve Bank of India

Guantao Yu
Research Fellow
Research Institute of Finance and Banking
People's Bank of China

*Also served as panelist.
†Speaker